The Calculator Cookbook

Mark Saks, an associate professor of mathematics at the Community College of Philadelphia, has worked as an operations research and statistical consultant and has developed stochastic (probability) mathematical models for a consulting firm.

MARK SAKS

THE CALCULATOR COOKBOOK

A SPECTRUM BOOK

PRENTICE-HALL, INC., Englewood Cliffs, New Jersey 07632

Library of Congress Cataloging in Publication Data

Saks, Mark.
   The calculator cookbook.

   "A Spectrum Book."
   Includes index.
   1. Calculating — machines.   I. Title.
QA75.S3116   1983   510'.285'42   83-4536
ISBN 0-13-110395-4
ISBN 0-13-110387-3 (pbk.)

This book is available at a special discount when ordered in
bulk quantities. Contact Prentice-Hall, Inc., General
Publishing Division, Special Sales, Englewood Cliffs, N.J. 07632.

10   9   8   7   6   5   4   3   2   1

ISBN 0-13-110395-4

ISBN 0-13-110387-3 {PBK}

Editorial production and design by Alberta Boddy
Manufacturing buyer: Cathie Lenard
Cover design: Hal Siegel

Prentice-Hall International, Inc., *London*
Prentice-Hall of Australia Pty. Limited, *Sydney*
Prentice-Hall Canada Inc., *Toronto*
Prentice-Hall of India Private Limited, *New Delhi*
Prentice-Hall of Japan, Inc., *Tokyo*
Prentice-Hall of Southeast Asia Pte. Ltd., *Singapore*
Whitehall Books Limited, *Wellington, New Zealand*
Editora Prentice-Hall do Brasil Ltda., *Rio de Janeiro*

To my friends,
of whom I am fortunate to have so many.

Contents

Preface *xiii*

1
Basic Arithmetic *1*

Calculator Display *1*
Arithmetic Operations *3*
Using the Constant K *3*
Entry Systems *4*
Recommendations for Features *5*
Chain Operations *6*
Hierarchy *7*
Signed Numbers *9*
Combined Operations *10*
Parentheses *11*
Scientific Notation *13*
Simple Percentage *17*

2
Elementary Algebra *31*

Basic Functions $\boxed{x^2}$ $\boxed{\sqrt{x}}$ $\boxed{1/x}$ *31*
Substitution in Simple Expressions and Formulas *33*
Powers and Roots *35*
Linear Equations and Proportions *39*
Quadratic Equations *41*
Laws of Exponents and Radicals *44*
Logarithms *47*
Progressions *50*
Solved Problems *55*

3
Trigonometry *84*

Angular Measure *84*
Basic Trigonometric Functions *87*
Solving Right Triangles *90*
Sine and Cosine Laws *91*
Areas *93*
Miscellaneous Trigonometric Computations *96*
Inverse Trigonometric Functions *97*
Trigonometric Equations *101*
Polar Coordinates *103*
Solved Problems *108*

4
Statistics *147*

Preliminaries *147*
Averages and Variability *148*
Statistics for Sampling *157*
Inference (Hypothesis Testing) *160*
Chi Squared: χ^2 *166*
Regression (Least Squares) *170*
Analysis of Variance *179*
Solved Problems *186*

5
The Mathematics of Business and Finance *217*

Percent *217*
Markup, Discount, and Gross Profit Margin *218*
Simple Interest and Discount *221*
Compound Interest *223*
Annuities *225*
Amortization and Sinking Funds *230*
Depreciation *232*
Bonds *236*
Solved Problems *238*

Index *281*

Preface

Why Was This Book Written?

If you've just bought a calculator but don't know how to use it for the problems you have, you are not alone. Repeatedly I am asked by students and acquaintances alike how they can use their calculators to solve their own individual problems. These are basically intelligent people, but somehow there is a gap between the mathematics they know or look up and the methods they must apply to use their calculators. This book bridges the gap between the information in the owner's manual and the mathematics taught in the schools. It gives the reader a useful reference, a problem solver, and a collection of "recipes" for using the calculator; in other words—a "cookbook."

Who Is the Audience for This Book?

The level of the material in this book is primarily suitable for college students taking courses that contain any of the topics addressed in this book. Undergraduates can benefit most, but even to graduate students in nonmathematical disciplines who need a statistics course, the statistic chapter will be an extremely valuable aid. For students taking a course in the mathematics of finance, there is an invaluable chapter on that subject. High school students will find that Chapters 1 to 4 contain most of the material they are likely to study as well as some extra material. In other words, if you are a novice user of a calculator and require more than just a rudimentary acquaintance with your machine, this book is for you.

What Calculator Should I Have?

Most of this text was written from the standpoint of a scientific calculator with a single memory and hierarchical logic. Specifically, the Texas Instruments models TI–30 and TI–35 are typical, although almost any scientific calculator with algebraic logic can easily be adapted to the key sequences in this book. In the chapter on business and finance, the Texas Instruments Business Analyst I and Business Analyst II are discussed in detail, as well as the former models. The Business Analyst II also has versatile statistical functions that will make the topics in the statistics chapter more accessible should you want to study both topics, although the TI–35 can be used for almost all topics with only slight inconvenience in certain special applications.

What Can I Get out of This Book?

This book provides:

- A summary of all pertinent mathematical results and formulas.
- A vast variety of examples illustrating the basic results.
- Summary tables of formulas and keystroke sequences for easy reference and review.
- Hundreds of solved problems similar to those that you are likely to encounter.

The book is a resource to complement the traditional textbook presentation on each subject, as well as a ready reference for ideas either overlooked or forgotten and requiring a quick review of the essentials. I emphasize teaching an efficient use of the nonprogrammable scientific or business calculator in a practical way.

What About Programmable Calculators?

This book does not cover programming, but it does provide a source of formulas that you may want to program should you own a programmable model. Many good books on programming calculators are directed at programming strategies. This book is directed at picking the right formulation for standard problems requiring calculator solution.

I have made a great effort to make this book as useful to the serious neophyte user of a calculator as possible. I developed just for this book a few new techniques tailored to the calculator. For example, I give a shortcut technique for analysis of variance for balanced experimental designs in the statistics chapter. It is my sincerest hope that the contents that follow will give the reader an improved ability to use the full computational power that the handheld calculator can provide.

1

Basic Arithmetic

Calculator Display

Two displays are available on most calculators—the floating-point display used for decimals and the scientific notation (exponential) display used to display very large or very small numbers. (Some calculators have only floating-point displays, which severely limits their usefulness.)

The floating-point display consists of 8 (or more) digits with a decimal point (.) and a minus sign (−) for negative numbers. On most of the newer calculators, the minus sign as well as the decimal "floats." On some devices, the (−) is fixed at the left side of the display.

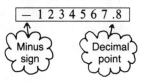

Example To enter 74.006 onto the display, key 74.006. If you wish to make it negative, key $\boxed{+/-}$, or on some calculators $\boxed{\text{CHS}}$, which changes the sign.

Example To prepare the calculator for a new entry, either key $\boxed{=}$ (which leaves the previous display, but readies the keyboard) or $\boxed{C}$ (also shown on a dual key as $\boxed{\text{ON/C}}$, which zeroes the display and readies the keyboard. Another method is to turn the calculator OFF and then ON, which also clears all memories (except on some continuous-memory or constant-memory units).

Example The displays $\boxed{\quad 0.2453}$ and $\boxed{\quad -0.2453}$ show the numbers 0.2453 and -0.2453, respectively.

    The scientific notation display shows numbers of the form 7.23×10^{17} by displaying the 7.23 and the 17 separately. The base 10 is not displayed. The number 7.23×10^{17} means 723000000000000000., that is, 7.23 with the decimal point moved 17 places to the right. This is much too big for the display. The scientific notation display would show the number like this:

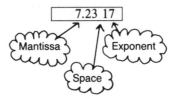

The details of scientific notation will be reviewed shortly. We shall examine only some of the mechanics at the moment.

Example To enter 7.23×10^{17} onto the display, key 7.23 $\boxed{\text{EE}}$ 17.

Example To enter 540,600,000. into the calculator, think of it as 5.406, but with the decimal moved 8 places to the right. Hence we enter it as 5.406 $\boxed{\text{EE}}$ 8.

Example To convert a scientific notation display back to floating-point mode (i.e., decimal form), use the sequence

$$\boxed{\times}\ 1\ \boxed{\text{INV}}\ \boxed{\text{EE}}\ \boxed{=}$$

(On some calculators $\boxed{\text{INV}}\ \boxed{\text{EE}}$ or $\boxed{\text{INV}}\ \boxed{\text{EE}}\ \boxed{=}$ is enough, but internal precision is lost on some models. On other models, specifically, the TI–30 manufactured by Texas Instruments, these shortcuts will not work because of an additional exponential shift feature built in.) For example, enter 7.08×10^5 by keying 7.08 $\boxed{\text{EE}}$ 5 $\boxed{=}$ and then read on the display $\boxed{\quad 7.08\ 05}$. Now change this to floating point by keying

$$\boxed{\times}\ 1\ \boxed{\text{INV}}\ \boxed{\text{EE}}\ \boxed{=}$$

and the display shows

$$\boxed{\quad 708000}$$

Arithmetic Operations

The arithmetic operations are $\boxed{+}$, $\boxed{-}$, $\boxed{\times}$, and $\boxed{\div}$ and are used in conjunction with the $\boxed{=}$ key. The numbers keyed in conjunction with these are called the *operands*; the numbers produced by the calculator are referred to as the *results*. The results may be sums, differences, products, or quotients, respectively.

Example To add 4.25 + 7.06, key 4.25 $\boxed{+}$ 7.06 $\boxed{=}$; the result is 11.31.

Example To perform the division 17)204, read it as "204 *divided by* 17" and key 204 $\boxed{\div}$ 17 $\boxed{=}$; the result is $\boxed{\quad 12 \quad}$

Example Multiply $(-1.008) \times (5.7)$ by using the $\boxed{+/-}$ key for the negative number. (*Caution*: The $\boxed{-}$ is *not* used here.)

$$1.008 \boxed{+/-} \boxed{\times} 5.7 \boxed{=}$$

and the result is $\boxed{\quad -5.7456 \quad}$

Example Subtract $8.6 - (-5.02)$ by keying the following:

$$8.6 \boxed{-} 5.02 \boxed{+/-} \boxed{=}$$

Notice that one minus sign is $\boxed{-}$ and the other is $\boxed{+/-}$ for the numerical sign. The result is 13.62.

Using the Constant $\boxed{K}$

The *constant key* $\boxed{K}$ is for repeated use of the same number as a multiplier, divisor, addend, or subtrahend. (It can also be used in conjunction with powers, which will be discussed in Chapter 2.) The key sequences for its use are as follows:

$r \boxed{+} \boxed{K}$ adds the number r to each subsequent entry

$r \boxed{-} \boxed{K}$ subtracts the number r from each subsequent entry

$r \boxed{\times} \boxed{K}$ multiplies the number r times each subsequent entry

$r \boxed{\div} \boxed{K}$ divides the number r *into* each subsequent entry

To complete the operation, a second number (operand) is entered, and then $\boxed{=}$ is keyed. (*Caution*: The $\boxed{-}$ and the $\boxed{\div}$ work in an order opposite to what you might ordinarily expect.)

Some calculators have an *automatic constant*; that is, the constant mode is always in operation. It can work in either of two ways: either the number keyed in immediately *before* the operation is treated as the constant, as in the manual constant just discussed, or on some calculators the number keyed in immediately *after* the operation is treated as the constant. In either case, the operation is completed by entering the second number and keying $\boxed{=}$. We will discuss the use of the manual constant. Check your own calculator to see how it sets up a constant and then adapt to the techniques shown here.

Example Add 4 to each of the numbers 7, 9.3, and -8.05, using $\boxed{K}$, by first keying 4 $\boxed{+}$ $\boxed{K}$ to set up the constant; then key

7 $\boxed{=}$	and read the result	$\boxed{\qquad 11.}$
9.3 $\boxed{=}$	and read the result	$\boxed{\qquad 13.3}$
8.05 $\boxed{+/-}$ $\boxed{=}$	and read the result	$\boxed{\qquad -4.05}$

This process could be continued for as many additional numbers as desired.

Example Divide 69.2, 92.2, and -0.014 by 4 by first keying 4 $\boxed{\div}$ $\boxed{K}$ to set up the constant divisor 4; then key the subsequent entries (dividends) followed by $\boxed{=}$. (When using the constant only, it is helpful to remember that $\boxed{\div}$ is read as "divided into." Usually it is read as "divided *by*." This can be a source of confusion, so make certain that you understand the distinction.)

To continue, now that the constant divisor is set up, key

69.2 $\boxed{=}$	and read the result	$\boxed{\qquad 17.3}$
92.2 $\boxed{=}$	and read the result	$\boxed{\qquad 23.05}$
.014 $\boxed{+/-}$ $\boxed{=}$	and read the result	$\boxed{\qquad -0.0035}$

Entry Systems

There are basically three kinds of entry systems: arithmetic, AOS* (algebraic operating system), and RPN (reverse Polish notation). Although a highly useful and efficient system, we do not discuss the RPN system in this text. Its main value lies with programmability, so it is too esoteric for most readers of this text for practical use. Also, an informal survey indicates that most students are purchasing either arithmetic or AOS devices. The RPN system is recognized by an *enter* key $\boxed{ENT}$ and the lack of an equals key.

For most of this text, the AOS system is used. It cannot be distinguished from the arithmetic system by looking at the keyboard. It is an

*A trademark of Texas Instruments, Inc.

internal logic that preserves the normal algebraic hierarchy (order) of operations. The specifics of this are covered under the Hierarchy section. This system is used in many (but not all) of the calculators manufactured by Texas Instruments as scientific calculators. Some later models of other manufacturers also use this system, but earlier models do not. Some earlier models by Texas Instruments have a small quirk in the system wherein the power function is not included in the hierarchical logic as in later models. For the novice who is purchasing a calculator or is using one seriously for the first time, or if you are borrowing an old calculator, check its logic out carefully as you go through this text. Any strange deviations are likely due to eccentricities in logic as the calculator design has evolved. You are better off buying a recent model such as the TI-30, TI-35, and so on.

To see if you have an AOS system, key the following: 2 $\boxed{+}$ 4 $\boxed{\times}$ 5 $\boxed{=}$. If you got an answer of 22, you have an AOS system. If you got an answer of 30, you have an arithmetic system. We shall refer to these as *entry systems*. Actually, the designations refer to the internal logic, but the reality is that the logic affects the way the numbers must be entered.

Recommendations for Features

Since there are literally hundreds of calculators on the market, it is impossible to write a practical text that covers all of them. This text is written for the most part for a calculator with AOS logic or arithmetic logic with parentheses and memory. Here are the features that are considered important, and in many cases essential, to make this text of any value to the reader:

AOS (preferred) or arithmetic system $\boxed{+}$ $\boxed{-}$ $\boxed{\times}$ $\boxed{\div}$ with $\boxed{=}$
Parentheses $\boxed{(}$ $\boxed{)}$; change sign key $\boxed{+/-}$ or $\boxed{\text{CHS}}$
Memory (one or more) $\boxed{\text{STO}}$ $\boxed{\text{RCL}}$ $\boxed{\text{SUM}}$
Percent $\boxed{\%}$ with add-on and discount feature
Manual constant $\boxed{\text{K}}$
Scientific notation entry $\boxed{\text{EE}}$ or $\boxed{\text{exp}}$
Basic algebraic functions $\boxed{1/x}$ $\boxed{\sqrt{x}}$ $\boxed{x^2}$
Logarithmic functions $\boxed{\ln x}$ $\boxed{\log}$
Power function $\boxed{y^x}$
Trigonometric functions $\boxed{\sin}$ $\boxed{\cos}$ $\boxed{\tan}$

If you don't have all these and are going to take or are taking a physics course, or a mathematics course beyond elementary algebra, you should probably invest in a new calculator with these features. The exception to this advice is if you are interested mainly in statistics or the business and finance mathematics, in which case certain specialized calculators would be more useful.

The LED (light-emitting diode) versions of most calculators are generally the least expensive. The LCD (liquid-crystal display) versions cost more but are more compact and the batteries last longer (and are also much more expensive when they do need replacement). If you elect the LED version, a rechargeable battery is an unnecessary luxury. In fact, if you are using it more as a portable calculator, it is more convenient to pop in a new battery if it discharges than to recharge. In fact you usually won't carry the recharger with you. You should always keep a spare battery in the refrigerator and carry another one with you.

For students of business and finance, the TI Business Analyst I is used primarily in Chapter 5. It is an LED unit and has an arithmetic entry system with parentheses that will be useful for understanding the structure of pertinent formulas. It does not have as many features as the Business Analyst II (an LCD device), which unfortunately does not have parentheses. The LED version is about half the price as well. If you have a Business Analyst II already, it should be easy to adapt it to most of the discussion in Chapter 6, but there are several small operating differences.

For statistics (Chapter 4), a more specialized calculator is most convenient. Almost any calculator with Stat functions will do, but one in which Σx and Σx^2 can be recalled (not just $\bar{x}$ and σ) is a more useful tool when doing analysis of variance and linear regression. If linear regression capability is built in, so much the better. The TI Business Analyst II has both business and statistical capability, but is somewhat deficient for general calculations because of the lack of parentheses. This difficulty can be overcome, but somewhat inconveniently.

The main point is that if you are looking for an inexpensive, nonprogrammable calculator that does everything, you probably won't find it. You should purchase the least expensive model that meets your current needs. You may even end up purchasing several calculators, but at a cost much less than for an expensive model that is more sophisticated than you need. Then, when you know what your specialty will be, buy the most convenient calculator that does the job. You may want a programmable device by that time.

Chain Operations

Sometimes we want to repeat the same operation but with different numbers. Each time the operation is keyed it acts like an $\boxed{=}$, completes the previous operation, and prepares for the next entry. This is not generally true if the operations are different (see Hierarchy).

Example   To multiply $5 \times 4 \times 3 \times 2$, key the sequence

$$5 \boxed{\times} 4 \boxed{\times} 3 \boxed{\times} 2 \boxed{=} \text{ and read } \boxed{\qquad 120 \qquad}$$

Notice that the last function is $\boxed{=}$, which completes the chain. It is not necessary to clear once $\boxed{=}$ is pressed. The calculator is automatically ready for the next calculation.

Example   To add $5 + 4 + 3 + 2$, key the obvious sequence

$$5 \boxed{+} 4 \boxed{+} 3 \boxed{+} 2 \boxed{=} \text{ and read } \boxed{\qquad 14 \qquad}$$

Example   Addition may be chained with subtraction. To compute $18 - 5 + 2 - 8 + 6$, key

$$18 \boxed{-} 5 \boxed{+} 2 \boxed{-} 8 \boxed{+} 6 \boxed{=} \text{ and get } \boxed{\qquad 13 \qquad}$$

Note: Addition or subtraction may *not* be chained with multiplication or division without regard to certain ordering rules (again, see Hierarchy).

The chaining of addition and subtraction can be used to balance your checkbook. Deposits are added; checks drawn on the account are subtracted. The result is the balance.

Hierarchy

The AOS (algebraic operating system) has a built in *hierarchy* (order of operations) that may be different from the order in which the keys are pressed. For instance, multiplication will be completed before addition, even if the $\boxed{+}$ is keyed before the $\boxed{\times}$.

Example   When we key $2 \boxed{+} 4 \boxed{\times} 5 \boxed{=}$ on an AOS calculator, the addition is not done until the multiplication, $4 \times 5 = 20$, is completed, even though the $\boxed{+}$ was keyed first. Then the 20 is added to the 2, giving a result of 22.

On an arithmetic entry system there is no hierarchy for the four basic operations, and they are done in the order in which they are entered. On that type of calculator when we key $\boxed{\times}$, the $\boxed{+}$ is automatically completed (rather than held pending as in the AOS system), so we get $2 + 4 = 6$, which is then multiplied by 5 to get a result of 30.

If you do this calculation on your calculator, the answer will tell you which type of operating system you have.

We shall summarize the AOS hierarchy in this section. The hierarchy for an AOS system is given in Table 1-1. Functions on the upper part of the table are done before functions on the lower part.

8 **TABLE** 1-1. Hierarchy for an Algebraic Operating System (AOS)

Basic Arithmetic

FUNCTIONS	KEYS	DISCUSSED IN CHAPTER
Parentheses; these can change the normal order	$($ $)$	1
Single variable functions; immediately replace display values	$1/x$ x^2 $\sqrt{x}$	2
	sin cos tan	3
	%	1
	lnx log	2
Powers and roots	y^x INV y^x (i.e., $\sqrt[x]{y}$)	2
Multiplication and division	$\times$ $\div$	1
Addition and subtraction	$+$ $-$	1
equals	$=$	1

Important Observation It is not necessary to memorize this table. Except for parentheses, functions are located on the keyboard according to the hierarchy. Notice that multiplication and division appear above addition and subtraction on your keyboard. Functions appearing above other functions are done first, unless they happen to be on the same level of the hierarchy, in which case they are done in the order entered.

Example The expression $3 \times 4 + 6 \div 3$ can have several different meanings. Two of the more obvious are as interpreted by the arithmetic and AOS logics. Each would give a different result.

Arithmetic System

KEY	DISPLAY	EXPLANATION
3 $\times$ 4 $+$	12.	3×4 completed
6 $\div$	18.	The 6 is added now
3 $=$	6.	Division by 3 completed

Thus the arithmetic logic would interpret the expression as a string where each operation is completed as soon as the next operation is entered, giving a result of 6.

KEY	DISPLAY	EXPLANATION
3 $\boxed{\times}$ 4 $\boxed{+}$	12.	3 $\times$ 4 completed
6 $\boxed{\div}$	6.	The entry 6 waits for division
3 $\boxed{=}$	14.	6 $\div$ 3 = 2 added to 12

What AOS has done is $(3 \times 4) + (6 - 3) = 14$. On the other hand, the arithmetic system has done $[(3 \times 4) + 6] - 3 = 6$. If we actually want the answer given by the AOS system and we have an arithmetic logic calculator, we must compute the appropriate expression using parentheses or the memory. (Memory will be discussed in Chapter 2.)

Signed Numbers

With respect to sign, there are three types of numbers: positive, negative, and zero. Zero (0) is neither positive nor negative. Affixing a $+$ or $-$ sign in front of it does not change its value. The negative numbers are a *mirror image* of the positive numbers, with 0 being the dividing point. This description refers to the usual representation of the numbers as being ordered on the real number line, and the numbers together are referred to as *signed numbers*.

Zero

Negatives	*Positives*

$\dots -3 \quad -2 \quad -1 \quad -0 \quad +1 \quad +2 \quad +3 \dots$

The calculator does not designate positive with a plus but puts no symbol in front of (to the left of) the digits. Negatives are designated by preceding the digits with a minus $(-)$ sign.

The rules for addition and subtraction of signed numbers conform to the geometry of the number line and the mirror-image arrangement. The calculator takes these rules into account automatically. Briefly these rules are:

Positive + positive	= positive	$7 + 3 = 10$
Negative + negative	= negative	$-7 + (-3) = -10$
Positive + negative	Sign of number = with largest absolute value	$\begin{cases} 7 + (-3) = 4 \\ -7 + 3 = -4 \end{cases}$

The rules for multiplication and division are different and are actually simpler. Briefly, the sign of the result is $+$ if the signs of both operands (numbers) are the same (i.e., $+ +$ or $- -$); the result is negative

(−) if the signs of the operands are different (+ − or − +), with the order being irrelevant.

Example (a) $(-7)(-6) = (-7) \times (-6) = +42$
(b) $(-12) \div (-3) = +4$
On a calculator (a) would be calculated as

$$7 \; \boxed{+/-} \; \boxed{\times} \; 6 \; \boxed{+/-} \; \boxed{=}$$

Note the multiplication *implied* by adjacent parentheses. The $\boxed{+/-}$ key following each number inserts the minus sign.
  Expression (b) is calculated similarly as

$$12 \; \boxed{+/-} \; \boxed{\div} \; 3 \; \boxed{+/-} \; \boxed{=}$$

Notice that parentheses are only to clarify the expressions and are not needed here in the calculation.

Combined Operations

Very often more than one operation appears in an expression. We shall discuss some of those that can be easily evaluated without parentheses. Parentheses will be discussed in the next section.

Example The expression $7 + 2 \times 5$ is calculated on an AOS system as

$$7 \; \boxed{+} \; 2 \; \boxed{\times} \; 5 \; \boxed{=}$$

The result is 17. If you enter it in this order on an arithmetic system, you get 45, which is wrong! To avoid this, do the multiplication first:

$$2 \; \boxed{\times} \; 5 \; \boxed{+} \; 7 \; \boxed{=}$$

which is what the expression means anyway. If we did not have the hierarchy rules, the expression would be ambiguous and we would always need parentheses in order to clarify it.

Example $6 \div 3 + 3$ is calculated as $6 \; \boxed{\div} \; 3 \; \boxed{+} \; 3 \; \boxed{=}$, and the answer is 5 no matter which entry system you have. If the expression to be calculated were

$$\frac{6}{3 + 3}$$

then even though the fraction bar means ÷ and seems to come before the +, in fact the addition must be done first. By hand, the arithmetic is

$$\frac{6}{3+3} = \frac{6}{6} = 6 \div 6 = 1$$

To do this on a calculator requires keys other than the four basic operations (i.e., parentheses or memory or reciprocal). These will be discussed later in detail. The calculation, using parentheses, would look like this:

$$6 \;\boxed{\div}\; \boxed{(}\; 3 \;\boxed{+}\; 3 \;\boxed{)}\; \boxed{=}$$

and, in fact, the right parenthesis could be omitted.

Example   (4.3/1.7)(5) + 6.2 is easily calculated as 4.3 $\boxed{\div}$ 1.7 $\boxed{\times}$ 5 $\boxed{+}$ 6.2 $\boxed{=}$, and the result is 18.847059. If the problem were written as 6.2 + (4.3/1.7)(5), it could still be calculated the same way. If you have an AOS system, the $\boxed{+}$ could be entered first, but *not* on an arithmetic system.

In general, the rule for the four basic operations is multiplication and division are to be done before addition and subtraction, unless there are parentheses (or other notation) to indicate otherwise. If you have an AOS system, this is taken care of automatically.

Parentheses

The parentheses keys $\boxed{(}$ and $\boxed{)}$ are flags that tell the calculator to first compute the expression contained within the parentheses. The left parenthesis $\boxed{(}$ is the initial indicator; the right one $\boxed{)}$ acts somewhat like an equals and says "go ahead and compute everything that came before until you reach $\boxed{(}$."

Example   The expression 3 × (5 + 8) has the meaning shown in the following diagram:

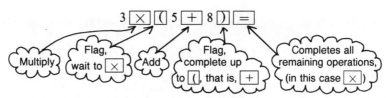

If we left out the right parenthesis $\boxed{)}$, the equals would cause *both* $\boxed{+}$ and $\boxed{\times}$ to be completed. The first parenthesis $\boxed{(}$ is still needed to tell the calculator to wait until the addition is done before doing the multiplication. That is, 3 $\boxed{\times}$ $\boxed{(}$ 5 $\boxed{+}$ 8 $\boxed{=}$ would give the same result.

Example   (7 + 5.1) × 4.2 is computed as $\boxed{(}$ 7 $\boxed{+}$ 5.1 $\boxed{)}$ $\boxed{\times}$ 4.2 $\boxed{=}$, giving a result of 50.82. Notice that the parentheses cause the addition to be done before the multiplication. On an AOS system, if we left the parentheses out, the multiplication would have been done first. On an arithmetic system, the addition would have been done first, since it was entered first.

To avoid the use of parentheses in this example, we could use $\boxed{=}$ to do what the parentheses do:

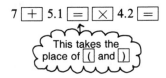

$$7 \boxed{+} 5.1 \boxed{=} \boxed{\times} 4.2 \boxed{=}$$

This takes the place of $\boxed{(}$ and $\boxed{)}$

Sometimes parentheses in expressions imply a multiplication and no parentheses need to be keyed on the calculator.

Example   8(4.7) means 8×4.7 and is calculated as $8 \boxed{\times} 4.7 \boxed{=}$, giving a result of 37.6. Note that no parentheses were keyed.

Example   (3.6)(1.2)/1.3 means $3.6 \boxed{\times} 1.2 \boxed{\div} 1.3 \boxed{=}$, giving a result of 3.3230769. Notice that no parentheses were keyed.

Parentheses are also used to set off negative numbers for clarity but are not keyed on the calculator.

Example $(-3) + 8.2(1.9)$ is calculated as $3 \boxed{+/-} \boxed{+} 8.2 \boxed{\times} 1.9 \boxed{=}$, giving 12.58 if you have an AOS system. If you have an arithmetic system, you must do the multiplication first:

$$8.2 \boxed{\times} 1.9 \boxed{+} 3 \boxed{+/-} \boxed{=}$$

in order to get the same result.

Example $7.5 - (-2.9)$ is calculated as $7.5 \boxed{-} 2.9 \boxed{+/-} \boxed{=}$, giving 10.4. Notice that no parentheses were needed and also that the minus signs had different meanings.

Example   If we try to compute $3 + 4[6 - 5(3 + 14)]$, we would try to key

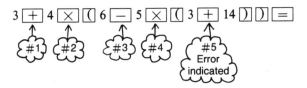

$$3 \boxed{+} 4 \boxed{\times} \boxed{(} 6 \boxed{-} 5 \boxed{\times} \boxed{(} 3 \boxed{+} 14 \boxed{)} \boxed{)} \boxed{=}$$

#1   #2   #3   #4   #5 Error indicated

As soon as we key the $\boxed{+}$ after the 3 inside the parentheses, we get an error indication. The reason is that the sequence of parentheses has caused too many operations to be pending (stored) before the computing begins. The last $\boxed{+}$ would have been the fifth operation, as indicated. Most calculators have a limit of four. If this is the case on your calculator, it can be overcome by starting at the *inner* parentheses and working your way out. That is, start with the 3 + 14. This is done as follows:

$$3 \boxed{+} 14 \boxed{)} \boxed{\times} 5 \boxed{+/-} \boxed{+} 6 \boxed{)} \boxed{\times} 4 \boxed{+} 3 \boxed{=}$$

and the result is −313. Notice that no left parentheses were needed, but certainly could have been included. The right parentheses acted like intermediate $\boxed{=}$ signs, which in fact could have been used in place of the parentheses in this example.

Example To compute $\dfrac{18}{2 \times 3}$, note that the fraction bar acts like parentheses as well as a division symbol. We calculate

$$18 \boxed{\div} \boxed{(} 2 \boxed{\times} 3 \boxed{)} \boxed{=} \quad \text{and get} \quad \boxed{3}.$$

We could even avoid parentheses by noticing that

$$\frac{18}{2 \times 3} = \frac{18}{2} \times \frac{1}{3} = \frac{18}{2} \div 3 = 18 \div 2 \div 3$$

so we key $18 \boxed{\div} 2 \boxed{\div} 3 \boxed{=}$. That is, we think of the original expression as "18 divided by 2, and then divided by 3." *Caution:* Notice that we do *not* key $18 \boxed{\div} 2 \boxed{\times} 3 \boxed{=}$, which gives 27, the *wrong answer*.

Example To compute $\dfrac{14 \times 45}{21 \times 5}$ without parentheses, key

$$14 \boxed{\times} 45 \boxed{\div} 21 \boxed{\div} 5 \boxed{=}$$

With parentheses, key

$$14 \boxed{\times} 45 \boxed{\div} \boxed{(} 21 \boxed{\times} 5 \boxed{=}$$

Notice that the right parenthesis is omitted since it was unnecessary. Had it been included, the intermediate product 21 × 5 = 105 would have been computed before the final result of 6 was obtained.

Scientific Notation

Scientific notation is a means of expressing very large or very small numbers in a convenient, systematic way. A number in this notation is expressed in two parts, the *mantissa*, which contains the significant digits, and the *exponent* (or *characteristic*), which gives information about the size of the number, that is, the location of the decimal point. The form looks like this:

$$M \times 10^p$$

The mantissa M is a decimal number less than 10 in absolute value, (i.e., between -10 and $+10$). The exponent p is written with base 10 and can be any integer. On the calculator it is limited to two digits, so it can go from -99 to $+99$. For instance, 7.03×10^{12} and 8.5×10^{-38} are expressions in scientific notation.

The *value* and rules for doing arithmetic with numbers in this form depend on the properties of the following pattern of *powers of* 10.

ten $=$	$10^1 =$	10
hundred $=$	$10^2 =$	100
thousand $=$	$10^3 =$	1000
ten thousand $=$	$10^4 =$	10,000

$$= 10^n = \underbrace{100 \ldots 0}_{n \text{ zeros}}$$

tenth $=$	$10^{-1} =$	0.1
hundredth $=$	$10^{-2} =$	0.01
thousandth $=$	$10^{-3} =$	0.001
ten thousandth $=$	$10^{-4} =$	0.0001

$$= 10^{-n} = \underbrace{0.00 \ldots 01}_{\substack{n \text{ zeros,} \\ \text{counting the} \\ \text{units place}}}$$

Notice that the absolute value of the exponent (power) equals the number of zeros in both cases, as long as the negative powers are written with a zero in the units (ones) place. Otherwise, for negative powers we would have $(n-1)$ zeros.

If we multiply any decimal number by these powers of ten, the effect is that multiplication by 10^k moves the decimal point k places (to the left, if k is negative, and to the right if k is positive).

Example

$3.42 \times 10^5 = 342000.$ (decimal moved 5 places to the right)

$3.42 \times 10^{-5} = 0.0000342$ (decimal moved 5 places to the left)

Thus 3.42×10^5 can be thought of as "3.42 with the decimal really five places to the right of where we see it in 3.42." The calculator would display the two numbers as $\boxed{\quad 3.42\ 05\quad}$ and $\boxed{\quad 3.42-05\quad}$, respectively.

Numbers in scientific notation are entered into the calculator by using the $\boxed{\text{EE}}$ key. EE stands for "enter exponent." Depending on the calculator model, there may be slight variations in the way this key works. On some calculators the key may look this way instead: $\boxed{\text{exp}}$. It would be treated the same way as the $\boxed{\text{EE}}$ key.

Example 7.32×10^6 is entered onto the display by keying

$7.32 \boxed{\text{EE}} 6$ and we read $\boxed{\quad 7.32\ 06\quad}$

Notice that the $\boxed{\times}$ key is not used. Before entering another number or continuing with a calculation, it is necessary to key $\boxed{=}$ or whatever operation one is performing.

Example 5.007×10^{-4} is entered as 5.007 $\boxed{EE}$ 4 $\boxed{+/-}$ and is displayed as

$$\boxed{\quad 5.007 - 04\quad}$$

Example -4.8×10^{-53} is entered as 4.8 $\boxed{+/-}$ $\boxed{EE}$ 53 $\boxed{+/-}$ and is displayed as

$$\boxed{\quad -4.8 - 53\quad}$$

Notice that neither a $\boxed{\times}$ nor the number 10 is keyed. The $\boxed{EE}$ takes care of this.

Once a number is entered onto the display, arithmetic is done as usual, whether the number is in scientific notation or not.

Example $(5 \times 10^6)(8.2 \times 10^{-3}) = (5 \times 10^6) \times (8.2 \times 10^{-3})$ is calculated as

$$5\ \boxed{EE}\ 6\ \boxed{\times}\ 8.2\ \boxed{EE}\ 3\ \boxed{+/-}\ \boxed{=}$$

The result is $\boxed{\quad 4.1\ 04\quad}$, which means 4.1×10^4. To convert to decimal form, we move the decimal the number of places indicated by the exponent, that is, four places to the right in this case, and get 41,000. The calculator can do this for you if desired by keying

$$\boxed{\times}\ 1\ \boxed{INV}\ \boxed{EE}\ \boxed{=}$$

On some calculators just keying $\boxed{INV}$ $\boxed{EE}$ will do it. Some calculators with *automatic* scientific notation will convert to decimal form automatically; you have no choice.

Example   To calculate $3 \times 10^5 - 10^4$, notice that the term $10^4 = 1 \times 10^4$ and thus that part can be entered as 1 $\boxed{EE}$ 4. Hence the expression in toto is calculated as

$$3\ \boxed{EE}\ 5\ \boxed{-}\ 1\ \boxed{EE}\ 4\ \boxed{=}\quad \text{and we get}\quad \boxed{\quad 2.9\ 05\quad}$$

which means 2.9×10^5. To change this into floating-point (decimal) notation, key

$$\boxed{\times}\ 1\ \boxed{INV}\ \boxed{EE}\ \boxed{=}\quad \text{which yields}\quad \boxed{\quad 290000\quad}$$

Notice that the decimal has moved exactly five places to the right and the exponent has vanished. You can do this mentally instead of relying on the calculator.

Example   To multiply $4,000,000,000 \times 320,000$ on your calculator, you must enter the 4 billion in scientific notation since it is too large to enter directly. Thus the decimal point that is *understood* in 4 billion after the last zero must be placed *behind* the 4 as 4.0, and then the 4.0 must be multiplied by the power of 10 that "tells" the decimal point where it really belongs (nine places to the right). Hence $4,000,000,000. = 4.0 \times 10^9$, and the zero only helps us to see where the decimal point is. It can also be written as 4×10^9, and hence the calculation is done as

$$4 \boxed{\text{EE}} \ 9 \boxed{\times} \ 320000 \boxed{=} \quad \text{and we read} \quad \boxed{1.28 \ 15}$$

which means 1.28×10^{15}. This cannot be converted on your calculator to floating point since it is too big to fit on the display in that form. On paper, however, one can move the decimal 15 places to the right and write $1,280,000,000,000,000.$

15 places

This number is read "one quadrillion, two hundred eighty trillion" which is clearly quite cumbersome. Hence we use scientific notation and merely read the symbols: "one-point-two-eight times ten-to-the-15th-power." Once we get to the higher powers, the old Latin names get to be both a numerical and linguistic nightmare, so we favor the symbolic names that scientific notation provides.

Numbers similar to scientific notation can also be entered using the $\boxed{\text{EE}}$ key. For instance 253×10^2 is *not* in scientific notation since 253 is more than 10, the limit for the mantissa. We call this more generally *exponential notation*. We could key $253 \boxed{\text{EE}} 2$ and it would be on the display. If we then key $\boxed{=}$, it is automatically converted to scientific notation, and we read $\boxed{\quad 2.53 \ 04}$ (unless you have automatic scientific notation, in which case it is converted to floating-point notation, specifically $25,300.$).

Caution: Do not enter a mantissa with more than five digits as the *integer* part of the number with the entry technique shown. You will get the wrong number entered.

Example $234,455 \times 10^2$ *cannot* be entered as $234455 \boxed{\text{EE}} 2 \boxed{=}$. If you try it, it will *seem* right, but here is what happens:

Key	Display
$234455 \boxed{\text{EE}}$	234455.
2	2344552.
$\boxed{=}$	2.3446 06

The displayed value *appears* to be correct, but if one looks at the display before $\boxed{=}$ was keyed, one sees that an exponential form was not there. Whereas the last value displayed seems to be the correct number in scientific notation with the last significant digit rounded up, in fact it is not. To see this, we convert to floating-point notation by keying

$$\boxed{\times}\ 1\ \boxed{\text{INV}}\ \boxed{\text{EE}}\ \boxed{=}\quad \text{and we get}\quad \boxed{2344552}$$

which is *not* what $234{,}455 \times 10^2$ equals. We should have 23445500. To enter the proper number try the following:

$$234455\ \boxed{\times}\ 1\ \boxed{\text{EE}}\ 2\ \boxed{=}$$

What we have done is enter $234455 \times 1 \times 10^2$, which equals the original number since the 1 does not affect the value; but what is different is that the mantissa is now 1, which is only one digit. If one now converts to floating point using the technique above, one would get the correct result.

Example Enter 2.34455×10^2 by simply keying $2.34455\ \boxed{\text{EE}}\ 2\ \boxed{=}$. This will be correct since the integer part of the mantissa is only one digit, even though the entire mantissa is six digits.

Simple Percentage

The word *percent* means "per hundred" or hundredths. The calculator expresses percentage as a decimal; for example, 6% means 6 hundredths = .06 in decimal notation. The percent key $\boxed{\%}$ has several functions. Its simplest is to move the decimal point two places to the left, which changes a percentage into a decimal. It does *not* change *into* a percent, but does aid in computing a *percentage* of some number.

Here is a summary of what the percent key can do:

1. (*number*) $\boxed{\%}$ divides the number keyed by 100 by moving the decimal point two places to the left; for example, 12 $\boxed{\%}$ becomes 0.12 on the display.
2. (*number*) $\boxed{\times}$ (*r*) $\boxed{\%}$ $\boxed{=}$ takes *r*% of a number; for example, 200 $\boxed{\times}$ 6 $\boxed{\%}$ $\boxed{=}$ takes 6% of 200, which equals 12.
3. (*number*) $\boxed{\div}$ (*r*) $\boxed{\%}$ $\boxed{=}$ divides a number by *r*%; for example, 300 $\boxed{\div}$ 6 $\boxed{\%}$ $\boxed{=}$ divides 300 by 6%, computing $300 \div 0.06 = 5000$.

Two very useful functions that novices tend to overlook are the add-on and discount capabilities.

4. (*number*) $\boxed{+}$ (*r*) $\boxed{\%}$ $\boxed{=}$ takes *r*% of a number and adds it to the original number, (i.e., increases the number by *r*%). For example, 200 $\boxed{+}$ 6 $\boxed{\%}$ $\boxed{=}$ adds 6% of 200 to 200, which gives $12 + 200 = 212$.

5. (*number*) $\boxed{-}$ (*r*) $\boxed{\%}$ $\boxed{=}$ takes *r*% of a number and then subtracts it from the original number; for example, 200 $\boxed{-}$ 6 $\boxed{\%}$ $\boxed{=}$ takes 6% of 200 and then subtracts it from 200 and computes $200 - 12 = 188$. That is, 200 is *discounted* by 6%.

There are three basic components to simple percentage problems: (1) the rate *R*, given as a percent (%); (2) the base *B*, which is the quantity of which a percentage (or part) is being considered; and (3) the percentage *P*, which is usually a part of the base having the same units as the base. For example, 20 is 10% of 200. The rate is 10%, the base is 200, and the percentage (or part) is 20. If the rate is more than 100%, the percentage (part) would in fact be more than the base (which explains why the word "part" is not generally used).

The relationship among these three quantities is expressed algebraically by the following formulas:

$$P = R \times B, \qquad R = P \div B, \qquad B = P \div R$$

and can be remembered by the following mnemonic device, sometimes referred to as the magic circle:

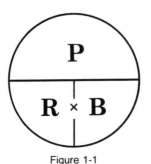

Figure 1-1

To use it, cover up the quantity that you want with your finger and the formula for it appears; for example, if you want *R*, cover the *R* in the diagram and read

$$\frac{P}{B}$$

which means $P \div B$.

Here are examples of the three basic percentage problems.

Example   What is 30% of 80? We know $R = 30\%$ and $B = 80$, and we want to compute *P*. By the formula $P = R \times B = 30\% \times 80$, so we key

$$30 \boxed{\%} \boxed{\times} 80 \boxed{=}$$

or, equivalently, we can key

$$80 \; \boxed{\times} \; 30 \; \boxed{\%} \; \boxed{=}$$

and get 24. Thus 24 is 30% of 80.

Example   576 is what percent of 3200? Here we know $P = 576$ and $B = 3200$, and we want to compute the rate R. Since $R = P/B = P \div B$, we simply key

$$576 \; \boxed{\div} \; 3200 \; \boxed{=}$$

and get 0.18. We must now interpret 0.18 as 18%. (Do *not* use the percent key to get the number as a percent. In fact, using the key does just the opposite. If you want the calculator to display the number of percent units when the decimal is displayed, multiply by 100.)

Example   Six is 20% of what number? Here we know the percentage $P = 6$ and the rate $R = 20\%$, and wish to compute the base B. Since $B = P/R = P \div R$, we simply key

$$6 \; \boxed{\div} \; 20 \; \boxed{\%} \; \boxed{=}$$

and get 30. Thus we have found that 6 is 20% of 30.

It is most important to identify the base when considering percentage problems that involve increase or decrease. The base is usually the *old* value. Some examples will make this intuitive idea clear.

Example   A dress that sold for $120 is now on sale for $80. What is the percent discount? The discount in dollars is $40. This is to be compared to the old price (the base) of $120. Thus the discount rate is $R = P \div B$, so we key

$$40 \; \boxed{\div} \; 120 \; \boxed{=} \quad \text{and read} \quad \boxed{.33333333}$$

which is 33.333333% = $33\frac{1}{3}\%$. If we had mistakenly used $80 as the base, we would have the wrong result.

Example   A drill press that sold for $80 last year has gone up in price to $120. What is the percent increase? The increase in dollars is $40, which is to be compared to the old price of $80 to get the rate $R = P \div B$, so we key $40 \; \boxed{\div} \; 80 \; \boxed{=}$ and get 0.5, which we interpret as 50%.

Notice that the two examples have the same numbers but different results due to the different base identification.

Solved Problems

BASIC OPERATIONS

1. Compute $2 + 4 \times 5$ on the calculator.

The expression means that 4 is to be multiplied by 5 and the result added to 2 since, unless parentheses indicate otherwise, multiplication is done before addition. Thus key

$$4 \boxed{\times} 5 \boxed{+} 2 \boxed{=} \quad \text{and the result is} \quad \boxed{22}$$

If you have an AOS system, the calculation can be done in the order given:

$$2 \boxed{+} 4 \boxed{\times} 5 \boxed{=}$$

which will *not* work with an arithmetic entry system. In that case you must either use the first method shown, or use parentheses:

$$2 \boxed{+} \boxed{(\!(} 4 \boxed{\times} 5 \boxed{=}$$

Notice that the right parenthesis was omitted. If it had been included, the intermediate product, $4 \times 5 = 20$, would have been displayed and then the $\boxed{=}$ would have completed the pending operation (addition).

2. Show that $(5 \times 8) \div 2 = 5 \times (8 \div 2)$.

$\boxed{(\!(} 5 \boxed{\times} 8 \boxed{)\!)} \boxed{\div} 2 \boxed{=}$ giving the result $\boxed{20}$. $5 \boxed{\times} \boxed{(\!(} 8 \boxed{\div} 2$ $\boxed{)\!)} \boxed{=}$ gives the same result.

3. Show that $(8 \div 2) \times 5 \neq 8 \div (2 \times 5)$.

$\boxed{(\!(} 8 \boxed{\div} 2 \boxed{)\!)} \boxed{\times} 5 \boxed{=}$ gives the result $\boxed{20}$. $8 \boxed{\div} \boxed{(\!(} 2 \boxed{\times} 5$ $\boxed{)\!)} \boxed{=}$ gives a different result: $\boxed{0.8}$.

4. Show how to calculate $8 \div (2 \times 5)$ without using parentheses keys.

$8 \div (2 \times 5)$ means $8/(2 \times 5)$, which equals $^8/_2 \times ^1/_5$, which in turn equals $(8/2) \div 5 = (8 \div 2) \div 5$. Thus we can compute it as $8 \boxed{\div}$ $2 \boxed{\div} 5 \boxed{=}$, giving $\boxed{0.8}$.

5. Convert the fraction $^5/_8$ into a decimal.

$^5/_8$ means 5 divided by 8. Thus calculate

$$5 \boxed{\div} 8 \boxed{=} \quad \text{which gives} \quad \boxed{0.625}$$

Thus $^5/_8 = 0.625$.

6. Add the fractions $\frac{1}{2} + \frac{1}{4}$ on your calculator, expressing the result as a decimal.

If you have an AOS system, divisions are automatically done before additions, so we simply key

1 $\div$ 2 $+$ 1 $\div$ 4 $=$ which gives | 0.75 |

You would get the wrong answer if you tried this on an *arithmetic* entry system. In this case, parentheses would be useful:

1 $\div$ 2 $+$ $($ 1 $\div$ 4 $=$

If you have no parentheses, you can accumulate (add) in the memory. There are several type of memory configurations. Here are two typical versions. First, clear the memory; then key

1 $\div$ 2 $=$ M+ 1 $\div$ 4 $=$ M+ MR

In another popular memory configuration, the calculation would take the following form:

1 $\div$ 2 $=$ STO 1 $\div$ 4 $=$ SUM RCL

Most, but not all, calculators with the latter configurations have parentheses. Clearly, the AOS system is best for this type of calculation.

7. Using your calculator, do the division 83)947 giving quotient and remainder.

83)947 means 947 $\div$ 83; thus compute 947 $\div$ 83 $=$ and the result is 11.409639. The quotient is the integer part of the result, that is, 11. The remainder is in decimal form and represents the integer remainder divided by 83. Thus, to get the whole number remainder, first remove the 11 by subtraction and then multiply the result by 83:

$-$ 11 $=$ $\times$ 83 $=$ which gives | 34 |

Thus 83 goes into 947 eleven times with a remainder of 34. In fraction form this can be interpreted as

$$\frac{947}{83} = 11\frac{34}{83}$$

8. Multiply 3 $\times$ 4.2 $\times$ 1.07 $\times$ 0.002.

Key 3 $\times$ 4.2 $\times$ 1.07 $\times$ .002 $=$. The product is | 0.026964 |.

9. Subtract ½ — ⅓, giving the result as a decimal.

If you have an AOS entry system, key

$$1 \boxed{\div} 2 \boxed{-} 1 \boxed{\div} 3 \boxed{=}$$

The result should be $\boxed{.16666667}$ or, if your calculator does not round off the last place, you may get $\boxed{.16666666}$. If you have an arithmetic entry system, you may have to use parentheses or the memory as in Problem 6. Yet another approach in this special case is to use the reciprocal key since both numerators are 1s:

$$2 \boxed{1/\times} \boxed{-} 3 \boxed{1/\times} \boxed{=}$$

10. Compute (a) 252 ÷ 3 ÷ 4 and (b) 252 ÷ (3 ÷ 4).

(a) Compute directly 252 $\boxed{\div}$ 3 $\boxed{\div}$ 4 $\boxed{=}$ and get the result 21. You have actually computed (252 ÷ 3) ÷ 4.

(b) If you have parentheses, key

$$252 \boxed{\div} \boxed{(\!(} 3 \boxed{\div} 4 \boxed{=}$$

and get the result 336. If you don't have parentheses, you must realize that 3 ÷ 4 is done first and the result divided *into* 252. Of course, 3 divided by 4 is so simple that the result can be done mentally or at least remembered. If the numbers were more complex, a memory would be useful, or a reciprocal key could be used as follows:

$$3 \boxed{\div} 4 \boxed{\div} 252 \boxed{=} \boxed{1/x}$$

What we have done here is divide *by* 252 and then the reciprocal gives the result as if we divided *into* 252.

If you don't have any of these keys, then you must really understand the numerical structure and realize that 3 ÷ 4 is just 3/4, and dividing 252 by 3/4 is the same as multiplying 252 by 4/3 (or 4 ÷ 3). Thus we could key

$$252 \boxed{\times} 4 \boxed{\div} 3 \boxed{=}$$

and again get the result 336.

SIGNED NUMBERS

11. Compute —(2.3 — 1.1).

Key 2.3 $\boxed{-}$ 1.1 $\boxed{=}$ $\boxed{+/-}$. The result is —1.2. If you don't have a key to change sign, you must place the — sign yourself. If you are going to work with signed numbers, you will want such a key. In this example, however, even if you have the key, you may just want to subtract and place the sign yourself.

12. Compute $-2.3 - 1.1$.

Key 2.3 $\boxed{+/-}$ $\boxed{-}$ 1.1 $\boxed{=}$. The result is -3.4. If you don't have a $\boxed{+/-}$ key, you must know that $-2.3 - 1.1 = -(2.3 + 1.1)$. Then just add and place the minus sign yourself.

13. Compute $1.8 - (-.3)$.

Key 1.8 $\boxed{-}$ .3 $\boxed{+/-}$ $\boxed{=}$, giving the result 2.1. Notice that parentheses are not needed in calculating. Alternatively, realize that $1.8 - (-.3) = 1.8 + .3$, so one can just add.

14. Compute $7.2 \div (-1.2)$.

Key 7.2 $\boxed{\div}$ 1.2 $\boxed{+/-}$ $\boxed{=}$, giving the result -6. *Caution: Do not use parentheses and the minus key.* (Even though some calculators will give you the correct answer if you do this, most will not. The method shown is preferred.)

15. Compute $-8.2 \times (-7.3)$.

Key 8.2 $\boxed{+/-}$ $\boxed{\times}$ 7.3 $\boxed{+/-}$ $\boxed{=}$, giving the result 59.86. Since a negative times a negative is a positive, we could have just keyed 8.2 $\boxed{\times}$ 7.3 $\boxed{=}$.

SCIENTIFIC NOTATION

16. Multiply $(5 \times 10^{28}) \times (6 \times 10^{17})$.

Key 5 $\boxed{EE}$ 28 $\boxed{\times}$ 6 $\boxed{EE}$ 17 $\boxed{=}$ and read $\boxed{\quad 3.\ 46}$, which is interpreted as 3×10^{46}. This represents a 3 followed by 46 zeros.

17. Multiply $10^{12} \times 10^{7}$ on your calculator.

Method 1 10 $\boxed{y^x}$ 12 $\boxed{\times}$ 10 $\boxed{y^x}$ 7 $\boxed{=}$. The result is $\boxed{\quad 1.\ 19}$ (i.e., $1 \times 10^{19} = 10^{19}$).

Method 2 Since $10^{12} = 1 \times 10^{12}$, we can enter the numbers using scientific notation as follows: 1 $\boxed{EE}$ 12 $\boxed{\times}$ 1 $\boxed{EE}$ 7 $\boxed{=}$, and again we get $1 \times 10^{19} = 10^{19}$, which represents a 1 followed by 19 zeros.

18. Multiply $200,000,000 \times 0.0000012345$ on your calculator.

The numbers are too big to enter directly. However, since $200,000,000 = 2 \times 10^8$ and $0.0000012345 = 1.2345 \times 10^{-6}$, we can enter the numbers using scientific notation and then multiply as follows:

$$2 \boxed{EE} 8 \boxed{\times} 1.2345 \boxed{EE} 6 \boxed{+/-} \boxed{=}$$

and we get $\boxed{\quad 2.469\ 02}$, which represents 2.469×10^2. We can change this into decimal notation by keying the following sequence:

$$\boxed{\times} 1 \boxed{INV} \boxed{EE} \boxed{=}$$

(On some calculators $\boxed{\text{INV}}$ $\boxed{\text{EE}}$ will do.) The result is 246.9, which could certainly have been obtained mentally by merely interpreting the power of 10 as moving the decimal point.

19. Perform the following multiplications:

(a) $(6.2 \times 10^{81}) \times (4.7 \times 10^9)$

(b) $10^{12} \times 10^{60}$

(c) $(7.4 \times 10^{63}) \times (9.26 \times 10^{52})$

(a) Key 6.2 $\boxed{\text{EE}}$ 81 $\boxed{\times}$ 4.7 $\boxed{\text{EE}}$ 9 $\boxed{=}$ and read $\boxed{\quad 2.914 \ 91\ }$, which represents 2.914×10^{91}.

(b) This can be done mentally using the rules of exponents, giving $10^{12+60} = 10^{72}$. To use the calculator for this, we enter

$$1 \ \boxed{\text{EE}} \ 12 \ \boxed{\times} \ 1 \ \boxed{\text{EE}} \ 60 \ \boxed{=}$$

and read $\boxed{\quad 1. \ 72\ }$, which is $1 \times 10^{72} = 10^{72}$.

(c) If we try to enter this in a manner similar to part (a), we get $\boxed{\text{Error}}$ or some display indication that we have violated the limits of the calculator. In this case it is because of *overflow* (the answer is too big). Thus we must do some of the work ourselves. We know that $10^{63} \times 10^{52} = 10^{63+52}$. Thus key 63 $\boxed{+}$ 52 $\boxed{=}$ and get the exponent $\boxed{\quad 115.\ }$.

Then key 7.4 $\boxed{\times}$ 9.26 $\boxed{=}$ to get the *mantissa* $\boxed{\quad 68.524\ }$, and thus the answer is 68.524×10^{115}. But this is *not* in *scientific* notation since 68.524 is bigger than 10. We shift the decimal and get 6.8524, and then increase the exponent by 1 to compensate for the decrease in the mantissa. The result in scientific notation is therefore 6.8524×10^{116}.

20. Compute $(8.7 \times 10^7) + (2.3 \times 10^2)$ and give the result in floating-point (decimal) notation.

First key 8.7 $\boxed{\text{EE}}$ 7 $\boxed{+}$ 2.3 $\boxed{\text{EE}}$ 2 $\boxed{=}$ and read $\boxed{\quad 8.7 \ 07\ }$, which is just the first number entered! The problem is that the second number is only significant in the hundreds place, which does not appear in the exponential form in this example. The calculator has, however, retained it internally. To see this, we change to floating-point notation. With the number still displayed, key $\boxed{\times}$ 1 $\boxed{\text{INV}}$ $\boxed{\text{EE}}$ $\boxed{=}$ (on some calculators $\boxed{\text{INV}}$ $\boxed{\text{EE}}$ will do it). The result is 87000230.

21. Compute $10^3 - 10^{-3}$.

Recall that $10^3 = 1 \times 10^3$. Thus we key

$$1 \ \boxed{\text{EE}} \ 3 \ \boxed{-} \ 1 \ \boxed{\text{EE}} \ 3 \ \boxed{+/-} \ \boxed{=} \quad \text{and read} \quad \boxed{\quad 1. \ 03\ }$$

which is just $1 \times 10^3 = 10^3$. This is just the first number! The reason for this is that 10^{-3} is so small compared to 10^3 that it does not show up in this form. We change to floating point to demonstrate this fact. Key $\boxed{+}$ 1 $\boxed{\text{INV}}$ $\boxed{\text{EE}}$ $\boxed{=}$ (or on some calculators just $\boxed{\text{INV}}$ $\boxed{\text{EE}}$) and read $\boxed{999.999}$.

22. Compute $(-4.3 \times 10^{23}) \div (-5.4 \times 10^{-24})$.

Key 4.3 $\boxed{+/-}$ $\boxed{\text{EE}}$ 23 $\boxed{\div}$ 5.4 $\boxed{+/-}$ $\boxed{\text{EE}}$ 24 $\boxed{+/-}$ $\boxed{=}$ and read $\boxed{7.963\ 46}$, which represents 7.963×10^{46}.

23. Compute $(-4.3 \times 10^{23}) \times (-5.4 \times 10^{-24})$.

Key 4.3 $\boxed{+/-}$ $\boxed{\text{EE}}$ 23 $\boxed{\times}$ 5.4 $\boxed{+/-}$ $\boxed{\text{EE}}$ 24 $\boxed{+/-}$ $\boxed{=}$ and read $\boxed{2.322\ 00}$, which represents $2.322 \times 10^0 = 2.322 \times 1 = 2.322$.

24. Calculate $(4.31 \times 10^6)(873.12 + 5 \times 10^{-3})$.

Notice that the parentheses imply a multiplication that must be calculated explicitly. The multiplication by powers of 10 is handled using scientific notation. Simply key 4.31 $\boxed{\text{EE}}$ 6 $\boxed{\times}$ $\boxed{(}$ 873.12 $\boxed{+}$ 5 $\boxed{\text{EE}}$ 3 $\boxed{+/-}$ $\boxed{)}$ $\boxed{=}$ and read $\boxed{3.7632\ 09}$, which represents 3.7632×10^9.

USE OF THE CONSTANT $\boxed{\text{K}}$

25. Multiply 9.3 by each of the following: 8.1, 0.3, and 5.2.

The constant multiplier is 9.3, which we set up as 9.3 $\boxed{\times}$ $\boxed{\text{K}}$. We then successively key

$$8.1 \boxed{=} \quad \text{and read the result} \quad \boxed{75.33}$$

$$.3 \boxed{=} \quad \text{and read the result} \quad \boxed{2.79}$$

$$5.2 \boxed{=} \quad \text{and read the result} \quad \boxed{48.36}$$

26. Add 3022 to each of the following numbers: 403, -850, and 6.3×10^3.

First key 3022 $\boxed{+}$ $\boxed{\text{K}}$, which sets up the constant addend. Then key successively

$$403 \boxed{=} \quad \text{and read} \quad \boxed{3425.}$$

$$850 \boxed{+/-} \boxed{=} \quad \text{and read} \quad \boxed{2172.}$$

$$6.3 \boxed{\text{EE}} 3 \boxed{=} \quad \text{and read} \quad \boxed{9.322\ 03}$$

To get this last result in floating-point (decimal) form, also key $\boxed{\times}$ 1 $\boxed{\text{INV}}$ $\boxed{\text{EE}}$ $\boxed{=}$ and get 9322. This process will, however, cancel the constant entry. You are better off doing this mentally if you have still other numbers to add.

27. Divide each of the following by 8.03; 16.06, -92.7, and 6.2×10^{-5}.

First set up the divisor 8.03 by keying 8.03 $\boxed{\div}$ $\boxed{\text{K}}$. Notice that in this case $\boxed{\div}$ is interpreted as *divided into*. Usually it is read as divided by. Then key each of the successive dividends:

16.06 $\boxed{=}$ and the result is $\boxed{\text{2.}}$

92.7 $\boxed{+/-}$ $\boxed{=}$ and read $\boxed{-11.544209}$

6.2 $\boxed{\text{EE}}$ 5 $\boxed{+/-}$ $\boxed{=}$ and read $\boxed{7.721-06}$, which is 7.721×10^{-6}

If we want this in decimal form, we key $\boxed{\times}$ 1 $\boxed{\text{INV}}$ $\boxed{\text{EE}}$ $\boxed{=}$ and get .00000772. (This cancels the constant. Notice that in this case we *lost* the digit 1 at the end. Actually, it is still contained internally in the calculator.)

COMBINED OPERATIONS

28. Calculate $\dfrac{802 + 4.7}{12.06}$

The fraction bar acts like parentheses. Thus we can key

$\boxed{(}$ 802 $\boxed{+}$ 4.7 $\boxed{)}$ $\boxed{\div}$ 12.06 $\boxed{=}$ and read $\boxed{66.890547}$

Alternatively, we could key

802 $\boxed{+}$ 4.7 $\boxed{=}$ $\boxed{\div}$ 12.06 $\boxed{=}$

If you have an *arithmetic* (i.e., sequential) entry system, the first equal sign could be omitted and one could simply key

802 $\boxed{+}$ 4.7 $\boxed{\div}$ 12.06 $\boxed{=}$

since each pending operation is immediately completed. This will *not* work on an AOS system. You would get a wrong result.

29. Calculate $\dfrac{200}{4.2 + 8.7}$

Again the fraction bar acts like parentheses, so key

200 $\boxed{\div}$ $\boxed{(}$ 4.2 $\boxed{+}$ 8.7 $\boxed{)}$ $\boxed{=}$ and read $\boxed{15.503876}$

This right parenthesis $\boxed{)}$ can be omitted.

30. Compute $\dfrac{6.2(4.3)}{3.1} - 9.8$.

Key 6.2 $\boxed{\times}$ 4.3 $\boxed{\div}$ 3.1 $\boxed{-}$ 9.8 $\boxed{=}$ and read the result, -1.2.

31. Compute $\dfrac{6.2}{3.1}(4.3 - 9.8)$.

Note the implied multiplication times the difference inside the parentheses. Here we key

6.2 $\boxed{\div}$ 3.1 $\boxed{\times}$ $\boxed{(}$ 4.3 $\boxed{-}$ 9.8 $\boxed{)}$ $\boxed{=}$

and read the result, −1.1. The right parenthesis $\boxed{)}$ could be omitted. The left parenthesis cannot. If you don't have parentheses, you must do the subtraction first:

$$4.3 \boxed{-} 9.8 \boxed{=} \boxed{\times} 6.2 \boxed{\div} 3.1 \boxed{=}$$

(If you have an arithmetic entry system, the first $\boxed{=}$ could be omitted.)

32. Calculate $\dfrac{6.3}{4.02} + 7.1(0.03)$.

With an AOS system, key

$$6.3 \boxed{\div} 4.02 \boxed{+} 7.1 \boxed{\times} .03 \boxed{=}$$

and read the result, 1.7801642. If you have an arithmetic entry system, parentheses are useful:

$$6.3 \boxed{\div} 4.02 \boxed{+} \boxed{(} 7.1 \boxed{\times} .03 \boxed{)} \boxed{=}$$

(If you have an arithmetic system without parentheses, the memory could be used. If you don't have memory capacity, there are some slightly inconvenient methods that involve rearranging the expression first. Better advice would be to use scratch paper in lieu of memory or buy a more convenient calculator.)

SIMPLE PERCENTAGE

33. Compute each of the following: (a) 63% of 742; (b) $^2/_5$% of 80; (c) 215% of 96; and (d) 6¾ % of 58.

(a) $63 \boxed{\%} \boxed{\times} 742 \boxed{=}$ and read the result, 467.46.

(b) $2 \boxed{\div} 5 \boxed{=} \boxed{\%} \boxed{\times} 80 \boxed{=}$ and read the result, 0.32.

(c) $215 \boxed{\%} \boxed{\times} 96 \boxed{=}$ and read the result, 206.4.

(d) $3 \boxed{\div} 4 \boxed{+} 6 \boxed{=} \boxed{\%} \boxed{\times} 58 \boxed{=}$ and read the result, 3.915.

34. How much is 24 increased by 12%?

Method 1   First compute 12% of 24 and then add the result to 24: $12 \boxed{\%} \boxed{\times} 24 \boxed{=}$ and read $\boxed{2.88}$, and now add $\boxed{+} 24 \boxed{=}$ and read the final result, $\boxed{26.88}$.

Method 2   Using the add-on feature of the calculator, this can be done in a sequential fashion reading intermediate results as follows:

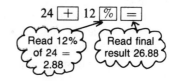

35. 12 is what percent of 25?

Compute the ratio $\dfrac{12}{25}$ and then interpret as a percent.

12 $\boxed{\div}$ 25 $\boxed{=}$ and read the display $\boxed{\quad 0.48 \quad}$

This can be interpreted as 48%. (If you wanted the calculator to display 48, multiply the displayed value by 100, which would move the decimal point to the right. *Caution*: Do *not* use the $\boxed{\%}$ key to change *into* percent. The percent key changes a given percent into a decimal for calculations.)

36. 2 is what percent of 8¼?

We want the ratio 2/8¼, which can be calculated as

2 $\boxed{\div}$ $\boxed{(}$ 1 $\boxed{\div}$ 4 $\boxed{+}$ 8 $\boxed{)}$ $\boxed{=}$

or if you can mentally change 8¼ into 8.25, then key

2 $\boxed{\div}$ 8.25 $\boxed{=}$ and in either case read $\boxed{\ .24242424\ }$, which we

round to two decimal places and then interpret as approximately 24%.

37. 14 is 60% of what number?

We compute 14 $\boxed{\div}$ 60 $\boxed{\%}$ $\boxed{=}$ and get $\boxed{\ 23.333333\ }$. (If you are alert, you will recognize this as $23\frac{1}{3}$.)

38. The retail price of gasoline has increased from 55¢ per gallon to $1.25 per gallon. What percent increase is this?

The increase in cents is calculated as 125 $\boxed{-}$ 55 $\boxed{=}$, which is 70 cents. With this number still displayed, calculate a ratio by keying $\boxed{\div}$ 55 $\boxed{=}$ and read $\boxed{\ 1.2727273\ }$. This is interpreted as approximately 127%. What has been computed is the quantity

$$\frac{125 - 55}{55}$$

and then, mentally, this ratio is changed to a percent.

MISCELLANEOUS TECHNIQUES

39. Enter the number 888666. $\times$ 10² into the calculator using the $\boxed{\text{EE}}$ key.

If you try to enter this number directly, you won't get the correct entry since the mantissa contains an integer part of more than five digits, the limit of most calculators. There are two practical ways of handling this situation:

Method 1 Change the number given mentally into scientific notation, 8.88666 × 10⁷, and enter it as

$$8.88666 \boxed{EE}\; 7 \boxed{=}$$

and read the display $\boxed{8.8867\ 07}$. To check that this
is correct, change to floating-point form by keying

$$\boxed{\times}\; 1 \boxed{INV} \boxed{EE} \boxed{=}\quad \text{and read}\quad \boxed{88866600}$$

Method 2 Since 888666. × 10² = 888666 × 1 × 10², simply key

$$888666 \boxed{\times}\; 1 \boxed{EE}\; 2 \boxed{=}$$

If you convert to floating point as shown in method 1,
you will see that the same number has been entered.

(If you attempt 888666 $\boxed{EE}$ 2 and then change to floating point,
you will see that the wrong number has been entered. This quirk
may be corrected on future versions of the calculator logic by some
manufacturers.)

40. Add the long multidigit numbers 843256075843 and 6578111254 on
the calculator without losing any digits.

The strategy is to use your calculator on parts of the addition problem and then merge the two results. This is done by partitioning the
numbers as shown. The partitioning is arbitrary, except that the individual pieces should be short enough to fit onto the calculator display.

$$84325\,|\,6075843$$
$$+\quad 657\,|\,8111254$$

$$1\,|\,4187097 \leftarrow 6075843 \boxed{+} 8111254 \boxed{=}$$

$$84325 \boxed{+} 657 \boxed{=} \rightarrow 84982\,|$$

$$84983\,|\,4187097 \quad \text{Add by hand. This is easy}$$
since there is only one
overlapping pair of digits.

41. Multiply 897,888 × 78,022 on your calculator retaining all digits.

If we did this in the ordinary way, we would get this in scientific notation. Instead notice that 78,022 = 78,000 + 22. Thus we first
multiply 897,888 by 78 and then append three zeros to the result.
Then we multiply by 22 and add it to the previous expression
obtained. What we have done is to rewrite the problem like this:

$$897{,}888 \times (78{,}000 + 22) = 897{,}888 \times 78{,}000 + 897{,}888 \times 22$$
$$897888 \boxed{\times} 78 \boxed{=}\quad \text{which gives } 70{,}035{,}264$$
$$897888 \boxed{\times} 22 \boxed{=}\quad \text{which gives } 19{,}753{,}536$$

We then append three zeros to the first result and add the second result to it. This can be done by the partitioning technique, as shown:

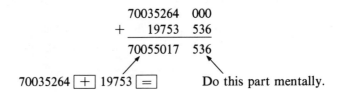

$$\begin{array}{r} 70035264 \quad 000 \\ +\quad 19753 \quad 536 \\ \hline 70055017 \quad 536 \end{array}$$

70035264 $\boxed{+}$ 19753 $\boxed{=}$ Do this part mentally.

2
Elementary Algebra

Basic Functions $\boxed{x^2}$ $\boxed{\sqrt{x}}$ $\boxed{1/x}$

The function $\boxed{x^2}$ *squares* the number in the display: that is, it multiplies the number by itself.

Example Keying 1.5 $\boxed{x^2}$ will give the result $\boxed{2.25}$. This means that $1.5^2 = (1.5) \times (1.5) = 2.25$. The letter x on the key refers to the number displayed before it is pressed, in this case 1.5.

Squaring any number will *never* give a negative result. The result is always positive except when $x = 0$, since $0^2 = 0$.

The function $\boxed{\sqrt{x}}$ takes the *square root* of the number on display. It answers the question, "what number squared, gives x?"

Example What number squared is 256? The answer is $\sqrt{256}$. To compute this, key 256 $\boxed{\sqrt{x}}$ and read $\boxed{16.}$ This is correct since we can easily check that $16^2 = 16 \times 16 = 256$.

In other words, $\boxed{\sqrt{x}}$ does just the opposite of $\boxed{x^2}$. In fact, when x is nonnegative, they are inverse functions.

31

Example

Notice that the square root has undone what the square did.

When x (the displayed number) is negative and you square it, and then take the square root, you will *not* get the minus sign back, since $\boxed{\sqrt{x}}$ gives only the positive square root, even though there are two square roots of any positive number.

Example First square -3.12: 3.12 $\boxed{+/-}$ $\boxed{x^2}$ and read $\boxed{9.7344}$. Now take the square root $\boxed{\sqrt{x}}$ and read $\boxed{3.12}$. Notice that we got $+3.12$, not -3.12. You must be aware of which sign you want to use when you take the square root and put it in manually if needed.

You *cannot* take the square root of a negative number. If you try you will get an error indication.

The function $\boxed{1/x}$ takes the *reciprocal* of the displayed number; that is, it divides the display value *into* the number 1.

Example To compute the reciprocal of 2.5, we want to calculate the value of $1/2.5$, so we simply key.

$$2.5 \boxed{1/x} \quad \text{and read} \quad \boxed{0.4}$$

Thus $1/2.5 = 0.4$.

The reciprocal is its own inverse. That is, it will undo itself. If we key it twice, it will take you back to the number at which you started.

Example

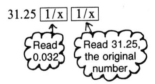

The reciprocal works on any number *except zero*. If 0 is on display and you key $\boxed{1/x}$, you will get an error indication.

A useful trick that makes use of the reciprocal is in the situation when you want to divide a number *already* on display *into* another number. This procedure makes use of the fact that

$$\frac{1}{(a/b)} = \frac{b}{a}$$

Just divide the displayed number *by* the second number, and then take the reciprocal.

Example If 16.42 is already displayed and we wish to divide it *into* 57.8, instead of starting over, divide *by* 57.8 and then take the reciprocal. To see how this would work, key

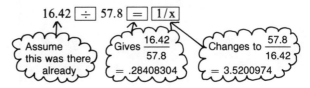

If you key 57.8 $\boxed{\div}$ 16.42 $\boxed{=}$, you will get the same result.

Substitution in Simple Expressions and Formulas

An algebraic expression is a numerical expression with letters used in place of numbers. The notation of algebra must be translated into the language of the calculator and the letters replaced with numbers when an actual calculation is to be done. Table 2-1 gives some of the most common elementary equivalences.

Table 2-1.

ALGEBRAIC	CALCULATOR EQUIVALENT	
$a + b$	$a \boxed{+} b \boxed{=}$	
ab	$a \boxed{\times} b \boxed{=}$	Arithmetic Functions
$\dfrac{a}{b}$	$a \boxed{\div} b \boxed{=}$	
$a - b$	$a \boxed{-} b \boxed{=}$	
$\sqrt{a}$	$a \boxed{\sqrt{x}}$	Algebraic Functions
a^2	$a \boxed{x^2}$	
$\dfrac{1}{a}$	$a \boxed{1/x}$	

The more common algebraic expressions are combinations of these. They are handled slightly differently in the two kinds of entry systems, AOS (which takes hierarchy into account automatically) and arithmetic systems (which perform operations sequentially in the order in which they are entered), as seen in Table 2-2. The main difference is that extra parentheses must sometimes be inserted with arithmetic systems. This can often be avoided by simply rearranging the terms of the given expression.

Table 2-2.

ALGEBRA	AOS SYSTEM	ARITHMETIC SYSTEM
$a + bc$	$a\boxed{+}b\boxed{\times}c\boxed{=}$	$a\boxed{+}\boxed{(}b\boxed{\times}c\boxed{=}$
		(or $b\boxed{\times}c\boxed{+}a\boxed{=}$)
$ab + cd$ (sum of products)	$a\boxed{\times}b\boxed{+}c\boxed{\times}d\boxed{=}$	$a\boxed{\times}b\boxed{+}\boxed{(}c\boxed{\times}d\boxed{=}$ (or use the memory)
$a + \dfrac{b}{c}$	$a\boxed{+}b\boxed{\div}c\boxed{=}$	$a\boxed{+}\boxed{(}b\boxed{\div}c\boxed{=}$
		(or $b\boxed{\div}c\boxed{+}a\boxed{=}$)
$\dfrac{1}{a+b}$	$1\boxed{\div}\boxed{(}a\boxed{+}b\boxed{=}$	Same as AOS
	(or $a\boxed{+}b\boxed{=}\boxed{1/x}$)	
$(a+b)(c+d)$ (product of sums)	$a\boxed{+}b\boxed{=}\boxed{\times}\boxed{(}$	$a\boxed{+}b\boxed{\times}\boxed{(}c\boxed{+}d\boxed{=}$
	$c\boxed{+}d\boxed{=}$	
ar^2	$a\boxed{\times}r\boxed{x^2}\boxed{=}$	Same as AOS
$\dfrac{1}{\sqrt{a}} = \sqrt{\dfrac{1}{a}}$	$a\boxed{\sqrt{x}}\boxed{1/x}$	Same as AOS
	(or $a\boxed{1/x}\boxed{\sqrt{x}}$)	
$ar^2 + br$	$a\boxed{\times}r\boxed{STO}\boxed{x^2}\boxed{+}$	$a\boxed{\times}r\boxed{STO}\boxed{x^2}$
	$b\boxed{\times}\boxed{RCL}\boxed{=}$	$\boxed{+}\boxed{(}b\boxed{\times}\boxed{RCL}\boxed{=}$

There are of course more complex expressions, but all are only variations, extensions, and combinations of those shown in the preceding table. If you carefully study how expressions like these are computed, you should have no trouble putting them together in more elaborate cases.

Example   If $f = \dfrac{S_1 S_2}{S_1 + S_2}$ and $S_1 = 25$, $S_2 = -100$, then to compute the value of f, substitute into the right-hand side:

$$\frac{(25)(-100)}{25 + (-100)} = \frac{25(-100)}{25 - 100}$$

and calculate:

$25\boxed{\times}100\boxed{+/-}\boxed{\div}\boxed{(}25\boxed{-}100\boxed{=}$ and read $\boxed{33.333333}$

Note the use of a parenthesis for the denominator.

Sometimes formulas or expressions are in tabular form to be evaluated for several values of the same variable (letter). If only one operation is involved, the constant $\boxed{K}$ can be useful.

Example   To complete the table of values of *W* corresponding to various values of *F*, where the value of *d* = 6.2 in all cases,

F	W = Fd
10.3	
15.7	
23.2	

set up the constant *d* as 6.2 $\boxed{\times}$ $\boxed{\text{K}}$ and key each subsequent entry followed by $\boxed{=}$:

$$10.3 \boxed{=} \quad \text{and record} \quad F = 63.86$$

$$15.7 \boxed{=} \quad \text{and record} \quad F = 97.34$$

$$23.2 \boxed{=} \quad \text{and record} \quad F = 143.84$$

Powers and Roots

Any expression of the form y^x is known as a *power function* when the exponent *x* is a constant and the base *y* is permitted to vary. When the base *y* is constant, it is called an *exponential function*.

Example   The expression y^5 is a power function. The expression 5^x is an exponential function.

Calculators compute numerical expressions, so we cannot refer to say 3^5 as a power function or an exponential function on the basis of the preceding definitions unless we know where it came from. However, when the constant is used in conjunction with the $\boxed{y^x}$ key, we can only make the power *x* constant, and hence we refer to this as the power function even when we are using it to evaluate exponential functions.

There is one important restriction on the value of *y* when using the power function: *y* may never be negative when entering it into the calculator. On the other hand, *x* can be any real number.

(One technical matter: the expression 0^0 is computed on the calculator as 1, but it is really *indeterminate*. However, for most elementary well-behaved functions, it will usually be 1; actually, it can be made to equal *any number*, which is why it is called an indeterminate form, which is studied in calculus. Some calculators will indicate an error.)

For positive integer powers (i.e., 1, 2, 3, . . .), the meaning of y^x is clear:

$$y^x = y \times y \times y \times \cdots \times y \quad (x \text{ times})$$

Thus, for positive integer powers, the power function is just a shorthand for a repeated multiplication. On the other hand, an expression like $y^{.27}$ cannot be defined in terms of elementary arithmetic operations.

35

The inverse of the power function is the *root* $^x\sqrt{y}$. It can also be expressed in the equivalent form $y^{1/x}$, which gives us two ways to calculate such expressions. Different calculators denote this function slightly differently. The most common two ways are

$$\boxed{\text{INV}}\ \boxed{\text{y}^\text{x}} \quad \text{and} \quad \boxed{\text{2nd}}\ \boxed{^x\sqrt{\text{y}}}$$

In both cases it is used in conjunction with $\boxed{=}$.

Example   To compute 3^5, key 3 $\boxed{\text{y}^\text{x}}$ 5 $\boxed{=}$ and read the answer, 243. Thus the fifth power of 3 is 243.

Example   To compute $^3\sqrt{8}$, key 8 $\boxed{\text{INV}}$ $\boxed{\text{y}^\text{x}}$ 3 $\boxed{=}$ and read the answer, 2. The cube root of 8 is 2. On some calculators the key sequence might look like this:

$$8\ \boxed{\text{2nd}}\ \boxed{^x\sqrt{\text{y}}}\ 3\ \boxed{=}$$

The following table summarizes the key sequences for computing powers and roots:

ALGEBRA	KEY SEQUENCE
a^b	a $\boxed{\text{y}^\text{x}}$ b $\boxed{=}$
$^b\sqrt{a}$	a $\boxed{\text{INV}}$ $\boxed{\text{y}^\text{x}}$ b $\boxed{=}$
	(or a $\boxed{\text{2nd}}$ $\boxed{^x\sqrt{\text{y}}}$ b $\boxed{=}$)
Equivalent form: $a^{1/b}$	a $\boxed{\text{y}^\text{x}}$ b $\boxed{1/\text{x}}$ $\boxed{=}$

Example   To compute $^3\sqrt{8}$ using the exponent form, we calculate $8^{1/3}$ by keying

$$8\ \boxed{\text{y}^\text{x}}\ 3\ \boxed{1/\text{x}}\ \boxed{=}$$

and we get the correct result, 2.

It is helpful to read $\boxed{\text{y}^\text{x}}$ as "raised to the power." a $\boxed{\text{y}^\text{x}}$ b $\boxed{=}$ would be read as "a raised to the power b is"; thus it is clear as you calculate that a^b is being computed. Otherwise, 3^5 and 5^3 could be easily confused.

More directly, remember that for powers the base is entered first, and for roots the radicand (the number inside the radical symbol) is entered first.

Unfortunately, when we use the constant $\boxed{\text{K}}$ in conjunction with the power function, the number x, the exponent, is entered first since it is the exponent that is being held constant. This is also true for roots, for it is the index of the radical that is held constant. That is, the symbol x is the quantity that is made constant in both cases and hence is entered first. The use of the constant with powers and roots is summarized in the following table:

ALGEBRA	CALCULATOR KEY SEQUENCE
y^p, p constant	p $\boxed{y^x}$ $\boxed{K}$ y $\boxed{=}$ (follow with subsequent values of y, and then $\boxed{=}$)
$\sqrt[p]{y}$, p constant	p $\boxed{INV}$ $\boxed{y^x}$ $\boxed{K}$ y $\boxed{=}$ (follow with subsequent values of y, and then $\boxed{=}$)
Equivalent form: $y^{1/p}$, p constant	p $\boxed{1/x}$ $\boxed{y^x}$ $\boxed{K}$ y $\boxed{=}$ (follow with subsequent values of y, and then $\boxed{=}$)

Notice that when using the constant caution must be exercised, since it is the power that is entered first. This is the opposite procedure than that used for single calculations.

Example To compute 2^3, 1.6^3, and 7^3, first key 3 $\boxed{y^x}$ $\boxed{K}$, which sets up 3 as the constant exponent. Then key

$$2 \boxed{=} \quad \text{and read} \quad 8. = 2^3$$
$$1.6 \boxed{=} \quad \text{and read} \quad 4.096 = 1.6^3$$
$$7 \boxed{=} \quad \text{and read} \quad 343. = 7^3$$

Example To compute $\sqrt[3]{2}$, $\sqrt[3]{1.6}$, and $\sqrt[3]{7}$, first key 3 $\boxed{INV}$ $\boxed{y^x}$ $\boxed{K}$, which will set up 3 as the root index. Then subsequently key

$$2 \boxed{=} \quad \text{and read} \quad 1.259921 \; = \sqrt[3]{2}$$
$$1.6 \boxed{=} \quad \text{and read} \quad 1.1696071 = \sqrt[3]{1.6}$$
$$7 \boxed{=} \quad \text{and read} \quad 1.9129312 = \sqrt[3]{7}$$

If we had started by keying 3 $\boxed{1/x}$ $\boxed{y^x}$ $\boxed{K}$, we would have been looking at the expressions as y raised to the $1/3$ power for various values of y and would get the same results.

One should be cautious when trying to evaluate expressions with negative bases, such as $(-6)^4$. If one tries to key 6 $\boxed{+/-}$ $\boxed{y^x}$ 4 $\boxed{=}$, an error condition is created because the restriction of bases for the power function to positive numbers only (or 0) has been violated. Nevertheless, the number does have a value. If you realize that $(-6)^4 = (-1)^4(6)^4 = 1(6)^4 = 6^4$, you can just compute 6^4 and get 1296. If you did not know this algebraic fact, you might think that $(-6)^4$ did not exist, which is not at all true.

On the other hand, don't think that you have only to take the positive base to the same power. For example, $(-6)^3$ is handled a bit differently. Notice that $(-6)^3 = (-1)^3(6)^3 = -1(6)^3 = -6^3$. Thus we compute 6^3 and place a minus sign in front of it. We would find that $(-6)^3 = -216$.

To summarize, *integer* powers of negative numbers are $+$ for even powers and are $-$ for odd powers. A similar principle applies to roots, except that even roots of negative numbers *do not exist* as real numbers (they are known as *imaginary numbers*), and odd roots are equal to the same root of the corresponding positive number, and then precede the result with a minus $(-)$ sign.

Example Compute $\sqrt[4]{-5}$ and $\sqrt[3]{-5}$. The $\sqrt[4]{-5}$ does not exist as a real number. The $\sqrt[3]{-5} = -\sqrt[3]{5}$, so we calculate

$$5 \boxed{\text{INV}} \boxed{y^x} 3 \boxed{=} \quad \text{and read} \quad \boxed{1.7099759}$$

so that $\sqrt[3]{5} = 1.7099759$ and hence $\sqrt[3]{-5} = -\sqrt[3]{5} = -1.7099759$. Notice that we placed the minus sign manually. We could have pressed the change sign key to have it displayed, but why bother unless the result is to be used immediately for a subsequent calculation?

If you tried to compute both quantities in the preceding example directly, you would get an error indication in both cases, and yet one exists and the other does not. You must rely on your mathematical knowledge in some cases, as well as the power of the calculator, or you can easily be misled.

A special situation concerns integer powers of 10. Numbers like 10^5 in an expression can be entered using the $\boxed{\text{EE}}$ key, as well as the $\boxed{y^x}$ key.

Example To compute 10^5 in two ways:
(1) Key $10 \boxed{y^x} 5 \boxed{=}$ and read the result, 100,000.
(2) $10^5 = 1 \times 10^5$, so key $1 \boxed{\text{EE}} 5 \boxed{=}$ and read $\boxed{1.\ 05}$.
This can be changed into floating point by keying $\boxed{\text{x}} 1 \boxed{\text{INV}} \boxed{\text{EE}} \boxed{=}$, and again the result is 100,000. The only difference in the two methods is the form in which the calculator treats the number in the course of the calculation.

However, other powers of 10 (e.g., $10^{2.7}$, $10^{1/12}$) all require $\boxed{y^x}$. Specifically, for fractional powers, there are two ways to handle the calculation since

$$y^{p/q} = \sqrt[q]{y^p}, \qquad p,\ q \text{ integers, } q \neq 0$$

For the form $y^{p/q}$, think of it as $y^{(p/q)}$; for the radical form, think of it as a power and a root taken in succession. These ideas are summarized in the following table:

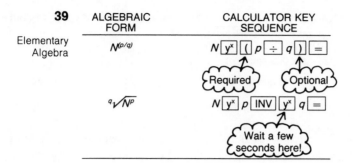

ALGEBRAIC FORM	CALCULATOR KEY SEQUENCE
$N^{(p/q)}$	$N\ \boxed{y^x}\ \boxed{(}\ p\ \boxed{\div}\ q\ \boxed{)}\ \boxed{=}$
$\sqrt[q]{N^p}$	$N\ \boxed{y^x}\ p\ \boxed{INV}\ \boxed{y^x}\ q\ \boxed{=}$

Linear Equations and Proportions

A *linear equation in one variable* is any equation that can be put in the form $ax = b$. A *proportion*, which is just the statement of equality of two ratios (fractions), is just a linear equation when one of the components of the proportion is unknown.

Using a calculator for equations simply involves solving algebraically for the variable as a numerical expression and then calculating.

Example Solve $3x - 7 = 30.2$. First add 7 to both sides:

$$\begin{array}{rcl} 3x - 7 & = & 30.2 \\ +7 & & +7 \\ \hline 3x & = & 37.2 \end{array}$$

Now divide both sides by 3, which cancels:

$$\frac{\cancel{3}x}{\cancel{3}} = \frac{37.2}{3}$$

Finally, calculate the expression formed on the right-hand side:

$$37.2\ \boxed{\div}\ 3\ \boxed{=}\quad \text{and read}\quad \boxed{12.4}$$

Thus $x = 12.4$ is the solution.

A more efficient way is to calculate while solving mentally. The concept of *transposing terms* is extremely useful here. Transposing terms involves moving a term to the other side of the equation and at the same time changing its sign.

A basic scheme for using transposition for mental calculation is illustrated next.

Elementary
Algebra

Solve $ax + b = c$

$ax \quad = c - b$ (transpose b)

$x \quad = \dfrac{c - b}{a}$ (divide by a)

$c \boxed{-} b \boxed{=}$

$\boxed{\div} a \boxed{=}$ (read solution)

The method indicated is used to get the solution without ever writing down the algebraic steps on the left. The whole process is done mentally, with the calculator keeping track of each step.

Example Solve $5x - 3 = 13$ without writing any algebraic steps by simply keying

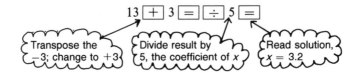

$$13 \boxed{+} 3 \boxed{=} \boxed{\div} 5 \boxed{=}$$

Transpose the -3; change to $+3$ — Divide result by 5, the coefficient of x — Read solution, $x = 3.2$

    Solving proportions uses basically the same procedure; that is, isolate the unknown by appropriate multiplication and/or division and then calculate. The basic form of a proportion is

$$\frac{x}{a} = \frac{b}{c}$$

To solve for x, multiply both sides by a:

$$\frac{(a)x}{a} = \frac{b(a)}{c}$$

and then calculate $b \boxed{\times} a \boxed{\div} c \boxed{=}$.

    It is easier to mentally think of the a as moving to the other side of the equation like this:

$$\frac{x}{} = \frac{a}{} \frac{b}{c}$$

so that you can mentally solve the proportion and go straight to the calculator.

Example To solve $a/x = b/c$ for x, mentally, we simply move terms as follows:

$$\frac{a}{} = \frac{x}{} \frac{b}{c} \quad \text{first move the } x$$

$$\frac{a}{b}\frac{c}{} = \frac{x}{}$$ Next move the b and c which isolates the x

Just think "the c moves to the top next to the a; b moves to the bottom, under the a and c." This procedure is simply based on the fact that such changes are equivalent to multiplying both sides of the equation by the same quantities.

Example Solve the proportion $4/x = 3.2/12$ mentally and calculate as you proceed. Think "the x moves to the top of the right side."

$$\frac{4}{} = \frac{3.2}{12}\frac{x}{}$$

Think "the 12 moves next to the 4," and calculate $4 \boxed{\times} 12$. Then "3.2 moves to the bottom," and compute $\boxed{\div} 3.2 \boxed{=}$. Read the result, $x = 15$.

Quadratic Equations

A *quadratic equation* is any equation that can be written in the form

$$ax^2 + bx + c = 0 \qquad (a \neq 0)$$

If the left-hand side can be *factored*, that is, written in the form $(x - r)$ $(x - s) = 0$, we can mentally see that $x = r$ and $x = s$ are the *roots* (solutions) of the equation, since when we substitute them (one at a time), they each make the expression equal zero:

Substituting r: $(r - r)(r - s) = 0(r - s) = 0$

Substituting s: $(s - r)(s - s) = (s - r)0 = 0$

Once one can factor the quadratic expression, there is virtually no need for the calculator, so we shall not discuss factoring techniques here. However, the theoretical concept of factoring gives us a useful computational technique for calculating one root if we already know what the other root is. If the roots are denoted by x_1 and x_2, then $(x - x_1)(x - x_2)$ $= 0$. If we multiply this out, we get

$$x^2 - (x_1 + x_2)x - x_1 x_2 = 0$$

If the original equation is $ax^2 + bx + c = 0$, we can make the coefficient of x^2 match the previous expression by dividing by a and get

$$x^2 + \frac{b}{a}x + \frac{c}{a} = 0$$

and compare with

$$x^2 - (x_1 + x_2)\, x + x_1 x_2 = 0$$

and see that the product of the roots $x_1 x_2$ must equal c/a, which is just the ratio of two of the coefficients.

Example   In the equation $3x^2 - 5x + 2 = 0$, the roots x_1 and x_2 (whatever their values) must satisfy the condition

$$x_1 x_2 = \frac{2}{3}$$

where the numbers 2 and 3 are taken from the coefficients in the quadratic equation.

If we know the value of one of the roots, we can use this result to find the other root by a simple division.

Example $x = -1$ is a root of the equation $2x^2 + 5x + 3 = 0$. To find the second root, use $x_1 x_2 = c/a$:

$$x_1 x_2 = \frac{3}{2} \qquad \text{where } x_1 = -1 \text{ (this was given)}$$

so that

$$(-1)x_2 = \frac{3}{2}$$

and we see that

$$x_2 = -\frac{3}{2}$$

The most important use of the calculator with quadratic equations is when the equation will not factor. In this case, the general equation has been solved for x to yield the two roots:

$$x = \frac{-b \pm \sqrt{b^2 - 4ac}}{2a} \qquad \text{(quadratic formula)}$$

where one root uses the minus $(-)$ sign and the other uses the plus $(+)$ sign of the radical. The letters a, b, and c are the coefficients of the original equation $ax^2 + bx + c = 0$.

Example   In the equation $x^2 - 3x + 5 = 0$, $a = 1$, $b = -3$, and $c = +5$. These values are then substituted in the formula for the roots, and the expression for the solution would look like this:

$$x = \frac{-(-3) \pm \sqrt{(-3)^2 - 4(1)\,(5)}}{2(1)}$$

The strategy for directly calculating the two roots using the formula is to compute the radical first, store it in the memory (so we won't have to compute it again), and then use it to complete the calculation of the two roots. The procedure is summarized as follows:

Step 1   Compute $\sqrt{b^2 - 4ac}$: b $\boxed{x^2}$ $\boxed{-}$ 4 $\boxed{\times}$ a $\boxed{\times}$ c $\boxed{=}$ $\boxed{\sqrt{x}}$

Step 2   Store it in memory: $\boxed{STO}$ (the value will remain displayed)

Step 3   Compute x_1: $\boxed{+}$ b $\boxed{+/-}$ $\boxed{=}$ $\boxed{\div}$ 2 $\boxed{\div}$ a $\boxed{=}$ (record x_1)

Step 4   Recall radical, change sign, compute x_2: $\boxed{RCL}$ $\boxed{+/-}$ $\boxed{+}$ b $\boxed{+/-}$ $\boxed{=}$ $\boxed{\div}$ 2 $\boxed{\div}$ a $\boxed{=}$ (record x_2)

Example   To solve the equation $2x^2 + 5x + 3 = 0$ using the quadratic formula, first note that $a = 2$, $b = 5$, and $c = 3$. When you substitute, you get

$$x = \frac{-5 \pm \sqrt{5^2 - 4(2)(3)}}{2(2)}$$

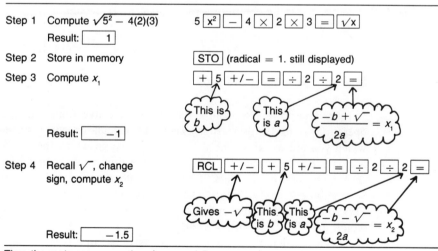

Step 1   Compute $\sqrt{5^2 - 4(2)(3)}$ 5 $\boxed{x^2}$ $\boxed{-}$ 4 $\boxed{\times}$ 2 $\boxed{\times}$ 3 $\boxed{=}$ $\boxed{\sqrt{x}}$
Result: $\boxed{\quad 1 \quad}$

Step 2   Store in memory $\boxed{STO}$ (radical = 1. still displayed)

Step 3   Compute x_1 $\boxed{+}$ 5 $\boxed{+/-}$ $\boxed{=}$ $\boxed{\div}$ 2 $\boxed{\div}$ 2 $\boxed{=}$

This is b This is a $\dfrac{-b + \sqrt{}}{2a} = x_1$

Result: $\boxed{\quad -1 \quad}$

Step 4   Recall $\sqrt{}$, change sign, compute x_2 $\boxed{RCL}$ $\boxed{+/-}$ $\boxed{+}$ 5 $\boxed{+/-}$ $\boxed{=}$ $\boxed{\div}$ 2 $\boxed{\div}$ 2 $\boxed{=}$

Gives $-\sqrt{}$ This is b This is a $\dfrac{-b - \sqrt{}}{2a} = x_2$

Result: $\boxed{\quad -1.5 \quad}$

Thus the roots are $x_1 = -1$ and $x_2 = -1.5$.

Some small effort can be saved in this procedure by use of the $\boxed{EXC}$ key, but if you are a novice at this, it could confuse an already

43

fairly complicated key sequence. However, for those who would like to know, the strategy is to store b immediately and then, once the radical is computed, key $\boxed{+}$ and, instead of storing it, exchange the radical for b, which is still in the memory. Then continue as before. All this does is save you the trouble of entering b a second time.

A much greater savings can be realized by using the product of roots theorem: $x_1 x_2 = c/a$. So instead of doing step 4, use the fact that $x_1 = -1$, and so $(-1)x_2 = 3/2 = 1.5$, and so $x_2 = -1.5$.

Laws of Exponents and Radicals

Several *laws of exponents* are used algebraically to manipulate and simplify various expressions. For calculation, they can be used to modify expressions to facilitate computation. These basic laws are as follows:

$$b^m \cdot b^n = b^{m+n} \qquad\qquad \left(\frac{a}{b}\right)^n = \frac{a^n}{b^n}, \qquad b \neq 0$$

$$\frac{b^m}{b^n} = b^{m-n}, \qquad b \neq 0$$
$$b^{-n} = \frac{1}{b^n}$$

$$(b^n)^m = b^{mn}$$

$$b^0 = 1, \qquad b \neq 0$$

$$(ab)^n = a^n b^n$$

For calculators, we have the additional restriction that, for entry using the power key, none of the bases may be negative.

Example Compute $(-3)^7$ by computing the equivalent expression -3^7 as

$$3 \ \boxed{y^x} \ 7 \ \boxed{=} \ \boxed{+/-} \quad \text{and read} \quad \boxed{\quad -2187\quad}$$

If we try to compute it directly as $3 \ \boxed{+/-} \ \boxed{y^x} \ \boxed{=}$, we get $\boxed{\quad \text{Error}\quad}$

It is important to realize that notation conventions indicate which operation is to be done first. Then the calculator entry system with which you are working will also affect the way in which the computation is done. For instance, $7x^3$ means that the number x is first cubed and then multiplied by 7. Thus, if we substitute $x = 2$ into the expression, we compute $7 \cdot 2^3 = 7 \cdot 8 = 56$. On the other hand, if we should see $(7x)^3$, then x is first multiplied by 7 and then cubed, thus, if $x = 2$, we would get $(7 \cdot 2)^3 = 14^3 = 2744$.

When calculating such expressions it is important to realize that the AOS system will automatically compute powers first (before multiplication), whereas arithmetic entry systems will compute things in exactly the order in which they are entered unless parentheses are employed.

Example   To compute $7x^3$ for $x = 2$ using the AOS system, key

$$7 \;\boxed{\times}\; 2 \;\boxed{y^x}\; 3 \;\boxed{=}$$

and the result is 56. If you had done this with an arithmetic system, the $\boxed{\times}$ would have been done first since it was entered first, and that would have given the wrong answer. For an arithmetic entry system, you have two choices for computing this quantity:

1. Use parentheses:

$$7 \;\boxed{\times}\; \boxed{(}\; 2 \;\boxed{y^x}\; 3 \;\boxed{=}$$

   Notice that the right-hand parenthesis was omitted. For this calculation its use is optional. If it had been included, then 2 cubed would have been displayed before the equals sign completed the calculation.

2. Reverse the entry order to correspond to the order in which the operations are intended to be done:

$$2 \;\boxed{y^x}\; 3 \;\boxed{\times}\; 7 \;\boxed{=}$$

Example   To compute $(7x)^3$ for $x = 2$ using the AOS system, we must override the preprogramming that does the cube first. This can be done in two ways:

1. Use parentheses:

$$\boxed{(}\; 7 \;\boxed{\times}\; 2 \;\boxed{)}\; \boxed{y^x}\; 3 \;\boxed{=} \quad \text{and read} \quad \boxed{2744}$$

2. Use an extra $\boxed{=}$:

$$7 \;\boxed{\times}\; 2 \;\boxed{=}\; \boxed{y^x}\; 3 \;\boxed{=}$$

   On an arithmetic entry system, we just enter the operations in the intended order:

$$7 \;\boxed{\times}\; 2 \;\boxed{y^x}\; 3 \;\boxed{=}$$

   Notice that on an AOS system, this last sequence would have computed $7x^3$ instead of $(7x)^3$ (see the previous example).

Example   Compute $(5^3)^2$ directly and then compute the equivalent form 5^6, which is found by using one of the laws of exponents.
To compute $(5^3)^2$, key

$$5 \;\boxed{y^x}\; 3 \;\boxed{y^x}\; 2 \;\boxed{=}$$

and find that the result is 15,625. To compute 5^6 key

$$5 \boxed{y^x}\ 6\ \boxed{=}$$

and the same result is obtained.

Table 2-3 illustrates some typical configurations with exponents and how to compute them. In all but the first two cases the AOS and arithmetic systems are done identically.

TABLE 2-3.

FORMULA	CALCULATOR KEY SEQUENCE
cb^p	$c \boxed{\times} b \boxed{y^x} p \boxed{=}$ (AOS system)
	$b \boxed{y^x} p \boxed{\times} c \boxed{=}$ (arithmetic)
$(cb)^p$	$c \boxed{\times} b \boxed{=} \boxed{y^x} p \boxed{=}$ (AOS system)
	$c \boxed{\times} b \boxed{y^x} p \boxed{=}$ (arithmetic)
$(b^p)^q$	$b \boxed{y^x} p \boxed{y^x} q \boxed{=}$
$b^{1/p}$	$b \boxed{y^x} p \boxed{1/x} \boxed{=}$
$b^{m/n} = (b^m)^{1/n}$	$b \boxed{y^x} \boxed{(} m \boxed{\div} n \boxed{=}$ or
	$b \boxed{y^x} m \boxed{y^x} n \boxed{1/x} \boxed{=}$
$b^{\sqrt{n}}$	$b \boxed{y^x} n \boxed{\sqrt{x}} \boxed{=}$

Another important fact about notation is that roots can be expressed either in radical notation or as fractional powers. The way you express it may affect the way you choose to compute it. For example,

$$\sqrt[n]{b} = b^{1/n}$$

may be computed in basically two ways:

1. Use the $\boxed{INV}\ \boxed{y^x}$ sequence (on some this is shown as $\boxed{2nd}\ \boxed{^x\sqrt{y}}$);

$$b \boxed{INV}\ \boxed{y^x}\ n\ \boxed{=}$$

2. Use the fractional power equivalent:

$$b \boxed{y^x}\ n\ \boxed{1/x}\ \boxed{=}$$

Example   To compute $\sqrt[5]{16,807}$, two methods may be used:

(1) $16807\ \boxed{INV}\ \boxed{y^x}\ 5\ \boxed{=}$ (or $16807\ \boxed{2nd}\ \boxed{^x\sqrt{y}}\ 5\ \boxed{=}$)

(2) $16807\ \boxed{y^x}\ 5\ \boxed{1/x}\ \boxed{=}$

and we find either way that $\sqrt[5]{16,807} = 7$.

Logarithms

A *logarithm* is the inverse of an exponential function. The base b of a logarithm corresponds to the base b of the exponential function. The notation for a logarithm is $\log_b N$. This logarithm is equal to the *power to which the base b must be raised to produce N*; that is,

$$\log_b N = p \qquad \text{provided that } b^p = N$$

Example $\text{Log}_2 8 = 3$ since $2^3 = 8$.

Example To evaluate $\log_4 16$, ask the question, To what power must we raise 4 (the base) to get 16?

$$4^{(?)} = 16$$

Clearly, the answer is 2. Thus $\log_4 16 = 2$. It is useful in understanding the logarithm concept to become accustomed to reading expressions such as this as "the power to which 4 must be raised to get 16 is 2."

Most scientific calculators have logarithms to either base 10 or base e, where e is Euler's notation for a special number known as the *natural base* ($e = 2.718281828$, approximately). It is called natural since it arises when analyzing many phenomena that occur in nature.

The number $\log_{10} a$ is computed by keying a $\boxed{\log}$. The natural logarithm $\log_e a$, which is also denoted by ln a, is computed as a $\boxed{\text{lnx}}$.

Example To compute $\log_{10} 5$, key 5 $\boxed{\log}$ and read $\boxed{\qquad 0.69897}$. To compute $\log_e 5$ = ln 5, key 5 $\boxed{\text{lnx}}$ and read $\boxed{1.6094379}$.

Some calculators do not have a base 10 logarithm key, but only a natural logarithm key. We shall discuss how calculations can be done using only the natural logarithm when the change of base formula is examined.

Logarithms were previously used for calculations that otherwise could not be easily done. In particular, since our number system is a base 10 system, it turns out that base 10 logarithms happened to be the most convenient, and extensive tables and interpolation methods were devised. For most purposes, calculators make that use obsolete.

Logarithms are still important for describing certain physical situations or for transformations of experimental data to make the data conform to certain theoretical assumptions when statistical analyses are done.

It is useful to know some general properties of logarithms. The three most commonly used properties are as follows:

1. Multiplication rule: $\log MN = \log M + \log N$.
2. Division rule: $\log M/N = \log M - \log N$.
3. Power rule: $\log M^n = n \log M$.

These three rules apply to logarithms of any base and can be used to simplify expressions to be evaluated or to solve equations that involve logarithms.

Example   The equation $\log_{10} x + \log_{10} (x + 21) = 2$ can be solved by using the multiplication rule to obtain the equivalent equation:

$$\log_{10} x(x + 21) = ?$$

Using the definition of logarithms in terms of powers, we get

$$10^2 = x(x + 21) = x^2 + 21x$$

and thus, putting the equation in standard quadratic form and noting that $10^2 = 100$, we obtain

$$x^2 + 21x - 100 = 0$$

which factors as $(x + 25)(x - 4) = 0$ and thus $x = -25$ or $x = +4$. But x may not be negative! That leaves $x = 4$. Checking this result in the original equation, we get

$$\log_{10} 4 + \log_{10} (4 + 21) \overset{?}{=} 2 \quad \text{(we hope!)}$$

Calculate to check:

$$4 \boxed{\log} \boxed{+} 25 \boxed{\log} \boxed{=} \quad \text{and read} \quad \boxed{2}$$

Thus the solution $x = 4$ checks upon substitution.

Some calculators have a $\boxed{\ln x}$ key but *not* a $\boxed{\log}$ key. This does not matter as far as the computational range of the calculator is concerned. Using the next theorem, we can obtain *any base* logarithm from any other. This is known as the *change of base formula*:

$$\log_B X = \frac{\log_c X}{\log_c B}$$

where B is the desired base and c is the known or directly computable base. On most calculators either $c = 10$ or $c = e$. Thus this formula reduces to two special cases:

$$\log_B X = \frac{\log_{10} X}{\log_{10} B}$$

$$\log_B X = \frac{\ln X}{\ln B}$$

Example   We can use $\boxed{\text{lnx}}$ to compute $\log_2 32$ by using the change of base formula as follows:

$$\log_2 32 = \frac{\ln 32}{\ln 2}$$

so key

$$32 \boxed{\text{lnx}} \boxed{\div} 2 \boxed{\text{lnx}} \boxed{=} \quad \text{and read} \quad \boxed{\quad 5 \quad}$$

(Actually, we knew beforehand that the result was $\log_2 32 = 5$, since $2^5 = 32$. We could also have used the $\boxed{\text{log}}$ key in the exact same manner to get the answer, since the change of base formula works for any base whatsoever.)

Example   If you don't have a $\boxed{\text{log}}$ key (and even if you do), you can compute $\log_{10} 7$ by using the $\boxed{\text{lnx}}$ key by using the change of base formula as follows:

$$\log_{10} 7 = \frac{\ln 7}{\ln 10}$$

so key

$$7 \boxed{\text{lnx}} \boxed{\div} 10 \boxed{\text{lnx}} \boxed{=} \quad \text{and read} \quad \boxed{.84509804}$$

To check this answer, keying $7 \boxed{\text{log}}$ gives the same result.

The inverse of $\log_{10} x$ is 10^x. Sometimes this is noted on a key or above it by $\boxed{10^x}$. More often one must key $\boxed{\text{INV}}$ $\boxed{\text{log}}$ to compute it. The power key may also be used, but that is inconvenient when the purpose is to take the inverse log of the displayed value.

Example   Compute $10^{4.3}$ by keying $4.3 \boxed{\text{INV}} \boxed{\text{log}}$ and read $\boxed{19952.623}$. If we compute it directly as

$$10 \boxed{y^x} 4.3 \boxed{=}$$

we get the same result.

The inverse of $\log_e x = \ln x$ is the function e^x. Sometimes $\boxed{e^x}$ appears as a key or, more typically, above the $\boxed{\text{lnx}}$ key as a second function. On many calculators we use the sequence $\boxed{\text{INV}}$ $\boxed{\text{lnx}}$ when the value of x is displayed.

Example   The number e^2 is computed by keying

$$2 \boxed{\text{INV}} \boxed{\text{lnx}} \quad \text{and reading} \quad \boxed{7.3890561}$$

On some key configurations the key sequence might look like

$$2 \boxed{\text{2nd}} \boxed{e^x}$$

If the e^x is on a separate key, the 2nd would be omitted.

Example Compute the approximate value of e by realizing that $e = e^1$; so key

$$1 \boxed{\text{INV}} \boxed{\text{lnx}} \quad \text{and read} \quad \boxed{2.7182818}$$

This is only a seven-decimal-place approximation.
(*Note*: The value of e computed and stored internally on some calculators is the following 11 digits: 2.7182818301. The last three digits are wrong. Actually, $e = 2.718281828459045. \ldots$ So there is an error, but only so far as the ninth decimal place is concerned, and not very large at that. This will not affect the eight-digit accuracy of most calculations to any significant extent.)

The use of the logarithm keys for computation is summarized in Table 2-4.

TABLE 2-4.

EXPRESSION	CALCULATOR KEY SEQUENCE
Base 10: $\log_{10} a$	$a \boxed{\text{log}}$
Base e (natural log): $\log_e a = \ln a$	$a \boxed{\text{lnx}}$
Any base: $\log_b a = \dfrac{\ln a}{\ln b}$	$a \boxed{\text{lnx}} \boxed{\div} b \boxed{\text{lnx}} \boxed{=}$
10^p	$p \boxed{\text{INV}} \boxed{\text{log}}$ or $p \boxed{\text{2nd}} \boxed{10^x}$
e^a	$a \boxed{\text{INV}} \boxed{\text{lnx}}$ or $a \boxed{\text{2nd}} \boxed{e^x}$

Note: The power function $\boxed{y^x}$ uses the logarithm internally to do its work. Since we cannot take a log of a negative number, that is why we cannot use a negative base for powers. For instance, 3^5 would be computed internally by using the fact that $\log 3^5 = 5 \log 3$, computing log 3, multiplying by 5, and finally taking the inverse log. Try it manually to understand what happens: $3 \boxed{\text{log}} \boxed{\text{x}} 5 \boxed{=} \boxed{\text{INV}} \boxed{\text{log}}$ and the result is 243. Keying $3 \boxed{y^x} 5 \boxed{=}$ will give the same result. If you try to compute $(-3)^5$, however, by either method, you get an error indication, since log (-3) does not exist. However, $(-3)^5 = -243$ does exist!

Progressions

When the natural numbers 1, 2, 3, 4, . . . can be substituted into the formula defining a function f, then the values $f(1)$, $f(2)$, $f(3)$, $f(4)$, . . . are said to form a *sequence* (or *progression*). $f(1)$ is called the first term, $f(2)$ is the second term, . . . , and $f(k)$ is the kth term.

Example   The formula $f(n) = 5n - 2$ defines a sequence with

$$f(1) = 5(1) - 2$$
$$f(2) = 5(2) - 2$$

.

.

.

$$f(k) = 5k - 2$$

The values of $f(n)$ are computed one at a time as

$$5 \boxed{\times} n \boxed{-} 2 \boxed{=}, \qquad \text{letting } n = 1, 2, 3, \ldots$$

Sometimes the constant $\boxed{K}$ can be utilized to simplify the generating of the sequence. For example, if $f(n) = n/3$, we divide each successive value of n by the same number, 3. Thus, first set up 3 as a constant divisor; then key successive values of n followed by $\boxed{=}$:

Step 1   Set up 3 as a constant divisor:

$$3 \boxed{\div} \boxed{K}$$

Step 2   Key 1 $\boxed{=}$ [read $f(1)$] 2 $\boxed{=}$ [read $f(2)$], ...

There are two special sequences known as *arithmetic* and *geometric progressions*. An arithmetic progression is a sequence of the form $f(n) = a_1 + (n - 1)d$, where a_1 is called the *first term* and d is a constant called the *difference*. It is so named because if we subtract any two successive terms we always get the same difference, which equals d. (Notice that f is a linear function of n.) The value of the nth term $f(n)$ is often denoted by the symbol a_n.

The arithmetic progression $f(n) = a_1 + (n - 1)d$ can be generated by starting with a_1 and then just adding the constant d to each successive term.

Example   If $a_1 = 2$ and $d = 3$, then the arithmetic sequence $a_1, a_2, a_3, \ldots$ is

$$a_1 = 2, \qquad a_2 = a_1 + d = 2 + 3 = 5, \qquad a_3 = 5 + 3 = 8,$$
$$a_4 = 8 + 3 = 11, \ldots$$

Thus 2, 5, 8, 11, . . . forms an arithmetic sequence. This is called the *recursive* formulation, wherein each term is generated from the previous term; that is,

$$a_{k+1} = a_k + d \quad \text{or} \quad f(k + 1) = f(k) + d$$

51

The usual form for the nth term of an arithmetic progression is

$$a_n = a_1 + (n - 1)d$$

which is used to derive various related quantities such as the sum of the first n terms, S_n. The formula is

$$S_n = n\frac{a_1 + a_n}{2}$$

This can be thought of as n times the average of the first and last terms.

Example Find the sum of the terms 2, 5, 8, 11, 14, 17, 20, and 23 by using the fact that these numbers form an arithmetic sequence (progression) of eight terms; so

$$S_8 = 8\frac{a_1 + a_8}{2} = 4\cancel{8}\frac{2 + 23}{\cancel{2}} = 4(25) = 100$$

The constant function $\boxed{K}$ is ideal for generating an arithmetic progession since we must only add a constant (the difference d). This is done as follows:

Step 1 Set up the difference d as a constant: $d\ \boxed{+}\ \boxed{K}$.
Step 2 Enter the first term and then successively key $\boxed{=}$ to generate the other terms:

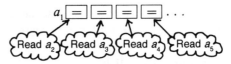

A *geometric progression* is just a sequence of the form $f(n) = a_1 r^{n-1} = a_n$ (note that this is an exponential function), a_1 is the first term, and r is called the *ratio* (so called because the ratio of two successive terms is a constant). The value of $f(n)$ is denoted by a_n and is called the nth term.

To generate a geometric progression, successively multiply the first term by the constant ratio r.

a_1

$a_2 = a_1 r$ { This is the recursive formulation

$a_3 = a_2 r = a_1 r \cdot r = a_1 r^2$ of a geometric progression

.

.

.

$a_{k+1} = a_k r = a_1 r^k$

Example Generate a geometric progression with $a_1 = 1$, $r = 2$ as follows:

$$a_1 = 1$$
$$a_2 = 1 \times 2 = 2$$
$$a_3 = 2 \times 2 = 4$$
$$a_4 = 4 \times 2 = 8$$

$$\cdot \qquad \cdot \qquad \cdot$$
$$\cdot \qquad \cdot \qquad \cdot$$
$$\cdot \qquad \cdot \qquad \cdot$$

Thus 1, 2, 4, 8, . . . forms a geometric progression with ratio $r = 2$. To generate this on a calculator, we could key

As an alternative procedure, we could utilize the constant $\boxed{K}$ by setting up $r = 2$ as a constant multiplier:

Step 1 Set up $r = 2$ as a constant multiplier.

$$2 \boxed{\times} \boxed{K}$$

Step 2 Enter the first term a_1 ($= 1$ here) and key $\boxed{=}$ to generate successive terms.

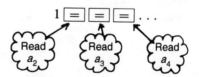

There are two cases for the sum S_n of a geometric progression:

1. General case: r is any real number $\neq 1$; n is finite.
2. Infinite case: $|r| < 1$, $n \to \infty$.

In the general case, the formula for the sum is

$$S_n = \frac{a_1(1 - r^n)}{1 - r}, \qquad r \neq 1$$

Example Find the sum of 1, 2, 4, 8, 16, 32, and 64 by noticing that these numbers form a geometric progression of seven terms. The ratio $r = 2$ is found by taking the ratio of any two consecutive terms, for example, $4/2 = 2$ or $16/8 = 2$ (any pair will do). The smallest terms are the easiest: $2/1 = 2$. The first term is $a_1 = 1$; hence

$$S_7 = \frac{a_1(1 - r^7)}{1 - r} = \frac{1(1 - 2^7)}{1 - 2} = \frac{1 - 2^7}{1 - 2} = \frac{1 - 2^7}{-1}$$

So compute (AOS system)

$$1 \boxed{-} 2 \boxed{y^x} 7 \boxed{=} \boxed{\div} 1 \boxed{+/-} \boxed{=}$$

and read the value of $S_7 = 127$. We could also have simplified the last expression even further:

$$\frac{1 - 2^7}{-1} = 2^7 - 1$$

and so key $2 \boxed{y^x} 7 \boxed{-} 1 \boxed{=}$

The ratio r may be positive or negative. A negative value of r will just make the sign of each consecutive term alternate. However, this poses a problem in the computation of S_n. (See problems 38 and 40.) In the infinite case, r is a fraction or decimal like $\frac{1}{2}$, $\frac{1}{4}$, 0.6, or 0.01. In that case $|r| < 1$, and the sum formula reduces to

$$S_\infty = \frac{a_1}{1 - r}$$

which is easily computed as $a_1 \boxed{\div} \boxed{(} 1 \boxed{-} r \boxed{=}$. If you don't have parentheses, use the memory like this:

$$1 \boxed{-} r \boxed{=} \boxed{STO} a_1 \boxed{\div} \boxed{RCL} \boxed{=}$$

Example Find the infinite sum of the geometric progression 1, $\frac{1}{2}$, $\frac{1}{4}$, . . . by noting that $a_1 = 1$, and $r = \frac{1}{2} = 0.5$, and thus

$$S_\infty = \frac{a_1}{1 - r} = \frac{1}{1 - .5} = \frac{1}{.5}$$

So key $.5 \boxed{1/x}$ and find that $S_\infty = 2$.

To summarize, the formulas that define arithmetic progressions (APs) and geometric progressions (GPs) are in two forms: functional, where the nth term is given by a formula in n, and recursive, where each term is generated by the previous term. See Table 2-5.

TABLE 2-5. Summary of Formulas
for Arithmetic and Geometric Progressions

ARITHMETIC PROGRESSIONS

$f(n) = a_n = a_1 + (n - 1)d$	Functional form
$a_{k+1} = a_k + d$	Recursive form
$S_n = n\dfrac{a_1 + a_n}{2}$	Sum of n terms

GEOMETRIC PROGRESSIONS

$f(n) = a_n = a_1 r^{n-1}$	Functional form
$a_{n+1} = a_n r$	Recursive form
$S_n = a_1 \dfrac{1 - r^n}{1 - r}, \quad r \neq 1$	Finite sum of n terms
$S_\infty = \dfrac{a_1}{1 - r}, \quad |r| < 1$	Infinite sum

Solved Problems

BASIC FUNCTIONS $\boxed{x^2}$ $\boxed{\sqrt{x}}$ $\boxed{1/x}$

1. Compute each of the following: (a) 3.7^2; (b) $(-3.7)^2$; (c) -3.7^2.
   (a) 3.7^2 means 3.7×3.7, so key 3.7 $\boxed{x^2}$ and read 13.69.
   (b) $(-3.7)^2$ means $(-3.7) \times (-3.7)$, so key 3.7 $\boxed{+/-}$ $\boxed{x^2}$ and
   again read 13.69, since a negative squared is positive.
   (c) $(-3.7^2$ means $-(3.7 \times 3.7)$, so we key 3.7 $\boxed{x^2}$ $\boxed{+/-}$ and read
   -13.69.
   Notice that $(-3.7)^2 \neq -3.7^2$ but instead has opposite sign.

2. Compute $(3 + \sqrt{8.4})^2$.
   We first evaluate the expression inside the parentheses and then
   square it:

   $$3 \boxed{+} 8.4 \boxed{\sqrt{x}} \boxed{=} \boxed{x^2} \quad \text{and read} \quad \boxed{34.789652}$$

   We could have used parentheses instead of the $\boxed{=}$ key:

   $$\boxed{(} 3 \boxed{+} 8.4 \boxed{\sqrt{x}} \boxed{)} \boxed{x^2}$$

   We would get the same answer. Be careful not to complete the addition before you have taken the square root of 8.4.

3. Compute $(8.3 \times 10^2)^2$.
   We enter the number in scientific notation and square:

   $$8.3 \boxed{EE} 2 \boxed{x^2} \quad \text{and the result is} \quad \boxed{6.889\ 05}$$

   This is equivalent to $6.889 \times 10^5 = 688,900$.

4. Compute $(1/5.9) + 8.06$.

We take the reciprocal of 5.9 and then add 8.06:

$$5.9 \boxed{1/x} \boxed{+} 8.06 \boxed{=} \quad \text{and read} \quad \boxed{8.2294915}$$

5. Compute (a) $\dfrac{1}{6.2} + \dfrac{1}{7.5}$ and (b) $\dfrac{1}{6.2 + 7.5}$.

For (a) key $6.2 \boxed{1/x} \boxed{+} 7.5 \boxed{1/x} \boxed{=}$ and read $\boxed{.29462366}$.

For (b) we add first, so key $6.2 \boxed{+} 7.5 \boxed{=} \boxed{1/x}$ and read $\boxed{0.0729927}$.

6. Compute $\dfrac{1}{5 + (1 + \dfrac{1}{\sqrt{5}})^2}$.

We start inside the parentheses, square the result, add 5, and lastly take the reciprocal, since the quantity computed is in the denominator with 1 in the numerator:

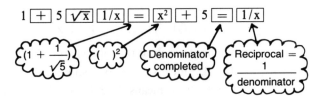

We could also have computed the denominator as written by using parentheses and then again taking the reciprocal.

$$5 \boxed{+} \boxed{(} \boxed{(} 1 \boxed{+} 5 \boxed{\sqrt{x}} \boxed{1/x} \boxed{)} \boxed{x^2} \boxed{=} \boxed{1/x}$$

The answer is .14095571.

7. Compute $\dfrac{5 + 7}{\dfrac{1}{5} + \dfrac{1}{7}}$

The fraction bar also acts like parentheses, so we key

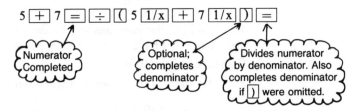

The result is 35.

8. If $x = -3$, $y = 2.1$, and $z = 4.5$, evaluate (a) $3x - y + 2z$; (b) $x(y - z)$; (c) $xy + (y/z)$.

(a) On an AOS calculator, we evaluate $3(-3) - 2.1 + 2(4.5)$ as

$$3 \boxed{x} 3 \boxed{+/-} \boxed{-} 2.1 \boxed{+} 2 \boxed{\times} 4.5 \boxed{=}$$

and the result is -2.1. On an arithmetic calculator, we need parentheses after the $\boxed{+}$ or else the 2 would be added before it was multiplied by the 4.5, which would be wrong. For that key,

$$3 \boxed{\times} 3 \boxed{+/-} \boxed{-} 2.1 \boxed{+} \boxed{(} 2 \boxed{\times} 4.5 \boxed{)} \boxed{=}$$

(b) Here we evaluate $-3(2.1 - 4.5)$ and for either system key

$$3 \boxed{+/-} \boxed{\times} \boxed{(} 2.1 \boxed{-} 4.5 \boxed{)} \boxed{=}$$

The result is 7.2. The right parenthesis could be omitted.

(c) Here we evaluate $(-3)(2.1) + (2.1/4.5)$. On an AOS system, key

$$3 \boxed{+/-} \boxed{\times} 2.1 \boxed{+} 2.1 \boxed{\div} 4.5 \boxed{=} \quad \text{and read}$$
$$\boxed{-5.8333333}$$

On an arithmetic system we again need parentheses:

$$3 \boxed{+/-} \boxed{\times} 2.1 \boxed{+} \boxed{(} 2.1 \boxed{\div} 4.5 \boxed{)} \boxed{=}$$

9. If $x = 8.3$, $y = 2.1$, and $z = 3.2$, evaluate (a) $2x + (y/z)$ and (b) $(2x + y)/z$.

To compute (a), which equals $2(8.3) + (2.1/3.2)$ on an AOS system, key

$$2 \boxed{\times} 8.3 \boxed{+} 2.1 \boxed{\div} 3.2 \boxed{=}$$

On an arithmetic system we need parentheses after the $\boxed{+}$. In either case, the result is 17.25625.

To compute (b), which equals $[2(8.3) + 2.1]/3.2$ on an AOS system, key

$$2 \boxed{\times} 8.3 \boxed{+} 2.1 \boxed{=} \boxed{\div} 3.2 \boxed{=}$$

In this case an arithmetic system would be simpler, since the first $\boxed{=}$ could be omitted. The result is 5.84375. Notice that the two expressions are similar, but definitely not equal!

10. In the formula $F = \frac{9}{5}C + 32$, let $C = 8$ and compute F.

$$F = \frac{9}{5}(8) + 32$$

so we key $9 \boxed{\div} 5 \boxed{\times} 8 \boxed{+} 32 \boxed{=}$, giving the result $F = 46.4$.

11. In the formula $H = [KA(t_2 - t_1)]/L$, let $K = .92$, $A = 10$, $t_2 = 35.2$, $t_1 = 12.7$, and $L = .1$, and compute the value of H.

We evaluate the expression as $[.92(10)(35.2 - 12.7)]/.1$, which is keyed as

$$.92 \boxed{\times} 10 \boxed{\times} \boxed{(\!(} 35.2 \boxed{-} 12.7 \boxed{)} \boxed{\div} .1 \boxed{=}$$

and so $H = 2070$.

12. In the formula $F = ma$, if $a = 6.2$, complete the table for the various values of m given.

m	$F = ma$
10.0	
10.2	
10.4	
11.0	

We use the constant, since a is the same on each line. First we set up the constant multiplier by keying $6.2 \boxed{\times} \boxed{K}$, and then we enter each value of m followed by an equal sign:

$10 \boxed{=}$ and read that $F = 62$

$10.2 \boxed{=}$ and read that $F = 63.24$

$10.4 \boxed{=}$ and read that $F = 64.48$

$11 \boxed{=}$ and read that $F = 68.2$

These values would be recorded in the table as they are read.

13. In the formula $T = (L/K) \times (H/A)$, if $L = 0.2$, $K = 2.7 \times 10^{-3}$, and $H/A = 18.7 \times 10^{-4}$, compute T.

Notice that H/A is already given as a single value, so we compute the expression

$$\frac{0.2}{2.7 \times 10^{-3}} \times 18.7 \times 10^{-4}$$

by keying

.2 $\boxed{\div}$ 2.7 $\boxed{\text{EE}}$ 3 $\boxed{+/-}$ $\boxed{\times}$ 18.7 $\boxed{\text{EE}}$ 4 $\boxed{+/-}$ $\boxed{=}$

and read the result $\boxed{\;\;1.3852\;\;-01\;}$, which is interpreted as 1.3852 $\times$ 10^{-1} = 0.13852. If we use the calculator to make this conversion by keying $\boxed{\times}$ 1 $\boxed{\text{INV}}$ $\boxed{\text{EE}}$ $\boxed{=}$, we get .13851852. These extra decimals are meaningless in application.

14. Complete the following table making use of the constant key:

t	$16t^2$
5.14	
1.1×10^5	
$.87 \times 10^{-3}$	
2048	

First set up the 16 as a constant by keying 16 $\boxed{\times}$ $\boxed{\text{K}}$, and then enter each value of t, square it, and press $\boxed{=}$ to complete the calculation:

5.14 $\boxed{x^2}$ $\boxed{=}$ $\boxed{\;\;422.7136\;\;}$

1.1 $\boxed{\text{EE}}$ 5 $\boxed{x^2}$ $\boxed{=}$ $\boxed{\;\;1.936\;\;11\;\;}$

.87 $\boxed{\text{EE}}$ 3 $\boxed{+/-}$ $\boxed{x^2}$ $\boxed{=}$ $\boxed{\;\;1.211\;\;-05\;\;}$

2048 $\boxed{x^2}$ $\boxed{=}$ $\boxed{\;\;6.7109\;\;07\;\;}$

Notice that the last result is in scientific notation, even though the number was entered in floating point. This is because the previous entry put the calculator in scientific notation mode. If one wanted the answer in floating-point notation at this point, simply key $\boxed{\times}$ 1 $\boxed{\text{INV}}$ $\boxed{\text{EE}}$ $\boxed{=}$ and the result is 67108864.

15. Evaluate $P = (mv^2/r) - mg$, if $m = 8$, $v = 12.7$, $r = 9$, and $g = 32.2$.

After substituting, we must evaluate the expression

$$\frac{8(12.7)^2}{9} - 8(32.2)$$

by keying (AOS system)

8 $\boxed{\times}$ 12.7 $\boxed{x^2}$ $\boxed{\div}$ 9 $\boxed{-}$ 8 $\boxed{\times}$ 32.2 $\boxed{=}$ and read
$\boxed{\;\;-114.23111\;\;}$

If you have an arithmetic system, you must insert a parenthesis $\boxed{(}$ immediately after the $\boxed{-}$ to tell the calculator to do the multiplication before it subtracts.

16. Compute $\sqrt[3]{3.27}$ in two ways.

First, we can simply key 3.27 $\boxed{\text{INV}}$ $\boxed{\text{y}^\text{x}}$ 3 $\boxed{=}$. On some calculators it may instead look like this:

$$3.27 \boxed{\text{2nd}} \boxed{\sqrt[x]{\text{y}}} \boxed{=}$$

which is really the same method. The result is 1.4842803.

A second method is to realize that $\sqrt[3]{3.27} = (3.27)^{1/3}$ and compute it as such:

$$3.27 \boxed{\text{y}^\text{x}} 3 \boxed{1/\text{x}} \boxed{=}$$

The sequence 3 $\boxed{1/\text{x}}$ computes $^1/_3$ which is used as the exponent.

17. Compute $(43.8)^{5/8}$. Also express this quantity using radical notation. One method is to first compute the fifth power and then take the eighth root:

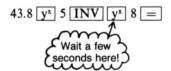

$$43.8 \boxed{\text{y}^\text{x}} 5 \boxed{\text{INV}} \boxed{\text{y}^\text{x}} 8 \boxed{=}$$

Wait a few seconds here!

The result is 10.615032.

Another method is to use parentheses to compute the 5/8 and use it as a power:

$$43.8 \boxed{\text{y}^\text{x}} \boxed{(} 5 \boxed{\div} 8 \boxed{)} \boxed{=}$$

Of course, we get the same result. Thus $43.8^{5/8} = \sqrt[8]{43.8^5} = 10.615032$.

18. Compute $5^{2/3} - 2.1^{3/4}$.

The most direct way is to use parentheses and view the expression given as

$$5^{(2/3)} - 2.1^{(3/4)}$$

and calculate it (AOS system) as follows:

$$5 \boxed{\text{y}^\text{x}} \boxed{(} 2 \boxed{\div} 3 \boxed{)} \boxed{-} 2.1 \boxed{\text{y}^\text{x}} \boxed{(} 3 \boxed{\div} 4 \boxed{)} \boxed{=}$$

If you have an arithmetic system, you must be careful. When you key the y^x function after the 2.1, the minus does not wait. To avoid this problem, you must use an additional $\boxed{(}$ after the $\boxed{-}$:

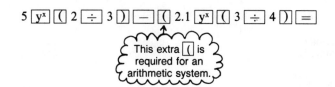

The result is 1.1795439.

19. Compute $\sqrt[5]{-12.8}$

If we try to compute this directly, we get an error indication. The reason for this is that negatives may not be used as the base for the power function. Yet the number does have a value. You can "pull" the minus sign past *odd* roots and realize that this equals $-\sqrt[5]{12.8}$ and compute accordingly: 12.8 $\boxed{\text{INV}}$ $\boxed{y^x}$ 5 $\boxed{=}$ $\boxed{+/-}$, and read the results, -1.6651064. This method will *not* work for even roots.

20. Compute $(4.6 \times 10^{12})^{1/3}$

It is not necessary to use the power function for the twelfth power (although we could), since it is just part of the scientific notation. Only the 1/3 power requires it:

4.6 $\boxed{\text{EE}}$ 12 $\boxed{y^x}$ 3 $\boxed{1/x}$ $\boxed{=}$ gives the result $\boxed{\text{1.6631 04}}$

which means 1.6631×10^4. We can change this into floating-point notation and even get a few extra decimal places by keying $\boxed{\times}$ 1 $\boxed{\text{INV}}$ $\boxed{\text{EE}}$ $\boxed{=}$; we get 16631.035.

If you don't have an $\boxed{\text{EE}}$ key on your calculator (and even if you do), you could have keyed

10 $\boxed{y^x}$ 12 $\boxed{\times}$ 4.6 $\boxed{=}$ $\boxed{y^x}$ 3 $\boxed{1/x}$ $\boxed{=}$

LINEAR EQUATIONS
AND PROPORTIONS

21. Solve the following proportion for x:

$$\frac{x}{4.375} = \frac{4.5}{75}$$

First solve algebraically by multiplying both sides by 4.375, which cancels on the left side:

$$(4.375)\,\frac{x}{4.375} = \frac{4.5}{75}\,(4.375)$$

and then calculate the resulting expression for x:

4.5 $\boxed{\div}$ 75 $\boxed{\times}$ 4.375 $\boxed{=}$ and read $\boxed{\text{0.2625}}$

22. Solve the following proportion for N:

$$\frac{26}{N} = \frac{4.125}{.06}$$

A technique to solve for N that can be envisioned mentally to actually avoid writing new equations (although we do so here) is to *exchange means* and get (try to see how this can be done mentally)

$$\frac{26}{4.125} = \frac{N}{.06}$$

and then multiply both sides by .06 giving

$$(.06)\frac{26}{4.125} = N$$

Now compute:

$$.06 \boxed{\times} 26 \boxed{\div} 4.125 \boxed{=} \quad \text{and read} \quad \boxed{.37818182}$$

which is N. (Another technique to solve for N is to take reciprocals of both sides of the proportion and then multiply both sides by 26.)

23. If three cans of peas cost 57¢, how much do two cans cost?

This is a proportion problem; the unknown is the cost of two cans. Put the unknown in the numerator for convenience:

$$\frac{57¢}{3 \text{ cans}} = \frac{x¢}{2 \text{ cans}}$$

Now we solve for x and get $x = (2)(57/3)$ and we compute:

$$2 \boxed{\times} 57 \boxed{\div} 3 \boxed{=}$$

and $x = 38$¢ for two cans.

24. In the equation $y = mx$, if $y = 3.4008$ and $x = 1.04$, compute m.

First substitute and get $3.4008 = m(1.04)$. Solving for m, we get

$$m = \frac{3.4008}{1.04}$$

Thus we simply compute $3.4008 \boxed{\div} 1.04 \boxed{=}$ and get $m = 3.27$.

25. Solve the equation $2.3x + 5.1 = 17.98$ for x.

One can solve the equation algebraically and then do the calculation at the final step. But a faster way is to start solving it mentally, performing each calculation on your calculator as you proceed. The table indicates how this can be done at each step:

ALGEBRAIC SOLUTION	CORRESPONDING KEY SEQUENCE
$2.3x = 17.98 - 5.1$	$17.98 \boxed{-} 5.1 \boxed{=}$
$x = \dfrac{17.98 - 5.1}{2.3}$	$\boxed{\div} 2.3 \boxed{=}$
$x = 5.6$	Read $\boxed{5.6}$

Notice that an $\boxed{=}$ was needed to complete the subtraction before the division by 2.3 took place. On an arithmetic system it could have been omitted.

If desired, one can solve the equation on paper until the ultimate expression for x is obtained and then start the calculation. The idea here, however, is to visualize each operation being done and then do it on the calculator without having to write anything down (i.e., "subtract 5.1, now divide by 2.3"). Then one can just record the result. For more complex equations it may be useful to record the algebraic steps, but for simple equations such as this, the steps can be done mentally with the aid of the calculator.

26. Solve $(x + 2.6)/4.7 + 2.5 = 6.3$.

We may either solve algebraically and then compute the expression obtained or calculate as we proceed. In fact, this can be done mentally even for this apparently more complicated equation, as shown next:

ALGEBRAIC SOLUTION	CORRESPONDING KEY SEQUENCE
$\dfrac{x + 2.6}{4.7} + 2.5 = 6.3$	No operation, yet; this is the original equation
$\dfrac{x + 2.6}{4.7} = 6.3 - 2.5$	$6.3 \boxed{-} 2.5 \boxed{=}$
$x + 2.6 = 4.7(6.3 - 2.5)$	$\boxed{\times} 4.7$
$x = 4.7(6.3 - 2.5) - 2.6$	$\boxed{-} 2.6 \boxed{=}$
$x = 15.26$	Read $\boxed{15.26}$

One could just solve the equation and then do the calculations indicated at the last step. The key sequence would be exactly the same as the one shown if you started inside the parentheses and worked your way out. As an alternative, one could evaluate the final expression as

$$4.7 \boxed{\times} \boxed{(} 6.3 \boxed{-} 2.5 \boxed{)} \boxed{-} 2.6 \boxed{=}$$

The first method given is somewhat neater.

27. Solve $1.2(x + 1.3) = 12.624$.

Instead of "multiplying out" the left side and then proceeding as usual, just *divide first* by 1.2; then subtract 1.3 and you will have solved for x.

ALGEBRAIC SOLUTION	CORRESPONDING KEY SEQUENCE
$1.2(x + 1.3) = 12.624$	No operation; original equation
$(x + 1.3) = \dfrac{12.624}{1.2}$	$12.624 \boxed{\div} 1.2$
$x = \dfrac{12.624}{1.2} - 1.3$	$\boxed{-} 1.3 \boxed{=}$
$x = 9.32$	Read $\boxed{\quad 9.32 \quad}$

28. Solve the equation $(8.7/9.6)x = 5.1/2.2$.

Multiply both sides by the reciprocal of the coefficient of x to clear fractions from the left side:

$$\frac{\cancel{9.6}}{\cancel{8.7}} \frac{\cancel{8.7}}{\cancel{9.6}} x = \frac{5.1}{2.2} \frac{9.6}{8.7}$$

This can be done mentally by envisioning the numbers that are in the fraction on the left side being moved to the opposite position on the right side. (Look at equation carefully.) The ultimate calculation is the same in either case:

$$5.1 \boxed{\div} 2.2 \boxed{\times} 9.6 \boxed{\div} 8.7 \boxed{=}$$

and we find that $x = 2.5579937$. (If the proportion came from some application where the numbers in the proportion were measured quantities, we would round the result to 5.6.)

QUADRATIC EQUATIONS

29. Solve $x^2 - 7.52x - 57.434 = 0$ using the quadratic formula.

For this equation, $a = 1$, $b = -7.52$, and $c = -57.434$ which when substituted into the quadratic formula yields

$$x = \frac{-(-7.52) \pm \sqrt{(-7.52)^2 - 4(1)(-57.434)}}{2(1)}$$

Before going to the calculator, simplify a bit by hand using the rules for signed numbers:

$$x = \frac{7.52 \pm \sqrt{7.52^2 + 4(57.434)}}{2}$$

First we compute the quantity under the radical sign since it will be needed for both the + and the − sign and store it in the memory:

7.52 $\boxed{x^2}$ $\boxed{+}$ 4 $\boxed{\times}$ 57.434 $\boxed{=}$ $\boxed{\sqrt{x}}$ $\boxed{\text{STO}}$ (for an AOS system)*

The number 16.92 is now stored in the memory. It is the value of the square root. Now we add it to 7.52, then divide by 2,

$\boxed{+}$ 7.52 $\boxed{=}$ $\boxed{\div}$ 2 $\boxed{=}$

and read the first root $x_1 = 12.22$. Now use the minus sign for the square root by first recalling it from memory; then change the sign and proceed as before:

$\boxed{\text{RCL}}$ $\boxed{+/-}$ $\boxed{+}$ 7.52 $\boxed{=}$ $\boxed{\div}$ 2 $\boxed{=}$

We find that the second root $x_2 = -4.7$.

30. Solve $x^2 + 3x + 1$ and check using the product of roots theorem. The quadratic formula gives

$$x = \frac{-3 \pm \sqrt{3^2 - 4(1)(1)}}{2(1)} = \frac{-3 \pm \sqrt{9 - 4}}{2} = \frac{-3 \pm \sqrt{5}}{2}$$

Up to this point, hand calculation was faster than entering the numbers into the calculator. Now we evaluate the final result to get a decimal approximation of the roots:

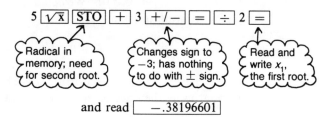

and read $\boxed{\quad -.38196601\quad}$

At this point the first root is on the display and the radical is in the memory. Since we will need the first root for our check, we save it and retrieve the radical from the memory at the same time by keying $\boxed{\text{EXC}}$, which exchanges the display value with the number in the memory, in this case $\sqrt{5}$.

*If you have an arithmetic system, insert a $\boxed{(}$ after the $\boxed{+}$.

$$\boxed{\text{EXC}}\ \boxed{+/-}\ \boxed{+}\ 3\ \boxed{+/-}\ \boxed{=}\ \boxed{\div}\ 2\ \boxed{=}$$

and we find that the second root $x_2 = -2.618034$. The product of the two roots equals $c/a = 1/1 = 1$, and we check this by multiplying the value of x_2 (now on display) by the value of x_1 (now in the memory):

$$\boxed{\times}\ \boxed{\text{RCL}}\ \boxed{=}\ \text{ and the display reads }\ \boxed{ 1}$$

(*Note*: Instead of using the theorem to check the results, we could have used it to compute x_2 once we knew x_1. Since we know that it must be true in this equation that $x_1 x_2 = 1$, we solve for x_2 and get

$$x_2 = \frac{1}{x_1} = \frac{1}{-.38196601}$$

Thus, while x_1 is on display, just key $\boxed{1/x}$ and read x_2.)

31. In the equation $x^2 - 0.2x - 3.99 = 0$, if $x_1 = 2.1$, compute x_2.

We know that $x_1 x_2 = c/a = -3.99/1 = -3.99$. Thus, solving for x_2, $(2.1)x_2 = -3.99$ implies that $x_2 = -3.99/2.1$, and we simply key

$$3.99\ \boxed{+/-}\ \boxed{\div}\ 2.1\ \boxed{=}\ \text{ and read }\ \boxed{ -1.9}$$

Thus we find that $x_2 = -1.9$ using only a simple division.

32. Check that $x = -1.9$ is actually a root of $x^2 - 0.2x - 3.99 = 0$ by substitution.

We calculate the quantity $(-1.9)^2 - 0.2\,(-1.9) - 3.99$, and if -1.9 is a root, we should get zero as a result:

$$1.9\ \boxed{+/-}\ \boxed{x^2}\ \boxed{-}\ .2\ \boxed{\times}\ 1.9\ \boxed{+/-}\ \boxed{-}\ 3.99\ \boxed{=}$$

We do, in fact, get zero (0). We could have simplified this considerably by reducing the signs to

$$1.9^2 + 0.2(1.9) - 3.99$$

before calculating. This is usually advisable provided that you are adept at using the rules of signs. We would key

$$1.9\ \boxed{x^2}\ \boxed{+}\ .2\ \boxed{\times}\ 1.9\ \boxed{-}\ 3.99\ \boxed{=}$$

which is much simpler. These two methods will only work for *AOS* systems. If you have an arithmetic system, these will not give the correct result. You must insert parentheses for the product, that is, $1.9^2 + (0.2(1.9)) - 3.99$. Also, the right parenthesis *cannot* be omitted:

$$1.9\ \boxed{x^2}\ \boxed{+}\ \boxed{(}\ .2\ \boxed{\times}\ 1.9\ \boxed{)}\ \boxed{-}\ 3.99\ \boxed{=}$$

If you rearrange the terms and place the product last, you may omit the right parenthesis. To be safe, if you have an arithmetic system it is better to include parentheses whenever you have a combination of operations unless you are very certain of the order in which the calculator will perform the operations.

33. Solve $x^4 - 10x^2 + 18 = 0$, which is quadratic in form.

The equation is a *quartic* (fourth degree) but can be thought of as quadratic in x^2 since it can be written as

$$(x^2)^2 - 10\ (x^2) + 18 = 0$$

We first solve for x^2 using the quadratic formula:

$$x^2 = \frac{-(-10) \pm \sqrt{(-10)^2 - 4(1)(18)}}{2(1)}$$

$$= \frac{10 \pm \sqrt{10^2 - 4(18)}}{2}$$

Now we calculate, and to save a bit of time we store $b = 10$ in the memory; then, after we use it to compute the radical (square root) term, we store the radical in memory by using the exchange key so that we can use the value $b = 10$ to add and finish computing the first root:

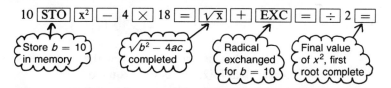

$$10\ \boxed{STO}\ \boxed{x^2}\ \boxed{-}\ 4\ \boxed{\times}\ 18\ \boxed{=}\ \boxed{\sqrt{x}}\ \boxed{+}\ \boxed{EXC}\ \boxed{=}\ \boxed{\div}\ 2\ \boxed{=}$$

Store $b = 10$ in memory $\sqrt{b^2 - 4ac}$ completed   Radical exchanged for $b = 10$ Final value of x^2, first root complete

and read the first value of $x^2 = 7.6457513$. (At this point we could compute the second root by using the product of roots theorem: just divide the first root *into* 18 in this case. We shall proceed, however, with the more naive approach of completing evaluation of the quadratic formula.)

At this point, compute the two corresponding values of x itself by taking the square root of the value of x^2 in the display by keying $\boxed{\sqrt{x}}$ and reading 2.7650952. Thus two roots of the quartic are $x = +2.7650952$ and $x = -2.7650952$. To get the other roots, remember that the radical is still stored in the memory, so we recall it and use it with a minus sign in the quadratic formula:

$$\boxed{RCL}\ \boxed{+/-}\ \boxed{+}\ 10\ \boxed{=}\ \boxed{\div}\ 2\ \boxed{=} \quad \text{and read} \quad \boxed{2.3542487}$$

which is another value of x^2. Now take the square root by again keying $\boxed{\sqrt{x}}$ and read 1.5343561. Thus two more values of x, roots of the quartic, are $x = +1.5343561$ and $x = -1.5343561$.

LAWS OF EXPONENTS AND RADICALS

34. Evaluate $4x^3$ and $(4x)^3$ for $x = 2.1$.

At $x = 2.1$, $4x^3 = 4(2.1)^3$. If you have an AOS system, key

$$4 \boxed{\times} 2.1 \boxed{y^x} 3 \boxed{=} \quad \text{and read} \quad \boxed{37.044}$$

The AOS system causes the 2.1 to be cubed first, as it should be, and then completes the multiplication by 4. If you have an arithmetic system, *you* must cube first; hence key

$$2.1 \boxed{y^x} 3 \boxed{\times} 4 \boxed{=}$$

To compute $(4x)^3$ at $x = 2.1$, the multiplication must be done first. On an AOS system, key

$$4 \boxed{\times} 2.1 \boxed{=} \boxed{y^x} 3 \boxed{=} \quad \text{and read} \quad \boxed{592.704}$$

or for either AOS or arithmetic, you could key

$$\boxed{(} 4 \boxed{\times} 2.1 \boxed{)} \boxed{y^x} 3 \boxed{=}$$

On arithmetic entry systems only, this could be shortened to

$$4 \boxed{\times} 2.1 \boxed{y^x} 3 \boxed{=}$$

(Notice that on an AOS system this would have computed $4(2.1)^3$ rather than $[4(2.1)]^3$, as was required.)

35. Compute $(5^{.2})^{.3}$ and also $5^{.06}$ showing that they are equal, and hence demonstrating the law that $(5^a)^b = 5^{ab}$.

To compute $(5^{.2})^{.3}$, key $5 \boxed{y^x} .2 \boxed{y^x} .3 \boxed{=}$ and read $\boxed{1.1013826}$
To compute $5^{.06}$, key $5 \boxed{y^x} .06 \boxed{=}$ and read the same result.

36. Compute $5^{.2^{.3}}$.

This expression means $5^{(.2^{.3})}$, and no special law of exponents applies to simplify it. It must be computed as written. (Compare this expression with the one in Problem 35.) There are two approaches to the calculation:

1. Use parentheses:

$$5 \boxed{y^x} \boxed{(} .2 \boxed{y^x} .3 \boxed{=} \quad \text{and read} \quad \boxed{2.69953}$$

2. Use the memory by computing $.2^{.3}$ first, store it, and then compute 5 to that power by recalling it from memory when needed:

$$.2 \boxed{y^x} .3 \boxed{=} \boxed{STO} \; 5 \boxed{y^x} \boxed{RCL} \boxed{=}$$

and again the result is 2.69953.

37. Compute $5^{1/6}$.

Method 1 $5 \boxed{y^x} 6 \boxed{1/x} \boxed{=}$

Method 2 Notice that $5^{1/6} = \sqrt[6]{5}$ and key

$$5 \boxed{INV} \boxed{y^x} 6 \boxed{=}$$

On some calculators the key configuration may look like

$$5 \boxed{2nd} \boxed{\sqrt[x]{y}} 6 \boxed{=}$$

The result is 1.3076605 using any method.

38. Compute $5^8(5^{.7})\sqrt{5}$.

Method 1 Direct calculation:

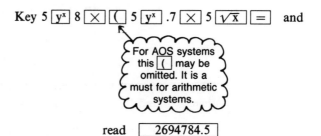

Key $5 \boxed{y^x} 8 \boxed{\times} \boxed{(} 5 \boxed{y^x} .7 \boxed{\times} 5 \boxed{\sqrt{x}} \boxed{=}$ and

For AOS systems this $\boxed{(}$ may be omitted. It is a must for arithmetic systems.

read $\boxed{\quad 2694784.5 \quad}$

Method 2 First, use the laws of exponents to simplify the expression. Note that $\sqrt{5} = 5^{\frac{1}{2}} = 5^{.5}$, and thus we have

$$5^8(5^{.7})(5^{.5}) = 5^8(5^{1.2}) = 5^{9.2}$$

Hence key $5 \boxed{y^x} 9.2 \boxed{=}$, and the result is identical.

39. Compute $6^{-2/3}(36)^3$.

Method 1 Direct calculation:

$$6 \boxed{y^x} \boxed{(} 2 \boxed{\div} 3 \boxed{)} \boxed{+/-} \boxed{\times} \boxed{(} 36 \boxed{y^x} 3 \boxed{=}$$

Method 2 First, simplify by noticing that $36 = 6^2$, and hence

$$6^{-2/3}(36)^3 = 6^{-2/3}(6^2)^3 = 6^{-2/3}(6^6) = 6^{5\,1/3} = 6^{16/3}$$

so key

$$6 \boxed{y^x} \boxed{(\!(} 16 \boxed{\div} 3 \boxed{)\!)} \boxed{=}$$

The result in both cases is 14129.93.

40. Compute $(5^3 \times 4.2^6)/3^7$. Key

$$5 \boxed{y^x} 3 \boxed{\times} \boxed{(\!(} 4.2 \boxed{y^x} 6 \boxed{)\!)} \boxed{\div} \boxed{(\!(} 3 \boxed{y^x} 7 \boxed{=}$$

(If you have an AOS system, all the parentheses may be omitted.)
The result is 313.73067.

41. Compute $5^6 + 5^3$.

No special formula is applicable. This must be computed directly:

$$5 \boxed{y^x} 6 \boxed{+} \boxed{(\!(} 5 \boxed{y^x} 3 \boxed{=} \quad \text{and read} \quad \boxed{15750}$$

The parenthesis may be omitted for AOS systems. If you have an
arithmetic system, it is required here.

42. Compute $(1.2^7 \times 5 \times 10^8)/(4^6 \times 5.2^4)$.

Notice that the quantity 5×10^8 can be handled using the $\boxed{EE}$ key
since it is really scientific notation. Hence key

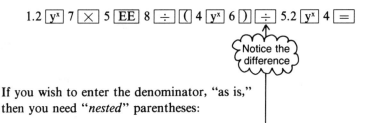

If you wish to enter the denominator, "as is,"
then you need "*nested*" parentheses:

$$1.2 \boxed{y^x} 7 \boxed{\times} 5 \boxed{EE} 8 \boxed{\div} \boxed{(\!(} \boxed{(\!(} 4 \boxed{y^x} 6 \boxed{)\!)} \boxed{\times} \boxed{(\!(} 5.2 \boxed{y^x} 4 \boxed{=}$$

In the first method the product in the denominator is treated as two
successive divisions. In the second method it is entered as a multiplication inside parentheses. Answer: $\boxed{5.9823 \ 02}$.

43. Compute $(0.52)^{12}/(0.52)^{-4}$.

Method 1 Direct calculation:

$$.52 \boxed{y^x} 12 \boxed{\div} \boxed{(\!(} .52 \boxed{y^x} 4 \boxed{+/-} \boxed{=} \quad \text{and read}$$
$$\boxed{.00002858}$$

If you want this in scientific notation, key

$$\boxed{EE} \boxed{=} \quad \text{and read} \quad \boxed{2.828 \ -05}$$

Thus the result is $0.00002858 = 2.858 \times 10^{-5}$.

Method 2 Algebraic simplification before computing: Subtracting exponents, we get $(0.52)^{12-(-4)} = (0.52)^{16}$; thus key

$$.52 \boxed{y^x} \ 16 \boxed{=}$$

and get the same result.

44. Compute $(3^{\sqrt{2}})^{\sqrt{8}}$.

Method 1 Direct calculation:

$$3 \boxed{y^x} \ 2 \boxed{\sqrt{x}} \boxed{y^x} \ 8 \boxed{\sqrt{x}} \boxed{=} \quad \text{and read}$$
$$\boxed{80.999999}$$

Method 2 Simplify first; then compute $(3^{\sqrt{2}})^{\sqrt{8}} = 3^{\sqrt{16}} = 3^4$. So key $3 \boxed{y^x} \ 4 \boxed{=}$ and read $\boxed{ 81}$. This is the exact answer. What this demonstrates is that taking roots and powers can introduce *roundoff error* even in simple problems. Moreover, algebraic changes can reduce it.

45. Compute $1/^5\sqrt{2}$.

Method 1 Direct calculation: key

$$2 \boxed{INV} \boxed{y^x} \ 5 \boxed{=} \boxed{1/x} \boxed{=} \quad \text{and read}$$
$$\boxed{.87055056}$$

On some calculators, even though it is exactly the same procedure, the key configuration looks like this:

$$2 \boxed{2nd} \boxed{^x\sqrt{y}} \ 5 \boxed{=} \boxed{1/x} \boxed{=}$$

Method 2 Change the quantity to power notation:

$$\frac{1}{^5\sqrt{2}} = \frac{1}{2^{1/5}} = 2^{-1/5}$$

and so calculate either

$$2 \boxed{y^x} \ 5 \boxed{1/x} \boxed{=} \boxed{1/x} \quad \text{for the positive exponent form}$$

or

$$2 \boxed{y^x} \ 5 \boxed{1/x} \boxed{+/-} \boxed{=} \quad \text{for the negative exponent form.}$$

46. Compute $^5\sqrt{-3.71293}$.

If we try to enter this directly we get an error indication because the calculator will not accept negative radicands. Since the index 5 is an odd number, the root of this negative number will be negative. More specifically, $^5\sqrt{-3.71293} = -^5\sqrt{+3.71293}$; thus key

3.71293 $\boxed{\text{INV}}$ $\boxed{y^x}$ 5 $\boxed{=}$ and read $\boxed{1.3}$

We can then key $\boxed{+/-}$ to display the $(-)$ sign of the actual answer, or (more easily) just write it down. Hence

$$\sqrt[5]{-3.71293} = -1.3$$

(*Caution*: This technique is not exactly the same if the index were even; for example, $\sqrt[4]{-7.2}$ does *not* exist, but $\sqrt[5]{-7.2}$ does!)

LOGARITHMS

47. Evaluate and round to four decimal places (a) $\log_{10} 5$; (b) $\log_{10} 0.042$; (c) $\log_{10} (2.1 + 5.6^2)$; (d) $\log_{10} (2.1 - 5.6^2)$.

(a) Key 5 $\boxed{\log}$ and read $\boxed{0.69897}$. To four decimal places this is 0.6990.
(b) Key .042 $\boxed{\log}$ and read $\boxed{-1.3767507}$. Thus, to four decimal places, $\log_{10} 0.042 = -1.3768$.
(c) Key 2.1 $\boxed{+}$ 5.6 $\boxed{x^2}$ $\boxed{=}$ $\boxed{\log}$ and read $\boxed{1.5245259}$. Rounded to four decimal places, this is 1.5245.
(d) Key 2.1 $\boxed{-}$ 5.6 $\boxed{x^2}$ $\boxed{=}$ $\boxed{\log}$ and read $\boxed{\text{Error}}$. (d) is undefined!

If you don't have a $\boxed{\log}$ key, but only a $\boxed{\ln x}$ key, use the formula

$$\log_{10} N = \frac{\ln N}{\ln 10}$$

by first computing ln 10 and storing the result; then use $\boxed{\ln x}$ in place of $\boxed{\log}$ in the preceding calculations. Then divide by ln 10 by recalling it from the memory. For example, (a) could be computed as:

Step 1   Compute ln 10 and store it in memory for all subsequent calculations.

$$10 \boxed{\ln x} \boxed{\text{STO}}$$

Step 2   To calculate $\log_{10} 5$, we can now key

$$5 \boxed{\ln x} \boxed{\div} \boxed{\text{RCL}} \boxed{=}$$

48. To what power must we raise 10 to get 23.442288?
This asks the question $10^x = 23.442288$? In terms of logarithms, this says $x = \log_{10} 23.442288$, and so key

23.442288 $\boxed{\log}$ and read $\boxed{\quad 1.37 \quad}$

If you only have a natural log key, use it instead and divide the result by ln 10.

23.442288 $\boxed{\ln x}$ $\boxed{\div}$ 10 $\boxed{\ln x}$ $\boxed{=}$

49. Use the logarithm key to compute $10^{4.6}$.
Since $10^{4.6} = $ antilog(4.6), the inverse log (base 10 of course), key

4.6 $\boxed{\text{INV}}$ $\boxed{\log}$ and read $\boxed{\quad 39810.717 \quad}$

If you only have a natural log key, this is a bit more difficult. You must first express the quantity desired in terms of the natural logarithm:

$$10^{4.6} = \ln^{-1}(\ln 10^{4.6}) = \ln^{-1}(4.6 \ln 10)$$

where $\ln^{-1}$ is the inverse natural log. Thus key 10 $\boxed{\ln x}$ $\boxed{\times}$ 4.6 $\boxed{=}$ $\boxed{\text{INV}}$ $\boxed{\ln x}$. (On many calculators $\boxed{\text{INV}}$ $\boxed{\ln x}$ is represented as $\boxed{\text{2nd}}$ $\boxed{e^x}$.)

50. Evaluate $[4.2(8.05)^5]/99.8$ using logarithms.

First take the log of the expression; expand using the rules of logarithms. Evaluate using the calculator, and finally take the inverse log (i.e., antilogarithm) of that result:

$$\log \frac{4.2(8.05)^5}{99.8} = \log 4.2 + 5 \log 8.05 - \log 99.8$$

and so key

4.2 $\boxed{\log}$ $\boxed{+}$ $\boxed{(}$ 5 $\boxed{\times}$ 8.05 $\boxed{\log}$ $\boxed{-}$ 99.8 $\boxed{\log}$ $\boxed{=}$

Then, with the number computed still displayed, key $\boxed{\text{INV}}$ $\boxed{\log}$. (On some calculators this looks like $\boxed{\text{2nd}}$ $\boxed{10^x}$), and the result is 1422.6503. A direct calculation will verify this result. If you have only a natural log key, use it instead of the base 10 log and at the end take the inverse natural log. We do not have to use ln 10 here since we are taking inverses after taking logs, which brings us back to the original numerical scale no matter which base logarithm is used.

51. Solve $\log_{10} x = 5.2$ for x.
This equation just says that 5.2 is the power to which 10 must be raised to yield x. That is,

$$10^{5.2} = x$$

So key 10 $\boxed{y^x}$ 5.2 $\boxed{=}$. Or we could use 5.2 $\boxed{INV}$ $\boxed{log}$ instead, and the result is 158489.32.

52. Solve $\log_x 100 = 10$ for x to two decimal places.

Here we want to find the base. This requires some algebraic manipulation: $\log_x 100 = 10$ means that $x^{10} = 100$, and so $x = \sqrt[10]{100} = 100^{1/10}$. And so simply key 100 $\boxed{y^x}$ 10 $\boxed{1/x}$ $\boxed{=}$ Or you could key 100 $\boxed{INV}$ $\boxed{y^x}$ 10 $\boxed{=}$ In either case, read $\boxed{1.5848932}$. Thus $x = 1.58$, approximately.

53. Evaluate $\log_2 512$.

Using the change of base formula

$$\log_2 512 = \frac{\log 512}{\log 2} \quad \text{and also} \quad = \frac{\ln 512}{\ln 2}$$

So key

$$512 \;\boxed{log}\; \boxed{\div}\; 2\; \boxed{log}\; \boxed{=}$$

or else key

$$512 \;\boxed{lnx}\; \boxed{\div}\; 2\; \boxed{lnx}\; \boxed{=}$$

and either way we find that $\log_2 512 = 9$. To check, $2^9 = 512$.

54. Solve $\ln x = 1.65$ for x to three decimal places.

Since $\ln x = \log_e x = 1.65$, x is the number we get when we raise e to the 1.65 power. Thus

$$x = e^{1.65}$$

Evaluate this as either 1.65 $\boxed{INV}$ $\boxed{lnx}$ or 1.65 $\boxed{2nd}$ $\boxed{e^x}$, depending on your key configuration, and find that $x = 5.207$, rounded to three decimal places.

Another way to look at this equation is to raise both sides as powers of e; that is, take inverse logs of both sides: $e^{\ln x} = e^{1.65}$, and since they are inverses, $e^{\ln x} = x$; hence, once again we deduce that $x = e^{1.65}$.

55. Solve for x if $e^x = 0.579$.

Since $e^x = 0.579$, taking natural logs of both sides, $\ln e^x = \ln 0.579$, and since they are inverses, $\ln e^x = x$. Thus $x = \ln 0.579$, and we key

$$.579 \;\boxed{lnx}\; \quad \text{and read} \quad \boxed{-0.5464528}$$

which is the value of x.

56. Solve for x if $5^x = 12$.

Take logs of both sides and use the power rule: $\ln 5^x = \ln 12$, which implies that $x \ln 5 = \ln 12$. Solving for x, we divide both sides by $\ln 5$ and get $x = \ln 12/\ln 5$; so key

$$12 \boxed{\ln x} \boxed{\div} 5 \boxed{\ln x} \boxed{=} \quad \text{and read} \quad \boxed{1.5439593}$$

If you use $\boxed{\log}$ instead of $\boxed{\ln x}$, the ultimate result is the same.

57. Solve the equation $1.24^{3x} = 5.2$ for x to three decimal places.

Taking natural logarithms (or any logarithm) of both sides, $\ln 1.24^{3x} = \ln 5.2$, and then applying the power rule, $3x \ln 1.24 = \ln 5.2$. Finally, isolate x by dividing both sides of the equation by $3 \ln 1.24$, and get

$$x = \frac{\ln 5.2}{3 \ln 1.24}$$

Thus calculate the right-hand side as

$$5.2 \boxed{\ln x} \boxed{\div} 3 \boxed{\div} 1.24 \boxed{\ln x} \boxed{=}$$

or, if you wish, use parentheses:

$$5.2 \boxed{\ln x} \boxed{\div} \boxed{(} 3 \boxed{\times} 1.24 \boxed{\ln x} \boxed{=}$$

The result is

$$\boxed{2.5547364}$$

Thus, to three decimal places, $x = 2.555$.

58. Solve for x to three decimal places: $6(5^{3x-1}) = 4^{-x}$.

First take logarithms of both sides (any log will do), and then apply the rules for logarithms and some algebra:

$$\ln 6 + (3x - 1)\ln 5 = -x \ln 4$$
$$(3x - 1)\ln 5 + x \ln 4 = -\ln 6$$
$$3x \ln 5 + x \ln 4 = \ln 5 - \ln 6$$
$$x(3 \ln 5 + \ln 4) = \ln 5 - \ln 6$$
$$x = \frac{\ln 5 - \ln 6}{3 \ln 5 + \ln 4}$$

This may be now calculated, as is, or it can be simplified even further into the equivalent expression:

$$x = \frac{\ln (5/6)}{\ln (4 \cdot 5^3)}$$

For the first expression for x, key

5 [lnx] [−] 6 [lnx] [=] [÷] [(] 3 [×] 5 [lnx] [+] 4 [lnx] [=]

For the second, simplified expression, key

5 [÷] 6 [=] [lnx] [÷] [(] 5 [yˣ] 3 [×] 4 [)] [lnx] [=]

and, in either case, read [−.02933758]. Thus $x = -0.029$ to three decimal places.

59. Solve for x to four decimal places: $\dfrac{1}{\sqrt{2\pi}}\, e^{-x^2/2} = 0.39$.

Use a little algebra and then take the natural log of both sides as follows:

$$e^{-x^2/2} = \sqrt{2\pi}(0.39)$$

$$\ln e^{-x^2/2} = \ln[\sqrt{2\pi}(0.39)]$$

Since $\ln(\ )$ and $e^{(\ )}$ are inverses of each other, we get

$$\frac{-x^2}{2} = \ln[\sqrt{2\pi}(0.39)]$$

$$x^2 = -2 \ln[\sqrt{2\pi}(0.39)]$$

$$x = \pm\sqrt{-2 \ln[\sqrt{2\pi}(0.39)]}$$

We shall compute the positive square root. The negative square root is also an answer, but has the same absolute value, so no additional computation is necessary. Starting with the innermost quantities, key

2 [×] [π] [=] [√x̄] [×] .39 [=] [lnx] [×] 2 [=] [+/−] [√x̄]

and read [.21293195]. Thus $x = \pm 0.2129$ to four decimal places.

PROGRESSIONS

60. Compute the first four terms of the sequence given by the formula $f(n) = 2/(n^2 + 3)$; that is, compute $f(1)$, $f(2)$, $f(3)$, and $f(4)$.

$$f(1) = \frac{2}{(n^2 + 3)}:$$ 2 [÷] [(] 1 [x²] [+] 3 [=] and read [0.5]

$f(2) = \dfrac{2}{2^2 + 3}$: $2 \boxed{\div} \boxed{(} \boxed{(} 2 \boxed{x^2} \boxed{+} 3 \boxed{=}$ and read $\boxed{.28571429}$

$f(3) = \dfrac{2}{3^2 + 3}$: $2 \boxed{\div} \boxed{(} \boxed{(} 3 \boxed{x^2} \boxed{+} 3 \boxed{=}$ and read $\boxed{.16666667}$

$f(4) = \dfrac{2}{4^2 + 3}$: $2 \boxed{\div} \boxed{(} \boxed{(} 4 \boxed{x^2} \boxed{+} 3 \boxed{=}$ and read $\boxed{.10526316}$

Thus the first four terms of the sequence are (to four decimal places) 0.5, .286, .167, and .105. If we computed by hand, we would get the fractions $\frac{1}{2}$, $\frac{2}{7}$, $\frac{1}{6}$, $\frac{2}{19}$.

61. Compute the first five terms of the sequence $f(n) = n^2 + 3$.

In this case we can use the constant to simplify the calculations. First set up the 3 as an addition constant by keying $3 \boxed{+} \boxed{K}$, and then key

$1 \boxed{x^2} \boxed{=}$ and the first term is 4

$2 \boxed{x^2} \boxed{=}$ and the second term is 7

$3 \boxed{x^2} \boxed{=}$ and the third term is 12

$4 \boxed{x^2} \boxed{=}$ and the fourth term is 19

$5 \boxed{x^2} \boxed{=}$ and the fifth term is 28

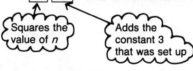

Squares the value of n Adds the constant 3 that was set up

If you don't have a constant key, you must key $\boxed{+}$ 3 after squaring; that is, the general sequence without the constant is

$$n \boxed{x^2} \boxed{+} 3 \boxed{=}$$

which must be computed for $n = 1, 2, 3, 4, 5$.

62. Find the 35th term of the arithmetic sequence (progression)

$$3, \ 3^2/_5, \ 3^4/_5, \ 4^1/_5, \ \ldots$$

For this sequence, $a_1 = 3$, $d = \frac{2}{5}$, and $n = 35$. Then the 35th term is given by using the formula

$$a_n = a_1 + (n - 1)d$$

Compute $n - 1$ mentally, which is easy since $n - 1 = 35 - 1 = 34$. Hence

$$a_{35} = 3 + 34(^2/_5)$$

and so key

$$34 \boxed{\times} 2 \boxed{\div} 5 \boxed{+} 3 \boxed{=} \quad \text{and read} \quad \boxed{10.2}$$

Since $0.2 = {}^1/_5$, $a_{35} = 10.2 = 10^1/_5$.

63. Generate the first eight terms of the arithmetic sequence $-2, 3, 8, \ldots$.

The first term is $a_1 = -2$ and the difference $d = 5$. Thus we want to add 5 to each successive term. If you have a constant key, set up 5 as an additive constant by keying $5 \boxed{+} \boxed{K}$. Then key $\boxed{=}$ seven times, writing each term that appears:

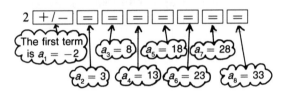

64. In an arithmetic sequence, if $a_3 = 8$ and $a_7 = 28$, compute a_{50}.

Since, in general, $a_n = a_1 + (n - 1)d$, the preceding facts yield, upon substitution,

$$a_3 = a_1 + (3 - 1)d$$

and since $a_3 = 8$, we get $8 = a_1 + 2d$.

$$a_7 = a_1 + (7 - 1)d$$

and since $a_7 = 28$, we get $28 = a_1 + 6d$. Subtracting the first equation from the second, we get $20 = 4d$; hence $d = 5$. Substituting this value into the first equation (or you could use the second), we get

$$8 = a_1 + 2(5) = a_1 + 10$$

Solving, we get $a_1 = -2$. Now that we have found d and a_1, we can find a_{50} by again using the general equation and substituting for those values that we now know:

$$a_{50} = a_1 + (50 - 1)d = -2 + 49(5)$$

and so compute

$$5 \boxed{\times} 49 \boxed{-} 2 \boxed{=} \quad \text{and read} \quad \boxed{\quad 243. \quad}$$

Thus $a_{50} = 243$.

65. Compute the sum of the first 50 terms of the arithmetic sequence 3, 5, 7, 9, ...

We first need to find $a_{50} = a_1 + (50 - 1)d = 3 + 49(2)$; so key $49 \boxed{\times} 2 \boxed{+} 3 \boxed{=}$ and we find that $a_{50} = 101$. *Leave this value displayed.* Now

$$S_n = n \frac{a_1 + a_n}{2}$$

and so

$$S_{50} = 50 \frac{a_1 + a_{50}}{2} = 50 \frac{3 + 101}{2}$$

Thus, key since $a_{50} = 101$ is still displayed, key

$$\boxed{+} 3 \boxed{=} \boxed{\times} 50 \boxed{\div} 2 \boxed{=}$$

and we find that $S_{50} = 2600$.

66. Compute the sum of the integers from 1 to 1,000,000.

This is just an arithmetic sequence with $a_1 = 1$ and $d = 1$, and we want to find $S_{1,000,000}$.

$$S_{1,000,000} = 1,000,000 \frac{1 + 1,000,000}{2}$$

so key

$$1 \boxed{+} 1000000 \boxed{=} \boxed{\div} 2 \boxed{\times} 1000000 \boxed{=} \quad \text{and read} \quad \boxed{5. \ 11}$$

Thus the sum is 5×10^{11}, which is a 5 followed by 11 zeros, that is, 500,000,000,000. (The exact answer is really 500,000,500,000. We are off by 500,000 because of roundoff in scientific notation.)

67. Find the tenth term of the geometric progression 2, −6, 18, ...

First compute the ratio r by forming the ratio of any two consecutive terms, for instance, the first two,

$$r = \frac{-6}{2}$$

and so key 6 $\boxed{+/-}$ $\boxed{\div}$ 2 $\boxed{=}$ and leave the result $r = -3$ displayed. *Do not clear.* Now $a_n = a_1 r^{n-1}$ and so

$$a_{10} = a_1 r^9 = 2(-3)^9$$

and $r = -3$ is still displayed. Since on the calculator we cannot take a power of a negative number, we must realize that $(-3)^9 = -3^9$, and so we must make the displayed value positive before taking the ninth power, multiply by 2, and finally place the minus sign manually by just writing it down. We key (with $r = -3$ still displayed)

$\boxed{+/-}\ \boxed{y^x}\ 9\ \boxed{\times}\ 2\ \boxed{=}$ and read $\boxed{39366}$.

Thus we place the minus sign in front of this answer and $a_{10} = -39{,}366$. If we had tried to compute the expression first obtained for the tenth term directly, we would have an error indication. Thus we had to algebraically account for the sign in order to perform the calculation.

68. In a geometric progression $a_3 = 18$, $a_9 = 13{,}122$. Find a_1 and r.

Substituting the given facts into the general formula $a_n = a_1 r^{n-1}$, we get

$$a_3 = 18 = a_1 r^{(3-1)} = a_1 r^2$$

and

$$a_9 = 13{,}122 = a_1 r^{(9-1)} = a_1 r^8$$

Dividing equations,

$$\frac{\cancel{a_1} r^8}{\cancel{a_1} r^2} = \frac{13{,}122}{18}$$

$$r^6 = \frac{13{,}122}{18}$$

and solving,

$$r = \sqrt[6]{\frac{13{,}122}{18}}$$

So to compute r, key 13122 $\boxed{\div}$ 18 $\boxed{=}$ $\boxed{INV}$ $\boxed{y^x}$ 6 $\boxed{=}$ and find that $r = 3$. Using the first equation, substitute this value for r:

$$18 = a_1 r^2 = a_1 (3)^2 = 9a_1$$

Thus $a_1 = {}^{18}/_9 = 2$, which is found mentally in this case. If the numbers are more complicated, the division can be done on the calculator.

69. For the geometric progression 3, 0.6, 0.12, . . ., find the sixth term a_6 and the sum of the first six terms S_6.

First we must find the quantity r by computing the ratio of two consecutive terms; that is, $r = a_{n+1}/a_n$. In this case

$$r = \frac{0.6}{3}$$

and so key .6 $\boxed{\div}$ 3 $\boxed{=}$ and find that $r = 0.2$. Note that the first term $a_1 = 3$, and since $a_n = a_1 r^{n-1}$, we have, upon substitution,

$$a_6 = a_1 r^5 = 3(.2)^5$$

Thus key

.2 $\boxed{y^x}$ 5 $\boxed{\times}$ 3 $\boxed{=}$ and read $\boxed{0.00096}$

Thus $a_6 = 0.00096$. Now

$$S_n = \frac{a_1(1 - r^n)}{1 - r}$$

and so

$$S_6 = \frac{a_1(1 - r^6)}{1 - r} = \frac{3(1 - .2^6)}{1 - .2}$$

To compute this as stated, key

3 $\boxed{\times}$ $\boxed{(}$ 1 $\boxed{-}$ $\boxed{(}$ .2 $\boxed{y^x}$ 6 $\boxed{=}$ $\boxed{\div}$ $\boxed{(}$ 1 $\boxed{-}$ .2 $\boxed{=}$

It would be easier to compute $1 - .2 = .8$ mentally and then to compute $1 - .2^6$ first when computing, as follows:

1 $\boxed{-}$ $\boxed{(}$ .2 $\boxed{y^x}$ 6 $\boxed{=}$ $\boxed{\times}$ 3 $\boxed{\div}$ .8 $\boxed{=}$

Using either method, the result is 3.74976.

70. In a geometric progression, if $a_1 = 7$ and $r = -.2$, compute S_8 accurate to three decimal places.

$$S_n = \frac{a_1(1 - r^n)}{1 - r} \quad \text{and so} \quad S_8 = \frac{7[1 - (-.2)^8]}{1 - (-.2)}$$

One must exercise caution here. When you try to compute $(-.2)^8$ directly, you will get an error indication. You must note *before* calculating that $(-.2)^8 = +.2^8$, since the power is even. Thus we actually calculate this simplified expression (where the denominator has already been mentally evaluated):

$$S_8 = \frac{7(1 - .2^8)}{1.2}$$

Key

$$1 \boxed{-} \boxed{(\!(} .2 \boxed{y^x} 8 \boxed{=} \boxed{\times} 7 \boxed{-} 1.2 \boxed{=} \quad \text{and read} \quad \boxed{5.8333184}$$

Thus, accurate to three decimal places, $S_8 = 5.833$.

As an alternative method, if we wanted to generate the progression as well, we could have used the constant key to facilitate generating the progression and used the memory to accumulate the sum of the generated terms, recalling the final sum once the eight terms required were generated.

71. Sum the infinite number of terms of the geometric progression 2, .4, .08, ...

First find the ratio $r = .4/2 = .2$ and note that $a_1 = 2$. Thus

$$S_\infty = \frac{a_1}{1 - r} = \frac{2}{1 - .2}$$

so key $2 \boxed{\div} \boxed{(\!(} 1 \boxed{-} .2 \boxed{=}$ and find that $S_\infty = 2.5$.

72. Insert a number x between 6 and 150 so that the three numbrs form a geometric progression.

If the three numbers are to be in a geometric progression, then successive ratios must be equal (to the ratio r for the progression). Thus

$$\frac{x}{6} = \frac{150}{x}$$

and hence, solving for x, $x^2 = 6(150)$ and thus $x = \sqrt{6(150)}$. Thus key

$$6 \boxed{\times} 150 \boxed{=} \boxed{\sqrt{x}} \quad \text{and read} \quad \boxed{30}$$

Therefore, the numbers 6, 30, 150 form a geometric progression, with ratio (incidentally) $r = 5$.

73. If $f(1) = 3$ and $f(n + 1) = 3f(n) - 1$, compute the first four terms of the sequence.

The first term is given as $f(1) = 3$. To find the remaining terms, we successively substitute in the recursion formula that is given:

$f(1 + 1) = f(2) = 3f(1) - 1 = \quad 3(3) - 1 = \quad 8 \qquad 3 \boxed{\times} 3 \boxed{-} 1 \boxed{=}$

$f(2 + 1) = f(3) = 3f(2) - 1 = \quad 3(8) - 1 = 23 \qquad 3 \boxed{\times} 8 \boxed{-} 1 \boxed{=}$

$f(3 + 1) = f(4) = 3f(3) - 1 = 3(23) - 1 = 68 \qquad 3 \boxed{\times} 23 \boxed{-} 1 \boxed{=}$

Thus the first four terms, each derived from the previous one, are 3, 8, 23, 68. This is neither an arithmetic nor a geometric sequence.

3
Trigonometry

Angular Measure

Whereas in plane geometry the measure of an angle was from 0° to 180°, here the concept is extended to any real number. Various scales can be used to do this, depending on different applications. In this text we utilize only the first three listed:

1. *Degree-minute-second* (DMS) is used in certain engineering applications. A circle is divided into 360 equal angular units called *degrees*. A *minute* is just $\frac{1}{60}$ of a degree (1 degree = 60 minutes). A *second* is $\frac{1}{60}$ of a minute (1 minute = 60 seconds).

2. *Decimal degrees* is essentially the same system except that, instead of minutes and seconds, fractional parts of a degree are expressed as a decimal fraction of a degree. This is the system used for calculation on calculators.

3. *Radians* are numerical units that compare arc length with the radius of a circle as a ratio. Thus one whole circle would be 2π radians. This unit of measure is used in both applied and theoretical work since it greatly simplifies certain formulas.

4. *Grads* (or grades) and *mils* are used in military applications. A *grad* is 1/100 of a right angle. A *mil* is 1/1600 of a right angle or 1/16 of a grad. (The mil was originally formulated to be an angle that would subtend an

arc equal to 1/1000 of a radius, but since that would have divided the circle into 6283.1853 units, this number was for convenience increased to 6400, and so a "mil" actually subtends an arc equal to 0.00098175 times the length of a radius, very close to 0.001. Hence we still keep the name "mil," which means "thousandth.")

Although many calculators have the capability of using the grade or grad measure, as it is now known, we shall not cover its use because its applications are very specialized.

The first thing to note is a method of changing a degree-minute-second angle into decimal degrees. We show it only for AOS systems, which most scientific calculators have. Some older versions may use an arithmetic (sequential) entry system and parentheses must then be inserted around each division. The idea is to represent each minute as 1/60 of a degree and each second as 1/3600 of a degree (rather than 1/60 of a minute). Hence if we have $D°M'S''$ (D degrees, M minutes, S seconds), key

$$D \boxed{+} M \boxed{÷} 60 \boxed{+} S \boxed{÷} 3600 \boxed{=}$$

and the displayed number will be in decimal degrees.

Example To change 56°12′18″ into decimal degrees, key

$$56 \boxed{+} 12 \boxed{÷} 60 \boxed{+} 18 \boxed{÷} 3600 \boxed{=}$$

and find that the equivalent angle is 56.205°.

If for some reason you wish to go from decimal degrees to the DMS scale, the procedure is to take the decimal part times 60 minutes to get the number of minutes; then any fraction of a minute left over is multiplied by 60 seconds to find out how many seconds this represents. A procedure for accomplishing this is contained in the next example, which should clarify the explanation just given.

Example To change 56.205° into DMS units, take the decimal part and multiply by 60: .205 $\boxed{\times}$ 60 $\boxed{=}$ and read $\boxed{\quad 12.3}$ and record 12′. Subtract the 12: $\boxed{-}$ 12 $\boxed{=}$, and then multiply the result by 60: $\boxed{\times}$ 60 $\boxed{=}$ and read $\boxed{\quad 18.}$. Record 18″. Thus 56.205° = 56°12′18″.

Some calculators do both conversions automatically by using a key labeled

$$\rightarrow D.MS$$

$$\boxed{\rightarrow DEG}$$

To use it on the previous examples, one would do the following:

Example   To change 56°12′18″ into decimal degrees, key 56.1218 $\boxed{\to\text{DEG}}$.
To change 56.205° into DMS, key 56.205 $\boxed{\text{2nd}}$ $\boxed{\text{D.MS}}$ and read
$\boxed{56.1218}$, which is interpreted as the DMS unit 56°12′18″.

Since most calculators do not have this feature, convenient as it is, and because those that do have it may have various key configurations we shall ignore it henceforth. Don't let that stop you from using it if, in fact, your calculator has this capability.

A *radian* is the ratio of the length of an arc to the radius of a circle. For a full circle, the arc length is the entire circumference $C = 2\pi r$. Thus the ratio of this to a radius is

$$\frac{\text{arc}}{\text{radius}} = \frac{C}{r} = \frac{2\pi r}{r} = 2\pi$$

Thus a full circle (360°) $= 2\pi$ radians, and 180° $= \pi$ radians. Hence, to change degrees to radians, multiply by $\pi/180$ and to change from radians to degrees multiply by $180/\pi$.

Example   36° is $36 \times (\pi/180) = \pi/5$ radians. On a calculator we would compute

$$36 \boxed{\times} \boxed{\pi} \boxed{\div} 180 \boxed{=} \quad \text{and read} \quad \boxed{.62831853}$$

If you compute $\pi/5$ you get the same result, so this is the decimal approximation to the radian measure of 36°.

Example   One radian is $1 \times (180/\pi)$ degrees. To compute this, key

$$180 \boxed{\div} \boxed{\pi} \boxed{=} \quad \text{and read} \quad \boxed{57.29578}$$

Thus 1 radian $= 57.29578°$ approximately. In the DMS system of angular notation, this would be 57°17′44.8″.

If an angle θ is expressed in *radians*, the arc length s (see Figure 3-1) that subtends that angle is related to the angle by the simple equation

$$s = r\theta$$

Figure 3-1 Arc Length

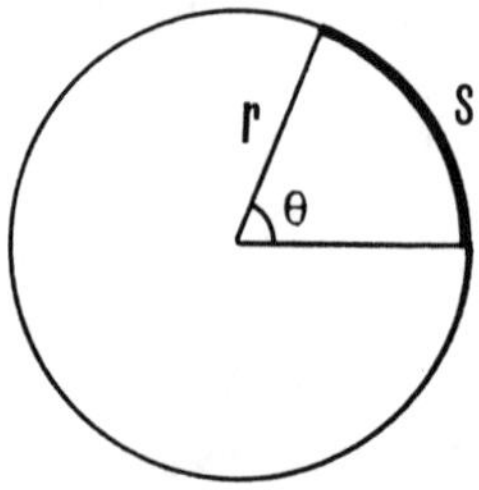

If θ is in radians, the area of the sector defined by the angle (see Figure 3-2) is given by the simple formula

$$A = \tfrac{1}{2}\,r^2\theta$$

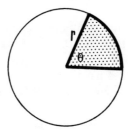

Figure 3-2 Area of Sector

Example In a circle of radius 8, an angle of 1 radian intercepts an arc of length

$$s = r\theta = 8(1) = 8 \text{ units}$$

and sweeps out a sector of area

$$A = \tfrac{1}{2}\,r^2\theta = \tfrac{1}{2}\,(8)^2(1) = \tfrac{1}{2}\,(64) = 32 \text{ square units}$$

Basic Trigonometric Functions

There are various formulations of trigonometric functions. The most common are ratios in right triangles, projections of winding functions on a unit circle, and series definitions. It may be helpful in using the calculator to think of a quasi-definition of these functions to simply be the output of the calculator upon pressing certain keys and then relating this to the mathematical definition depending upon the situation. Since the calculator is an application tool, we shall only give the triangle definition, but note that it is not entirely satisfactory nor general from a mathematical viewpoint. Refer to Figure 3-3.

Figure 3-3

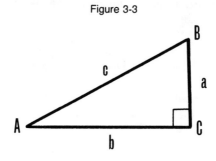

Sine function: $\sin A = \dfrac{a}{c}$; $\sin B = \dfrac{b}{c}$

Cosine function: $\cos A = \dfrac{b}{c}$; $\cos B = \dfrac{a}{c}$

Tangent function: $\tan A = \dfrac{a}{b}$; $\tan B = \dfrac{b}{a}$

These three functions are computed by entering the angle in question onto the display and then pressing either $\boxed{\sin}$, $\boxed{\cos}$, or $\boxed{\tan}$ as desired. Since the angle may be expressed in degrees, radians, or even grads, the calculator must have some way to tell them apart. For example, the display $\boxed{2.53}$ could mean 2.53°, 2.53 radians, or 2.53 grads, which are all different angles. The $\boxed{\text{DRG}}$ key provides the solution to this dilemma. When the calculator is turned on, it is set to *degree mode*. This means that the calculator will interpret a displayed value as degrees. The letters D, R, and G on the key stand for degrees, radians, and grads, respectively. Each time you press the $\boxed{\text{DRG}}$ key, the calculator changes mode in the cyclic order degrees → radians → grads, and then back to degrees again. This is shown in the following diagram:

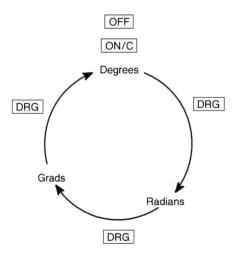

The calculator indicates on the display which mode it is in by a symbol. On LED (light-emitting diode) versions, no symbol indicates degrees, a single apostrophe (') indicates radians, and a double apostrophe (") indicates grads.

$\boxed{2.53}$ $\boxed{'2.53}$ $\boxed{''2.53}$
Degrees   Radians   Grads

Very Important: When pressing $\boxed{\text{DRG}}$, it *does not change* from each unit to the other, but merely *tags* the entered number with the desired unit.

If your calculator has an LCD (liquid-crystal display), the indicators will be abbreviations DEG, RAD, and GRA actually shown on the display. On some of these calculators, nothing is shown to indicate degrees. (See your owner's manual or just experiment.)

On some older calculators, grads are not included and a slide switch is the method of changing mode. In this case, no display indication is provided, nor is it needed, for the position of the switch will tell you which mode you are in. However, if you have such a calculator, you must be very alert to the operating mode that you are in.

Example   Turn on the calculator and you are in degree mode, so to compute sin 20°, key 20 [sin] and read [.34202014]. Now if we wanted to compute sin 20ʳ instead, where the symbol 20ʳ means 20 radians, first change to radian mode:

$$\boxed{\text{DRG}} \ 20 \ \boxed{\text{sin}} \quad \text{and read} \quad \boxed{.91294525}$$

Notice that the number 20 is read as a different angle in each case when you compute the sine, and hence you get a different result. At this point you are still in radian mode. To get back to degree mode, either press [DRG] twice or turn the calculator off and then on again.

The other three basic trigonometric functions, cotangent, secant, and cosecant, have no special keys on the calculator. To compute them, we must use the *reciprocal relations*:

$$\text{Cotangent: } \cot A = \frac{1}{\tan A} \quad \text{and so key} \quad A \ \boxed{\text{tan}} \ \boxed{1/x}$$

$$\text{Secant: } \sec A = \frac{1}{\cos A} \quad \text{and so key} \quad A \ \boxed{\text{cos}} \ \boxed{1/x}$$

$$\text{Cosecant: } \csc A = \frac{1}{\sin A} \quad \text{and so key} \quad A \ \boxed{\text{sin}} \ \boxed{1/x}$$

Example   To compute cot 5° in degree mode, key

$$5 \ \boxed{\text{tan}} \ \boxed{1/x} \quad \text{and read} \quad \boxed{11.430053}$$

Thus cot 5° = 11.43 approximately.

Example   To evaluate sec 18°20′, first change into decimal degrees, then compute the cosine, and finally take the reciprocal to get the secant as required. Key

$$18 \ \boxed{+} \ 20 \ \boxed{\div} \ 60 \ \boxed{=} \quad \text{and read} \quad \boxed{18.333333} \quad \text{(decimal degrees)}$$

Then key

$\boxed{\cos}$ $\boxed{1/x}$ and read $\boxed{1.0534714}$

Thus sec 18°20′ = 1.0535, rounded to four decimal places.

Solving Right Triangles

Trigonometric functions are commonly used to compute unknown parts of right triangles when certain other parts are known. The basic idea is to set up a ratio definition of a trigonometric function that involves two known quantities and a single unknown quantity. Then solve for the unknown. An important extra fact is that the sum of the acute angles is 90°, which can be used to find one acute angle if the other is known.

Example   To compute c, b, and B in the right triangle of Figure 3-4, follow the procedure indicated by the equations and key sequences:

EQUATION	KEY SEQUENCE	DISPLAY
To find angle B: $B = 90° - A$ $= 90° - 23°$ To find b, set up the tangent relation: $\dfrac{5.7}{b} = \tan A = \tan 23°$ and solve $b = \dfrac{5.7}{\tan 23°}$ To find c, set up the sine relation: $\dfrac{5.7}{c} = \sin 23°$ and solve $c = \dfrac{5.7}{\sin 23°}$	90 $\boxed{-}$ 23 $\boxed{=}$ 5.7 $\boxed{\div}$ 23 $\boxed{\tan}$ $\boxed{=}$ 5.7 $\boxed{\div}$ 23 $\boxed{\sin}$ $\boxed{=}$	67. 13.428359 14.588037

Figure 3-4

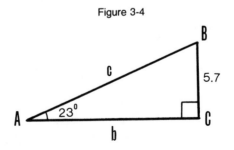

Thus $B = 67°$, $b = 13.43$, and $c = 14.59$ approximately. To mentally confirm the result, notice that, for an angle as small as A, c should be only slightly bigger than b, which is the case.

More complicated equations might arise in the analysis of such problems, but the basic concept of the method of solution will be similar to that shown in the preceding example.

Sine and Cosine Laws

The *law of sines* and the *law of cosines* are equations that relate the angles of *any* triangle to the lengths of the sides. The law of sines is usually stated as

$$\frac{\sin A}{a} = \frac{\sin B}{b} = \frac{\sin C}{c}$$

where a, b, and c are the sides and A, B, and C are the corresponding angles opposite those sides. This is really three equations, since we may look at any pair of ratios and set them equal.

Example   If angle $A = 125°$, angle $C = 35°$, and side $b = 7.6$, we can use the law of sines to solve for the other two sides. First find the third angle: $B = 180° - A - C = 180° - 125° - 35° = 20°$. Now that we know an angle and an opposite side (b and B), we can set up a sine law equation for each of the other sides:

$$\frac{\sin B}{b} = \frac{\sin C}{C} \quad \text{which gives} \quad \frac{\sin 20°}{7.6} = \frac{\sin 35°}{c}$$

$$\frac{\sin B}{b} = \frac{\sin A}{a} \quad \text{which gives} \quad \frac{\sin 20°}{7.6} = \frac{\sin 125°}{a}$$

Figure 3-5

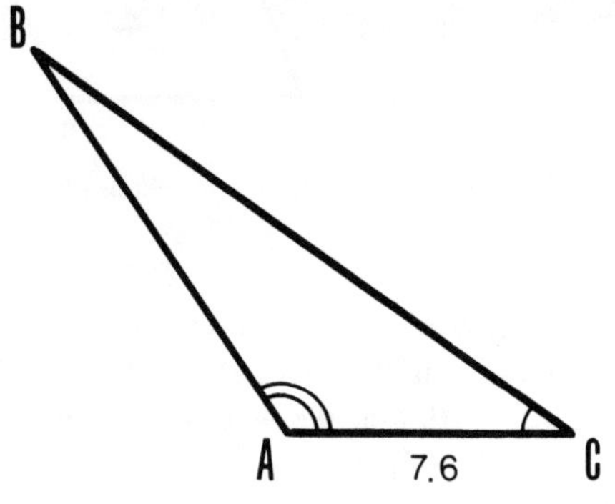

These can now be solved for a and c.

$$a = \frac{7.6 \sin 125°}{\sin 20°}, \qquad c = \frac{7.6 \sin 35°}{\sin 20°}$$

Since both expressions contain $7.6/\sin 20°$, we can save a little time by computing it first and storing it in memory:

7.6 $\boxed{\div}$ 20 $\boxed{\sin}$ $\boxed{=}$ $\boxed{\text{STO}}$ $\boxed{\times}$ 125 $\boxed{\sin}$ $\boxed{=}$
and read a: $\boxed{\quad 18.202307 \quad}$

Now recall the stored value to help compute c:

$\boxed{\text{RCL}}$ $\boxed{\times}$ 35 $\boxed{\sin}$ $\boxed{=}$ and read c: $\boxed{\quad 12.745392 \quad}$

The sine law is used when one side and two angles are given. When only one, or even no angle is given, the cosine law is usually appropriate. The law of cosines can be given by three formulas. These are really the same except for the labeling of the sides and angles (i.e., if we renamed everything, we would get one formula from another). Refer to Figure 3-6.

$$c^2 = a^2 + b^2 - 2ab \cos C$$
$$b^2 = a^2 + c^2 - 2ac \cos B$$
$$a^2 = b^2 + c^2 - 2bc \cos A$$

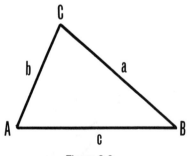

Figure 3-6

The law of cosines is sometimes referred to as a generalization of the Pythagorean theorem. If, in the first formula, $C = 90°$, then $\cos C = \cos 90° = 0$, and we would have simply $c^2 = a^2 + b^2$, the Pythagorean relationship. It may be helpful for memorization purposes to think of the law of cosines as being the Pythagorean theorem with an adjustment

for the "included angle" not being a right angle. You need only memorize one of these formulas and then just relabel any given triangle to suit
the one you remembered.

There are three situations when the Cosine Law may be used:

1. Given two sides and the angle included.
2. Given three sides.
3. Given two sides and an opposite angle. This is the ambiguous case. There
   will be possibly two answers, one answer, or even no answer for any particular data.

Techniques for applying the formulas in these cases are given in the
solved problems.

Areas

When we are not given the altitude of a triangle, we can often find it using trigonometry and so deduce the area K of any triangle if we have
enough other information.

Example If we are given two sides a and b and the included angle C (see Figure
3-7), we can find the altitude h by the relation $h = a \sin C$. Since the
area $K = \frac{1}{2} bh$, we get

$$K = \frac{1}{2} ab \sin C$$

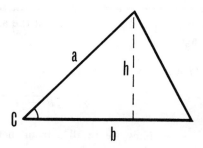

Figure 3-7

There are still other situations. If we are given two angles and a
side, we can also find the area. Suppose we are given side a, angle A and
angle B (see Figure 3-8). We can find angle $C = 180° - A - B$. Also
$h = a \sin C$ is the altitude to side b, which can itself be found by using
the sine law:

$$\frac{b}{\sin B} = \frac{a}{\sin A}$$

which implies that

$$b = \frac{a \sin B}{\sin A}$$

Thus the area

$$K = \frac{1}{2} bh = \frac{1}{2} \left(\frac{a^2 \sin B \sin C}{\sin A} \right)$$

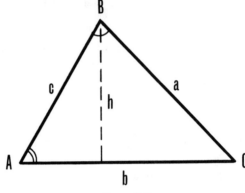

Figure 3-8

The most famous formula, Heron's formula, is the case of three given sides:

$$\text{Area} = \sqrt{s(s - a)(s - b)(s - c)}$$

where $s = \frac{1}{2}(a + b + c)$ is called the *semiperimeter*, which means half of the perimeter. The calculation of the area by this formula proceeds in two stages:

Step 1 Compute s and store:

$$a \boxed{+} b \boxed{+} c \boxed{=} \boxed{\div} 2 \boxed{=} \boxed{\text{STO}}$$

Now we recall s from memory as needed in the second stage.

Step 2 Compute the area (s is still displayed from step 1).

$$\boxed{\times} \boxed{(\!(} \boxed{\text{RCL}} \boxed{-} a \boxed{)} \boxed{\times} \boxed{(\!(} \boxed{\text{RCL}} \boxed{-} b \boxed{)} \boxed{\times} \boxed{(\!(}$$
$$\boxed{\text{RCL}} \boxed{-} c \boxed{=} \boxed{\sqrt{x}}$$

and we can then read the area (see Problem 33). Although this key sequence appears to be complicated, if you just realize that each time $\boxed{\text{RCL}}$ is pressed s is displayed, then the key sequence looks just like the preceding algebraic formula.

There are also areas related to circles that involve trigonometric functions. They are easily derived based on the area of a sector, $A = \frac{1}{2} r^2 \theta$, θ in radians, and the basic formula for the area of a triangle.

Example The area of a circular *segment* equals the area of a sector minus that of a triangle (see Figure 3-9). The area of the sector is $\frac{1}{2} r^2 \theta$. The altitude of the triangle is $r \cos \theta/2$ and *half* of the base is $r \sin \theta/2$; thus the area of the triangle is just the product of these two quantities:

$$r \sin \theta/2 \cdot r \cos \theta/2 = \frac{1}{2} r^2 \sin \theta$$

The equality is from a *double-angle* formula. Thus the area of the segment is

$$A_{segment} = \frac{r^2}{2} (\theta - \sin \theta), \quad \theta \text{ in radians}$$

This can also be converted into a formula in degrees by writing

$$A_{segment} = \frac{r^2}{2} (\frac{\pi \theta^\circ}{180} - \sin \theta^\circ), \quad \theta^\circ = \theta \text{ in degrees}$$

Figure 3-9

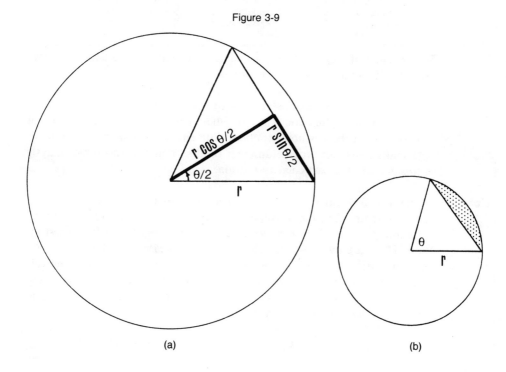

(a)   (b)

A nice thing about the first formula is that θ in radians need not be entered twice. It could be changed to radians during the course of the calculation, which is done in the *radian mode*:

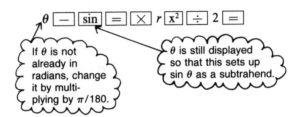

If θ is not already in radians, change it by multiplying by $\pi/180$.

θ is still displayed so that this sets up $\sin \theta$ as a subtrahend.

Miscellaneous Trigonometric Computations

Most calculations involve the three basic trigonometric functions or their reciprocals, with the *argument* (i.e., angle) θ expressed in either degrees or radians. When radians are in use, the symbol $\pi \doteq 3.1415927$ often appears to alert you to the mode. Failure to have the calculator in the proper mode is probably the most frequent source of error.

Example   Compute $\sin \pi/3$ by keying

Puts calculator in radian mode

Computes $\pi/3$

$\sin \pi/3$ displayed $= .86602541$

If we did not key $\boxed{\text{DRG}}$, placing the calculator in radian mode, we would still get an answer—a wrong one!

Another type of calculation is to find the angle when the value of the trigonometric function is given. Since there are an infinite number of answers when there is no restriction, different restrictions on the admissible solution set can provide different results. You must do some analysis depending on the particular restriction.

Example   If $\cos x = 3/4$ and $x + y = \pi/4$, then if we restrict $0 \le y \le \pi/2$ to find y we must first find the possible values of x (in radians) and then substitute into $y = (\pi/4) - x$, making sure that the results satisfy the restriction. There are two possible values of x in this case, x_1 and x_2, which are negatives of each other in this case (see Figure 3-10). However, the calculator gives only the positive value when we key $\boxed{\text{DRG}}$ .75 $\boxed{\text{INV}}$ $\boxed{\cos}$ $\boxed{\text{STO}}$ and read $x_1 = .72273425$ radians. Now we compute the first value of y, $y_1 = (\pi/4) - x_1$, by keying

$$\boxed{\pi}\ \boxed{\div}\ 4\ \boxed{-}\ \boxed{\text{RCL}}\ \boxed{=} \quad \text{and read} \quad y_1 = .06266392 \text{ radians}$$

Since x_2 is just the negative of x_1 (i.e., $x_2 = -x_1$), then

$$y_2 = \frac{\pi}{4} - x_2 = \frac{\pi}{4} - (-x_1) = \frac{\pi}{4} + x_1$$

so just *add* x_1 (still in memory) to $\pi/4$:

$\boxed{\pi}\ \boxed{\div}\ \boxed{4}\ \boxed{+}\ \boxed{\text{RCL}}\ \boxed{=}$ and read $y_2 = 1.5081324$ radians

The values of y_1 and y_2 are indicated in the diagram. If we tried any other possible values of x by adding (or subtracting) multiples of 2π, we would have exceeded the range of values specified for y.

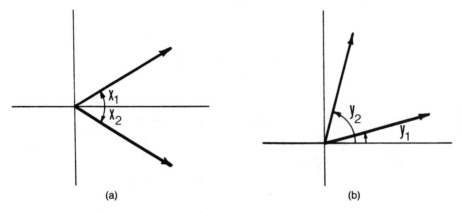

(a)   (b)

Figure 3-10 (a) Values of $x = \cos^{-1}(3/4)$; (b) Corresponding Values of $y = \pi/4 - x$

Inverse Trigonometric Functions

If we limit the domain (angle values) of the trigonometric functions in certain ways, these functions will have inverses. Otherwise, we would have (as we ordinarily do) more than one angle that produces the same value. The inverse problem is to compute the angle when the function value is given. The inverse trigonometric functions are automatically restricted on the calculator to the *principal values*. These are not the same for each function (see Figure 3-11).

Notice that the inverse sine and the inverse tangent have *almost* the same set of principal values except for the endpoints, which are excluded for the inverse tangent. Notationally, these range values can be expressed as

$$R(\mathrm{Sin}^{-1}) = \{y \mid -\frac{\pi}{2} \leq y \leq +\frac{\pi}{2}\} = \{\theta \mid -90° \leq 0 \leq +90°\}$$

$$R(\mathrm{Cos}^{-1}) = \{y \mid 0 \leq y \leq \pi\} = \{0 \mid 0 \leq 0 \leq 180°\}$$

$$R(\mathrm{Tan}^{-1}) = \{y \mid -\frac{\pi}{2} < y < +\frac{\pi}{2}\} = \{\theta \mid -90° < \theta < +90°\}$$

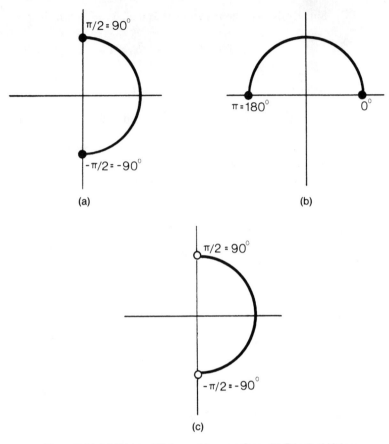

Figure 3-11 (a) Principal Values of Inverse Sine; (b) Principal Values
of Inverse Cosine; (c) Principal Values of Inverse Tangent

The reason that the inverse tangent does not include the endpoint
values is that those numbers are not in the domain of definition of the
tangent function itself. There are several different notations for inverse
functions. Notationally, when a capital letter is used, it commonly refers
to only the principal value, whereas when a small letter is used it refers
to the entire set of values. An old, now almost obsolete notation is the
arc notation. For instance, Arcsin refers to the measure of the circular
arc that gives a specified sine value (principal value in this case). That is,
Arcsin 0.5 refers to the arc that gives a sine equal to 0.5. That arc is
$\pi/6$, which is in fact the radian measure of 30°. Thus the equivalent notations

$$\text{Arcsin } 0.5 = \text{Sin}^{-1} 0.5 = \left(\frac{\pi}{6}\right)^{\text{r}} = 30°$$

can be read as "the angle whose sine is 0.5 is $\pi/6$ radians or 30°."

We shall use the notation Sin⁻¹ exclusively, and avoid the arc notation. The arc notation still appears on the keyboards of some calculators,
and you should interpret it as INV for the purpose of following this text.
The various common key configurations for these inverse functions are
shown in Table 3-1.

TABLE 3-1.

FUNCTION	KEY SEQUENCE	OTHER KEY CONFIGURATIONS	
Sin⁻¹y	y ⎢INV⎢ ⎢sin⎢	y ⎢arc⎢ ⎢sin⎢	y ⎢2nd⎢ ⎢sin⁻¹⎢
Cos⁻¹y	y ⎢INV⎢ ⎢cos⎢	y ⎢arc⎢ ⎢cos⎢	y ⎢2nd⎢ ⎢cos⁻¹⎢
Tan⁻¹y	y ⎢INV⎢ ⎢tan⎢	y ⎢arc⎢ ⎢tan⎢	y ⎢2nd⎢ ⎢tan⁻¹⎢

If the value of y is not in the range of the original trigonometric function, then we get an error indication.

Example   If we compute, in degree mode, Sin⁻¹ (0.5) by keying .5 ⎢INV⎢ ⎢sin⎢, we
find that an angle of 30° is the result. That is, Sin⁻¹ (0.5) = 30°. However, if we forget the decimal point, and key 5 ⎢INV⎢ ⎢sin⎢, we get ⎢ Error⎢
since there is no angle θ such that sin θ = 5.

The other three trigonometric functions also have inverses for appropriately restricted ranges, but there are usually no sec⁻¹, csc⁻¹, or cot⁻¹
keys, so we must combine other functions to compute these. For example, because sec x = 1/cos x, if we are given the value of y = sec x and
want to compute the value of x = Sec⁻¹y, we must notice that

$$y = \sec x = 1/\cos x \quad \text{implies that} \quad \cos x = \frac{1}{y}$$

and hence, x = Cos⁻¹ (1/y) provided that we carefully check that the
range values are consistent. We shall not do a complete analysis of that
here, but are merely indicating the idea behind the formulas. Consequently, putting all the preceding information together, we find that

$$\text{Sec}^{-1} y = \text{Cos}^{-1}\left(\frac{1}{y}\right)$$

and so we can compute the inverse cosecant by using the inverse cosine
in conjunction with the reciprocal function. In a similar manner, one can
deduce that

$$\text{Csc}^{-1} y = \text{Sin}^{-1}\left(\frac{1}{y}\right)$$

However, for $\text{Cot}^{-1} y$ the situation is not so simple, because its range is not the same as the range of $\text{Tan}^{-1} y$. After some simple analysis, the ultimate result is that we have two cases depending on whether y is positive or negative. When y is negative, we must add 180° or π radians in order to put the result in the proper quadrant to be consistent with the definition of the principal value of the inverse cotangent. The results, with key sequences, are summarized in Table 3-2.

TABLE 3-2.

FUNCTION	KEY SEQUENCE
$\text{Sec}^{-1} y = \text{Cos}^{-1}(1/y)$	y ⌗1/x⌗ ⌗INV⌗ ⌗cos⌗
$\text{Csc}^{-1} y = \text{Sin}^{-1}(1/y)$	y ⌗1/x⌗ ⌗INV⌗ ⌗sin⌗
$\text{*Cot}^{-1} y = \begin{cases} \text{Tan}^{-1}(1/y), & y > 0 \\ \pi + \text{Tan}^{-1}(1/y), & y < 0 \\ \quad \text{or in degree mode} \\ 180° + \text{Tan}^{-1}(1/y), & y < 0 \end{cases}$	y ⌗1/x⌗ ⌗INV⌗ ⌗tan⌗ (any mode y positive) ⌗π⌗ ⌗+⌗ y ⌗1/x⌗ ⌗INV⌗ ⌗tan⌗ ⌗=⌗ (radian mode, y negative) 180 ⌗+⌗ y ⌗1/x⌗ ⌗INV⌗ ⌗tan⌗ ⌗=⌗ (degree mode, y negative)

*Another formula is $\text{Cot}^{-1} x = \pi/2 - \text{Tan}^{-1} x$ (radian mode) or $\text{Cot}^{-1} \theta = 90° - \text{Tan}^{-1} \theta$ (degree mode).

Example To compute $\text{Cot}^{-1} 3.7$, key 3.7 ⌗1/x⌗ ⌗INV⌗ ⌗tan⌗ and read ⌗15.124007⌗. Thus $\text{Cot}^{-1} 3.7 = 15.124°$ approximately. If we were in radian mode, we would get a different numerical result, which would be the same angle expressed in radians. To compute $\text{Cot}^{-1}(-3.7)$, we note that the argument is negative; hence we use the form $\text{Cot}^{-1} y = 180° + \text{Tan}^{-1}(1/y)$ if we want the result in degrees, and key

180 ⌗+⌗ 3.7 ⌗+/−⌗ ⌗1/x⌗ ⌗INV⌗ ⌗tan⌗ ⌗=⌗   and read ⌗164.87599⌗

Thus $\text{Cot}^{-1}(-3.7) = 164.88°$ approximately and is in the second quadrant, as it should be. Had we not added the 180° we would have had an answer in the fourth quadrant because that is where the inverse tangent has its range. That would have been wrong.

One must always be cognizant of the range and domain values when using the calculator; otherwise, there could be trouble. If we are in the first quadrant, there is no problem. Elsewhere, however, even for simple situations, sometimes something unexpected can happen.

Example First compute sin 105° by keying 105 ⌗sin⌗. Then compute the inverse sine: ⌗INV⌗ ⌗sin⌗ and read ⌗75⌗. It might be expected that we would get 105° back; however, 105° is not in the range of the inverse sine.

Most calculators will compute the basic functions for a very wide range of input values (see your owner's manual for specifics), but all inverse calculations are necessarily restricted to principal values. Thus we do not get the input value back unless it is itself a principal value. This concept can be used in conjunction with changing modes to perform degree–radian conversions for angles in the first and fourth quadrants ($-90°$ to $+90°$) using the sine function and its inverse. The general calculation scheme is as follows:

1. Display angle in whatever units it is given and select the matching mode.
2. Take the sine of the angle by keying $\boxed{\text{sin}}$.
3. Change the mode to the units to which you wish to change.
4. Take the inverse sine by keying $\boxed{\text{INV}}$ $\boxed{\text{sin}}$.

Example   To change 30° into radian measure, start in degree mode, since that is the unit of the given quantity, and then key

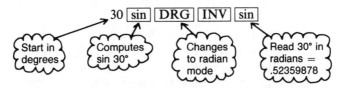

The result actually represents $\pi/6$ radians. To confirm this, multiply the result by 6 and read the decimal value of π.

Example   To change $\pi/12$ radians to degrees, start in radian mode:

1. Turn on calculator; then key $\boxed{\text{DRG}}$ once. You should now be in radian mode. Look for display indicator.
2. Enter $\pi/12$ by keying $\boxed{\pi}$ $\boxed{\div}$ 12 $\boxed{=}$ (read $\boxed{\quad.26179939}$).
3. Take the sine: $\boxed{\text{sin}}$; and read the display value $\boxed{\quad.25881904}$.
4. Change to degree mode: $\boxed{\text{DRG}}$ $\boxed{\text{DRG}}$ (this key is pressed twice).
5. Take the inverse sine: $\boxed{\text{INV}}$ $\boxed{\text{sin}}$.

We find that $\pi/12$ radians $= 15°$.
Caution   This method works only in the first and fourth quadrants. If you wanted to use this technique to convert 120° to radians, for example, it would not work properly since 120° is in the second quadrant. However, a similar implementation of the cosine function would work, since the principal values of the inverse cosine are in the first and second quadrant.

Trigonmetric Equations

Solving equations involving trigonometric functions cannot be summarized by a general formula as can be done for linear or quadratic equations. However, one can make the statement that most solutions rely on the periodic property of the functions and on an understanding of the inverse functions. Restrictions that cut the solution set down to a finite number often are involved.

Example   The solution set of $2 \sin x - \sqrt{3} = 0$ is found by first solving as $\sin x = \sqrt{3}/2$ and then noting that two values that work for x are 60° and 120°. In radians, this is $\pi/3$ and $2\pi/3$. Thus the entire solution set (adding multiples of the circle) is

$$\{x \mid x = \frac{\pi}{3} + 2k\pi \text{ or } x = \frac{2\pi}{3} + 2k\pi, \ k \text{ any integer}\}$$

or in degrees

$$\{x \mid x = 60° + 360°k \text{ or } x = 120° + 360°k, \ k \text{ any integer}\}$$

The entire set of solutions even between 0° and 360° is *not* automatically produced by the calculator. The values produced depend on the particular function involved and its principal values. Sometimes we cannot get even a single solution in a particular restricted range without doing a little extra work. In other words, you must know what you are doing and not be under the misapprehension that the calculator obviates the need to think.

Example   To find the solution set of $2 \sin x + \sqrt{3} = 0$ in the range $0° \leq x \leq 360°$, first solve the equation as

$$\sin x = -\frac{\sqrt{3}}{2} \quad \text{and hence;} \quad x = \sin^{-1}\left(-\frac{\sqrt{3}}{2}\right)$$

If we try to compute the solution as 3 $\boxed{\sqrt{x}}$ $\boxed{\div}$ 2 $\boxed{=}$ $\boxed{+/-}$ $\boxed{\text{INV}}$ $\boxed{\sin}$, we will get −60°, which we denote as x_p, the principal value. But $x_p = -60°$ is not in the desired range specified for the equation. Refer to Figure 3-12 to see how to get two solutions x_1 and x_2 in the required range from the principal value x_p. The angle x_1 has the same terminal side as x_p, so $x_1 = x_p + 360°$ and so $x_1 = -60° + 360° = 300°$. Notice also in Figure 3-12(c) that $x_2 = 180° + \mid x_p \mid = 180° + 60° = 240°$. For more complicated numbers, these same computations would be done on the calculator.

The following examples illustrate but a few of the more common situations. These situations may be further complicated by multiple angles, quadratic equations, or the appearance of more than one trigonometric function in a single equation. A variety of situations is illustrated in the solved problems. The exposition is hardly comprehensive since the object of this section is mainly to illustrate how the calculator should be applied in various circumstances. When both an algebraic and a trigono-

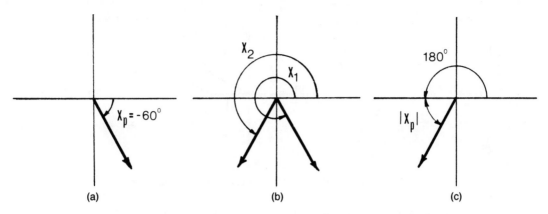

(a)   (b)   (c)

Figure 3-12 (a) Principal Value Produced by the Calculator; (b) Required Angles, $0° \leq x \leq 360°$; (c) Showing that $x_2 = 180° + |x_p|$

metric function of the same variable appear in the same equation, numerical techniques must usually be applied. Detailed discussion of these topics is beyond the scope of this book.

Polar Coordinates

Polar coordinates provide an alternative method for locating a point in the plane. The location information is contained in two numbers, r and θ, where r is a distance and θ is an angle. The basis for reference is a fixed point O called the *pole* or *polar origin* and a fixed ray (half-line) emanating from the pole, called the *polar axis* or $0°$ *ray*. Refer to Figure 3-13, which shows the rectangular coordinate system and the polar coordinate system graphically, in order to orient yourself to this concept.

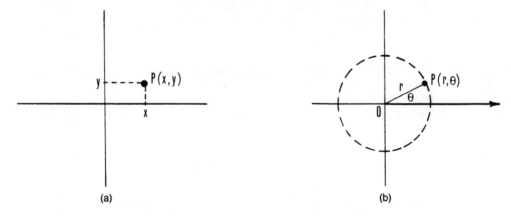

(a)   (b)

Figure 3-13 (a) Rectangular Coordinates; (b) Polar Coordinates

To locate a point $P(r, \theta)$ on a polar graph, move r units along the polar axis and then follow the coordinate circle (see Figure 3-14) along an arc that measures an angle θ.

103

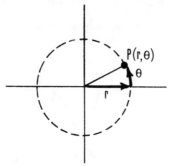

Figure 3-14 Locating a Point in Polar Coordinates

Example To locate (plot) the point $P(2, \pi/4) = P(2, 45°)$, move $+2$ units along the polar axis and then move counterclockwise along the coordinate circle of radius 2 until the arc defines an angle of $\pi/4$ radians or $45°$ (see Figure 3-15).

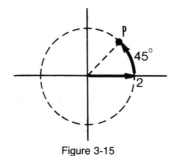

Figure 3-15

One complication with polar coordinates is that they are not unique. That is, the same point can be labeled in more than one way. This is because the distance r can be positive or negative, and the angle θ can be supplemented by multiples of $360°$ and still describe the same geometric location.

Example If we plot $(2, 30°)$ and $(-2, 210°)$, we get the same point (see Figure 3-16).

Figure 3-16

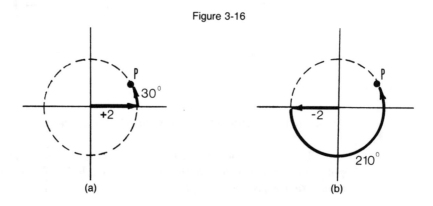

(a)   (b)

In general (r, θ) and $(-r, \theta + 180°)$, or $(-r, \theta + \pi)$ in radians, represent the same point. Even more generally, we can have an infinite number of representations by just going "full circle" as often as desired by adding or subtracting multiples of 2π (i.e., 360°). Thus we get that the point $(r, \theta + 2k\pi)$ and $(-r, \theta + (2k + 1)\pi)$, where k is any integer, both represent the same point (r, θ). However, we do *not* say that these ordered pairs are "equal" since they contain different numbers.

Once the concept of polar coordinates is understood, the primary calculation problem is conversion between rectangular and polar coordinates. Some calculators have built-in conversion functions, but most do not. These built-in conversions will be discussed briefly; however, the main emphasis will be on the transformation equations.

To change a point (r, θ) into rectangular coordinates (x, y), use the transformation equations

$$x = r \cos \theta$$

$$y = r \sin \theta$$

The angle θ may be in degrees or radians, and r may be either positive or negative. Make sure that your calculator is in the right angular mode.

Example To change $(5, \pi/12)$ to rectangular coordinates, first put the calculator into radian mode (since θ is obviously in radians):

$\boxed{\text{DRG}}$ (make certain that radians are indicated by the display)

Compute $\theta = \pi/12$ and store in memory:

$\boxed{\pi}$ $\boxed{\div}$ 12 $\boxed{=}$ $\boxed{\text{STO}}$ (the numerical value of θ is displayed)

Compute $x = r \cos \theta$ (note that you start with θ already displayed):

$\boxed{\cos}$ $\boxed{\times}$ 5 $\boxed{=}$ (read the value of $x = 4.8296291$)

Compute $y = r \sin \theta$ (θ must be recalled from memory first):

$\boxed{\text{RCL}}$ $\boxed{\sin}$ $\boxed{\times}$ 5 $\boxed{=}$ (read the value of $y = 1.2940952$)

Thus $(x, y) = (4.83, 1.29)$ approximately.

If your calculator has automatic conversion capability, the preceding conversion is easy, but the register used to store $r = 5$ for conversion is also used to compute $\pi/12$. Thus one must be careful to compute $\theta = \pi/12$ first, store it, and recall it when needed for the conversion routine. Not every calculator has the same key configuration, so your particular keyboard may not exactly resemble the following notation below, but it should be similar. The register key may look like this $\boxed{\updownarrow}$ or like this $\boxed{\leftrightarrow}$ or even like this $\boxed{x\, \colon y}$. The actual conversion key may be one single key that can convert in two directions and may look something like this:

$$\begin{array}{cc} P \to R & R \to P \\ \boxed{R \to P} \quad \text{or like this} \quad \boxed{P \to R} \end{array}$$

The conversion may be performed by two separate keys labeled xy or $r\theta$, written above two other keys; hence, they are "called" by preceding them with the 2nd function key.

Basically, the technique is the following: to convert (r, θ) to (x, y)

1. Enter r; press the register key (see preceding paragraph).
2. Enter θ; press the conversion key and read x (convert *into* rectangular).
3. Press the register key again and read y.

If some calculation is necessary first for either quantity, you may not do it during this routine, but only before you begin the procedure. Also, the calculator mode will correspond to the units that the angle is given in. When you must do a calculation first, store the result in the memory and then recall it when it must be entered for the conversion routine.

One difficulty with automatic conversion is that on some calculators negative values of r are not admissible. Then you must either use the positive value and make adjustments or resort to the transformation equations. A graph is helpful under these circumstances.

Because of the variety of calculator formats, we shall say no more about this useful feature except to refer you to your owner's manual and to note, in some of the solved problems, when special adjustments are needed if you try to use this feature.

To convert from rectangular into polar coordinates, we use the transformation equations:

$$r^2 = x^2 + y^2 \quad \text{or more directly} \quad r = \pm\sqrt{x^2 + y^2}$$

$$\theta = \tan^{-1}\left(\frac{y}{x}\right), \quad \text{where } \theta \text{ is the value in the appropriate quadrant}$$

Depending on which sign is chosen for r, the value of θ will vary accordingly. Choosing r positive is recommended for convenience.

Example To convert $P(3, 2)$ into polar coordinates (see Figure 3-17), first compute

$$r = +\sqrt{x^2 + y^2} = \sqrt{3^2 + 2^2} = \sqrt{9 + 4} = \sqrt{13}$$

To find θ, use $\theta = \tan^{-1}(y/x) = \tan^{-1}(2/3)$. Since the point is in the first quadrant, we can compute θ directly as

$$2 \boxed{\div} 3 \boxed{=} \boxed{\text{INV}} \boxed{\text{tan}}$$

and if we are in degree mode, we get $\theta = 33.690067°$. If we were in radian mode, the same key sequence would give $\theta = 0.550026$ radians. Thus, $P(3, 2) = P(\sqrt{13}, 33.7°)$ or, in radians, $P(\sqrt{13}, 0.588')$ approximately. One may also choose to replace $\sqrt{13}$ with its decimal approximation, 3.6055513, or some rounded version of it.

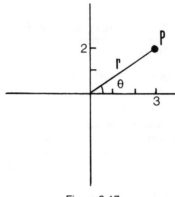

Figure 3-17

Example   To convert $(-2, 1)$ into polar coordinates, first compute $r = \sqrt{(-2)^2 + (1)^2} = \sqrt{5}$. If we try to compute the angle

$$\theta = \tan^{-1}\left(\frac{y}{x}\right) = \tan^{-1}\left(\frac{1}{-2}\right) = \tan^{-1}(-0.5)$$

then we would calculate (degree mode) $.5 \boxed{+/-} \boxed{\text{INV}} \boxed{\text{tan}}$ and read $\boxed{-26.565051}$. But this value is in the *fourth quadrant*. We need to get the corresponding value in the second quadrant where the point is located (see Figure 3-18). Thus we add 180° by keying $\boxed{+} 180 \boxed{=}$ and read the correct result, $\boxed{153.43495}$. Thus $\theta = 153.4°$ approximately. If we were in radian mode, we would add π instead of 180. Thus in polar coordinates the point is $(\sqrt{5}, 153.4°)$, or if we choose to approximate $\sqrt{5}$, then we write $(2.236, 153.4°)$. If we did the calculation in radian mode, we would first compute $\theta = -.46364761$ radians, and the minus sign would indicate that we may be in the wrong quadrant. Then, upon adding π, we would get the correct result, $\theta = 2.677945$ radians.

A summary of polar–rectangular convertions is given in Table 3-3.

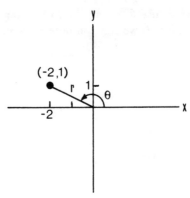

Figure 3-18

TABLE 3-3. Summary of Polar–Rectangular Conversions

Polar to rectangular:	Key sequence:
$x = r \cos \theta$	r ⊠ θ ⌷cos⌷ ⌷=⌷ (read x)
$y = r \sin \theta$	r ⊠ θ ⌷sin⌷ ⌷=⌷ (read y)
Alternative method: the radius r is used as a constant multiplier. Also, θ is stored and recalled as required.	θ ⌷STO⌷ r ⊠ ⌷K⌷ (set up constants)
	⌷RCL⌷ ⌷cos⌷ ⌷=⌷ (read x)
	⌷RCL⌷ ⌷sin⌷ ⌷=⌷ (read y)

Rectangular to polar:
$$r = \sqrt{x^2 + y^2}$$

x ⌷x²⌷ ⌷+⌷ y ⌷x²⌷ ⌷=⌷ ⌷√x⌷ (read $r > 0$)

$$\theta = \begin{cases} \text{Tan}^{-1}\left(\dfrac{y}{x}\right), \; \theta \in \text{I, IV*} \\[2mm] \text{Tan}^{-1}\left(\dfrac{y}{x}\right) + 180°, \; \theta° \in \text{II, III} \\[2mm] \text{Tan}^{-1}\left(\dfrac{y}{x}\right) + \pi^r, \; \theta^r \in \text{II, III,} \\ \quad (\theta \text{ in radians}) \end{cases}$$

y ⌷÷⌷ x ⌷=⌷ ⌷INV⌷ ⌷tan⌷ (read $\theta°$ or θ')

y ⌷÷⌷ x ⌷=⌷ ⌷INV⌷ ⌷tan⌷ ⌷+⌷ 180 ⌷=⌷ (read $\theta°$)

y ⌷÷⌷ x ⌷=⌷ ⌷INV⌷ ⌷tan⌷ ⌷+⌷ ⌷π⌷ ⌷=⌷ (read θ^r)

*The Roman numerals refer to the quadrant in which θ is located.

Solved Problems

ANGULAR MEASURE

1. Change 32°14′53″ into decimal degrees.

Since $1' = (1/60)°$ and $1'' = (1/60)' = (1/60)(1/60)° = (1/3600)°$, we have

$$\left(32 + \frac{14}{60} + \frac{53}{3600}\right)°$$

so we compute (AOS system)

32 $\boxed{+}$ 14 $\boxed{\div}$ 60 $\boxed{+}$ 53 $\boxed{\div}$ 3600 $\boxed{=}$ and read $\boxed{32.248056}$

Thus 32°14′53″ = 32.25° approximately.

2. Express 19.345° in terms of degrees, minutes, and seconds.
First find the minutes:

.345 $\boxed{\times}$ 60 $\boxed{=}$ and read $\boxed{20.7}$

Thus we have 20.7 minutes. Take the fractional part of the minutes and convert it to seconds: .7 $\boxed{\times}$ 60 $\boxed{=}$, and we find that we have 42 seconds. Thus the final result is 19.345° = 19°20′42″.

3. Change −42°12′ into decimal degrees.

We must be careful to realize that the minus sign applies to the whole expression, not just the 42. Thus we proceed as if it were a positive angle and then change the sign:

42 $\boxed{+}$ 12 $\boxed{\div}$ 60 $\boxed{=}$ $\boxed{+/-}$ and read $\boxed{-42.2}$

Thus −42°12″ = −42.2°.

4. Change the radian measure $7\pi/16$ to (decimal) degree form.
To change radians to degrees, multiply by $180/\pi$; thus we have

$$\frac{7\pi}{16} \times \frac{180}{\pi} = \frac{7(180)}{16}$$

Notice that π cancels. Thus simply key 7 $\boxed{\times}$ 180 $\boxed{\div}$ 16 $\boxed{=}$ and we get 78.75° as the answer.

5. Change 72.352° to radians, correct to three decimal places.
To change degrees to radians, multiply by $\pi/180$; thus key

72.352 $\boxed{\times}$ $\boxed{\pi}$ $\boxed{\div}$ 180 $\boxed{=}$ and read $\boxed{1.2627806}$

Thus 72.352° = 1.263 radians, approximately.

6. Change 217°43′24″ to radians, correct to four decimal places.

First convert to decimal degrees and then multiply by $\pi/180$:

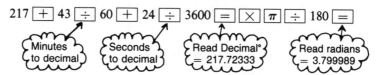

Thus 217°43′24″ = 3.8000 radians, correct to four decimal places.

7. Change each of the following radian measures to degrees: (a) 2.14, (b) .08, (c) $\sqrt{3} + 1$, (d) $\pi/36$.

Since we have several quantities to convert, first compute the conversion factor $180/\pi$, store it in memory, and recall as needed.

$$180 \boxed{\div} \boxed{\pi} \boxed{=} \boxed{\text{STO}} \quad (\text{read: } \boxed{57.29578})$$

(a) $2.14 \boxed{\times} \boxed{\text{RCL}} \boxed{=}$ and read 122.61297°.
(b) $.08 \boxed{\times} \boxed{\text{RCL}} \boxed{=}$ and read 4.5836624°.
(c) $3 \boxed{\sqrt{x}} \boxed{+} 1 \boxed{=} \boxed{\times} \boxed{\text{RCL}} \boxed{=}$ and read 156.53498°.
(d) $\boxed{\pi} \boxed{\div} 36 \boxed{\times} \boxed{\text{RCL}} \boxed{=}$ and read 5°.

8. Find the arc length in a circle of radius 3.47 meters intercepted by a central angle of 2 radians.

Use the formula for arc length, $s = r\theta = 3.47(2)$. Thus simply key $3.47 \boxed{\times} 2 \boxed{=}$ and find that the arc length $s = 6.94$ meters.

9. Find the area of the sector subtended by the arc described in Problem 8.

Use the formula for area, $A = 1/2\ r^2\theta$, θ in radians. Thus, merely substitute

$$A = \frac{(3.47)^2(2)}{2} = 3.47^2$$

So key $3.47 \boxed{x^2}$ and read $\boxed{12.0409}$. Thus $A = 12.0409$ square meters $= 12.0409$ m².

10. Find the angle, in degrees, minutes, and seconds, of the central angle that subtends an arc of 5 inches in a circle of radius 10 inches (see Figure 3-19).

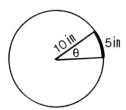

Figure 3-19

Since $s = r\theta$, we get

$$\theta = \frac{s}{r} = \frac{5}{10} = .5 \text{ (radian)}$$

Thus we convert .5 radian into degrees by multiplying by $180/\pi$:

$$.5 \boxed{\times} 180 \boxed{\div} \boxed{\pi} \boxed{=} \quad \text{and read} \quad \boxed{28.64789}$$

This is 28.64789 degrees. Leave this number displayed. There are 28°
plus a decimal part. To get minutes, subtract the 28 and then multiply the resulting decimal part by 60 (minutes):

$$\boxed{-}\;28\;\boxed{=}\;\boxed{\times}\;60\;\boxed{=}\quad\text{and we get}\quad\boxed{38.873385}$$

Thus 38 is the minutes. The decimal part represents the seconds.
Subtract the 38 to get the decimal, which is then multiplied by 60
(seconds) to get the seconds:

$$\boxed{-}\;38\;\boxed{=}\;\boxed{\times}\;60\;\boxed{=}\quad\text{and read}\quad\boxed{54.403122}$$

This represents the seconds. Putting these results together, we get
$\theta = 28°38'54.4''$, approximately.

11. The area of a sector of a circle is 355.68 mm² and the arc length that
defines that sector is 22.8 mm. (a) Find the radius of the circle in
millimeters, and (b) the central angle of the sector in both radians
and degrees.

The area $A = \frac{1}{2}r^2\theta$, and the arc length $s = r\theta$. If we take their ratio,

$$\frac{A}{s} = \frac{\frac{1}{2}r^2\theta}{r\theta} = \frac{1}{2}r$$

If we now solve this for r,

$$r = \frac{2A}{s} = \frac{2(355.68)}{22.8}$$

which we calculate:

$$2\;\boxed{\times}\;355.68\;\boxed{\div}\;22.8\;\boxed{=}\quad\text{and read}\quad\boxed{31.2}$$

Hence $r = 31.2$ mm. To find the central angle θ, solve $s = r\theta$ for θ.
Thus

$$\theta = \frac{s}{r} = \frac{22.8}{31.2}$$

So key

$$22.8\;\boxed{\div}\;31.2\;\boxed{=}\quad\text{and read}\quad\boxed{.73076923}\quad\text{(leave displayed)}$$

Hence $\theta = .73$ radian, approximately. To change this displayed value to degrees, multiply by $180/\pi$:

$$\boxed{\times}\;180\;\boxed{\div}\;\boxed{\pi}\;\boxed{=}\quad\text{and read}\quad\boxed{41.869993}$$

Rounded to 2 decimals, $\theta = 41.87°$ approximately.

Trigonometry   **12.** For the triangle in Figure 3-20, compute the six trigonometric functions of the angle θ indicated.

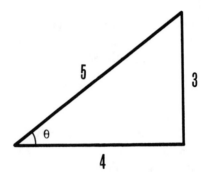

Figure 3-20

Use of the reciprocal relations will shorten calculation:

$$\sin \theta = \frac{3}{5}, \quad \csc \theta = \frac{1}{\sin \theta}: \quad 3\boxed{\div}5\boxed{=} \quad (\text{read } \sin \theta) \qquad \boxed{1/\text{x}} \quad (\text{read } \csc \theta)$$

$$\cos \theta = \frac{4}{5}, \quad \sec \theta = \frac{1}{\cos \theta}: \quad 4\boxed{\div}5\boxed{=} \quad (\text{read } \cos \theta) \qquad \boxed{1/\text{x}} \quad (\text{read } \sec \theta)$$

$$\tan \theta = \frac{3}{4}, \quad \cot \theta = \frac{1}{\tan \theta}: \quad 3\boxed{\div}4\boxed{=} \quad (\text{read } \tan \theta) \qquad \boxed{1/\text{x}} \quad (\text{read } \cot \theta)$$

The results are

$$\sin \theta = 0.6, \qquad \csc \theta = 1.6666667$$

$$\cos \theta = 0.8, \qquad \sec \theta = 1.25$$

$$\tan \theta = 0.75, \qquad \cot \theta = 1.3333333$$

13. Evaluate sec 24°.

There is no secant key, but since $\sec \theta = 1/\cos \theta$, compute the cosine and then take the reciprocal. In degree mode, key

$$24 \boxed{\cos} \boxed{1/\text{x}} \quad \text{and read} \quad \boxed{1.0946363}$$

Thus sec 24° = 1.0946363.

14. Compute tan 810°.

Trying to key 810 $\boxed{\tan}$, we get $\boxed{\text{Error}}$. This indicates that the quantity is undefined. The sense in this case is that the result is infinite.

15. Evaluate cos 59°12′.

First change to decimal degrees: 59 $\boxed{+}$ 12 $\boxed{\div}$ 60 $\boxed{=}$. Then, in degree mode, take the cosine $\boxed{\cos}$ and read the result: $\boxed{.51204287}$.

16. Evaluate (a) sin 7° and (b) sin 7.

(a) With the calculator in degree mode, key 7 $\boxed{\sin}$ and read $\boxed{.12186934}$.

(b) We must be in radian mode. Press $\boxed{DRG}$ 7 $\boxed{\sin}$ and this time read $\boxed{0.6569866}$.

Notice that the key sequences are basically the same, but the different modes cause the sine function to interpret the number 7 as a different quantity, first as 7 degrees, then as 7 radians.

17. Evaluate (a) sin (1/8)° and (b) $\dfrac{1}{\sin 8°}$.

(a) Key 8 $\boxed{1/x}$ $\boxed{\sin}$ and read $\boxed{.00218166}$.

(b) Key 8 $\boxed{\sin}$ $\boxed{1/x}$ and read $\boxed{7.1852965}$.

The second answer is, in fact, csc 8°. Notice that changing the order of the two function keys entirely changes the quantity that is calculated.

18. Calculate (a) tan 2 and (b) tan (π + 2).

(a) There is no degree symbol (°), which indicates that the calculator should be put in radian mode: $\boxed{DRG}$. Then key

$$2 \;\boxed{\tan}\quad \text{and read}\quad \boxed{-2.1850399}$$

(b) Still in radian mode, key $\boxed{\pi}$ $\boxed{+}$ 2 $\boxed{=}$ $\boxed{\tan}$ and the result will be identical to part (a). Thus it has been demonstrated that (within the accuracy of the calculator) tan (π + 2) = tan 2.

19. Evaluate sec [π − (π/3)].

Now π − (π/3) = (2π/3) and so we just calculate sec (2π/3) in radian mode. If the calculator is in degree mode, key first $\boxed{DRG}$. Then key

$$2 \;\boxed{\times}\; \boxed{\pi}\; \boxed{\div}\; 3 \;\boxed{=}\; \boxed{\cos}\; \boxed{1/x}\quad \text{and read}\quad \boxed{-2.}$$

SOLVING RIGHT TRIANGLES

20. In the right triangle of Figure 3-21, a = 12.6 and angle A = 38°. Find b, c, and angle B.

For right triangles, since the sum of the *acute* angles is 90°, we have $A + B$ = 90°; hence, B = 90° − A = 90° − 38° = 52°, which can be done either mentally or on the calculator.

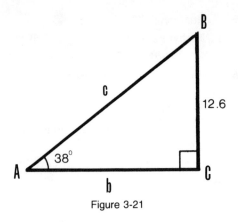

Figure 3-21

To find b, realize that $a/b = \tan A$; hence $12.6/b = \tan 38°$. Solving for b,

$$b = \frac{12.6}{\tan 38°}$$

Hence key

12.6 ⌈÷⌉ 38 ⌈tan⌉ ⌈=⌉ and read ⌈ 16.127265 ⌉ (leave displayed)

To determine the hypotenuse c, several relations may be useful. It is more convenient to use the derived quantity b, since it is already displayed; however, be warned that using derived quantities can often introduce *roundoff errors* into subsequent calculations. That is not the case here if we use the value computed (and *not* reentered). Since $b/c = \cos A$, then $c = b/\cos A = b/\cos 38°$, and b is already on display. Thus simply key

⌈÷⌉ 38 ⌈cos⌉ ⌈=⌉ and read ⌈ 20.465792 ⌉

(*Note*: If we had reentered b manually, 16.127265, we would have computed 20.465793 for c, because the internal guard digits computed while computing b would not be present. Thus an error in the sixth decimal place would be introduced.)

To use only given values, use $a/c = \sin A$ and so $c = 12.6/\sin 38°$. Keying 12.6 ⌈÷⌉ 38 ⌈sin⌉ ⌈=⌉ gives again $c = 20.465792$.

21. In the right triangle of Figure 3-22, if $c = 5.72$ and angle $A = 21°\,17'12''$, find sides a and b and angle B.

Find angle B in the DMS system, since that is how the problem is stated. $B = 90° - 21°17'12'' = 89°59'60'' - 21°17'12'' = 68°42'48''$. Note the convenient equivalent of 90°. This calculation may be done mentally as three separate subtractions or on the calculator:

Degrees: 89 $\boxed{-}$ 21 $\boxed{=}$
Minutes: 59 $\boxed{-}$ 17 $\boxed{=}$
Seconds: 60 $\boxed{-}$ 12 $\boxed{=}$

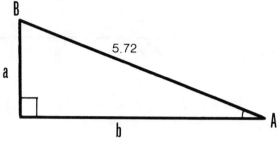

Figure 3-22

(If your calculator has automatic conversion, this can be done faster by converting to decimal degrees, subtracting from 90°, and then converting back. If it does not have this feature, the preceding method is easier.)

To continue solving for the other quantities, we need angle A in decimal degrees, so we convert:

21 $\boxed{+}$ 17 $\boxed{\div}$ 60 $\boxed{+}$ 12 $\boxed{\div}$ 3600 $\boxed{=}$ and read $\boxed{21.286667}$

Store it in memory: $\boxed{\text{STO}}$. This is done because the number will be used twice. In fact, even if it were only to be used once, it will be more convenient to recall it from memory (and more accurate) than to reenter it as needed. Since

$$\frac{a}{5.72} = \sin A, \qquad a = 5.72 \sin A$$

and since angle A is stored in memory, key

5.72 $\boxed{\times}$ $\boxed{\text{RCL}}$ $\boxed{\sin}$ $\boxed{=}$ and read a: $\boxed{2.0765568}$

Now $b/5.72 = \cos A$, so $b = 5.72 \cos A$, and again since A is stored in memory, key

5.72 $\boxed{\times}$ $\boxed{\text{RCL}}$ $\boxed{\cos}$ $\boxed{=}$ and read b: $\boxed{5.3297572}$

Thus $B = 68°42'48''$, $a = 2.08$, and $b = 5.33$ approximately.

22. If $a = 4.2$ and angle $A = 23°$, find the area of the triangle of Figure 3-23.

115

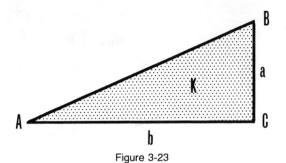

Figure 3-23

The area $K = \frac{1}{2} ab$ and we know $a = 4.2$. Also $a/b = \tan A$; thus $b = a/\tan A$. Hence the area

$$K = \frac{1}{2} a\left(\frac{a}{\tan A}\right) = \frac{a^2}{2 \tan A} = \frac{(4.2)^2}{2 \tan 23°}$$

So calculate

$$4.2 \boxed{x^2} \boxed{\div} \boxed{(} 2 \boxed{\times} 23 \boxed{\tan} \boxed{=} \text{ in degree mode}$$

Thus, rounded to one decimal place, $K = 20.8$ square units. Alternatively, the calculation can be done as

$$4.2 \boxed{x^2} \boxed{\div} 2 \boxed{\div} 23 \boxed{\tan} \boxed{=}$$

where no parenthesis is needed since we look at the expression as two divisions.

23. Given that the hypotenuse $c = 9.2$ and the base $b = 5.8$, find the altitude a, angle A, and angle B for the right triangle shown of Figure 3-24.

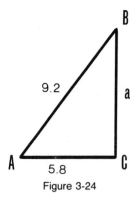

Figure 3-24

We may find a by using the Pythagorean theorem; thus

$$a = \sqrt{c^2 - b^2} = \sqrt{9.2^2 - 5.8^2}$$

so key

$$9.2 \boxed{x^2} \boxed{-} 5.8 \boxed{x^2} \boxed{=} \boxed{\sqrt{x}} \quad \text{and read} \quad \boxed{7.1414284}$$

(During the calculation notice that $a = \sqrt{51}$ exactly.)
We could use this derived value of a to compute functions of the angles, but it is a better practice computationally to use given quantities when possible. Thus, referring to the triangle,

$$\cos A = \frac{5.8}{9.2} \quad \text{and so} \quad A = \text{Cos}^{-1}\left(\frac{5.8}{9.2}\right)$$

and we compute

$$5.8 \boxed{\div} 9.2 \boxed{=} \boxed{\text{INV}} \boxed{\cos} \quad \text{and read} \quad \boxed{50.917793}$$

which is left displayed. Thus $A = 50.9°$ approximately. To get angle B, subtract the displayed value from 90° as follows:

$$\boxed{+/-} \boxed{+} 90 \boxed{=} \quad \text{and read} \quad \boxed{39.082207}$$

Thus angle $B = 39.1°$ approximately. (Note that here we did use a derived quantity, angle A, to compute angle B. However, since the difference was not close to zero, no important errors were introduced numerically. If we evaluated angle $B = \text{Sin}^{-1}(5.8/9.2)$, which are given quantities, we would get exactly the same result.)

We did not need the Pythagorean theorem for a if we wanted to get it from the computed value of angle B, since $a = 9.2 \cos B$. So when angle B is displayed, just key $\boxed{\cos} \boxed{\times} 9.2 \boxed{=}$ and we have a simple way to get a knowing one of the angles.

24. The top of a flagpole is sighted from a point 100 feet from its base and 5.2 feet above the horizontal, and an angle of elevation of 33°14′ is measured. Find the height of the flagpole.

First draw a diagram (see Figure 3-25) and note that the height of the pole is equal to the length of leg a plus 5.2 ft. Thus solve for a and add 5.2. Now

$$\frac{a}{100} = \tan A = \tan 33°14′$$

To compute this, change to decimal degrees: $33 \boxed{+} 14 \boxed{\div} 60 \boxed{=}$. Then complete the calculation of a:

$$\boxed{\tan} \boxed{\times} 100 \boxed{=} \quad \text{to get} \quad \boxed{65.521288}$$

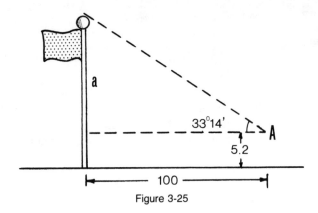

Figure 3-25

Then add the extra height:

$$\boxed{+}\ 5.2\ \boxed{=}\quad \text{which gives}\quad \boxed{70.721288}$$

Thus the flagpole is about 70.7 feet high.

25. A surveyor has the task of measuring the height of a hill (see Figure 3-26) and does it by measuring the acute angles $A = 34.7°$ and $B = 42.6°$ from two points A and B so that the distance measured between them is found to be $AB = 786$ ft. How does the surveyor compute the height of the hill and what is it?

First draw a diagram as shown in Figure 3-26(b), and then set up equations using the cotangent function:

$$\frac{x + 786}{H} = \cot 34.7°$$

$$\frac{x}{H} = \cot 42.6°$$

Figure 3-26

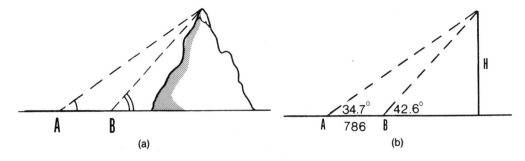

(a)   (b)

Subtracting equations, we get

$$\frac{786}{H} = \cot 34.7° - \cot 42.6°$$

Solving this equation for H,

$$H = \frac{786}{\cot 34.6° - \cot 42.6°}$$

To compute this, since there is no cotangent key, we must use the sequence $\boxed{\tan}\ \boxed{1/x}$ when we want the cotangent since it is just the reciprocal of the tangent. Thus key

$$786\ \boxed{\div}\ \boxed{(}\ 34.7\ \boxed{\tan}\ \boxed{1/x}\ \boxed{-}\ 42.6\ \boxed{\tan}\ \boxed{1/x}\ \boxed{=}$$
$$\text{and read}\ \boxed{2203.5844}$$

Thus the hill is 2203 feet high.

SINE AND COSINE LAWS

26. In the acute triangle shown of Figure 3-27, $a = 11.47$ mm, $b = 15.62$ mm, and the angle included between them is $C = 51°$. Compute c, angle A, and angle B.

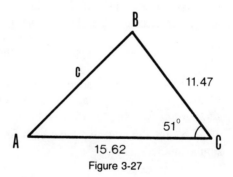

Figure 3-27

Since we are given two sides and the included angle, the cosine law applies, and we have

$$c^2 = a^2 + b^2 - 2ab \cos C$$
$$= 11.47^2 + 15.62^2 - 2(11.47)\,(15.62) \cos 51°$$

We compute this quantity and then take the square root to get c:

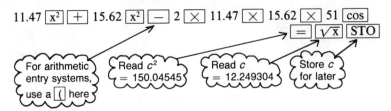

11.47 $\boxed{x^2}$ $\boxed{+}$ 15.62 $\boxed{x^2}$ $\boxed{-}$ 2 $\boxed{\times}$ 11.47 $\boxed{\times}$ 15.62 $\boxed{\times}$ 51 $\boxed{\cos}$

$\boxed{=}$ $\boxed{\sqrt{x}}$ $\boxed{\text{STO}}$

For arithmetic entry systems, use a $\boxed{(}$ here

Read c^2 = 150.04545

Read c = 12.249304

Store c for later

Thus $c = 12.25$ mm, rounded to two decimal places; however, leave it displayed to full accuracy to be used in the next calculation.

To compute angle A, use the form of the cosine law that involves $\cos A$; that is, $a^2 = b^2 + c^2 - 2bc \cos A$. Solving for $\cos A$,

$$\cos A = \frac{b^2 + c^2 - a^2}{2bc}$$

Now with c still displayed, square it (to get full accuracy) and continue, completing the calculation of $\cos A$, and then finally take the inverse cosine to get angle A.

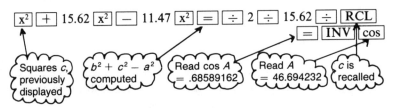

$\boxed{x^2}$ $\boxed{+}$ 15.62 $\boxed{x^2}$ $\boxed{-}$ 11.47 $\boxed{x^2}$ $\boxed{=}$ $\boxed{\div}$ 2 $\boxed{\div}$ 15.62 $\boxed{\div}$ $\boxed{\text{RCL}}$

$\boxed{=}$ $\boxed{\text{INV}}$ $\boxed{\cos}$

Squares c, previously displayed

$b^2 + c^2 - a^2$ computed

Read $\cos A$ = .68589162

Read A = 46.694232

c is recalled

Thus $A = 46.694232°$, which is still displayed; $C = 51°$ was given. So to compute angle B at this point, recall that $A + B + C = 180°$; thus subtract A and C from 180°, with A still displayed as follows:

$\boxed{+/-}$ $\boxed{-}$ 51 $\boxed{+}$ 180 $\boxed{=}$ and read $\boxed{82.305768}$

Notice that 180° was added last rather than starting with it to take advantage of the fact that angle A was already displayed. Thus $c = 12.25$ mm, $A = 46.7°$, and $B = 82.3°$ approximately.

Note: Angle B could also have been found using the cosine law in a similar manner:

$$\cos B = \frac{a^2 + c^2 - b^2}{2ac}$$

and then take the inverse cosine. The fact that the sum of the angles is 180° can be used as a check.

27. In the triangle of Figure 3-28, $a = 92.5$, $b = 48.2$, and $c = 105.6$. What are the three interior angles in decimal degrees?

The law of cosine can be used as three formulas to find the cosines of each of the angles and then the inverse cosine taken to compute the angles themselves.

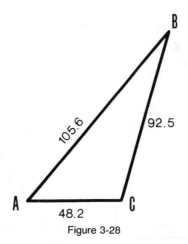

Figure 3-28

$$\cos A = \frac{b^2 + c^2 - a^2}{2bc} = \frac{48.2^2 + 105.6^2 - 92.5^2}{2(48.2)(105.6)}$$

so key

48.2 $\boxed{x^2}$ $\boxed{+}$ 105.6 $\boxed{x^2}$ $\boxed{-}$ 92.5 $\boxed{x^2}$ $\boxed{=}$ (this is the numerator)

$\boxed{\div}$ 2 $\boxed{\div}$ 48.2 $\boxed{\div}$ 105.6 $\boxed{=}$ (dividing by the denominator)

$\boxed{\text{INV}}$ $\boxed{\cos}$ and read angle A: $\boxed{\quad 61.108919}$. The other angles are computed in an analogous manner using the other two forms of the cosine law, substituting appropriately. The results are $B = 27.143922$ and $C = 91.747159$. If we round these to one decimal place, we get $A = 61.1°$, $B = 27.1°$, and $C = 91.7°$. If we were to add these rounded values to check, we would get 179.9°, which shows that rounded values will not produce a perfect check.

28. In a triangle, $b = 32.5$, $c = 39.2$, and angle $B = 40°12'$. Find a, angle A, and angle C.

The diagram of Figure 3-29(a) is a *tentative* diagram, since this is the case of two sides and a *non*included angle, which can possibly produce two solutions. It is not drawn to scale and is only a guide to setting up formulas. It may in fact turn out that the configuration may not even be possible, but we never know until we do the calculation.

Since we know angle B, use the form of the cosine law that involves $\cos B$: $b^2 = a^2 + c^2 - 2ac \cos B$, which we rearrange to write as a *quadratic equation* with unknown a, the side for which we are asked to solve.

$$a^2 - (2c \cos B)a + (c^2 - b^2) = 0$$

121

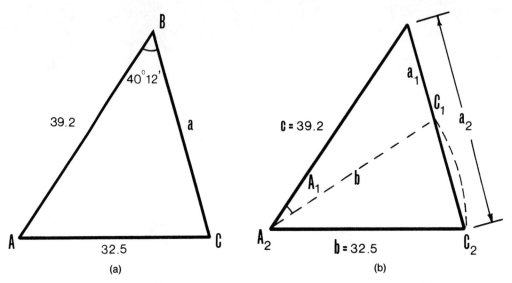

Figure 3-29 (a) Tentative Diagram; (b) Two Possible Solutions (Not to scale)

Applying the quadratic formula, we solve this for a:

$$a = \frac{-(-2c \cos B) \pm \sqrt{(-2c \cos B)^2 - 4(1)(c^2 - b^2)}}{2(1)}$$

This expression can be simplified somewhat with a little algebra and using the identify $\sin^2 B = 1 - \cos^2 B$.

$$a = \frac{2c \cos B \pm \sqrt{4c^2 \cos^2 B - 4c^2 + 4b^2}}{2}$$

$$= \frac{2c \cos B \pm 2\sqrt{c^2(\cos^2 B - 1) + b^2}}{2}$$

$$= c \cos B \pm \sqrt{b^2 - c^2 \sin^2 B} = c \cos B \pm \sqrt{b^2 - (c \sin B)^2}$$

Now substitute the known values:

$$a = 39.2 \cos 40°12' \pm \sqrt{32.5^2 - (39.2 \sin 40°12')^2}$$

First compute the radical (square root) and store it in memory, to be recalled when needed to use the minus sign. In order to do this, change to decimal degrees:

$$40 \boxed{+} 12 \boxed{\div} 60 \boxed{=} \quad \text{and read} \quad \boxed{40.2}$$

Thus $40°12' = 40.2°$. Evaluate the radical and store. Use $40.2°$ for the angle.

32.5 $\boxed{x^2}$ $\boxed{-}$ 39.2 $\boxed{x^2}$ $\boxed{\times}$ 40.2 $\boxed{\sin}$ $\boxed{=}$ $\boxed{\sqrt{x}}$ $\boxed{STO}$ reading $\boxed{8.0258269}$

Now add it to the first term

$\boxed{+}$ 39.2 $\boxed{\times}$ 40.2 $\boxed{\cos}$ $\boxed{=}$ and read $\boxed{37.966631}$

Now, with this still displayed, we can subtract the radical as

$\boxed{-}$ 2 $\boxed{\times}$ $\boxed{RCL}$ $\boxed{=}$ and get $\boxed{21.914977}$

[This is a clever way to subtract something you have just added. If you have $a + b$ and want $a - b$, just subtract $2b$; that is, $(a + b) - 2b = a - b$.]

Thus we have two answers for a: $a_1 = 21.91$ and $a_2 = 37.97$ approximately. Thus two configurations are possible [see Figure 3-29(b)], since only angle B is fixed. Thus, corresponding to each value of a, there are corresponding values of angle A and angle C, which we shall denote by A_1, A_2 and C_1, C_2. In each case, we use the cosine law to solve for the included angle and then subtract from 180° to get the third angle.

For $a_1 = 21.914977$, use (to solve for angle C_1):

$$c^2 = a_1^2 + b^2 - 2a_1 b \cos C_1$$

and solve for $\cos C_1$.

$$\cos C_1 = \frac{a_1^2 + b^2 - c^2}{2a_1 b} = \frac{21.914977^2 + 32.5^2 - 39.2^2}{2(21.914977)(32.5)}$$

To calculate this, use all the digits for a_1, store it for the later division (to save time), and finally take the inverse cosine to get angle C_1.

21.914977 $\boxed{STO}$

$\boxed{x^2}$ $\boxed{+}$ 32.5 $\boxed{x^2}$ $\boxed{-}$ 39.2 $\boxed{x^2}$ $\boxed{=}$ $\boxed{\div}$ 2 $\boxed{\div}$ $\boxed{RCL}$ $\boxed{\div}$ 32.5 $\boxed{=}$ $\boxed{INV}$ $\boxed{\cos}$ and read $\boxed{90.004979}$

(This could be converted to 90°00′18″.) This says that angle C_1 is just about a right angle. Now to get angle A_1, subtract this and angle B from 180°.

$\boxed{+/-}$ $\boxed{-}$ 40.2 $\boxed{+}$ 180 $\boxed{=}$ and read $\boxed{49.795021}$

which can be converted to 49°47′42″, approximately.

For $a_2 = 37.966631$ use the formula,

$$\cos C_2 = \frac{a_2^2 + b^2 - c^2}{2a_2 b} = \frac{37.966631^2 + 32.5^2 - 39.2^2}{2(21.914977)(32.5)}$$

which is calculated in the same manner, and get for angle $C_2 = 67.080266°$ or, converted to DMS, $67°04'49''$. For corresponding angle A_2, $72.719734°$, or converted to the DMS system, $72°43'11''$, is the result.

29. In the triangle of Figure 3-30, $b = 25$, angle $A = 46°$, and angle $C = 72°$. Compute a, c, and angle B.

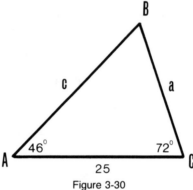

Figure 3-30

Since we are given two angles and the included side, the law of sines is the appropriate formula. To find a use,

$$\frac{a}{\sin A} = \frac{b}{\sin B}$$

but compute angle B first. Clearly, $B = 62°$.

Angle B was computed by subtracting from $180°$: $180 \boxed{-} 46 \boxed{-} 72 \boxed{=}$. Thus, solving for a,

$$a = \frac{b \sin A}{\sin B} = \frac{25 \sin 46°}{\sin 62°}$$

To compute this quantity in degree mode, key

$25 \boxed{\times} 46 \boxed{\sin} \boxed{\div} 62 \boxed{\sin} \boxed{=}$ and read $\boxed{20.367568}$

We could use the cosine law to find c now, but it is actually easier to use the sine law again. This time use

$$\frac{c}{\sin C} = \frac{b}{\sin B}$$

which implies that

$$c = \frac{b \sin C}{\sin B} = \frac{25 \sin 72°}{\sin 62°}$$

(Notice that we did not use the derived side a, which, if we had entered rounded, could introduce roundoff error. If, however, we use all the digits of a, no appreciable error is introduced.)

To continue with the calculation of c, key

25 $\boxed{\times}$ 72 $\boxed{\sin}$ $\boxed{\div}$ 62 $\boxed{\sin}$ $\boxed{=}$ and read $\boxed{\quad 26.928453 \quad}$

A Computational Note: Notice that the only difference between these two calculations is one angle (A or C):

$$a = \frac{b}{\sin B} \sin A \quad \text{and} \quad c = \frac{b}{\sin B} \sin C$$

Thus, as an alternative method, we could compute

b $\boxed{\div}$ B $\boxed{\sin}$ $\boxed{\times}$ $\boxed{\text{STO}}$ A $\boxed{\sin}$ $\boxed{=}$

which computes a and stores $b/\sin B$.

Then compute c by simply keying

C $\boxed{\sin}$ $\boxed{\times}$ $\boxed{\text{RCL}}$ $\boxed{=}$

30. Compute the width of the river diagrammed in Figure 3-31, where a rock R has been sighted from two points A and B 30 yards apart. The angles of sight are $A = 35°$ and $B = 132°$.

The strategy is to use the sine law to compute side $b = AR$ of triangle ABR and then use it for the calculation of the river width $D = b$

Figure 3-31

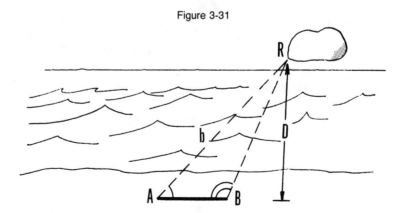

sin A. Also, since the sum of the interior angles is 180°, angle $R =$ 13°. So

$$\frac{b}{\sin B} = \frac{AB}{\sin R} \quad \text{and hence} \quad b = \frac{AB \sin B}{\sin R} = \frac{30 \sin 132°}{\sin 13°}$$

Now $D/b = \sin A$ and hence $D = b \sin A = b \sin 35°$. Substituting the expression obtained for b, we get

$$D = \frac{30 \sin 132°}{\sin 13°} \sin 35°$$

To compute this, key

30 $\boxed{\times}$ 132 $\boxed{\sin}$ $\boxed{\times}$ 35 $\boxed{\sin}$ $\boxed{\div}$ 13 $\boxed{\sin}$ $\boxed{=}$
and read $\boxed{\quad 56.845747 \quad}$

Then, to the nearest tenth of a yard, the width $D = 56.8$ yards.

AREAS

31. Find the area of the triangle shown in Figure 3-32, where angle $A = $ 23°, angle $C = 41°$, and side $a = 14.7$.

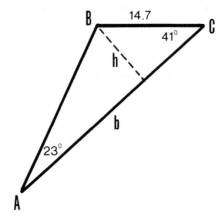

Figure 3-32

First compute $h = 14.7 \sin 41°$:

14.7 $\boxed{\times}$ 41 $\boxed{\sin}$ $\boxed{=}$ $\boxed{\text{STO}}$ and read $\boxed{\quad 9.6440677 \quad}$

which was stored in memory as well. Now we apply the sine law to compute

$$b = \frac{a}{\sin A} \sin B = \frac{14.7}{\sin 23°} \sin 116°$$

by keying

14.7 $\boxed{\div}$ 23 $\boxed{\sin}$ $\boxed{\times}$ 116 $\boxed{\sin}$ $\boxed{=}$ and read $\boxed{\qquad 33.814231 \qquad}$

which is left displayed. Now since h is stored in memory and b is displayed, and the area $K = \frac{1}{2}hb$, we compute

$\boxed{\times}$ $\boxed{\text{RCL}}$ $\boxed{=}$ and read K: $\boxed{\qquad 163.05337 \qquad}$

As an alternative procedure, if you don't wish to do this in stages, we may use the formula

$$K = \frac{a^2 \sin B \sin C}{2 \sin A} = \frac{14.7^2 \sin 116° \sin 41°}{2 \sin 23°}$$

Since we are given two angles and a side, as in the first part, the third angle is just the difference between 180° and the other two angles. The key sequence is

14.7 $\boxed{x^2}$ $\boxed{\times}$ 116 $\boxed{\sin}$ $\boxed{\times}$ 41 $\boxed{\sin}$ $\boxed{\div}$ 2 $\boxed{\div}$ 23 $\boxed{\sin}$ $\boxed{=}$

(Be sure to pause a few seconds each time you press the $\boxed{\sin}$ key to allow the calculator time to do its work.)

32. Compute the area of the triangle of Figure 3-33, where $a = 50.7$, $b = 65.2$, and angle $C = 26°$.

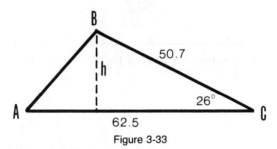

Figure 3-33

First notice that the altitude $h = a \sin C = 50.7 \sin 26°$. Thus the area $K = \frac{1}{2}hb = \frac{1}{2}(50.7)(\sin 26°)(65.2)$, or just use the formula $K = \frac{1}{2}ab \sin C$, which is the same thing. To compute this, key

50.7 $\boxed{\times}$ 26 $\boxed{\sin}$ $\boxed{\times}$ 65.2 $\boxed{\div}$ 2 $\boxed{=}$

and read the area K: $\boxed{\quad 724.5486 \quad}$ in square units.

33. The triangle of Figure 3-34 has sides $a = 5.8$, $b = 9.3$, and $c = 12.5$. Compute the area of the triangle.

Since three sides are given, we use Heron's formula:

$$K = \sqrt{s(s-a)(s-b)(s-c)}, \quad \text{where } s = \frac{1}{2}(a+b+c)$$

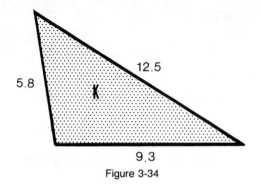

Figure 3-34

First we compute the semiperimeter s and store it in memory:

5.8 $\boxed{+}$ 9.3 $\boxed{+}$ 12.5 $\boxed{=}$ $\boxed{\div}$ 2 $\boxed{=}$ $\boxed{\text{STO}}$;   read $s = 13.8$

Now we use the stored value in the formula by recalling it when s is needed in the expression for area:

$$K = \sqrt{s(s - 5.8)(s - 9.3)(s - 12.5)}$$

We key (with $s = 13.8$ still displayed)

$\boxed{\times}$ $\boxed{(}$ $\boxed{\text{RCL}}$ $\boxed{-}$ 5.8 $\boxed{)}$ $\boxed{\times}$ $\boxed{(}$ $\boxed{\text{RCL}}$ $\boxed{-}$ 9.3 $\boxed{)}$ $\boxed{\times}$ $\boxed{(}$ $\boxed{\text{RCL}}$
$\boxed{-}$ 12.5 $\boxed{=}$ $\boxed{\sqrt{x}}$

and read the area K: $\boxed{\text{25.413382}}$.

Hence the area $K = 25.4$ square units, approximately.

34. Compute the area of the shaded segment of the circle shown in Figure 3-35 if the radius $r = 8.3$ and the central angle $\theta = 68°$.

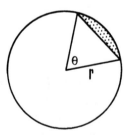

Figure 3-35

The formula for the area of the sector is

$$A = \frac{r^2}{2} (\theta - \sin \theta), \qquad \text{where } \theta \text{ is in } \textit{radians}$$

(We could look up the formula of the sector with the angle in degrees, but it is slightly easier to use radians. In fact, the degree formula essentially changes the angle into radians without explicitly saying so.)

First set the calculator to *radian mode* by pressing [DRG] once. Now change 68° to radians:

$$68 \; \boxed{\times} \; \boxed{\pi} \; \boxed{\div} \; 180 \; \boxed{=} \; \boxed{\text{STO}}$$

Now that the angle is in memory, complete the calculation of the formula;

$$8.3 \; \boxed{x^2} \; \boxed{\div} \; 2 \; \boxed{\times} \; \boxed{(} \; \boxed{\text{RCL}} \; \boxed{-} \; \boxed{\text{RCL}} \; \boxed{\sin} \; \boxed{=}$$

and read *A*: [8.943301]

This could be omitted since θ is still on display

Thus the area $A = 8.94$ square units, approximately.

35. If line segment *PQ* is tangent to the circle at *P*, with radius $r = 7.3$ and central angle $\theta = 38°$ as shown in Figure 3-36, compute the shaded area that is the part of triangle *OPQ* that lies outside the circle.

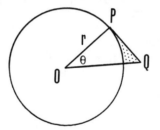

Figure 3-36

Notice that $PQ/r = \tan \theta$; thus $PQ = r \tan \theta$. Also, the area of the sector determined by θ is $\frac{1}{2} r^2 \theta$, θ in radians. The area of triangle *OPQ* is $\frac{1}{2} r \cdot PQ = \frac{1}{2} r \cdot r \tan \theta = \frac{1}{2} r^2 \tan \theta$ using the relation noted and the fact that a tangent to a circle must be perpendicular to the radius at the point of tangency. The required shaded area, therefore, is

$$\text{triangle } OPQ - \text{sector} = \frac{r^2}{2} \tan \theta - \frac{r^2}{2} \theta = \frac{1}{2} r^2 (\tan \theta - \theta)$$

where θ is in radians. Thus, to calculate change $\theta = 38°$ to radian measure, put the calculator in radian mode (since we are computing a function of an angle expressed in radians), and compute:

1. Set to radian mode: [DRG].
2. Change θ to radians: $38 \; \boxed{\times} \; \boxed{\pi} \; \boxed{\div} \; 180 \; \boxed{=} \; \boxed{\text{STO}}$.

3. Compute shaded area using the derived formula, recalling the value of θ stored in step 2, as required. Note that θ, in radians, is still displayed at this point:

$$\boxed{\text{tan}}\ \boxed{-}\ \boxed{\text{RCL}}\ \boxed{=}\ \boxed{\times}\ 7.3\ \boxed{x^2}\ \boxed{\div}\ 2\ \boxed{=}$$
$$\text{and read}\ \boxed{\quad 3.1457222 \quad}$$

Thus the shaded area is approximately 3.15 square units.

MISCELLANEOUS
TRIGONOMETRIC COMPUTATIONS

36. Compute each of the following to four-decimal-place accuracy: (a) tan $5\pi/12$; (b) sin$(.3\pi)$; (c) sin 2.6; (d) sin 38°.

Since the calculator starts in degree mode, it is most convenient to start with (d) first, for it is the only one with the argument (i.e., angle) expressed in degrees:

$$38\ \boxed{\text{sin}}\ \ \text{and read}\ \ \boxed{\quad .61566148 \quad}$$

Now change to radian mode by keying $\boxed{\text{DRG}}$ once. Now
(a) $5\ \boxed{\times}\ \boxed{\pi}\ \boxed{\div}\ 12\ \boxed{=}\ \boxed{\text{tan}}$ and read $\boxed{\quad 3.7320508 \quad}$.
(b) $.3\ \boxed{\times}\ \boxed{\pi}\ \boxed{=}\ \boxed{\text{sin}}$ and read $\boxed{\quad 0.809017 \quad}$.
(c) $2.6\ \boxed{\text{sin}}$ and read $\boxed{\quad .51550137 \quad}$.
In part (c) notice that 2.6 does not contain the four-degree symbol and so it represents 2.6 *radians*. So, to four-place accuracy, the results are (a) 3.7321, (b) .8090, (c) .5155, and (d) .6157.

37. Compute

$$\frac{\tan 46° + \tan 27°}{1 - \tan 46° \tan 27°}$$

In this (somewhat contrived) problem, if you notice that the form looks like the formula for the tangent of the sum of two angles, you soon realize that it equals

$$\tan(46° + 27°)$$

and so simply key

$$46\ \boxed{+}\ 27\ \boxed{=}\ \boxed{\text{tan}}\ \ \text{and read}\ \ \boxed{\quad 3.2708526 \quad}$$

which is much simpler than a direct calculation of the original expression.

38. If sin $x = {}^2/_3$ and $x + y = \pi/3$, then find y accurate to four decimal places, provided that y satisfies the condition $|y| < \pi$.

Since $x + y = \pi/3$, $y = (\pi/3) - x$, so we must first find admissible values of x and subtract from $\pi/3$ to get y. Since no degrees are mentioned, the quantities are in radians, so set your calculator to radian mode (press $\boxed{\text{DRG}}$ once). While in radian mode, do the following:

1. Find $x = \sin^{-1}(2/3)$:

$$2 \boxed{\div} 3 \boxed{=} \boxed{\text{INV}} \boxed{\sin} \boxed{\text{STO}} \quad \text{reading} \quad \boxed{.72972766}$$

This is only one value of $x = x_1$ (first quadrant). It has been stored in memory. The second value will be found later.

2. Subtract the displayed value x_1 from $\pi/3$ to get the first value of $y = y_1$.

$$\boxed{+/-} \boxed{+} \boxed{\pi} \boxed{\div} 3 \boxed{=} \quad \text{reading} \quad \boxed{.31746989}$$

3. The second value of $x = x_2$ is found by subtracting x_1 from π. Figure 3-37 explains why. Recall that x_1 is in memory.

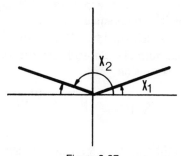

Figure 3-37

$$\boxed{\pi} \boxed{-} \boxed{\text{RCL}} \boxed{=} \quad \text{reading } x_2: \quad \boxed{2.411865}$$

4. Now subtract this value from $\pi/3$ to get $y = y_2$, the second value of y:

$$\boxed{+/-} \boxed{+} \boxed{\pi} \boxed{\div} 3 \boxed{=} \quad \text{and read } y_2: \quad \boxed{1.3646674}$$

Thus there are two values of y, $y_1 = .3175$, $y_2 = 1.3647$, both given in radians rounded to four decimal places.

39. If $\tan \theta = .35$, $0 < \theta < \pi/2$, compute (a) $\sin 3\theta$; (b) $\cos 3\theta$; (c) $\tan 3\theta$.

The calculator can be in any angular mode. Compute θ and then triple it. Store 3θ in memory. The calculation is shown in degree mode:

$$.35 \boxed{\text{INV}} \boxed{\tan} \boxed{\times} 3 \boxed{=} \boxed{\text{STO}} \quad \text{and read } 3\theta: \quad \boxed{57.870139}$$

With this value still displayed, key

(a) $\boxed{\text{sin}}$ and read sin 3θ = .84684486.

(b) $\boxed{\text{RCL}}\boxed{\text{cos}}$ and read cos 3θ = .53184001.

(c) $\boxed{\text{RCL}}\boxed{\text{tan}}$ and read tan 3θ = 1.5922925.

40. Given that sin $(\theta/3)$ = 0.42, $0 < \theta < 90°$, evaluate (a) cos θ; (b) sin 2θ; (c) cot $(\theta/2)$.

Various multiples of θ are needed. Since $\theta/3$ = Sin^{-1} (0.42), θ = 3 Sin^{-1} (0.42), which is stored in memory to be recalled as needed. Any mode may be used here, but the calculations are shown in degree mode. First compute θ and store:

$$.42 \boxed{\text{INV}}\boxed{\text{sin}}\boxed{\times}\ 3 \boxed{=}\boxed{\text{STO}}\quad \text{reading } \theta \quad \boxed{74.503763}$$

With the value of θ still displayed, compute

(a) cos θ: $\boxed{\text{cos}}$ reading $\boxed{.26717509}$.

(b) sin 2θ: $\boxed{\text{RCL}}\boxed{\times}\ 2 \boxed{=}\boxed{\text{sin}}$ and read $\boxed{.51492549}$.

(c) cot $\theta/2$: $\boxed{\text{RCL}}\boxed{\div}\ 2 \boxed{=}\boxed{\text{tan}}\boxed{1/x}$ and read $\boxed{1.3149771}$.

41. Find two exact expressions for sin 15° and confirm by calculation that they both equal sin 15°.

Notice that sin 15° = sin ½ (30°) = $\sqrt{(1 - \cos 30°)/2}$ using a half-angle formula. Substituting the exact value cos 30° = $\sqrt{3}/2$ gives the expression

$$\sin 15° = \sqrt{\frac{1 - (\sqrt{3}/2)}{2}} = \sqrt{\frac{2 - \sqrt{3}}{4}} = \frac{\sqrt{2 - \sqrt{3}}}{2}$$

Computing this expression, we get

$$2 \boxed{-}\ 3 \boxed{\sqrt{x}}\boxed{=}\boxed{\sqrt{x}}\boxed{\div}\ 2 \boxed{=}\quad \text{and read}\quad \boxed{.25881905}$$

On the other hand, sin 15° = sin (45° − 30°) = sin 45° cos 30° − cos 45° sin 30°, using the formula for the sine of the difference of two angles. Substituting exact values for each term of the expression yields

$$\frac{\sqrt{2}}{2}\frac{\sqrt{3}}{2} - \frac{\sqrt{2}}{2}\frac{1}{2} = \frac{\sqrt{6} - \sqrt{2}}{4}$$

This is computed by keying

$$6 \boxed{\sqrt{x}}\boxed{-}\ 2 \boxed{\sqrt{x}}\boxed{=}\boxed{\div}\ 4 \boxed{=}$$

and we get the same result as before. To confirm these results, compute sin 15° directly by keying 15 $\boxed{\text{sin}}$, and once again the identical result is obtained. Thus

$$\sin 15° = \frac{\sqrt{2 - \sqrt{3}}}{2} = \frac{\sqrt{6} - \sqrt{2}}{4}$$

42. Evaluate each of the following in both degrees and radians: (a) Sin^{-1} .83; (b) Cos^{-1} (-1); (c) Sin^{-1} ($2/\sqrt{3}$).

With the calculator in degree mode key:

(a) .83 $\boxed{\text{INV}}$ $\boxed{\text{sin}}$ and read Sin^{-1} .83 = 56.098738°.

(b) 1 $\boxed{+/-}$ $\boxed{\text{INV}}$ $\boxed{\text{cos}}$ and read Cos^{-1} (-1) = 180°.

(c) 2 $\boxed{\div}$ 3 $\boxed{\sqrt{x}}$ $\boxed{=}$ $\boxed{\text{INV}}$ $\boxed{\text{sin}}$ and read $\boxed{\text{Error}}$.
This is because $2/\sqrt{3} > 1$ and no sine is bigger than 1! Now change to radians by pressing $\boxed{\text{DRG}}$ once and then key:

(a) .83 $\boxed{\text{INV}}$ $\boxed{\text{sin}}$ and thus Sin^{-1} .83 = .97910768 radians.

(b) 1 $\boxed{+/-}$ $\boxed{\text{INV}}$ $\boxed{\text{cos}}$, and so Cos^{-1} (-1) = 3.1415927 radians. Notice that this is just the decimal value of π. Since part (c) is undefined in degrees, it certainly can not exist in radians.

43. Evaluate Tan^{-1} (sec 1.53) in both degrees and radians.

Since 1.53 is in radians, begin with the calculator in radian mode (press $\boxed{\text{DRG}}$ once after turning on calculator); then key

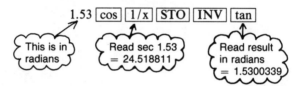

1.53 $\boxed{\text{cos}}$ $\boxed{1/x}$ $\boxed{\text{STO}}$ $\boxed{\text{INV}}$ $\boxed{\text{tan}}$

This is in radians

Read sec 1.53 = 24.518811

Read result in radians = 1.5300339

Now change to degree mode (press $\boxed{\text{DRG}}$ $\boxed{\text{DRG}}$) and then

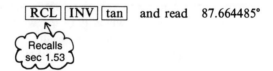

$\boxed{\text{RCL}}$ $\boxed{\text{INV}}$ $\boxed{\text{tan}}$ and read   87.664485°

Recalls sec 1.53

44. Use the calculator to confirm, to available accuracy, Machin's formula:

$$\frac{\pi}{4} = 4\tan^{-1}\left(\frac{1}{5}\right) - \tan^{1}\left(\frac{1}{239}\right)$$

(This formula was utilized in the year 1706 in connection with Gregory's infinite series for tan^{-1} to obtain 100 decimal places for π.)

First we shall compute $\pi/4$ and store it for comparison:

$$\boxed{\pi}\ \boxed{\div}\ 4\ \boxed{=}\ \boxed{\text{STO}}$$

Now put the calculator in radian mode by pressing $\boxed{\text{DRG}}$; then key

5 $\boxed{1/x}$ $\boxed{\text{INV}}$ $\boxed{\text{tan}}$ $\boxed{\times}$ 4 $\boxed{-}$ 239 $\boxed{1/x}$ $\boxed{\text{INV}}$ $\boxed{\text{tan}}$ $\boxed{=}$

and now compare the displayed value, ⬚.78539816 , with the stored value of $\pi/4$ by keying ⬚EXC⬚. This exchanges the display value with the memory. No *observable* change will occur, indicating that the values are equal.

45. Compute each of the following in both degrees and radians: (a) Cot⁻¹ (2.36); (b) Cot⁻¹ (−2.36).

First, in degree mode, compute expression (a), recalling that

$$\text{Cot}^{-1}\, x = \text{Tan}^{-1}\left(\frac{1}{x}\right)$$

provided that x is positive. Hence key

2.36 ⬚1/x⬚ ⬚INV⬚ ⬚tan⬚   and read   ⬚ 22.963773 ⬚

Thus Cot⁻¹ (2.36) = 23° approximately. Now for part (b), recall that, if x is negative,

$$\text{Cot}^{-1}\, x = 180° + \text{Tan}^{-1}\left(\frac{1}{x}\right)$$

and so for (b) key

2.36 ⬚+/−⬚ ⬚1/x⬚ ⬚INV⬚ ⬚tan⬚ ⬚+⬚ 180 ⬚=⬚
and read ⬚ 157.03623 ⬚

So Cot⁻¹(−2.36) = 157° approximately.

If you did not add the extra 180°, the value obtained would have been −22.963773, which is in the wrong quadrant for the principal value of Cot⁻¹. To get the results in radians, press ⬚DRG⬚ once, then for part (a) repeat the same key sequence given for the degree calculation but obtain .40079345 radian. However, for part (b) add π instead of 180°. That is, key

2.36 ⬚+/−⬚ ⬚1/x⬚ ⬚INV⬚ ⬚tan⬚ ⬚+⬚ ⬚π⬚ ⬚=⬚
and read ⬚ 2.7407992 ⬚

Thus Cot⁻¹(−2.36) = 2.74 radians approximately.

46. Compute the following in degrees: (a) Sec⁻¹ (2.81); (b) Sec⁻¹ (³/₅); (c) Csc⁻¹ $\sqrt{2}$; (d) Csc⁻¹ (−2/$\sqrt{3}$).

Since Sec⁻¹x = Cos⁻¹$(1/x)$ and Csc⁻¹x = Sin⁻¹$(1/x)$ for $|x| \geq 1$,
(a) 2.81 ⬚1/x⬚ ⬚INV⬚ ⬚cos⬚ , reading ⬚ 69.15311 ⬚.
(b) 3 ⬚÷⬚ 5 ⬚=⬚ ⬚1/x⬚ ⬚INV⬚ ⬚cos⬚ and read ⬚ Error ⬚. (This is because 3/5 < 1 and is therefore not in the domain of Sec⁻¹.)

(c) 2 $\boxed{\sqrt{x}}$ $\boxed{1/x}$ $\boxed{\text{INV}}$ $\boxed{\sin}$; then read $\boxed{45}$.

(d) 2 $\boxed{\div}$ 3 $\boxed{\sqrt{x}}$ $\boxed{=}$ $\boxed{+/-}$ $\boxed{1/x}$ $\boxed{\text{INV}}$ $\boxed{\sin}$ and read $\boxed{ -60}$.

Instead of using the reciprocal key for part (d), we could have done this step mentally since we had a fraction; that is,

$$\text{Csc}^{-1}\left(-\frac{3}{\sqrt{3}}\right) = \text{Sin}^{-1}\left(-\frac{\sqrt{3}}{2}\right)$$

Since to take the reciprocal of a fraction, we just invert it. Then we would just evaluate the right-hand expression and obtain the same result.

47. Show that $\cos(\text{Sin}^{-1}x)$ can be expressed without using trigonometric functions. Then evaluate both expressions for $x = .38$ to confirm the relation for this value of x.

First draw a diagram as in Figure 3-38 with $\theta = \text{Sin}^{-1}x$ in the first quadrant. The base length of the triangle is derived by applying the Pythagorean theorem. Notice that the diagram was constructed so that $\sin\theta = x/1 = x$. Now we want

$$\cos(\text{Sin}^{-1}x) = \cos\theta$$

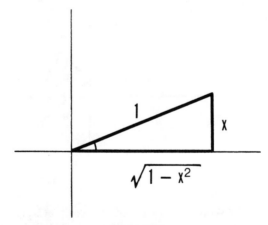

Figure 3-38

and so we simply read $\cos\theta$ from the triangle. Thus

$$\cos(\text{Sin}^{-1}x) = \sqrt{1 - x^2}$$

For $x = 0.38$, we compute $\sqrt{1 - .38^2}$ as

$$1 \boxed{-} .38 \boxed{x^2} \boxed{=} \boxed{\sqrt{x}} \boxed{\text{STO}}$$

storing the result for comparison. Now compute cos(Sin⁻¹ .38) by keying

.38 [INV] [sin] [cos]   and read   [.92498649]

Keying [EXC] will exchange this value for the previous value stored in the memory. The fact that no observable change occurs indicates that the results are the same for all decimal places.

BASIC TRIGONOMETRIC EQUATIONS

48. Find all solutions of $4 \cos x - 3 = 0$ such that $-\pi \leq x \leq \pi$.

The equation can be changed to $\cos x = ¾$ and, since the cosine is positive in the first and fourth quadrants, the solutions x_1 and x_2 are shown graphically in Figure 3-39. For x_1, the principal value, since $¾ = .75$ (either do this mentally or calculate it), we simply key

[DRG] .75 [INV] [cos]   and read x_1 in radians   [.72273425]

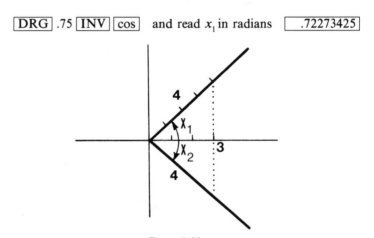

Figure 3-39

Looking at Figure 3-39, we see that x_2 is just the negative of the angle x_1, so the solution set, rounded to four decimal places, is {.7227, −.7227}. Radians were used since the limiting conditions in the problem were given in radians. The solutions could have been found in degrees by doing the same calculation in degree mode.

49. Find the solutions of $5.12 \sin x + 3.4 = 0$, such that $0 \leq x \leq 2\pi$.

The equation becomes $\sin x = -(3.4/5.12)$, and because the sine is negative, the solutions are in the third and fourth quadrants as shown in Figure 3-40(a). Note that the angles are both measured counterclockwise due to the limiting condition given with the equation. To get these values on the calculator, we don't get them directly. First put the calculator in radian mode (press [DRG] once).

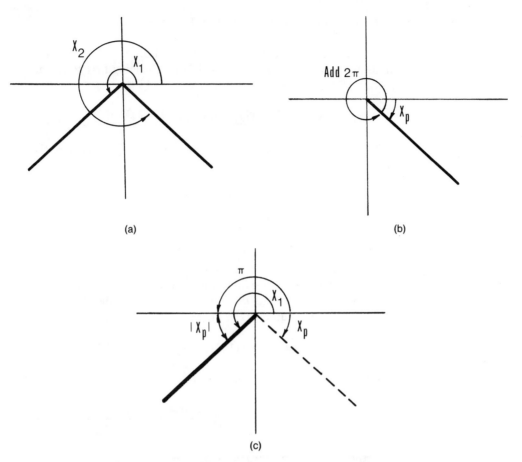

(a)

(b)

(c)

Figure 3-40 (a) Solution Set; (b) Principal Value x_p; (c) Showing that $x_1 = \pi + |x_p|$

Then key

$$3.4 \boxed{\div} 5.12 \boxed{=} \boxed{+/-} \boxed{\text{INV}} \boxed{\text{sin}} \quad \text{and read} \quad \boxed{-.72623924}$$

and store: $\boxed{\text{STO}}$. What this represents is the principal value of $x = x_p$ measured clockwise from the reference axis; hence the negative value. Although this is a solution, it is not between the specified limits, as required, so we use it to get the admissible solutions. By adding 2π we get the solution x_2 [see Figure 3-40(b)]. So key

$$\boxed{+} 2 \boxed{\times} \boxed{\pi} \boxed{=} \quad \text{and read } x_2: \quad \boxed{5.5569461}$$

Now to get x_1 we just add the absolute value of x_p to π. To do this, recall x_p from memory (that is why we stored it) and change sign to make it positive; then add π:

$$\boxed{\text{RCL}} \boxed{+/-} \boxed{+} \boxed{\pi} \boxed{=} \quad \text{and read } x_1: \quad \boxed{3.8678319}$$

Thus $x_1 = 3.8678'$ and $x_2 = 5.5569'$ approximately.

137

50. Solve the equation $4 \tan (2x - 1.5) = 3, 0 \leq x \leq 2\pi$.

We first change the equation to $\tan (2x - 1.5) = \frac{3}{4} = .75$ and compute the principal value of $(2x - 1.5)$ by changing first to radian mode (key $\boxed{\text{DRG}}$ once), and then key

$.75 \boxed{\text{INV}} \boxed{\tan} \boxed{\text{STO}}$ and read $\boxed{.64350111}$

Thus $(2x - 1.5)_p = .64350111$. The solution set $[x_k]$ satisfies the equation

$$(2x_k - 1.5) = (2x - 1.5)_p + k\pi, \quad k \text{ any integer}$$
$$= .64350111 + k\pi, \quad k \text{ any integer.}$$

Thus we add multiples of π to the principal value $(2x - 1.5)_p$ and solve each for $x = x_k$. The principal value has been stored previously in memory to facilitate this. We can solve for x in each equation by adding 1.5 and then dividing by 2. We therefore solve each of the following equations until the solution x exceeds 2π:

$$2x - 1.5 = .64350111: \boxed{\text{RCL}} \boxed{+} 1.5 \boxed{=} \boxed{\div} 2 \boxed{=}$$

Thus the solution $x_0 = 1.0717506$ radians.

$$2x - 1.5 = .64350111 + \pi: \boxed{\text{RCL}} \boxed{+} \boxed{\pi} \boxed{=} \boxed{\text{STO}} \boxed{+} 1.5 \boxed{=}$$
$$\boxed{\div} 2 \boxed{=}$$

and the solution $x_1 = 2.6425469$ radians.

Now we add another π to the *new* value stored in memory to solve

$$2x - 1.5 = .64350111 + 2\pi: \boxed{\text{RCL}} \boxed{+} \boxed{\pi} \boxed{=} \boxed{\text{STO}} \boxed{+}$$
$$1.5 \boxed{=} \boxed{\div} 2 \boxed{=}$$

and the solution $x_2 = 4.2133432$ radians.

Adding yet another π to the again new value stored in memory, we solve

$$2x - 1.5 = .64350111 + 3\pi: \boxed{\text{RCL}} \boxed{+} \boxed{\pi} \boxed{=} \boxed{\text{STO}} \boxed{+}$$
$$1.5 \boxed{=} \boxed{\div} 2 \boxed{=}$$

and the solution $x_3 = 5.7841395$ radians.

If we add any more multiples of π, the resulting values of x exceed $2\pi \doteq 6.28$ approximately. If we try to subtract multiples of π, the resulting solution is negative, again violating the restriction on the solution set. Thus, only the solutions x_0, x_1, x_2, x_3 satisfy $0 \leq x \leq 2\pi$.

51. Solve for all solutions of $\sin x = -.42$ to the nearest hundredth of a degree (see Figure 3-41).

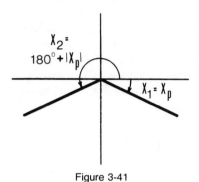

Figure 3-41

First we find the principal value of $x = x_p$ (in degree mode):

$.42 \boxed{+/-} \boxed{\text{INV}} \boxed{\sin}$ and read x_p: $\boxed{-24.834588}$

and then we find the third quadrant value by adding 180° to the absolute value of x_p:

$\boxed{+/-} \boxed{+} 180 \boxed{=}$ and read the value of x_2: $\boxed{204.83459}$

Thus the solution set consists of all numbers of the form

$$-24.83° + k \cdot 360° \quad \text{or} \quad 204.83° + k \cdot 360°$$

52. Solve the equation $4 \cos^2 x - 2 \cos x - 1 = 0$, $0 x \leqq 360°$.

This equation is quadratic in $\cos x$. To help clarify the solution by quadratic formula, let $u = \cos x$ so that the equation becomes

$$4u^2 - 2u - 1 = 0$$

and the solution for $u = \cos x$ is

$$u = \frac{-(-2) \pm \sqrt{(-2)^2 - 4(4)(-1)}}{2(4)} = \frac{2 \pm \sqrt{20}}{8}$$

$$= \frac{2 \pm 2\sqrt{5}}{8} = \frac{1 \pm \sqrt{5}}{4}$$

Thus either $u = (1 - \sqrt{5})/4$ or $u = (1 + \sqrt{5})/4$. Since $u = \cos x$, if we evaluate each of the right-hand sides on a calculator (included in the following calculations), we get

$$\cos x = -.30901699 \quad \text{or} \quad \cos x = .80901699$$

Solving the first of these (in degree mode), we key

$$1 \boxed{-} 5 \boxed{\sqrt{x}} \boxed{=} \boxed{\div} 4 \boxed{=} \boxed{\text{INV}} \boxed{\cos}$$

and read the principal value of x corresponding to the first value of u: $\boxed{ 108}$. Since this value of $u = \cos x$ is negative and the cosine is negative in both the second and third quadrants, we can obtain a second value for x by subtracting the first value from 360° in this case [see Figure 3-42(a)]. Thus key $360 \boxed{-} 180 \boxed{=}$ and the second value of x = $x_2 = 252°$.

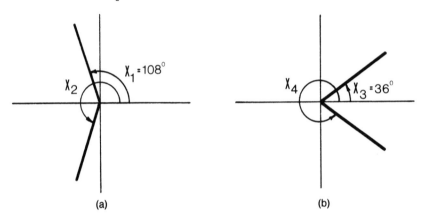

(a)   (b)

Figure 3-42 (a) Roots x Corresponding to $u = (1 - \sqrt{5})/4$; (b) Roots x Corresponding to $u = (1 + \sqrt{5})/4$

For the second root u of the quadratic equation, we also compute a principal value for x:

$$1 \boxed{+} 5 \boxed{\sqrt{x}} \boxed{=} \boxed{\div} 4 \boxed{=} \boxed{\text{INV}} \boxed{\cos} \quad \text{and read} \quad \boxed{ 36}$$

Thus $x_3 = 36°$, and since the cosine is positive and also in the fourth quadrant, and we want $0 \leq x < 360°$, subtract x_3 from 360° to get the root $x_4 = 324°$ [see Figure 3-42(b)]. Thus there are four roots: $x_1 = 108°$, $x_2 = 252°$, $x_3 = 36°$, and $x_4 = 324°$. If we try to check these results by substituting into the original equation, we get either 9.2×10^{-9} or 4×10^{-9} due to roundoff error. Recognize that these are close to zero and so the solutions essentially check up to the precision of the calculations.

53. Solve the equation $5 \sin x - 12 \cos x = 4$ in both radians and degrees.

One method for solving an equation containing both a sine and cosine is to introduce an artificial angle A by using the coefficients as follows. Divide both sides of the equation by $\sqrt{5^2 + (-12)^2} = 13$:

$$\frac{5}{13} \sin x - \frac{12}{13} \cos x = \frac{4}{13}$$

Notice from Figure 3-43(a) that $\cos A = {}^5\!/{}_{13}$ and $\sin A = -12/13$, so if we substitute in the preceding equation, it becomes

$$\cos A \sin x + \sin A \cos x = \frac{4}{13}$$

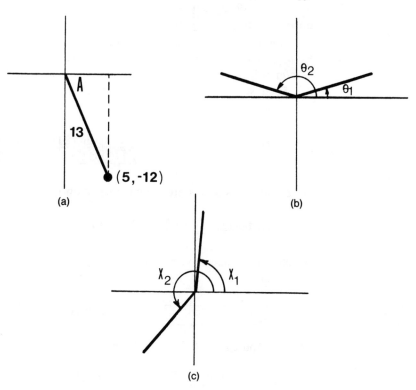

(a)

(b)

(c)

Figure 3-43 (a) Artificial Angle $A = \text{Sin}^{-1}(-12/13)$; (b) Values of $\theta = x + A$; (c) Solutions for $0 \le x \le 2\pi$

The left-hand side is just the sine of a sum (expanded); hence it can be written as

$$\sin (x + A) = \frac{4}{13}$$

If we denote $x + A$ by the symbol θ, the equation becomes

$$\sin \theta = \frac{4}{13}$$

which we shall solve for two values of θ, $\theta_1 = \text{Sin}^{-1} 4/13$, the principal value, and $\theta_2 = \pi - \theta_1$ [see Figure 3-43(b)]. This is done because the sine can be positive in both the first and second quadrants. Start in radian mode (press $\boxed{\text{DRG}}$ once), and then to compute θ_1 key

$$4 \boxed{\div} 13 \boxed{=} \boxed{\text{INV}} \boxed{\text{sin}} \quad \text{and read} \quad \boxed{.31276672}$$

Write this value down. Then, with this value still displayed, compute $\theta_2 = \pi - \theta_1$ by keying $\boxed{+/-} \boxed{+} \boxed{\pi} \boxed{=}$ and read and write down the result $\boxed{2.8288259}$.

We now proceed to obtain the corresponding values of $x = \theta - A$ by first computing $A = \text{Sin}^{-1}(-12/13)$. [Do *not* use $\text{Cos}^{-1}(5/13)$ or you will be in the wrong quadrant for angle A as we formulated it.] Then subtract this value of A from each of the values of θ obtained previously. With the calculator still in radian mode, key

$$12 \boxed{\div} 13 \boxed{+/-} \boxed{=} \boxed{\text{INV}} \boxed{\text{sin}} \boxed{\text{STO}} \quad \text{reading } A:$$
$$\boxed{-1.1760052}$$

Note that A has been stored in memory. Now compute $x_1 = \theta_1 - A$:

$$.31276672 \boxed{-} \boxed{\text{RCL}} \boxed{=} \quad \text{and read } x_1: \quad \boxed{1.4887719}$$

which is in radians. With this value displayed, also get it in degrees by keying

$$\boxed{\times} 180 \boxed{\div} \boxed{\pi} \boxed{=} \text{ and read } x_1 \text{ in degrees: } \boxed{85.300348}$$

Now compute $x_2 = \theta_2 - A$ by keying

$$2.8288259 \boxed{-} \boxed{\text{RCL}} \boxed{=} \quad \text{and read } x_2 \text{ in radians} \quad \boxed{4.0048311}$$

Then get x_2 in degrees:

$$\boxed{\times} 180 \boxed{\div} \boxed{\pi} \boxed{=} \quad \text{reading} \quad \boxed{229.45992}$$

Thus, in radians, the solution set is

$$\{x \mid x = x_1^r + 2k\pi \text{ or } x = x_2^r + 2k\pi\} = \{x \mid x = 1.489 + 2k\pi \text{ or } x = 4.005 + 2k\pi\}$$

and in degrees

$$\{x \mid x = x_1^\circ + k \cdot 360^\circ \text{ or } x = x_2^\circ + k \cdot 360^\circ\} = \{x \mid x = 85.3^\circ + 360^\circ \cdot k \text{ or } x = 229.46^\circ + 360^\circ \cdot k\}$$

54. Solve $\sin 3x = (1 + \sqrt{2})/3$, $0 \leq x < 360°$.

First solve for $3x = \sin^{-1}\!\left(\dfrac{1 + \sqrt{2}}{3}\right)$, noticing that there are two primary solutions, first and second quadrants (see Figure 3-44). In degree mode, key

$$1 \boxed{+} 2 \boxed{\sqrt{x}} \boxed{=} \boxed{\div} 3 \boxed{=} \boxed{\text{INV}} \boxed{\text{sin}} \boxed{\text{STO}} \quad \text{reading } 3x_1:$$
$$\boxed{53.584946}$$

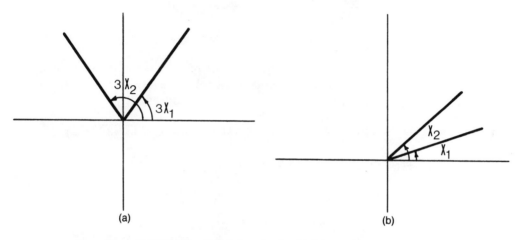

Figure 3-44 (a) Primary Solutions for $3x$; (b) Primary Solutions for x

This value is stored for later calculation. To find $3x_2$, subtract $3x_1$ from $180°$ (i.e., $3x_2 = 180° - 3x_1$). Thus, with $3x_1$ still displayed, key

$$\boxed{+/-} \boxed{+} 180 \boxed{=} \quad \text{and read} \quad \boxed{126.41505}$$

Thus $3x_2 = 126.42°$ approximately. Write down *all* the digits of $3x_2$ and save it for later. (If you have more than one memory, just store it in a second memory. $3x_1$ is already stored.)

Now the solutions corresponding to $3x_1$ are given by

$$[3x \mid 3x = 3x_1 + k \cdot 360°]$$

and to find the solutions for x that correspond, divide everything by 3:

$$[x \mid x = x_1 + k \cdot 120°]$$

To generate these solutions, recall $3x_1$, divide by 3 to get x_1, and store it:

$$\boxed{\text{RCL}} \boxed{\div} 3 \boxed{=} \boxed{\text{STO}} \quad \text{and read} \quad \boxed{17.861649}$$

which we denote by the symbol x_{11}. Now we generate the other solutions in the given range, setting up 120° as a constant addend and then adding it until we exceed the limit of 360°: 120 $\boxed{+}$ $\boxed{\text{K}}$. Then key

$\boxed{\text{RCL}}$ $\boxed{=}$ and read x_{12}: $\boxed{137.86165}$

$\boxed{=}$ and read x_{13}: $\boxed{257.86165}$

$\boxed{=}$ read the too large value $\boxed{377.86165}$ and ignore it

Now we get all the admissible values of x_2 by doing the same thing. Key in $3x_2$, which you wrote down before, divide by 3, store the result, and again set up 120° as a constant addend.

126.41505 $\boxed{\div}$ 3 $\boxed{=}$ $\boxed{\text{STO}}$ reading x_{21}: $\boxed{42.13835}$

Set up the constant addend: 120 $\boxed{+}$ $\boxed{\text{K}}$. Then key

$\boxed{\text{RCL}}$ $\boxed{=}$ and read x_{22}: $\boxed{162.13835}$

$\boxed{=}$ and read x_{23}: $\boxed{282.13835}$

$\boxed{=}$ read the too large value $\boxed{402.13835}$ and ignore it

Thus we have a total of six values of x in the desired range. To two decimal places, these are 17.86°, 137.86°, 257.86°, 42.14°, 162.14°, and 228.14°

POLAR COORDINATES

55. Express the point (7, 40°) in rectangular coordinates (see Figure 3-45).

Use the relations $x = r \cos \theta$ and $y = r \sin \theta$ by first setting up $r = 7$ as a multiplicative constant: 7 $\boxed{\text{x}}$ $\boxed{\text{K}}$. Then compute x:

40 $\boxed{\cos}$ $\boxed{=}$ and read x: $\boxed{5.3623111}$

and compute y:

40 $\boxed{\sin}$ $\boxed{=}$ and read y: $\boxed{4.4995133}$

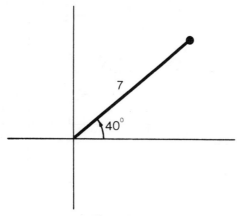

Figure 3-45

The $\boxed{=}$ completes the multiplication by 7. (These multiplications could have been done separately, but if r had many digits, the technique shown eliminates the necessity of entering it a second time. Yet another technique is to store r in the memory and then recall it as needed.) Thus, to two decimal places, $(x, y) = (5.36, 4.50)$.

56. Change the point $(-2, 1)$ to polar coordinates with $r > 0$, $0 \leq \theta \leq 180°$.

Use the formulas $r = \sqrt{x^2 + y^2}$ and $\theta = \tan^{-1}(y/x)$. To

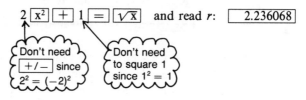

To compute θ, key

$1 \boxed{\div} 2 \boxed{+/-} \boxed{=} \boxed{INV} \boxed{\tan}$ and read $\boxed{-26.565051}$

which is in the wrong quadrant. Hence, add 180°:

$\boxed{+} 180 \boxed{=}$ and read θ: $\boxed{153.43495}$

(A quick glance at Figure 3-46 indicated that the first value obtained from the inverse tangent was in the wrong quadrant.) Thus, to two decimal places, $(r, \theta) = (2.24, 153.43°)$.

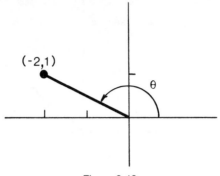

Figure 3-46

57. Express the point $(-3, 32°16')$ in rectangular coordinates.

First we change θ to decimal degrees and store the result for further use:

32 $\boxed{+}$ 16 $\boxed{\div}$ 60 $\boxed{=}$ $\boxed{\text{STO}}$ reading $\boxed{\quad 32.266667 \quad}$

Now since $x = r\cos\theta$, $y = r\sin\theta$, and $r = -3$, set up -3 as a multiplicative constant:

3 $\boxed{+/-}$ $\boxed{\times}$ $\boxed{\text{K}}$

Then key

$\boxed{\text{RCL}}$ $\boxed{\cos}$ $\boxed{=}$ and read x: $\boxed{\quad -2.5367177 \quad}$

$\boxed{\text{RCL}}$ $\boxed{\sin}$ $\boxed{=}$ and read y: $\boxed{\quad -1.6015815 \quad}$

Thus $(x, y) = (-2.54, -1.60)$ to two decimal places.

Note: If your calculator does polar into rectangular automatically, it probably does not accept a negative r. Enter it as $+3$ instead; then change both signs of the results.

4

Statistics

Preliminaries

This chapter covers classical statistical calculations. If you wish to do more than the most elementary of computations, you must have a calculator that can automatically compute means and standard deviations. There are various key configurations, so you may have to consult your owner's manual if your calculator is not exactly like the configurations discussed in this chapter. Basically, they are all very similar, consisting of a data entry key, $\boxed{\Sigma +}$ (or the key may just be labeled DATA), a key to compute the mean, $\boxed{\overline{x}}$ (or possibly $\boxed{\text{mean}}$), and a key to compute the standard deviation, of which there are two slightly different, but related, quantities. Such a key may be labeled $\boxed{\sigma}$ or possibly $\boxed{\sigma_n}$, $\boxed{\sigma_{n-1}}$, or $\boxed{\text{SD}}$ (in which case there is probably an associated key labeled $\boxed{\text{VAR}}$). These will all be discussed briefly, but only one of the configurations will be carried through all examples.

If you are studying statistics and will need least-squares regression and correlation, it would make things much easier if you had a calculator that had these automatically available.

Averages and Variability

If we have a set of data $x_1, x_2, \ldots, x_n$, a single number can be computed to represent an *average* or *central tendency* of the data. This number is somewhere between the smallest and largest values of the x_i, and its value depends on which of many possible averages is computed.

Several common averages are used in statistics (as well as some uncommon ones that we shall not consider here). We shall examine the following:

1. Arithmetic mean, $\bar{x}$ (weighted or unweighted)
2. Geometric mean (GM)
3. Harmonic mean (HM)
4. Midrange
5. Median $\widetilde{x}$
6. Mode

Each of these has specific applications. The two that are overwhelmingly encountered are the arithmetic mean and the median. The arithmetic mean is given by the formula

$$\bar{x} = \frac{1}{n} \sum_{1}^{n} x_i = \frac{\Sigma x}{n} = \frac{x_1 + x_2 + \cdots + x_n}{n}$$

where the symbol Σ means "take the sum."

Example   To compute the arithmetic mean of 2, 3, 8, 9, and 11, evaluate $(2 + 3 + 8 + 9 + 11)/5$, since there are $n = 5$ data values. Simply key

2 $\boxed{+}$ 3 $\boxed{+}$ 9 $\boxed{+}$ 11 $\boxed{=}$ $\boxed{\div}$ 5 $\boxed{=}$ and read $\bar{x} = 6.6$ on the display.

If you have statistics functions on your calculator, you might key

2 $\boxed{\Sigma +}$ 3 $\boxed{\Sigma +}$ 8 $\boxed{\Sigma +}$ 9 $\boxed{\Sigma +}$ 11 $\boxed{\Sigma +}$ $\boxed{\text{2nd}}$ $\boxed{\bar{x}}$

Notice that each time you key $\boxed{\Sigma +}$, the current value of n is displayed. You know that all the data are entered for this example when $n = 5$ is displayed.

Caution   On some calculators, when $\boxed{\Sigma +}$ is pressed, the arithmetic keys become locked; they don't do anything when pressed. (Not all calculators do this.) To unlock them, key $\boxed{\text{2nd}}$ $\boxed{\text{CSR}}$, which clears the data registers as well, or just turn the calculator off if you are finished with the calculation.

If you wish to include any additional data points, even after computing $\bar{x}$, as long as you have not yet cleared the registers, you can just continue with data entry using the $\boxed{\Sigma +}$ key.

Example Suppose that you have just computed $\bar{x} = 6.6$ using the data of the previous example and you discover that you forgot to enter a sixth data point $x_6 = 18$. Just key 8 $\boxed{\Sigma+}$ $\boxed{2nd}$ $\boxed{\bar{x}}$ and read the new value $\bar{x} = 8.5$.

On the other hand, if you computed the old value using the arithmetic functions (or if you didn't have statistical keys), get back the sum Σx by multiplying the old value of $\bar{x}$ by n; that is $\Sigma x = n\bar{x}$. Then add the additional value of x and divide by $n + 1$. If you are adding several, say k, additional values, do the same thing but divide by $n + k$. For this example, with $\bar{x} = 6.6$ still displayed, since it was computed from $n = 5$ values of x, key

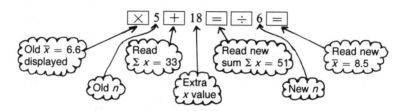

Symbolically, the formula for adding a single new x value x_{n+1} to an already computed value of $\bar{x}$ is

$$\bar{x}_{new} = \frac{n\bar{x}_{old} + x_{n+1}}{n + 1}$$

or, for adding k additional values $x_{n+1}, x_{n+2}, \ldots, x_{n+k}$,

$$\bar{x}_{new} = \frac{n\bar{x}_{old} + x_{n+1} + x_{n+2} + \cdots + x_{n+k}}{n + k}$$

Example Suppose $\bar{x} = 36.2$ has been computed for $n = 50$ values of x and two additional observations have just been recorded. To update to a new value of $\bar{x}$, if $x_{51} = 38.5$ and $x_{52} = 40.3$, compute

$$\bar{x}_{new} = \frac{n\bar{x}_{old} + x_{51} + x_{52}}{52} = \frac{50(36.2) + 38.5 + 40.3}{52}$$

by keying

50 $\boxed{\times}$ 36.2 $\boxed{+}$ 38.5 $\boxed{+}$ 40.3 $\boxed{=}$ $\boxed{\div}$ 52 $\boxed{=}$ and read $\bar{x}_{new}$:

$$\boxed{36.323077}$$

The *geometric mean* $\bar{x}_G$ (or GM) is the nth root of the product of all of the x values. That is,

$$\bar{x}_G = \sqrt[n]{x_1 \cdot x_2 \cdot \cdots \cdot x_n} = \left(\prod_{i=1}^{n} x_i\right)^{1/n}$$

where the symbol Π denotes "take the product." Another formulation for $\bar{x}_G$ is in terms of logarithms. Notice that

$$\log \bar{x}_G = \frac{\log x_1 + \log x_2 + \cdots + \log x_n}{n}$$

Thus the logarithm of the geometric mean is just the arithmetic mean of the logarithms of the individual values. Hence we have two ways to compute the geometric mean:

1. Directly, by multiplying the x's and then taking the nth root.
2. Add the logs of the x's, divide by n, and then take the antilog (inverse log) of the result. The statistical key $\boxed{\Sigma+}$ can simplify this procedure. This method is especially useful if the product is very large.

Example To compute the geometric mean of 2, 2.3, and 2.645 directly, key

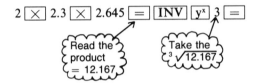

and $\bar{x}_G = 2.3$ exactly.

To do the same calculation using logarithms (you can use $\boxed{\log}$ in place of $\boxed{\ln x}$), key

$$2 \boxed{\ln x} \boxed{+} 2.3 \boxed{\ln x} \boxed{+} 2.645 \boxed{\ln x} \boxed{=} \boxed{\div} 3 \boxed{=} \boxed{\text{INV}} \boxed{\ln x}$$

An alternative method is to take the mean of the logs using the $\boxed{\Sigma+}$ key:

$$2 \boxed{\ln x} \boxed{\Sigma+} 2.3 \boxed{\ln x} \boxed{\Sigma+} 2.645 \boxed{\ln x} \boxed{\Sigma+} \boxed{\text{2nd}} \boxed{\bar{x}} \boxed{\text{INV}} \boxed{\ln x}$$

Here $\bar{x}$ is the arithmetic mean of the logarithms. Also, the key sequence $\boxed{\text{INV}} \boxed{\ln x}$ may appear as $\boxed{e^x}$ or possibly $\boxed{\text{2nd}} \boxed{e^x}$.

The *harmonic mean* $\bar{x}_H$ or *HM* is even less frequently encountered, but it does have its uses. It is simply defined to be the reciprocal of the arithmetic mean of the reciprocals of the x values. That is,

$$\bar{x}_H = \frac{1}{(\Sigma\, 1/x)/n} = \frac{n}{\Sigma\, 1/x} = \frac{n}{(1/x_1) + (1/x_2) + \cdots + (1/x_n)}$$

This can be computed directly or by using $\boxed{\Sigma+}$ on the reciprocals of the x values and then taking the reciprocal of the resulting $\bar{x}$.

Example   The harmonic mean of 2 and 8 is computed as

$$\bar{x}_H = \frac{1}{(1/2 + 1/8)/2}$$

by keying

$2\boxed{1/x}\boxed{+}8\boxed{1/x}\boxed{=}\boxed{\div}2\boxed{=}\boxed{1/x}$ and read $\bar{x}_H = 3.2$

The *midrange* of a set of data is the arithmetic mean of the smallest and largest values of the set. There is no common notation for the midrange so we use

$$\bar{x}_{\text{midrange}} = \frac{x_{\text{min}} + x_{\text{max}}}{2}$$

Example   For the data 2, 3, 8, 9, and 11, $x_{\text{min}} = 2$ and $x_{\text{max}} = 11$; thus

$$\bar{x}_{\text{midrange}} = \frac{2 + 11}{2} = \frac{13}{2} = 6.5$$

The *median* is just the middle number when the data are ordered. More precisely, the median is the fiftieth percentile, that number below which half of the population values are found. From the data we estimate the population median by choosing the middle number. There are special problems when the data are grouped. Since grouped data are used mostly for graphical display purposes currently (the ready availability of computers renders the method less necessary), we shall not take the space for a detailed discussion. The use of the calculator is minimal.

The *mode*, the most frequent value, may or may not be an indicator of the "center" of the data. If we have unimodal (one mode), fairly symmetric data, the mode is often a reasonable answer. No calculation is needed for the mode, only counting.

The *variability* or *dispersion* of the data is also important since vastly different distributions can have the same "center." Some common measures of dispersion or variability are the following:

1. *Range*
2. *Variance* and *standard deviation*
3. *Coefficient of variation*
4. *Mean absolute deviation* (about the median)

The *range* is given by the formula $R = x_{\text{max}} - x_{\text{min}}$ and is computed by a simple subtraction. It represents the total span of the data set. The *standard deviation* σ measures the dispersion of the data about the arith-

151

metic mean $\bar{x}$, and the *variance* is the square of the standard deviation. There are two standard deviation formulas, which are not equivalent for they describe two slightly different concepts.

If we know all of the x values in some population, the standard deviation is

$$\sigma_x = \sigma = \sqrt{\frac{\Sigma (x - \bar{x})^2}{N}} = \sqrt{\frac{(x_1 - \bar{x})^2 + \cdots + (x_N - \bar{x})^2}{N}}$$

where N is the number of objects in the population.

On the other hand, if we take a random sample of n objects from the population, we use the estimate of σ denoted by s or s_x and given by

$$s_x = s = \sqrt{\frac{\Sigma (x - \bar{x})^2}{n - 1}} = \sqrt{\frac{(x_1 - \bar{x})^2 + \cdots + (x_n - \bar{x})^2}{n - 1}}$$

where n is the number of objects in the sample.

The *variance* $\text{Var}(X) = \sigma_x^2 = \sigma^2$. Both of the preceding forms of the standard deviation can be computed directly using modified computational forms of the formulas. Some calculators can do them automatically. The key configurations differ slightly however. We shall describe some of the more common ones.

$\boxed{\sigma_n}$ or $\boxed{\sigma}$ computes $\sigma = \sigma_x$ (N divisor)

$\boxed{\sigma_{n-1}}$ or $\boxed{s}$ computes $s = s_x$ ($n - 1$ divisor)

On some calculators $\boxed{\text{VAR}}$ computes $\text{Var}(X) = \sigma_x^2$, and so to compute the standard deviation σ_x requires keying $\boxed{\text{VAR}}$ $\boxed{\sqrt{x}}$. Each of these keys is usually a second function and must be preceded by $\boxed{\text{2nd}}$. This is not uniformly true, so we shall omit the $\boxed{\text{2nd}}$ in key sequences with these functions. Also the key sequences will be clearer without it. A summary of the most common key configurations is given in Table 4-1.

TABLE 4-1.

STATISTIC	KEY CONFIGURATION	ALTERNATE CONFIGURATION
$\sigma = \sigma_x$	$\boxed{\sigma}$ or $\boxed{\sigma_n}$	$\boxed{\text{VAR}}$ $\boxed{\sqrt{x}}$
$s = s_x$	$\boxed{s}$ or $\boxed{\sigma_{n-1}}$	$\boxed{\text{SD}}$
$\sigma_x^2 = \text{Var}(X)$	$\boxed{\sigma}\boxed{x^2}$ or $\boxed{\sigma_n}\boxed{x^2}$	$\boxed{\text{VAR}}$
$s^2 = s_x^2$	$\boxed{s}\boxed{x^2}$ or $\boxed{\sigma_{n-1}}\boxed{x^2}$	$\boxed{\text{SD}}\boxed{x^2}$

These key sequences are effective only after the x data have been entered using $\boxed{\Sigma+}$ or $\boxed{\text{DATA}}$. The data entry sequence would typically look like this:

$$x_1 \boxed{\Sigma+} x_2 \boxed{\Sigma+} \ldots x_n \boxed{\Sigma+}$$

For some of the tables we shall write this more compactly, using sequence notation, as $[x_i \boxed{\Sigma+}]_{i=1}^{i=n}$ or simply $[x_i \boxed{\Sigma+}]$.

Example To compute the variance and standard deviation for the data 1, 2, 5, 7, and 8 using the statistical functions, first key

$$1 \boxed{\Sigma+} \; 2 \boxed{\Sigma+} \; 5 \boxed{\Sigma+} \; 7 \boxed{\Sigma+} \; 8 \boxed{\Sigma+}$$

and the display will show the number 5, which is n, the number of data points. To obtain the population standard deviation σ and variance $\sigma^2 = \text{Var}(X)$, key

$$\boxed{\sigma_n} \quad \text{and read} \quad \sigma = \sigma_x = 2.7276363$$

Then key $\boxed{x^2}$ and read $\text{Var}(X) = \sigma_x^2 = 7.44$. To compute these quantities, viewing the data as a sample (rather than the population), requires the $n - 1$ divisor, so instead we key

$$\boxed{\sigma_{n-1}} \quad \text{and read} \quad s = s_x = 3.0495901$$

Then key

$$\boxed{x^2} \quad \text{and read} \quad s^2 = s_x^2 = 9.3$$

Some statistics related to those just discussed that are often needed are $\Sigma\, x$, $\Sigma\, x^2$, and $\Sigma\, (x - \bar{x})^2$. In terms of the statistics $\bar{x}$ and σ^2 that we can compute automatically, it is easily shown that

$$\Sigma x = n\bar{x}, \qquad \Sigma\, x^2 = n(\bar{x}^2 + \sigma^2), \qquad \Sigma\, (x - \bar{x})^2 = n\sigma^2$$

The calculations of all the quantities just discussed are summarized in Table 4-2, which shows the calculations assuming that the functions $\boxed{\bar{x}}$ and $\boxed{\sigma_n}$ are available. The method that is used when these functions are not available is shown in the following table (see page 154).

Remark On the calculations in Table 4-2 where it is necessary to clear statistics registers by keying $\boxed{\text{2nd}}\ \boxed{\text{CSR}}$, you will lose the data that have been entered. Therefore, first compute the other statistics and record them before proceeding with those other sequences. Once you have done one of them, you cannot do the others since the data have been cleared. Modifications to avoid this somewhat are given in the solved problems. You could also just enter the previously recorded statistic required for the calculation.

If you don't have statistics functions built into your calculator, you are limited in what you can do conveniently. It is possible, however, to efficiently compute the same basic statistics by using certain modified formulas. A memory that can accumulate and a squaring function are required to enter the data.

TABLE 4-2. Calculation of Basic Statistics
on a Calculator with Special Statistics Functions

Enter data: x_1 $\boxed{\Sigma+}$ x_2 $\boxed{\Sigma+}$ x_3 $\boxed{\Sigma+}$ ... x_n $\boxed{\Sigma+}$ and read n	
STATISTIC	KEY SEQUENCE AFTER DATA ENTRY
Mean $= \bar{x} = \Sigma\, x/n$	$\boxed{\bar{x}}$
Standard deviation s_x $= \sqrt{\dfrac{\Sigma\,(x-\bar{x})^2}{n-1}}$; s_x^2 = variance	$\boxed{\sigma_{n-1}}$ (read s_x) $\boxed{x^2}$ (read s_x^2)
Population standard deviation; variance $\sigma = \sqrt{\dfrac{\Sigma\,(x-\bar{x})^2}{n}}$; σ^2	$\boxed{\sigma_n}$ (read σ) $\boxed{x^2}$ (read variance σ^2)
Sum of squared deviations $= \Sigma\,(x-\bar{x})^2$ $= \Sigma\,x^2 - n\bar{x}^2 = n\sigma^2$	$\boxed{\sigma_n}$ $\boxed{x^2}$ * $\boxed{\times}$ n $\boxed{=}$
Sum of data $= \Sigma\,x = n\bar{x}$	$\boxed{\bar{x}}$ † $\boxed{\times}$ n $\boxed{=}$
Sum of squares of data $=$ $\Sigma\,x^2 = n(\bar{x}^2 + \sigma^2)$	$\boxed{\bar{x}}$ $\boxed{x^2}$ $\boxed{STO}$ $\boxed{\sigma_n}$ $\boxed{x^2}$ $\boxed{SUM}$ $\boxed{RCL}$ ‡ $\boxed{\times}$ n $\boxed{=}$

* Some calculators are locked in statistical mode. If so, key $\boxed{2nd}$ $\boxed{CSR}$ in order to perform the multiplication.
† You may have to key $\boxed{2nd}$ $\boxed{CSR}$ to proceed with multiplication. Data are lost, however, if this is pressed.
‡ Key $\boxed{2nd}$ $\boxed{CSR}$ if necessary.

Calculation of s^2 and σ^2 rely on the algebraic identity

$$\Sigma\,(x - \bar{x})^2 = \Sigma\,x^2 - \frac{(\Sigma\,x)^2}{n} = \Sigma\,x^2 - n\bar{x}^2$$

which is derived in virtually every statistics book using simple algebraic substitutions and simplifications. The calculation is usually set up in a tabular format, which is useful to keep in mind when using a calculator to help keep track of what one is doing.

X	X^2
x_1	x_1^2
x_2	x_2^2
.	.
.	.
.	.
x_n	x_n^2
Totals $\Sigma\,x$	$\Sigma\,x^2$

$$\bar{x} = \frac{\Sigma\,x}{n}$$

$$\sigma^2 = \Sigma\,x^2 - \frac{(\Sigma\,x)^2}{n} = \Sigma\,x^2 - n\bar{x}^2$$

Thus, calculating the basic quantities depends on accumulating the x values and their squares. A convenient way is to sum the x's in the memory and the squares using the $\boxed{+}$ key. This is done as follows:

$$x_1 \boxed{\text{STO}} \boxed{x^2} \boxed{+} x_2 \boxed{\text{SUM}} \boxed{x^2} \boxed{+} x_3 \boxed{\text{SUM}} \boxed{x^2} \boxed{+} \ldots$$
$$x_n \boxed{\text{SUM}} \boxed{x^2} \boxed{=}$$

At this point any of the basic statistics can now be computed using the formulas. The basic method is summarized in Table 4-3.

TABLE 4-3. Calculation of Basic Statistics without Statistical Functions

Enter data to accumulate Σx and Σx^2 simultaneously:

$$x_1 \boxed{\text{STO}} [\boxed{x^2} \boxed{+} x_i \boxed{\text{SUM}}] \, {}_{i=2}^{i=n} \boxed{x^2} \boxed{=} \text{ (sequence notation)}$$

STATISTIC	COMPUTATION PROCEDURE
Σx Σx^2	Read Σx^2 now displayed. Write it down. Key $\boxed{\text{EXC}}$ and read Σx. (Σx^2 now in memory.) Write down the value of Σx and leave it displayed.
Mean $= \bar{x}$ $= \Sigma x / n$	Compute $\bar{x}$ by keying $\boxed{\div} n \boxed{=}$. Read $\bar{x}$ and write it down and leave it displayed.
Sum of squares $= \Sigma (x - \bar{x})^2$	To compute $\Sigma (x - \bar{x})^2 = \Sigma x^2 - n\bar{x}^2$ at this point key $\boxed{\text{EXC}} \boxed{-} n \boxed{\times} \boxed{\text{RCL}} \boxed{x^2} \boxed{=}$. Record if desired. Leave it displayed. (*Note:* This is for AOS systems. For sequential entry a $\boxed{(}$ in front of n is needed.)
Variance $= \sigma^2$ or s^2	Compute either the population variance σ^2 or the sample variance s^2 by dividing by either n or $n - 1$, respectively: $\boxed{\div} n \boxed{=}$ (read σ^2) or $\boxed{\div} (n - 1) \boxed{=}$ (read s^2) Leave number displayed and write it down.
Standard deviation $= \sigma$ or s	Compute the standard deviation by taking the square root of whichever variance you desired by keying $\boxed{\sqrt{x}}$ and read the corresponding standard deviation σ or s, respectively, depending on whether you divided by n or $n - 1$ previously.

Example   To compute the mean, variance, and standard deviation of the data 1, 2, 5, 7, and 8 without using built-in statistics, first enter the data by keying

$$1 \boxed{\text{STO}} \boxed{x^2} \boxed{+} 2 \boxed{\text{SUM}} \boxed{x^2} \boxed{+} 5 \boxed{\text{SUM}} \boxed{x^2} \boxed{+} 7 \boxed{\text{SUM}} \boxed{x^2} \boxed{+}$$
$$8 \boxed{\text{SUM}} \boxed{x^2} \boxed{=}$$

Read $\Sigma\ x^2 = 143$ on the display. $\Sigma\ x = 23$ is stored in memory. Press $\boxed{\text{EXC}}$ to display $\Sigma\ x = 23$ and at the same time put $\Sigma\ x^2 = 143$ in the memory. To compute $\bar{x}$ at this point, key $\boxed{\div}\ 5\ \boxed{=}$ since $n = 5$, and read $\bar{x} = 4.6$. With $\bar{x} = 4.6$ on the display and $\Sigma\ x^2 = 143$ in memory, to compute the sum of squared deviations using the formula $\Sigma\ x^2 - n\bar{x}^2$, key

$$\boxed{\text{EXC}}\ \boxed{-}\ 5\ \boxed{\times}\ \boxed{\text{RCL}}\ \boxed{x^2}\ \boxed{=}\ \boxed{\text{STO}}$$

The result has been stored in memory so that both variances and standard deviation can be computed. To compute σ^2 and σ just divide by 5, read the variance, and then take the square root. To get the sample statistics, divide by $n - 1 = 5 - 1 = 4$ by first recalling the sum of squares from memory. Again, taking the square root will give the standard deviation. The results are identical to the last example done with statistical functions since the same data were used.

The *coefficient of variation* is a relative measure of dispersion that is used to compare the variation of quantities that may be measured on entirely different scales. For example, one may want to ask whether blood glucose levels are more or less variable than free fatty acids. The quantity $CV = s/\bar{x}$ provides such a measure since it compares the standard deviation to the mean and dimensional units will cancel, which gives a pure number. To compute the coefficient of variation CV once you have computed $\bar{x}$ and s, get $\bar{x}$ displayed and s stored in memory; then key $\boxed{\div}\ \boxed{\text{RCL}}\ \boxed{=}$ and read CV.

The *mean absolute deviation* (or *average deviation*) about the median is given by the formula

$$\text{MAD} = \frac{\Sigma\ |\ x - \tilde{x}\ |}{n}$$

where $\tilde{x}$ is the median. In words this formula says that the MAD is the arithmetic mean of the absolute difference of each x value from the median $\tilde{x}$. When the median is the appropriate measure of central tendency, the MAD is usually the appropriate measure of dispersion. When the ungrouped estimate of the median is used, the preceding formula can be replaced by one that is easier to use in calculations:

$$\text{MAD} = \frac{\displaystyle\sum_{x_i > \tilde{x}} x_i - \sum_{x_i < \tilde{x}} x_i}{n}$$

This rather formidable looking formula just says to subtract the sum of the x value below the median from the sum of those values above the median and divide by n, the number of observations. If one of the values should happen to equal the median, the difference would be zero in the definition, so we just ignore it in this formula.

Example   For the data 1, 2, 5, 7, and 8, the median is $\tilde{x} = 5$. Thus

$$\text{MAD} = \frac{(7 + 8) - (1 + 2)}{5} = \frac{15 - 3}{5} = \frac{12}{5} = 2.4$$

This can be done on the calculator by first summing the values below the median in memory; then use $\boxed{+}$ to add the values above the median, and subtract the stored value from the sum. Then divide by $n = 5$. The calculation looks like this:

$$1 \boxed{\text{STO}} \ 2 \boxed{\text{SUM}} \ 7 \boxed{+} \ 8 \boxed{=} \ \boxed{-} \boxed{\text{RCL}} \boxed{=} \boxed{\div} \ 5 \boxed{=}$$

Statistics for Sampling

When one takes a simple random sample (SRS) from a population, it is very often for one of two purposes: (1) estimating the population mean μ by either point or interval estimates, or (2) testing some hypothesis about a presumed value of μ, usually denoted by μ_0. A sample size n will yield an arithmetic mean of the sample $\bar{x}_n$, which is called a *point estimate* of μ. However, a different sample will most likely produce a slightly different value of $\bar{x}_n$. The distribution of these possible values of $\bar{x}_n$ is called the *sampling distribution of $\bar{x}$*. If the SRS is from a population with mean μ_x and variance σ_x^2 the sampling distribution of $\bar{x}$ has mean $\mu_{\bar{x}} = \mu_x$ and variance $\sigma_{\bar{x}}^2 = \sigma_x^2/n$ provided that we are sampling from an infinite population or are sampling with replacement. We shall not cover sampling from a finite population without replacement, which forms the basis for survey sampling theory.

From the preceding distribution parameters, it can be shown that (unbiased) estimates of $\mu_{\bar{x}}$ and $\sigma_{\bar{x}}^2$ are $\bar{x}$ and $s_{\bar{x}}^2 = s_x^2/n$, respectively, and consequently $s_{\bar{x}} = s_x/\sqrt{n}$. The quantity $s_{\bar{x}}$ is called the *standard error of the mean $\bar{x}$*, and care should be taken not to confuse it with s_x, the standard error of the observation x, that is, the standard deviation of the sample.

To compute $s_{\bar{x}}$ just compute s_x and divide by $\sqrt{n}$.

Example   A sample of 12 observations has a standard deviation $s_x = 2.6$. The standard error of the mean is $s_{\bar{x}} = s_x/\sqrt{n} = 2.6/\sqrt{12}$, so compute

$$2.6 \boxed{\div} \ 12 \boxed{\sqrt{x}} \boxed{=} \quad \text{and read } s_{\bar{x}}: \quad \boxed{0.7505554}$$

Notice that $s_{\bar{x}} < s_x$, and this is always the case as long as $n > 1$, with equality if $n = 1$.

If Y is a random variable (usually $Y = X$ or $Y = \bar{x}$) and if μ_Y is the mean of the distribution of values of Y, and σ_Y is its standard error, very often a *Z score* is formed by transforming the random variable Y according to the equation $Z = (Y - \mu_Y)/\sigma_Y$. The Z scores represent the number of standard deviations that a value of Y is from its mean μ_Y.

157

Example   Let Y follow a distribution with mean $\mu_Y = 3$ and standard deviation $\sigma_Y = 1.6$. Then for a value $Y = 5$, the corresponding Z score is

$$Z = \frac{Y - \mu_Y}{\sigma_Y} = \frac{5 - 3}{1.6} = 1.25$$

which is computed as

$$5 \boxed{-} 3 \boxed{=} \boxed{\div} 1.6 \boxed{=} \quad \text{and read} \quad Z = 1.25$$

This Z score is interpreted by saying that $Y =$ is 1.25 standard deviations from the mean μ_Y. Alternatively, we may write that $Y = \mu_Y + 1.25\,\sigma_Y$.

If the random variable Y just discussed is chosen to be the sample mean $\bar{x}$, and if the sample size is relatively large, then the corresponding Z score is known to follow approximately a *standard normal (Gaussian) distribution* with mean $\mu_Z = 0$ and variance $\sigma_Z^2 = 1$. The quantity Z is given by the equation

$$Z = \frac{\bar{x} - \mu_{\bar{x}}}{\sigma_{\bar{x}}} = \frac{\bar{x} - \mu_x}{\sigma_x / \sqrt{n}}$$

A short table of the more commonly used *standard normal areas* is given in Figure 4-1.

Z \ Area	CUMULATIVE	CENTRAL	TWO-TAIL	UPPER TAIL
	z	−z z	−z z	z
1.645	0.950	0.900	0.100	0.050
1.960	0.975	0.950	0.050	0.025
2.326	0.990	0.980	0.020	0.010
2.576	0.995	0.990	0.010	0.005

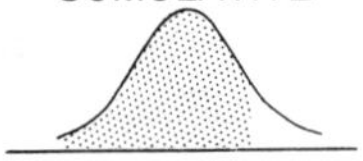

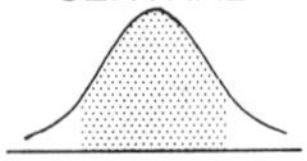

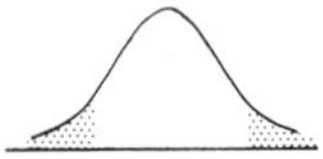

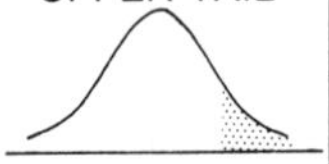

Figure 4-1

The central areas under the bell-shaped curves represent probabilities associated with the question of whether a certain interval contains the parameter in question (usually the mean μ), assuming that the random variable follows a normal distribution. Such an interval is called a *confidence interval*. A confidence interval for the parameter μ_x has the following form:

$$\bar{x} \pm z \frac{\sigma_x}{\sqrt{n}}$$

In interval notation the confidence interval can be represented as

$$[L, U] = [\bar{x} - \frac{z\sigma_x}{\sqrt{n}}, \ \bar{x} + \frac{z\sigma_x}{\sqrt{n}}]$$

where n = sample size, L = lower limit, and U = upper limit.

Example   In a sample of size $n = 20$, it was found that $\bar{x} = 4.6$ and $\sigma_x = 1.5$. A 95% confidence interval for μ_x would use the value $z = 1.96$ (see Figure 5-1, central area = 1.96). Thus a 95% confidence interval is computed as $\bar{x} \pm z\sigma_x/\sqrt{n} = 4.6 \pm (1.96)(1.5)/\sqrt{20}$. First compute the upper limit $U = \bar{x} + z\sigma_x/\sqrt{n}$ and store the quantity $z\sigma_x/\sqrt{n}$ in memory:

1.96 $\boxed{\times}$ 1.5 $\boxed{\div}$ 20 $\boxed{\sqrt{x}}$ $\boxed{+}$ $\boxed{\text{STO}}$ 4.6 $\boxed{=}$ and read U:

$\boxed{5.257404}$

To get the lower limit L, we use the trick of subtracting $z\sigma_x/\sqrt{n}$ *twice* from U, which is still displayed, by keying

$\boxed{-}$ 2 $\boxed{\times}$ $\boxed{\text{RCL}}$ $\boxed{=}$ and read L: $\boxed{3.942596}$

(If you have a sequential entry system and no parentheses, you can still do this by keying $\boxed{\text{EXC}}$ $\boxed{\times}$ 2 $\boxed{+/-}$ $\boxed{+}$ $\boxed{\text{RCL}}$ $\boxed{=}$.) The trick we used here was that, if you want $a \pm b$, compute $a + b$; then subtract $2b$ to get $a - b$. That is, $a + b - 2b = a - b$. This method can save re-entering values. A more straightforward method is to store $z\sigma_x/\sqrt{n}$ in memory, and then key

4.6 $\boxed{+}$ $\boxed{\text{RCL}}$ $\boxed{=}$ and read the upper limit U

4.6 $\boxed{-}$ $\boxed{\text{RCL}}$ $\boxed{=}$ and read the lower limit L

Thus a 95% confidence interval for μ_x is $[L, U] = [3.94, 5.26]$ to three decimal places.

A major problem is that we rarely know the value of σ_x, and we must estimate it from the sample by s_x. Since different samples will give different estimates s_x, we have yet another source of variation. This will make the confidence interval somewhat wider. The estimation is taken into account by using the Student t distribution rather than the normal distribution. The value used for t depends on a quantity known as *degrees of freedom* (*df*). For a simple random sample of size n, $df = n - 1$. Tables of t are readily available (look in the appendix of any statistics book). A portion of such a table is shown for a 95% confidence level.

$df = n - 1$	t
.	.
.	.
.	.
18	2.101
19	2.093
20	2.086
21	2.080
.	.
.	.

Example In a sample of size $n = 20$, suppose that $\bar{x} = 4.6$ and an estimated $s_x = 1.5$ is computed from the sample. Then a 95% confidence interval for μ_x uses $t(20 - 1) = t(19) = 2.093$ (from the table). The $df = 19$ are given in the parentheses. The interval has the form:

$$\frac{\bar{x} \pm t(19)s_x}{\sqrt{n}} = 4.6 \pm \frac{(2.093)(1.5)}{\sqrt{20}}$$

First compute $ts_x/\sqrt{n}$ and store it in memory:

 2.093 $\boxed{\times}$ 1.5 $\boxed{\div}$ 20 $\boxed{\sqrt{x}}$ $\boxed{=}$ $\boxed{\text{STO}}$ reading $\boxed{0.7020135}$

Now compute the lower limit L:

 4.6 $\boxed{-}$ $\boxed{\text{RCL}}$ $\boxed{=}$ reading $\boxed{3.8979865}$

Then compute the upper limit U:

 4.6 $\boxed{+}$ $\boxed{\text{RCL}}$ $\boxed{=}$ reading $\boxed{5.3020135}$

Thus a 95% confidence interval is approximately given by $[L, U] = [3.90, 5.30]$, slightly wider than the previous example because we used t this time instead of z.

 Parameters other than the mean can also be estimated by confidence intervals. The form of the confidence interval depends on the sampling distribution of the point estimate. Some simple examples are given in the solved problems.

Inference (Hypothesis Testing)

 Another purpose of sampling is to test an assumption or proposition. Sometimes we set up the assumption in such a way that, in order to demonstrate the desired result, our hope is that the sample will contradict that form of the assumption. This is often done when we hope to show that one thing is better than another. One makes the (tacit) assumption that they are alike and hope that the data collected show that this is unlikely. We say that the experimental data "reject the null hypothesis," the hypothesis of no difference.

We use the hypothesis together with the data or previous knowledge to create a *critical region*. If the observed statistic computed from the data is in the critical region, we reject the null hypothesis (H_0) in favor of an alternative hypothesis (H_1). Otherwise we accept the hypothesis H_0. (This does not prove that H_0 is true, only that we have insufficient evidence to deny the likelihood that it is correct.) Table 4-4 contains some common statistical tests of hypotheses. These are the classical tests usually covered in a first statistics course. The key sequences indicate a possible method of computing the test statistic given. Depending on the formulation of the problem and the calculator capability, certain modifications are possible.

Concerning the notation for the critical values shown in Table 4-4, if the level of significance of the test is α, then z_α refers to the ordinate of the left tail of a normal distribution that has area α. That is, the subscript will always refer to the area of the left tail. (Some authors do it the other way; that is, they let the subscript be the right tail. But the method given here is more common.)

Example The value $z_{.05}$ is the value of z that has a left tail area of .05; so from tables of the normal distribution we find that $z_{.05} = -1.645$ (see Figure 4-2).

Figure 4-2

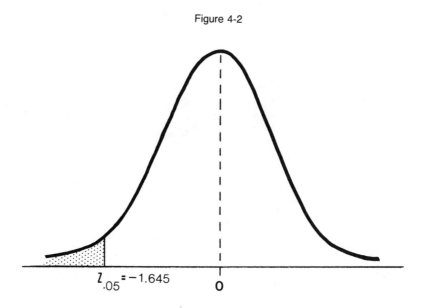

TABLE 4-4. Summary of Some Standard Tests of Classical Statistical Hypotheses

HYPOTHESIS	TEST STATISTIC	KEY SEQUENCE	CRITICAL VALUE
$H_0: p = p_0$ $H_1: p < p_0$ or $p > p_0$ Test of a specified proportion	$z = \dfrac{\hat{p} - p_0}{\sqrt{p_0 q_0/n}}$ $\hat{p} = \dfrac{\text{no. of successes}}{n}$ $q_0 = 1 - p_0$	1 $\boxed{-}$ p_0 $\boxed{=}$ $\boxed{\times}$ p_0 $\boxed{\div}$ n $\boxed{=}$ $\boxed{\sqrt{x}}$ $\boxed{\text{STO}}$ $\hat{p}$ $\boxed{-}$ p_0 $\boxed{=}$ $\boxed{\div}$ $\boxed{\text{RCL}}$ $\boxed{=}$	$z_{\alpha/2}$ and $z_{1-\alpha/2}$ (2-sided) z_α or $z_{1-\alpha}$ (1-sided) where z_α is the α percentile of the standard normal distribution
$H_0: p_1 = p_2$ $H_1: p_1 < p_2$ or $p_1 > p_2$ Test of equal proportions	$z = \dfrac{\hat{p}_1 - \hat{p}_2}{\sqrt{\bar{p}\,\bar{q}\left(\dfrac{1}{n_1} + \dfrac{1}{n_2}\right)}}$ where $\bar{p}$ = pooled proportion = $\dfrac{n_1\hat{p}_1 + n_2\hat{p}_2}{n_1 + n_2}$	1. Compute $\bar{p}$ and store: n_1 $\boxed{+}$ n_2 $\boxed{=}$ $\boxed{\text{STO}}$ x_1 $\boxed{+}$ x_2 $\boxed{=}$ $\boxed{\div}$ $\boxed{\text{RCL}}$ $\boxed{=}$ $\boxed{\text{STO}}$ where x_i = no. of successes = $n_i\hat{p}_i$; i = 1, 2 2. Compute z (with $\bar{p}$ stored). 1 $\boxed{-}$ $\boxed{\text{RCL}}$ $\boxed{=}$ $\boxed{\times}$ $\boxed{\text{RCL}}$ $\boxed{=}$ $\boxed{\text{STO}}$ n_1 $\boxed{1/x}$ $\boxed{+}$ n_2 $\boxed{1/x}$ $\boxed{=}$ $\boxed{\times}$ $\boxed{\text{RCL}}$ $\boxed{=}$ $\boxed{\sqrt{x}}$ $\boxed{\text{STO}}$ $\hat{p}_1$ $\boxed{-}$ $\hat{p}_2$ $\boxed{=}$ $\boxed{\div}$ $\boxed{\text{RCL}}$ $\boxed{=}$	Same critical values as the previous test. (*Note*: This test is equivalent to a χ^2 test of equal proportions.)
$H_0: \mu = \mu_0$ $H_1: \mu < \mu_0$ or $\mu > \mu_0$ σ known	$z = \dfrac{\bar{x} - \mu_0}{\sigma/\sqrt{n}}$ = $\dfrac{(\bar{x} - \mu_0)\sqrt{n}}{\sigma}$	First compute $\bar{x}$ from the data: $\bar{x}$ $\boxed{-}$ μ_0 $\boxed{=}$ $\boxed{\times}$ n $\boxed{\sqrt{x}}$ $\boxed{\div}$ σ $\boxed{=}$	Same critical values as the previous two tests.
$H_0: \mu = \mu_0$ $H_1: \mu < \mu_0$ or $\mu > \mu_0$ σ unknown (One Sample t test)	$t = \dfrac{\bar{x} - \mu_0}{s/\sqrt{n}}$ = $\dfrac{(\bar{x} - \mu_0)\sqrt{n}}{s}$ where s = sample standard deviation	First compute $\bar{x}$ and s: $\bar{x}$ $\boxed{-}$ μ_0 $\boxed{=}$ $\boxed{\times}$ n $\boxed{\sqrt{x}}$ $\boxed{\div}$ s $\boxed{=}$	$t_{\alpha/2}(n-1)$ and $t_{1-\alpha/2}(n-1)$ (2-sided) $t_\alpha(n-1)$ or $t_{1-\alpha}(n-1)$ (1-sided)

Hypotheses	Test statistic	Calculator keystrokes	Critical values
$H_0: \mu_1 = \mu_2$ $H_1: \mu_1 < \mu_2$ or $\mu_1 > \mu_2$ $\sigma_1 = \sigma_2 = \sigma$ (known)	$z = \dfrac{\bar{x}_1 - \bar{x}_2}{\sigma\sqrt{\dfrac{1}{n_1}+\dfrac{1}{n_2}}}$	n_1 $\boxed{1/x}$ $\boxed{+}$ n_2 $\boxed{1/x}$ $\boxed{=}$ $\boxed{\sqrt{x}}$ $\boxed{\text{STO}}$ $\bar{x}_1$ $\boxed{-}$ $\bar{x}_2$ $\boxed{=}$ $\boxed{\div}$ σ $\boxed{\div}$ $\boxed{\text{RCL}}$ $\boxed{=}$ The means $\bar{x}_i$ are first computed from the data.	$z_{\alpha/2}$ and $z_{1-\alpha/2}$ (2-sided) z_α or $z_{1-\alpha}$ (1-sided)
$H_0: \mu_1 = \mu_2$ $H_1: \mu_1 < \mu_2$ or $\mu_1 > \mu_2$ $\sigma_1 = \sigma_2 = \sigma$ (unknown)	$t = \dfrac{\bar{x}_1 - \bar{x}_2}{s_p\sqrt{\dfrac{1}{n_1}+\dfrac{1}{n_2}}}$ where $s_p^2 =$ $\dfrac{(n_1-1)s_1^2 + (n_2-1)s_2^2}{n_1 + n_2 - 2}$ (pooled variance)	1. Compute $\bar{x}_1, s_1, \bar{x}_2, s_2$ from the data. Then compute s_p: s_1 $\boxed{x^2}$ $\boxed{\times}$ $n_1 - 1$ $\boxed{=}$ $\boxed{\text{STO}}$ s_2 $\boxed{x^2}$ $\boxed{\times}$ $n_2 - 1$ $\boxed{=}$ $\boxed{\text{SUM}}$ $\boxed{\text{RCL}}$ $\boxed{\div}$ $n_1 + n_2 - 2$ $\boxed{=}$ $\boxed{\sqrt{x}}$ $\boxed{\text{STO}}$ 2. Compute t: n_1 $\boxed{1/x}$ $\boxed{+}$ n_2 $\boxed{1/x}$ $\boxed{=}$ $\boxed{\sqrt{x}}$ $\boxed{\times}$ $\boxed{\text{RCL}}$ $\boxed{=}$ $\boxed{\text{STO}}$ $\bar{x}_1$ $\boxed{-}$ $\bar{x}_2$ $\boxed{=}$ $\boxed{\div}$ $\boxed{\text{RCL}}$ $\boxed{=}$	$t_{\alpha/2}$ and $t_{1-\alpha/2}$ (2-sided) t_α or $t_{1-\alpha}$ (1-sided) All critical values with $df = n_1 + n_2 - 2$
$H_0: \sigma^2 = \sigma_0^2$ $H_1: \sigma^2 < \sigma_0^2$ or $\sigma^2 > \sigma_0^2$	$\chi^2 = \dfrac{(n-1)s^2}{\sigma_0^2}$	$(n-1)$ $\boxed{\times}$ s $\boxed{x^2}$ $\boxed{\div}$ σ_0^2 $\boxed{=}$ $(n-1)$ computed mentally; s computed first from data	$\chi^2_{1-\alpha}$ (1-sided) $\chi^2_{1-\alpha/2}$ and $\chi^2_{\alpha/2}$ (2-sided) $df = n - 1$
$H_0: \sigma_1^2 = \sigma_2^2$ $H_1: \sigma_1^2 < \sigma_2^2$ or $\sigma_1^2 > \sigma_2^2$	$F = \dfrac{s_1^2}{s_2^2}$	s_1 $\boxed{x^2}$ $\boxed{\div}$ s_2 $\boxed{x^2}$ $\boxed{=}$ s_i values computed from data first	$F_{\alpha/2}$ and $F_{1-\alpha/2}$ (2-sided; $df = n_1 - 1, n_2 - 1$) F_α or $F_{1-\alpha}$ (1-sided; $df = n_1 - 1, n_2 - 1$)
$H_0: \mu_1 = \mu_2$ $H_1: \mu_1 < \mu_2$ or $\mu_1 > \mu_2$	$t = \dfrac{\bar{d} - 0}{s_d/\sqrt{n}}$ $= \dfrac{\bar{d}\sqrt{n}}{s_d}$	$\bar{d}$ $\boxed{\times}$ n $\boxed{\sqrt{x}}$ $\boxed{\div}$ s_d $\boxed{=}$ $\bar{d}$ and s_d computed first from difference data	$t_{\alpha/2}$ and $t_{1-\alpha/2}$ (2-sided; $df = n - 1$) t_α or $t_{1-\alpha}$ (1-sided; $df = n - 1$)

If we are doing a two-sided (two-tailed) test and we desire a total area of α in the two tails, then the symmetric z values are denoted by $z_{\alpha/2}$ and $z_{1-\alpha/2}$. Figure 4-3 illustrates the relation of the subscript to the area.

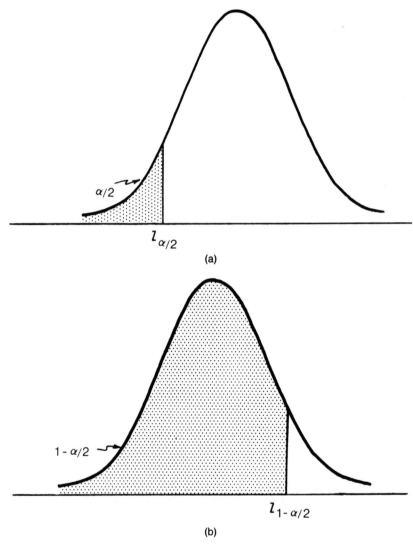

$\alpha/2$

$z_{\alpha/2}$

(a)

$1-\alpha/2$

$z_{1-\alpha/2}$

(b)

Figure 4-3

Example If $\alpha = .05$, then the z values for a two-tailed test are

$$z_{\alpha/2} = z_{.05/2} = z_{.025} = -1.96 \quad \text{and} \quad z_{1-\alpha/2} = z_{1-.05/2} = z_{.975} = +1.96$$

by referring to a table of normal areas.

For the t, F, and χ^2 distributions, the numbers in parentheses refer to the *degrees of freedom*. For example, $t_{.05}(9)$ means the fifth percentile of the t distribution with 9 degrees of freedom. From a table $t_{.05}(9) = -1.833$. The t distribution is symmetric about zero, thus $t_{.95}(9) = +1.833$. Since we are concerned with the computational methods, we assume that the reader is now taking, or has taken a basic statistics course and has such tables available. If not, look in the appendix of almost any elementary statistics text.

Before one actually applies a statistical method, one should be aware of the following:

1. The underlying assumptions (e.g., the type of sampling distribution required, the nature of the data).
2. Appropriateness of the method (i.e., does it answer the question actually asked? Is it the proper test?).
3. The *power* of the test. If a test is not powerful enough, it will not detect an actual difference. If it is too powerful, it will say that unimportant differences are statistically significant when in actuality the test is detecting *sampling noise*.

There are concepts that should be covered in any good statistics course. We shall refer to some of them at times in the solved problems, but we avoid a comprehensive discussion due to lack of space and the scope of this book.

Example   Two groups of weight-loss patients ($n_1 = 20$, $n_2 = 15$) had average weight losses of $\bar{x}_1 = 20.3$ and $\bar{x}_2 = 22.5$ pounds. Both groups are assumed to come from a population with a standard deviation in weight loss of 3 pounds. (This should actually be tested first in a real study.) We test the hypothesis that both group's weight losses are equal; that is, $H_0: \mu_1 = \mu_2$ against the alternative hypothesis $H_1: \mu_1 \neq \mu_2$, a two-sided test.

We compute the test statistic

$$z = \frac{\bar{x}_1 - \bar{x}_2}{\sigma \sqrt{\dfrac{1}{n_1} + \dfrac{1}{n_2}}} = \frac{20.3 - 22.5}{3 \sqrt{\dfrac{1}{20} + \dfrac{1}{15}}}$$

by keying

20 $\boxed{1/x}$ $\boxed{+}$ 15 $\boxed{1/x}$ $\boxed{=}$ $\boxed{\sqrt{x}}$ $\boxed{\times}$ 3 $\boxed{=}$ $\boxed{\text{STO}}$

20.3 $\boxed{-}$ 22.5 $\boxed{=}$ $\boxed{\div}$ $\boxed{\text{RCL}}$ $\boxed{=}$ and read z: $\boxed{-2.1469802}$

which we round to $z = -2.15$. Suppose we are testing at the level $\alpha = .05$, and since this is a two-tailed test we use as critical values $z_{\alpha/2} = z_{.05/2} = z_{.025} = -1.96$ and $z_{1-\alpha/2} = z_{1-0.25} = z_{.975} = +1.96$. Since the observed (computed) value of $z = -2.15 < z_{.025} = -1.96$, we reject the hypothesis H_0 and conclude that the two groups exhibit different mean weight loss.

Chi Squared: χ^2

A continuous variable X having positive values is said to have a *chi-squared* (or *chi square*) distribution, denoted by the symbol χ^2_v, where $v > 0$ is a positive integer called the *degrees of freedom*. When the variable X is the sum of the squares of v independent standard normal (Gaussian) variables, then X follows a χ^2 distribution with v degrees of freedom. Other statistics can be shown to (approximately) obey a chi-squared distribution, some of which will be discussed. Some uses of the chi-squared distribution are for the following:*

1. Testing the hypothesis $\sigma^2 = \sigma^2_0$ (see Table 5-4).
2. Goodness-of-fit tests.
3. Tests of association using contingency tables.

Example   *Goodness of fit*: A die is tossed 150 times with frequencies as shown in the table. We test the fairness of the die at the $\alpha = .05$ level by seeing how well the observed frequency distribution fits a theoretical uniform distribution.

Observed frequency	5	24	42	51	12	16
Expected frequency	25	25	25	25	25	25

The correct statistic that follows a χ^2 distribution with $n - 1 = 6 - 1 = 5$ degrees of freedom is

$$\chi^2 = \sum \frac{(O - E)^2}{E}$$

where O and E are corresponding observed and expected frequencies. When the numbers from the table are substituted, this becomes

$$\frac{(5 - 25)^2}{25} + \frac{(24 - 25)^2}{25} + \frac{(42 - 25)^2}{25} + \frac{(51 - 25)^2}{25} + \frac{(12 - 25)^2}{25} + \frac{(16 - 25)^2}{25}$$

*For other uses of χ^2, see Joseph L. Fleiss, *Statistical Methods for Rates and Proportions*, John Wiley & Sons, Inc., New York, 1973.

Since the denominator $E = 25$ happens to be the same for each term in this example, we can divide by it last. Key

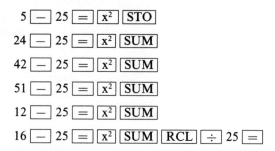

and read $\chi^2 = 64.64$, which is to be compared with a tabled value of χ^2 with 5 degrees of freedom at the $\alpha = .05$ level. This tabled value turns out to be $\chi^2_{table} = 11.07$, which the computed (observed) value exceeds. Thus we reject the null hypothesis (of a good fit) and conclude that the die (or the person throwing it) is not fair, since the nonconformance of the results to a uniform model is greater than that expected by chance.

Some algebra can provide a better computational form for the χ^2 formula. Since $\Sigma E = \Sigma O = n$, we can do the following algebra:

$$\chi^2 = \Sigma \frac{(O - E)^2}{E} = \Sigma \frac{(O^2 - 2OE + E^2)}{E}$$

$$= \Sigma \frac{O^2}{E} - 2 \Sigma O + \Sigma E = \Sigma \frac{O^2}{E} - 2n + n$$

$$= \Sigma \frac{O^2}{E} - n$$

Moreover, if E happens to be constant (it is not in general), as in the case of the uniform distribution (see preceding example), we can even divide by that common value last instead of dividing each O^2 separately by the corresponding value of E.

Example Using the shortcut formula on the data of the previous example, we have (factoring out $1/25$)

$$\chi^2 = \frac{1}{25} (5^2 + 24^2 + 42^2 + 51^2 + 12^2 + 16^2) - 150$$

Thus simply key

$$5\ \boxed{x^2}\ \boxed{+}\ 24\ \boxed{x^2}\ \boxed{+}\ 42\ \boxed{x^2}\ \boxed{+}\ 51\ \boxed{x^2}\ \boxed{+}\ 12\ \boxed{x^2}\ \boxed{+}\ 16\ \boxed{x^2}\ \boxed{=}\ \boxed{\div}$$
$$25\ \boxed{-}\ 150\ \boxed{=}$$

and once again read $\chi^2 = 64.64$.

Test of Equal Proportions If there are two categories between which we wish to compare the presence or absence of some characteristic, we usually display the data in a *two-way* table (*contingency* table). The χ^2 statistic is usually computed from this table using a special formula and has one degree of freedom. It can be shown to be equivalent to the square of the normal *z* statistic used to test equal proportions.

		Category		
		I	II	Total
Event	E	a	b	R_1
	Not E	c	d	R_2
	Total	K_1	K_2	n

The null hypothesis, symbolically, is H_0: $p_I(E) = p_{II}(E)$. That is, the proportion of those in category I that exhibit event E having occurred is the same as the proportion in category II. We could compute estimates of these proportions from the data and use the appropriate normal test (which is really better, since you do not tend to lose track of what the hypothesis and populations are), but our purpose is to present the chi-squared statistic that tests this hypothesis. The correct statistic is

$$\chi^2 = \frac{n(ad - bc)^2}{K_1 K_2 R_1 R_2}$$

where the K_i and the R_i are the column and row sums of the two-way table. This quantity is easy to compute on AOS entry systems, but if you have an arithmetic (sequential) entry system, the difference $ad - bc$ must be computed by using the memory like this:

$$a \boxed{\times} d \boxed{=} \boxed{\text{STO}} \; b \boxed{\times} c \boxed{=} \boxed{=} \boxed{+/-} \boxed{\text{SUM}} \boxed{\text{RCL}}$$

A clever trick is to use the algebraic identity

$$\left(\frac{ad}{c} - b\right)c = ad - bc$$

and compute (arithmetic entry systems only)

$$a \boxed{\times} d \boxed{\div} c \boxed{-} b \boxed{\times} c \boxed{=}$$

If we tried to compute it like this

$$a \boxed{\times} d \boxed{-} b \boxed{\times} c \boxed{=}$$

it would *not* give the correct answer on arithmetic systems, only on AOS systems. Of course, if parentheses are available, key a $\boxed{\times}$ d $\boxed{-}$ $\boxed{(}$ b $\boxed{\times}$ c $\boxed{=}$.

Example   To compute $15(7) - 13(5)$ for AOS systems key

$$15 \boxed{\times} 7 \boxed{-} 13 \boxed{\times} 5 \boxed{=}$$

and the result is 40. (If you have an arithmetic system, you would get the *wrong* answer of 460.) For arithmetic systems, think of the quantity as $\left(\dfrac{15(7)}{5} - 13 \right)$ 5, and so key

$$15 \boxed{\times} 7 \boxed{\div} 5 \boxed{-} 13 \boxed{\times} 5 \boxed{=}$$

and again read 40. (If you try this sequence on an AOS system, you get the *wrong* answer of -44.)

Example   For the following 2×2 contingency table, the calculation of χ^2 using both AOS and arithmetic entry systems is shown.

$$
\begin{array}{cc|c}
8 & 12 & 20 \\
7 & 13 & 20 \\
\hline
15 & 25 & 40
\end{array}
\qquad
\chi^2 = \frac{n(ad - bc)^2}{K_1 K_2 R_1 R_2} = \frac{40(8(13) - 7(12))^2}{15(25)(20)(20)}
$$

AOS calculation:

$$8 \boxed{\times} 13 \boxed{-} 7 \boxed{\times} 12 \boxed{=} \boxed{x^2} \boxed{\times} 40 \boxed{\div} 15 \boxed{\div} 25 \boxed{\div} 20 \boxed{\div}$$
$$20 \boxed{=}$$

Arithmetic calculation without parentheses, using the trick discussed in the previous example, yields

$$8 \boxed{\times} 13 \boxed{\div} 12 \boxed{-} 7 \boxed{\times} 12 \boxed{=} \boxed{x^2} \boxed{\times} 40 \boxed{\div} 15 \boxed{\div} 25 \boxed{\div}$$
$$20 \boxed{\div} 20 \boxed{=}$$

In either case, $\chi^2 = .1066667$.

Since our data are discrete counting data and the χ^2 distribution is really for a continuous variable (theoretically), you will sometimes come across *Yate's continuity correction*, which reduces the value of χ^2 that we compute to compensate somewhat for the discrepancy. The formula is

$$\chi^2_{\text{corrected}} = \frac{n(|\ ad - bc\ | - \frac{1}{2} n)^2}{K_1 K_2 R_1 R_2}$$

The absolute value is obtained by keying $\boxed{+/-}$ if the difference $ad - bc$ is negative, nothing if it is positive.

There is also a special formula for an $r \times k$ table, where the number of degrees of freedom is $(r - 1) \times (k - 1)$. If R_i are the row sums and C_j are the column sums, and the grand total is n, the expected value

169

for each cell $E_{ij} = R_iC_j/n$ is to be compared with the observed cell entry O_{ij}, so the formula for chi squared takes the form

$$\chi^2 = \sum_i \sum_j \frac{(O_{ij} - E_{ij})^2}{E_{ij}}$$

An algebraically equivalent formula that makes computation somewhat easier is

$$\chi^2 = n\left(\sum_i \frac{1}{R_i} \sum_j \frac{O_{ij}^2}{C_j} - 1 \right)$$

$$= n\left(\frac{1}{R_1} \sum_j \frac{O_{1j}^2}{C_j} + \frac{1}{R_2} \sum_j \frac{O_{2j}^2}{C_j} + \ldots + \frac{1}{R_r} \sum_j \frac{O_{rj}^2}{C_j} - 1 \right)$$

That is, going across each row, sum the observed value squared divided by the column total in which it appears and divide that total by the row total. After this is accumulated for each row, subtract 1 and multiply the whole thing by the grand total n. An example of the use of this formula is given in Problem 33 on page 205.

Regression (Least Squares)

A *regression model* in statistics considers the distribution of a variable when another (related) variable is held fixed, but at several different levels. For example, we might consider the drop in blood pressure for people when a drug (at several fixed dose levels) is administered. Notice that the dose would be fixed for a given individual. If neither variable can be controlled or observed at predetermined levels, the problem is described as a *correlation problem*.

The regression model usually discussed in a basic course is the *linear regression model*. If we have a variable Y that may depend (linearly) on a variable X, we assume each observation (x_i, y_i) satisfies the relation $y_i = \alpha + \beta x_i + \epsilon_i$. The goal of the least-squares procedure is to estimate α and β so that the corresponding estimate of y denoted by $\hat{y}$ satisfies the equation $\hat{y} = a + bx$, where $a = \hat{\alpha}$ and $b = \hat{\beta}$ are the least-squares estimates of α and β.

The least-squares estimates for α and β are the quantities a and b given by the following formulas:

$$b = \frac{n \sum x_iy_i - (\sum x_i)(\sum y_i)}{n \sum x_i^2 - (\sum x_i)^2} = \text{slope}$$

$$a = \bar{y} - b\bar{x} = y \text{ intercept}$$

Some calculators have automatic functions that compute these estimates of the parameters α and β, but there is a notation problem. Here are some of the more common notations:

$$y = mx + b, \quad m = \text{slope}; \ b = \text{intercept}$$
$$y = ax + b, \quad a = \text{slope}; \ b = \text{intercept}$$
$$y = a + bx, \quad b = \text{slope}; \ a = \text{intercept}$$
$$y = b_0 + b_1 x, \quad b_1 = \text{slope}; \ b_0 = \text{intercept}$$

The unfortunate thing is that most statistics books use the last two notations, while most calculators use the first or the second notation. On your calculator, if it has linear regression, note which letter stands for the slope and which for the intercept by looking in your owner's manual.

Table 4-5 shows the most common textbook notations compared with the most common calculator keyboard notation for the same statistics that are related to regression.

TABLE 4-5.

STATISTIC	TEXT NOTATION	CALCULATOR KEYBOARD
Equation	$y = a + bx$	$y = ax + b$
Slope	b	a (or m)
y-Intercept	a	b
Fitted y value	$\hat{y}$	y'
Fitted x value	$\hat{x}$	x'
Correlation	r or $\hat{\rho}$	r or CORR

Table 4-5 may not totally unravel the notation confusion, but will be a handy reference when using the calculator with your statistics text.

We shall summarize a method of calculating some common regression statistics for two kinds of calculators: (1) AOS entry system with mean and standard deviation, and (2) any entry system with regression statistics. First, however, we shall summarize some forms of some typical formulas for reference. The data will be denoted by uppercase letters X and Y. A handy notation is to denote the *deviations from the mean* by lowercase letters; that is, $x = X - \bar{X}$, $y = Y - \bar{Y}$. Then rather messy expressions such as $\sum (X - \bar{X})^2$ becomes $\sum x^2$ and the formula $\sum (X - \bar{X})(Y - \bar{Y})$ becomes $\sum xy$. The data for the formulas that follow are usually presented in a tabular form, which we give for reference in reading the formulas in Table 4-6.

The reference numbers (in parentheses) in Table 4-6, as well as in Table 4-7, appear in formulas. When using a formula, a reference number is to be replaced by the corresponding formula or the quantity computed using the corresponding formula.

TABLE 4-6.

Labels	DATA		SQUARES AND PRODUCTS		
	X	Y	X^2	Y^2	XY
	X_1	Y_1	X_1^2	Y_1^2	$X_1 Y_1$
	X_2	Y_2	X_2^2	Y_2^2	$X_2 Y_2$
	.	.	.	.	.
	.	.	.	.	.
	X_n	Y_n	X_n^2	Y_n^2	$X_n Y_n$
Totals	ΣX	ΣY	ΣX^2	ΣY^2	ΣXY
Ref. Nos.	(1)	(2)	(3)	(4)	(5)

TABLE 4-7. Formulas for Regression Statistics*

REF. NOS.	FORMULA	NAME
See Table 4-6 for (1) to (5)	$\bar{X} = \dfrac{\Sigma X}{n} = \dfrac{(1)}{n}; \ \bar{Y} = \dfrac{\Sigma Y}{n} = \dfrac{(2)}{n}$	Means
(6)	$\Sigma x^2 = \sum (X - \bar{X})^2 = \Sigma X^2 - (\Sigma X)^2/n = (3) - (1)^2/n$	X Sum of squares $= S_{xx}$
(7)	$\Sigma y^2 = \sum (Y - \bar{Y})^2 = \Sigma Y^2 - (\Sigma Y)^2/n = (4) - (2)^2/n$	Y Sum of squares $= S_{yy}$
(8)	$\Sigma xy = \sum (X - \bar{X})(Y - \bar{Y}) = \Sigma XY -$ $\Sigma X \Sigma Y/n = (5) - \dfrac{(1)(2)}{n}$	Sum of products $= S_{xy}$
(9)	$b = \Sigma xy / \Sigma x^2 = (8)/(6)$	Slope
(10)	$a = \bar{Y} - b\bar{X} = (\Sigma Y - b \Sigma X)/n = [(2) - (9)(1)]/n$	Y Intercept
(11)	$s_x^2 = \Sigma x^2/(n-1) = \sum (X - \bar{X})^2/(n-1) = (6)/(n-1)$	X variance of sample
(12)	$s_y^2 = \Sigma y^2/(n-1) = \sum (Y - \bar{Y})^2/(n-1) = (7)/(n-1)$	Y variance of sample
(13)	$\Sigma \hat{y}^2 = \sum (\hat{Y} - \bar{Y})^2 = (\Sigma xy)^2/\Sigma x^2 = (8)^2/(6)$	"Explained" sum of squares
(14)	$\sum (Y - \hat{Y})^2 = \Sigma y^2 - \Sigma \hat{y}^2 = S_{yy} - \Sigma \hat{y}^2 = (7) - (13)$	"Unexplained" sum of squares
(15)	$s_{y \cdot x}^2 = \sum (Y - \hat{Y})^2/(n-2) = (14)/(n-2)$	Mean square about regression
(16)	$s_{y \cdot x} = \sqrt{s_{y \cdot x}^2} = \sqrt{(15)}$	Standard error of estimate
(17)	$r = \Sigma xy / \sqrt{\Sigma x^2 \Sigma y^2} = (8)/\sqrt{(6)(7)}$	Correlation coefficient

*These are not the only relations between the given quantities, and we shall mention a few others while discussing computational procedures.

Keeping these formulas in mind (or at hand), we shall work the same numerical example for each of the two types of calculators that we consider here. If your calculator does not have statistical functions, compute the various quantities using the formulas directly. You will need to first compute the five totals shown in the data table before you can even get started. If you try this, you will probably run out and buy a calculator with regression, or at least mean and standard deviation built in.

Example   Ordered pairs (X, Y) are collected as data and regression statistics are computed in Figure 4-4. A scatterplot of the data is also shown.

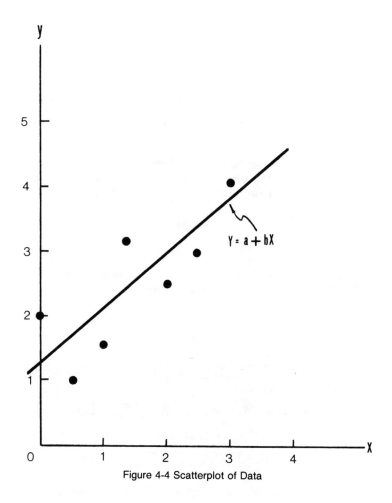

Figure 4-4 Scatterplot of Data

Before proceeding with the example, one important fact to note is that

$$(n - 1)s^2 = \sum (X - \bar{X})^2 = \Sigma \, x^2$$

so that to compute a sum of squares just square the $(n-1)$-weighted standard deviation and multiply the result by $n-1$. Since the standard deviations are automatically computed, this gives a faster way of computing than using the formulas in the table directly.

A. Calculation of Regression Statistics Using an AOS Entry System with Basic Statistics, but <u>Without</u> Built-In Regression Functions.

1. Compute n, $\bar{X}$, s_X, and $\Sigma\, x^2 = \sum (X - \bar{X})^2 = S_{xx}$. First enter the X data:

$$0\;\boxed{\Sigma+}\;.5\;\boxed{\Sigma+}\;1\;\boxed{\Sigma+}\;1.5\;\boxed{\Sigma+}\;2\;\boxed{\Sigma+}\;2.5\;\boxed{\Sigma+}\;3\;\boxed{\Sigma+}\quad\text{and}$$
read $n = 7$

Compute $\bar{X}$ by keying $\boxed{2\text{nd}}\;\boxed{\bar{x}}$ and read $\bar{X} = 1.5$.

Compute s_X by keying $\boxed{2\text{nd}}\;\boxed{\sigma_{n-1}}$ or $\boxed{2\text{nd}}\;\boxed{s}$ or $\boxed{2\text{nd}}\;\boxed{\text{SD}}$ and read

s_X: $\boxed{\quad 1.0801234 \quad}$. Since $(n-1)s_X^2 = \sum (X - \bar{X})^2$, we can square the

displayed value and multiply by $n - 1 = 7 - 1 = 6$ (computed mentally). On some calculators, in order to unlock the arithmetic functions, we must *clear statistics registers* before doing the multiplication; that is, key

$$\boxed{x^2}\;\boxed{2\text{nd}}\;\boxed{\text{CSR}}\;\boxed{\times}\;6\;\boxed{=}\quad\text{and read}\quad \Sigma\, x^2 = S_{xx} =$$
$$\sum (X - \bar{X})^2 = 7$$

We derived an additional benefit from pressing $\boxed{\text{CSR}}$: the statistics registers are clear for the next step.

2. Compute $\bar{Y}$, s_Y, and $\Sigma\, y^2 = \sum (Y - \bar{Y})^2 = S_{yy}$ by following the same procedure as in step 1, only using the Y data:

$$2\;\boxed{\Sigma+}\;1\;\boxed{\Sigma+}\;1.6\;\boxed{\Sigma+}\;3.2\;\boxed{\Sigma+}\;2.5\;\boxed{\Sigma+}\;3\;\boxed{\Sigma+}\;4.1\;\boxed{\Sigma+};$$
read $n = 7$

$\boxed{2\text{nd}}\;\boxed{\bar{x}}$ and read $\bar{Y}$: $\boxed{\quad 2.4857143 \quad}$

$\boxed{2\text{nd}}\;\boxed{\sigma_{n-1}}$ and read s_Y: $\boxed{\quad 1.0494897 \quad}$

$\boxed{x^2}\;\boxed{2\text{nd}}\;\boxed{\text{CSR}}\;\boxed{\times}\;6\;\boxed{=}$ and read $\Sigma\, y^2 = S_{yy}$: $\boxed{\quad 6.6085714 \quad}$

3. Now we must compute $\Sigma\, XY$ directly. Since this is for AOS, key

$$0\;\boxed{\times}\;2\;\boxed{+}\;.5\;\boxed{\times}\;1\;\boxed{+}\;1\;\boxed{\times}\;1.6\;\boxed{+}\;1.5\;\boxed{\times}\;3.2\;\boxed{+}$$
$$2\;\boxed{\times}\;2.5\;\boxed{+}\;2.5\;\boxed{\times}\;3\;\boxed{+}\;3\;\boxed{\times}\;4.1\;\boxed{=}\quad\text{and read}\;\Sigma\, XY =$$
31.7 exactly

4. Compute the sum of products $\Sigma\ xy = \sum (X - \bar{X})\ (Y - \bar{Y}) = \Sigma\ XY - $
$\Sigma\ X \Sigma\ Y/n = \Sigma\ XY - n\bar{X}\bar{Y}$ *(slightly altered formula). Since* $\Sigma\ XY$ is still
displayed, key $\boxed{-}\ n\ \boxed{\times}\ \bar{X}\ \boxed{\times}\ \bar{Y}\ \boxed{=}$, where previously computed values are to be substituted. For this example we use $\boxed{-}\ 7\ \boxed{\times}\ 1.5\ \boxed{\times}$
2.4857143 $\boxed{=}$ and read $\Sigma\ xy = S_{xy}$: $\boxed{\ 5.5999999\ }$ (Do not clear.) Notice
the apparent roundoff error inherent in using this revised form of the for-
mula. The correct result is actually 5.6 exactly. If you need more precision,
use the original formula, but this is easier to use.

5. Compute $b = \Sigma\ xy/\Sigma\ x^2$. Since $\Sigma\ xy$ should still be displayed, just key
$\boxed{\div}\ \Sigma\ x^2\ \boxed{=}\ \boxed{STO}$, where $\Sigma\ x^2 = 7$ was the value computed in step 1.
For this example we key specifically $\boxed{\div}\ 7\ \boxed{=}\ \boxed{STO}$ and read the slope
b: $\boxed{\ \ 0.8\ \ }$, which is stored in memory. Notice that the roundoff error in
the previous step did not hurt this result. We need b for the next step.

6. Compute the Y intercept $a = \bar{Y} - b\bar{X}$ by keying, in general $\bar{Y}\ \boxed{-}\ \boxed{RCL}$
$\boxed{\times}\ \bar{X}\ \boxed{=}$, where $\bar{Y}$ and $\bar{X}$ are the values previously calculated. For this
example, key

$$2.4857143\ \boxed{-}\ \boxed{RCL}\ \boxed{\times}\ 1.5\ \boxed{=}\quad \text{and read } a: \boxed{\ 1.2857143\ }$$

7. Compute the explained and unexplained sum of squares using the formulas

$$SS_{\text{explained}} = \Sigma\ \hat{y}^2 = (\Sigma\ xy)^2/\Sigma\ x^2 = (5.6)^2/7 = 4.48$$

and

$$SS_{\text{unexplained}} = \Sigma\ y^2 - SS_{\text{expl.}} = 6.6085714 - 4.48 = 2.1285714$$

by performing the indicated operations on the results from the previous
steps substituted into the formulas as shown.

8. Compute $s^2_{y \cdot x}$ and $s_{y \cdot x}$. We use the result of the previous step in the formula

$$S^2_{y \cdot x} = \frac{SS_{\text{unexpl.}}}{n - 2} = \frac{2.1285714}{7 - 2} = .4257143$$

and perform the division on the calculator. To get $s_{y \cdot x}$, take the square
root of the preceding result and get .6524678, the standard error of estimate.

9. Compute the correlation coefficient using the formula

$$r = \frac{\Sigma\ xy}{\sqrt{\Sigma\ x^2 \Sigma\ y^2}} = \frac{5.6}{\sqrt{7(6.6085714)}} = .8233514$$

by keying

$$5.6\ \boxed{\div}\ \boxed{(}\ 7\ \boxed{\times}\ 6.6085714\ \boxed{)}\ \boxed{\sqrt{x}}\ \boxed{=}$$

This procedure is obviously quite lengthy, but we include it for completeness. Clearly, if one wishes to do regression analysis with some moderate ease, a calculator designed for that purpose is needed. Some of these do not, however, give the sums of squares and products of the data (unless there are multiple memories). There is really no need for these summary statistics as far as the regression statistics are concerned. If you really need them, use the basic formulas, substitute the results that you will soon see how to get automatically, and solve for the desired quantity. For example, we know that $b = \Sigma\ xy/\Sigma\ x^2$. Moreover, $\Sigma\ xy = \Sigma\ XY - n\bar{X}\ \bar{Y} = b\ \Sigma\ x^2$, and thus $\Sigma\ XY = n\bar{X}\ \bar{Y} + b\ \Sigma\ x^2$, and all the quantities on the right-hand side are computed sometime during the other calculations. We shall not pursue this idea, but merely give it mention in case the reader should require it.

Example

B. *Calculation of Regression Statistics Using a Calculator with Regression Functions.* (If the summary statistics are available automatically, as they are on some multimemory calculators, one could just use the formulas given in Table 4-7.) We shall give a strategy for computing all pertinent statistics including the standard error of estimate, as well as explained and unexplained sum of squares (which are used for an analysis of variance approach to regression, not covered in this book.)

1. First place the calculator in regression mode. Some require that keys such as $\boxed{\text{2nd}}$ $\boxed{\text{LR}}$ be pressed; others just use the regular statistics functions together with an extra key. Often $\boxed{\text{x \textonehalf\ y}}$ is how that extra key appears. We shall assume this is the case. Enter the paired data by keying:

   0 $\boxed{\text{x \textonehalf\ y}}$ 2 $\boxed{\Sigma +}$ .5 $\boxed{\text{x \textonehalf\ y}}$ 1 $\boxed{\Sigma +}$ 1 $\boxed{\text{x \textonehalf\ y}}$ 1.6 $\boxed{\Sigma +}$ 1.5 $\boxed{\text{x \textonehalf\ y}}$
   3.2 $\boxed{\Sigma +}$

   2 $\boxed{\text{x \textonehalf\ y}}$ 2.5 $\boxed{\Sigma +}$ 2.5 $\boxed{\text{x \textonehalf\ y}}$ 3 $\boxed{\Sigma +}$ 3 $\boxed{\text{x \textonehalf\ y}}$ 4.1 $\boxed{\Sigma +}$

   and the value $n = 7$ is displayed.

2. Compute the means $\bar{X}$ and $\bar{Y}$ by simply keying

   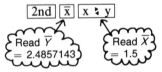

3. Compute the Y intercept a and the slope b. (Some calculators label them in reverse, since *their* model is $Y = aX + b$ and *ours* is $Y = a + bX$.) Just press the keys as shown:

   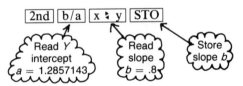

   (*Note*: Some calculators have separate keys $\boxed{\text{m}}$ for slope and $\boxed{\text{b}}$ for the intercept. Remember their b = intercept is our a.)

4. Compute the correlation coefficient r and the *coefficient of determination* r^2 by keying

$$\boxed{\text{2nd}}\ \boxed{\text{Corr}}\quad \text{and read } r: \quad \boxed{\quad 0.8233514 \quad}$$

$$\boxed{x^2}\quad \text{and read } r^2: \quad \boxed{\quad 0.6779075 \quad}$$

So far this is quite simple and automatic. The standard deviations s_X and s_Y are also automatic, but we must do some thinking to get $s_{y \cdot x}$ and, if desired, $S_{xx} = \Sigma\ x^2$, $S_{yy} = \Sigma\ y^2$, and $S_{xy} = \Sigma\ xy$.

5. Compute other related statistics if desired. Recall that at this point the slope b is stored in memory. The strategy depends on what you need.

   (a) If you only need s_X, s_Y, and $s_{y \cdot x}$, then there are two possible formulas that can be implemented.

   Method 1   Using the formula $s_{y \cdot x}^2 = \dfrac{n-1}{n-1}\ (s_Y^2 - b^2 s_X^2)$, we key

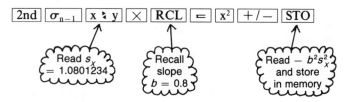

   Continuing,

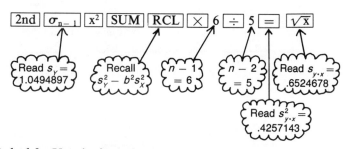

   Method 2   Use the formula

$$s_{y \cdot x}^2 = \frac{n-1}{n-2} s_Y^2 (1 - r^2).$$

   With r^2 still displayed (end of step 4), we proceed as follows:

$$\boxed{+/-}\ \boxed{\text{STO}}\ 1\ \boxed{\text{SUM}}\ \boxed{\text{2nd}}\ \boxed{\sigma_{n-1}}\ \boxed{x^2}\ \boxed{\times}\ 6\ \boxed{\div}$$
$$5\ \boxed{\times}\ \boxed{\text{RCL}}\ \boxed{=}$$

   Read $s_{y \cdot x}^2 = .4257143$; then key $\boxed{\sqrt{x}}$ and read $s_{y \cdot x} = .6524678$.

(b) If you want to compute the explained and unexplained sums of squares as well as the preceding statistics, a different strategy is required. We shall also compute $S_{xx} = \Sigma\ x^2$, $S_{yy} = \Sigma\ y^2$, and $S_{xy} = \Sigma\ xy$. First compute s_X^2 and multiply by $n - 1$ to get $\Sigma\ x^2$:

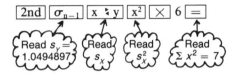

Now, since $b = \dfrac{\Sigma\ xy}{\Sigma\ x^2}$, $\Sigma\ xy = b\ \Sigma\ x^2$. Recall that $b = $ slope is stored in memory (unless you already tried part (a) of this step; if so, put $b = .8$ back into memory before proceeding). $\Sigma\ x^2$ should now be displayed, so key

$$\boxed{\times}\ \boxed{\text{EXC}}\ \boxed{=} \quad \text{and read } \Sigma\ xy = 5.6$$

Since we keyed the exchange key, Σx^2 is now in memory and $\Sigma\ xy$ is displayed. But $SS_{\text{explained}} = (\Sigma\ xy)^2 / \Sigma\ x^2$, so key

$$\boxed{x^2}\ \boxed{\div}\ \boxed{\text{RCL}}\ \boxed{=}\ \boxed{\text{STO}} \quad \text{and read } SS_{\text{explained}} = 4.48$$

which we have also stored in memory once obtaining it. That is because

$$SS_{\text{unexplained}} = S_{yy} - SS_{\text{explained}} = \Sigma\ y^2 - SS_{\text{explained}}$$

If we use the additional important fact that

$$S_{yy} = \Sigma\ y^2 = \Sigma\ (Y - \bar{Y})^2 = (n - 1)s_Y^2$$

then we key

Notice that during the preceding calculations we have displayed s_X, s_X^2, s_Y, s_Y^2, $\Sigma\ x^2$, $\Sigma\ y^2$, $\Sigma\ xy$, $SS_{\text{expl.}}$, and $SS_{\text{unexpl.}}$. Thus in order to compute $s_{y \cdot x}^2$ since the last quantity displayed is $SS_{\text{unexplained}}$, we divide by $n - 2 = 7 - 2 = 5$. Then take the square root to get the standard error of estimate.

Notice that $\bar{X}$, $\bar{Y}$, s_X, s_Y, a, b, and r are very easy to compute (steps 1 to 4). To do proper analysis and compute confidence intervals requires the standard error of estimate $s_{y \cdot x}$ and a bit more effort.

At this point we mention one other capability of calculators with regression statistics: computing estimated (and predicted) values from the least-squares regression line.

If you have not cleared the statistics registers, take an X value, say $X = 2$, and compute the corresponding estimate of Y, denoted $\hat{Y}$, by keying 2 ⌊2nd⌋ ⌊y'⌋ and read the *estimate* $\hat{Y} = 2.8857143$. Notice that the observed value, from the data table, is $Y = 2.5$. If we enter an X value not among the data, then the value of $\hat{Y}$ computed is called the *predicted value*. The calculator method is the same, but the confidence interval for the estimate would be slightly different. We could also do reverse prediction or estimation and compute an X value for a given Y value. For example, for $Y = 4$ we compute a prediction $\hat{X}$ by keying 4 ⌊2nd⌋ ⌊x'⌋ and read $\hat{X} = 3.3928571$. Figure 4-5 indicates the relation of these quantities to the fitted least-squares line.

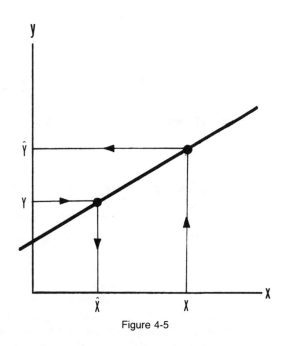

Figure 4-5

Analysis of Variance

In this section we shall not attempt to summarize the analysis of variance (ANOVA) theory, but will present an easy way of computing the ANOVA table for various balanced experimental designs. You must at least be acquainted with the standard ANOVA calculation to understand the contents of this section, as well as appreciate the savings in effort that is achieved by the methods of this discussion of analysis of variance.

The method relies on having a calculator that can automatically compute standard deviations. The fundamental relationship for this section is

$$\sum_{i=1}^{n} (Y - \bar{Y})^2 = n\sigma_Y^2$$

where Y is any statistic. It is precisely a sum of squares like this that comprises an ANOVA table. (When studying the theory, there are several models for ANOVA. However, the calculation is the same for all models that are commonly used. Only the significance tests and their interpretation may vary from model to model. It is not our purpose to discuss these models here. We shall only present a somewhat different computational procedure that, coupled with a good statistics book for interpretation and theory, should provide an easy but powerful tool.)

The data set $[X_1, X_2, \ldots, X_n]$ is usually entered with the key sequence

$$X_1 \boxed{\Sigma +} X_2 \boxed{\Sigma +} \ldots X_n \boxed{\Sigma +}$$

which we shall denote by the abbreviated symbol

$$[X_i \boxed{\Sigma +}]_{i=1}^{n}$$

for that key sequence. Then to compute the corresponding *sum of squares*, that is, $\Sigma (X - \bar{X})^2$, key $\boxed{2\text{nd}}$ $\boxed{\sigma_n}$ $\boxed{x^2}$ $\boxed{\times}$ n $\boxed{=}$. (On some calculators, in order to multiply you may have to clear statistics registers by keying $\boxed{2\text{nd}}$ $\boxed{\text{CSR}}$ just before keying $\boxed{\times}$, since the arithmetic keys may be locked.)

Important Note To clarify the key sequences that follow, the key symbol $\boxed{2\text{nd}}$ will be omitted in most cases, even though it may be the most common key configuration. By now it should be clear when this key should be pressed on your own calculator to obtain various results, such as the mean or standard deviation, and when it should not.

One-Way ANOVA We shall use the following notation for the data array $[X_{ij}]$:

X_{11}	$X_{12}\ldots$	X_{1k}	$C_j = \sum_{i=1}^{r} X_{ij} =$ sum of jth column
X_{21}	$X_{22}\ldots$	X_{2k}	
.	.	.	r = number of rows; k = number of columns
.	.	.	
.	.	.	Grand total $= \sum_i \sum_j X_{ij} = \sum_j C_j$
X_{r1}	$X_{r2}\ldots$	X_{rk}	
Totals C_1	$C_2\ldots$	C_k	Let $n = rk$ = total number of points X_{ij}

The *total sum of squares SST* is

$$\sum_{i}^{k}\sum^{r} (X_{ij} - \bar{X})^2 = kr\sigma_{\bar{X}}^2 = n\sigma_{\bar{X}}^2.$$

Thus to compute SST, follow these steps:

1. Enter data $[X_{ij} \boxed{\Sigma+}]_{i, j=1}^{r, k}$ and read n displayed.
2. Compute SST: $\boxed{\sigma_n} \boxed{x^2} \boxed{\times} \, n \, \boxed{=}$.

To get the *column sum of squares SSC*, it can be easily shown that

$$\text{SSC} = \Sigma(\bar{C}_j - \bar{X})^2 = \frac{k\sigma_C^2}{r}$$

where the symbol σ_C^2 denotes the variance of the k column sums computed as if they were ordinary data. Thus, to compute SSC, follow these steps:

1. Enter column sums as data: $[C_j \boxed{\Sigma+}]_{j=1}^{k}$
2. Compute SSC: $\boxed{\sigma_n} \boxed{x^2} \boxed{\times} \, k \, \boxed{\div} \, r \, \boxed{=}$.

An Important Observation Notice that SSC is computed in the same way as SST except that we divide by r, the number of entries that comprise each column sum. This is the first example of what will be a general principle in this section.

Finally, the residual or *error sum of squares SSE* is just the difference SSE = SST − SSC. The computation can be facilitated by using the memory. The following hypothetical numerical example illustrates the process.

Example We compute an ANOVA table for the following data.

Data:	3	2	8	6	$r = 3$
	2	2	7	5	$k = 4$
	6	5	3	2	$n = rk = 12$
Column totals:	11	9	18	13	

Step 1 First clear statistics registers $\boxed{\text{CSR}}$ and enter X data:

$3 \boxed{\Sigma+} 2 \boxed{\Sigma+} 6 \boxed{\Sigma+} 2 \boxed{\Sigma+} 2 \boxed{\Sigma+} 5 \boxed{\Sigma+} 8 \boxed{\Sigma+} 7$
$\boxed{\Sigma+} 3 \boxed{\Sigma+} 6 \boxed{\Sigma+} 5 \boxed{\Sigma+} 2 \boxed{\Sigma+}$

and read $n = 12$.

Step 2 Compute SST, store the result in memory, then clear statistics registers:

$$\boxed{\sigma_n}\ \boxed{x^2}\ ^*\ \boxed{\times}\ 12\ \boxed{=}\ \boxed{STO}\ \boxed{CSR}$$

and read SST = 52.25.

Step 3 Enter column data:

$$11\ \boxed{\Sigma+}\ 9\ \boxed{\Sigma+}\ 18\ \boxed{\Sigma+}\ 13\ \boxed{\Sigma+}$$

and read the number of columns $k = 4$.

Step 4 Compute SSC:

$$\boxed{\sigma_n}\ \boxed{x^2}\ ^*\ \boxed{\times}\ 4\ \boxed{\div}\ 3\ \boxed{=}$$

and read SSC = 14.916667.

Step 5 Compute SSE by subtraction in the memory. With SSC still displayed, key $\boxed{+/-}\ \boxed{SUM}\ \boxed{RCL}$ and read SSE = 37.333333.

If you followed the example step by step, you saw that the only things you must remember to do after entering data are (1) obtain σ, (2) square it, (3) multiply by the number of data items, and (4) divide by the number of X values comprising each data item. If the data are X's, no division is needed.

The one-way ANOVA is summarized next. The tables that follow summarize the two other most common designs: two-way ANOVA with a single entry in each cell and also with an equal number of replications in each cell. Some other possible designs in which this ANOVA shortcut can be used are given in the solved problems.

Summary of One-Way ANOVA

	DATA Categories		
	1	$\ldots j \ldots$	k
k columns	X_{11}	$\ldots$	X_{1k}
r entries	X_{21}		X_{2k}
per column	.	X_{ij}	.
	.		.
$n = rk$ = total	.		.
number of entries	X_{r1}	$\ldots$	X_{rk}
Totals:	C_1	$\ldots C_j \ldots$	C_k

*On some calculators you may have to press $\boxed{CSR}$ here which clears statistics registers as well as unlocks $\boxed{\times}$.

SOURCE	SS	ORDER*	DATA ENTRY	KEY SEQUENCE
Columns	SSC	(2)	$[C_j \boxed{\Sigma+}]_{j=1}^k$	$\boxed{\sigma_n}\,\boxed{x^2}\,\boxed{\times}\,k\,\boxed{\div}\,r\,\boxed{=}$
Error	SSE	(3)	Difference	$\boxed{+/-}\,\boxed{\text{SUM}}\,\boxed{\text{RCL}}$
Total	SST	(1)	$[X_{ij} \boxed{\Sigma+}]_{i,j=1,1}^{r,k}$	$\boxed{\sigma_n}\,\boxed{x^2}\,\boxed{\times}\,n\,\boxed{=}$
				$\boxed{\text{STO}}\,\boxed{\text{CSR}}$

*The number in parentheses indicates which line is to be *computed* first, second, and third. They are displayed in the standard format.

We have omitted mention of degrees of freedom, mean squares, and the statistical tests in this present discussion, but the solved problems illustrate the complete ANOVA table. The hardest part is to compute the sums of squares. This methodology makes that easy.

Summary of Two-Way ANOVA, Single Entry per Cell

DATA

			Total
X_{11}	...	X_{1k}	R_1
			.
	X_{ij}		R_i
			.
X_{r1}	...	X_{rk}	R_r

Total $\quad C_1 \quad ...\, C_j\, ... \quad C_k$

The calculation strategy is as follows:

1. Enter X data; get SST; store it.
2. Enter R data; get SSR; subtract from memory.
3. Enter C data; get SSC; subtract from memory.
4. SSE = SST − SSR − SSC now in memory.

Computational Procedure

SOURCE	SS	ORDER OF CALCULATION	DATA ENTRY	KEY SEQUENCE
Rows	SSR	(2)	$[R_i \boxed{\Sigma+}]_{i=1}^r$	$\boxed{\sigma_n}\,\boxed{x^2}\,\boxed{\times}\,r\,\boxed{\div}\,k\,\boxed{=}$*
				$\boxed{+/-}\,\boxed{\text{SUM}}\,\boxed{\text{CSR}}$
Columns	SSC	(3)	$[C_j \boxed{\Sigma+}]_{j=1}^k$	$\boxed{\sigma_n}\,\boxed{x^2}\,\boxed{\times}\,k\,\boxed{\div}\,r\,\boxed{=}$
Error	SSE	(4)	Difference	$\boxed{+/-}\,\boxed{\text{SUM}}\,\boxed{\text{RCL}}$
Total	SST	(1)	$[X_{ij} \boxed{\Sigma+}]_{1,1}^{r,k}$	$\boxed{\sigma_n}\,\boxed{x^2}\,\boxed{\times}\,n\,\boxed{=}\,\boxed{\text{STO}}$
				$\boxed{\text{CSR}}$

*Read SSR at this point.

As an example, we use the same numerical table but this time viewing it as a two-way table with both row and column sums:

3	2	8	6	19
2	2	7	5	16
6	5	3	2	16
11	9	18	13	

Since the numbers are the same as before, the calculations of SST = 52.25 and SSC = 14.92 are the same as before, only now SST should be stored in memory. The entire calculation is given next.

1. Compute SST:

$$3 \; \boxed{\Sigma+} \; 2 \; \boxed{\Sigma+} \; 8 \; \boxed{\Sigma+} \; 6 \; \boxed{\Sigma+} \; 2 \; \boxed{\Sigma+} \; 2 \; \boxed{\Sigma+} \; 7 \; \boxed{\Sigma+} \; 5 \; \boxed{\Sigma+}$$
$$6 \; \boxed{\Sigma+} \; 5 \; \boxed{\Sigma+} \; 3 \; \boxed{\Sigma+} \; 2 \; \boxed{\Sigma+} \quad (\text{read } n = 12) \; \boxed{\sigma_n} \; \boxed{x^2} \; \boxed{\times}$$
$$12 \; \boxed{=} \; \boxed{\text{STO}} \; \boxed{\text{CSR}}$$

(read SST = 52.25, which is stored in memory; The last key clears statistical registers so that the row data can be entered)

2. Compute SSR and subtract it from SST in the memory:

$$19 \; \boxed{\Sigma+} \; 16 \; \boxed{\Sigma+} \; 16 \; \boxed{\Sigma+} \quad (\text{read } r = 3)$$

$$\boxed{\sigma_n} \; \boxed{x^2} \; \boxed{\times} \; 3 \; \boxed{\div} \; 4 \; \boxed{=} \quad (\text{read SSR} = 1.5 \text{ exactly})$$

$$\boxed{+/-} \; \boxed{\text{SUM}} \; \boxed{\text{CRS}} \quad (\text{this subtracts SSR from the memory and } \boxed{\text{CSR}}$$
clears the statistics registers so that the column data can be entered next)

3. Compute SSC:

$$11 \; \boxed{\Sigma+} \; 9 \; \boxed{\Sigma+} \; 18 \; \boxed{\Sigma+} \; 13 \; \boxed{\Sigma+} \quad (\text{read } k = 4)$$

$$\boxed{\sigma_n} \; \boxed{x^2} \; \boxed{\times} \; 4 \; \boxed{\div} \; 3 \; \boxed{=} \quad (\text{read SSC} = 14.92)$$

4. Compute the error sum of squares by subtracting SSC, which is still displayed from the quantity in memory, which is currently SST − SSR.

$$\boxed{+/-} \; \boxed{\text{SUM}} \; \boxed{\text{RCL}} \quad (\text{read SSE} = 35.83)$$

Thus an ANOVA table, with degrees of freedom and sums of squares, would usually appear as follows:

SOURCE OF VARIATION	DEGREES OF FREEDOM	SUMS OF SQUARES
SSR	2	1.5
SSC	3	14.92
SSE	6	35.83
SST	11	52.25

Using this same technique, it is also possible to treat a two-way experiment with equal replication. In order to facilitate calculations, one must first construct, from the original X data table, a summary table that contains row, column, and cell totals.

Summary of Two Way ANOVA, Equal Number of Replications in Each Cell

Data

X_{111} X_{112} $\cdot$ $\cdot$ X_{11p}	$\cdots$ X_{ijk}	X_{1k1} X_{1k2} $\cdot$ $\cdot$ X_{1kp} $\cdot$ $\cdot$
X_{r11} X_{r12} $\cdot$ $\cdot$ X_{r1p}	$\cdots$	X_{rk1} X_{rk2} $\cdot$ $\cdot$ X_{rkp}

Summary Table

T_{11}	$\cdots$	T_{1k}	R_1
$\cdot$		$\cdot$	
$\cdot$	T_{ij}	$\cdot$	R_i
$\cdot$		$\cdot$	
T_{r1}	$\cdots$	T_{rk}	R_r
$C_1 \ldots$	$C_j \ldots$	C_k	

The symbols X_{ijk} mean the kth X value in cell (i, j). R_i and C_j are the sums of the rows and columns, respectively, each row or column being comprised of *cells* rather than single entries. The symbol T_{ij} is the total of all the X values in cell (i, j). That is,

$$T_{ij} = \sum_{k=1}^{p} X_{ijk} = X_{ij1} + X_{ij2} + \cdots + X_{ijp}$$

An example of how to apply the method is given in Problem 42. The concept is the same however. If we want the total sum of squares, we multiply σ^2 by $n = rkp$; for the row SS, multiply by r since there are r rows, but also divide by kp since each row total is actually the sum of k cells, each having p entries, for a total of kp X values comprising each row sum. Similarly, each column total is comprised of rp values and each cell total is comprised of p X values. Those quantities are the numbers that we divide by.

Table 4-8 is a summary table for this computational method.

TABLE 4-8. Computational Procedure

SOURCE OF VARIATION	SS	ORDER OF CALCULATION	DATA ENTRY	KEY SEQUENCE
Rows	SSR	(4)	$[R_i \boxed{\Sigma+}]$	$\boxed{\sigma_n}\boxed{x^2}\boxed{\times}\, r\boxed{\div}\, kp\boxed{=}$*$\boxed{+/-}\boxed{\text{SUM}}$ $\boxed{\text{CSR}}$
Columns	SSC	(5)	$[C_j \boxed{\Sigma+}]$	$\boxed{\sigma_n}\boxed{x^2}\boxed{\times}\, k\boxed{\div}\, rp\boxed{=}$*$\boxed{+/-}\boxed{\text{SUM}}$
Interaction	SSI	(6)	(2) − (4) − (5)	$\boxed{\text{RCL}}$
Subtotal	SS (cells)	(2)	$[T_{ij} \boxed{\Sigma+}]$	$\boxed{\sigma_n}\boxed{x^2}\boxed{\times}\, kr\boxed{\div}\, p\boxed{=}\boxed{+/-}\boxed{\text{SUM}}$ $\boxed{+/-}$
Exp. error	SSE	(3)	(1) − (2)	$\boxed{\text{EXC}}\boxed{\text{CSR}}$
Total	SST	(1)	$[X_{ijk} \boxed{\Sigma+}]$	$\boxed{\sigma_n}\boxed{x^2}\boxed{\times}\, n\boxed{=}\boxed{\text{STO}}\boxed{\text{CSR}}$

*Read and record SS value displayed at this point.

Solved Problems

AVERAGES AND VARIABILITY

1. Compute the arithmetic mean $\bar{x}$ and the median $\tilde{x}$ of the following data:

$$[5.7,\ 4.6,\ 9.6,\ 2.1,\ 35.3]$$

To get the median, the data must first be ordered:

$$2.1 \quad 4.6 \quad 5.7 \quad 9.6 \quad 35.3$$

The median $\tilde{x} = 5.7$, the middle number. To compute the mean, key

$$2.1\ \boxed{+}\ 4.6\ \boxed{+}\ 5.7\ \boxed{+}\ 9.6\ \boxed{+}\ 35.3\ \boxed{=}\ \boxed{\div}\ 5\ \boxed{=}$$

and read $\bar{x} = 11.46$. This could also be found using the statistics feature of some calculators, like this:

$$2.1\ \boxed{\Sigma+}\ 4.6\ \boxed{\Sigma+}\ 5.7\ \boxed{\Sigma+}\ 9.6\ \boxed{\Sigma+}\ 35.3\ \boxed{\Sigma+}\ \boxed{\text{2nd}}\ \boxed{\bar{x}}$$

Notice that the mean is much larger than the median. This is because the value $x = 35.3$ increased the mean, but did not affect the median.

2. The mean of 19 items was $\bar{x}_{19} = 4.26$. If an additional data point $x_{20} = 6.06$ is to be included among the items, what is the mean of the 20 items?

Use the formula

$$\bar{x}_{new} = \frac{n\bar{x}_{old} + x_{n+1}}{n + 1} = \frac{19(4.26) + 6.06}{20}$$

and compute

19 $\boxed{\times}$ 4.26 $\boxed{+}$ 6.06 $\boxed{=}$ $\boxed{\div}$ 20 $\boxed{=}$ reading $\bar{x}_{20} = 4.35$

3. Suppose the mean of 15 items is $\bar{x}_{15} = 8.92$ and three more data points $x_{16} = 7.03$, $x_{17} = 16.50$, and $x_{18} = 15.47$ are to be included. What is the mean $\bar{x}_{18}$ of the 18 items?

Use the formula

$$\bar{x}_{new} = \frac{nx_{old} + x_{n+1} + x_{n+2} + x_{n+3}}{n + 3}$$

$$= \frac{15(8.92) + 7.03 + 16.50 + 15.47}{18}$$

and compute

15 $\boxed{\times}$ 8.92 $\boxed{+}$ 7.03 $\boxed{+}$ 16.5 $\boxed{+}$ 15.47 $\boxed{=}$ $\boxed{\div}$ 18 $\boxed{=}$ and read $\bar{x}_{18} = 9.6$

4. Compute the geometric and harmonic mean of the data of Problem 1 and compare the result with the arithmetic mean previously computed.

The data are 2.1, 4.6, 5.7, 9.6, and 35.3 so that the geometric mean is given by the expression:

$$\bar{x}_G = \sqrt[5]{(2.1)(4.6)(5.7)(9.6)(35.3)}$$

which can be computed directly by keying

2.1 $\boxed{\times}$ 4.6 $\boxed{\times}$ 5.7 $\boxed{\times}$ 9.6 $\boxed{\times}$ 35.3 $\boxed{=}$ $\boxed{\text{INV}}$ $\boxed{y^x}$ 5 $\boxed{=}$

and read $\bar{x}_G$: $\boxed{\quad 7.1479184\quad}$. This could also have been computed by taking the arithmetic mean of the logarithms of the data and then taking the inverse log:

2.1 $\boxed{\log}$ $\boxed{+}$ 4.6 $\boxed{\log}$ $\boxed{+}$ 5.7 $\boxed{\log}$ $\boxed{+}$ 9.6 $\boxed{\log}$ $\boxed{+}$ 35.3 $\boxed{\log}$ $\boxed{=}$ $\boxed{\div}$ 5 $\boxed{=}$ $\boxed{\text{INV}}$ $\boxed{\log}$

This may seem longer, but the advantage is that, if we had many more data points, the direct method could easily overflow the calculator. For the harmonic mean we take the arithmetic mean of the reciprocals, and then take the reciprocal of the result:

2.1 $\boxed{1/x}$ $\boxed{+}$ 4.6 $\boxed{1/x}$ $\boxed{+}$ 5.7 $\boxed{1/x}$ $\boxed{+}$ 9.6 $\boxed{1/x}$ $\boxed{+}$ 35.3 $\boxed{1/x}$ $\boxed{=}$ $\boxed{\div}$ 5 $\boxed{=}$ $\boxed{1/x}$

The answer is $\bar{x}_H$: $\boxed{4.9924332}$

Comparing these results with that of Problem 1, we find that $\bar{x}_H < \bar{x}_G < \bar{x}$.

5. A man drives to his vacation spot at 60 mph and returns home via the same route at 40 mph. What is his average speed?

The answer is *not* 50 mph. The correct mean to use here is the harmonic mean since we are averaging rates. Thus we compute the harmonic mean of 40 and 60:

$$\bar{x}_H = \frac{1}{(1/60 + 1/40)/2}$$

by keying 60 $\boxed{1/x}$ $\boxed{+}$ 40 $\boxed{1/x}$ $\boxed{=}$ $\boxed{\div}$ 2 $\boxed{=}$ $\boxed{1/x}$ and find that the average speed is 48 mph.

6. The price of gasoline increased 3½ times in 5 years. What is the average percentage of increase per year?

This is a disguised geometric mean problem. Suppose that the actual rates for the 5 years are r_1, r_2, r_3, r_4, and r_5, and the original price is P. Then after 5 years the new price would be

$$P(1 + r_1)(1 + r_2)(1 + r_3)(1 + r_4)(1 + r_5) = 3.5P$$

The average rate is a decimal r such that

$$P(1 + r)^5 = 3.5P$$

In other words, the average rate is that rate which would have the same effect if the increase were the same each year. Solving for r, the initial price P cancels, and we get $r = \sqrt[5]{3.5} - 1$; so we compute

3.5 $\boxed{INV}$ $\boxed{y^x}$ 5 $\boxed{-}$ 1 $\boxed{=}$ and read r: $\boxed{0.2847352}$

which we interpret as approximately 28.5% per year.

7. A survey of 500 families produced the following data that summarize the number of children per family as a frequency distribution. Compute the arithmetic mean.

x = no. of children	0	1	2	3	4	5	6	7	8	9
f = no. of families with x children	70	90	105	85	75	40	25	7	2	1

This is computed as a weighted mean with the frequencies f as weights.

$$\bar{x} = \frac{\Sigma\,fx}{\Sigma\,f} = \frac{0\cdot70 + 1\cdot90 + 2\cdot105 + \cdots + 9\cdot1}{70 + 90 + 105 + \cdots + 1}$$

Since we are already told that the $\Sigma\,f = 500$, the denominator need not be computed, except as a check. If you have an AOS system, compute the sum of products in the numerator (leaving out $0\cdot70 = 0$ for convenience):

90 $\boxed{+}$ 2 $\boxed{\times}$ 105 $\boxed{+}$ 3 $\boxed{\times}$ 85 $\boxed{+}$ 4 $\boxed{\times}$ 75

$\boxed{+}$ 5 $\boxed{\times}$ 40 $\boxed{+}$ 6 $\boxed{\times}$ 25 $\boxed{+}$ 7 $\boxed{\times}$ 7 $\boxed{+}$ 8 $\boxed{\times}$ 2 $\boxed{+}$ 9 $\boxed{\times}$ 1 $\boxed{=}$

reading $\boxed{\qquad 1279.}$ Then divide by $\Sigma\,f = 500$:

$\boxed{\div}$ 500 $\boxed{=}$ and read $\bar{x} = 2.558$

8. For the following frequency distribution, compute the arithmetic mean, geometric mean, and the midrange.

x	1	3	5	7	11
f	8	15	7	4	2

The arithmetic mean is $\bar{x} = \Sigma\,fx/\Sigma f$. First compute $\Sigma f = 36$ and store that result in memory:

8 $\boxed{+}$ 15 $\boxed{+}$ 7 $\boxed{+}$ 4 $\boxed{+}$ 2 $\boxed{=}$ $\boxed{\text{STO}}$

Now compute $\Sigma\,fx$ (AOS systems):

1 $\boxed{\times}$ 8 $\boxed{+}$ 3 $\boxed{\times}$ 15 $\boxed{+}$ 5 $\boxed{\times}$ 7 $\boxed{+}$ 7 $\boxed{\times}$ 14 $\boxed{+}$ 11 $\boxed{\times}$ 2 $\boxed{=}$

and read $\Sigma\,fx = 138$. Divide this value, still displayed, by $\Sigma\,f$, still stored in memory:

$\boxed{\div}$ $\boxed{\text{RCL}}$ $\boxed{=}$ and read $\bar{x}$: $\boxed{\qquad 3.8333333}$

The geometric mean $\bar{x}_G = \sqrt[n]{x_1, x_2, \ldots x_{36}}$, but since the data are grouped by frequencies with five x values, we can rewrite the formula as

$$\bar{x}_G = \sqrt[n]{x_1^{f_1} \, x_2^{f_2} \, x_3^{f_3} \, x_4^{f_4} \, x_5^{f_5}}, \qquad \text{where } n = \Sigma f$$

$$= \sqrt[36]{1^8 (3)^{15} (5)^7 (7)^4 (11)^2}$$

This is more easily computed using logarithms:

$$\log \bar{x}_G = \frac{1}{36} (8 \log 1 + 15 \log 3 + 7 \log 5 + 4 \log 7 + 2 \log 11)$$

which we compute and then take the antilog (inverse log). Note first that log $1 = 0$, so the first term need not be keyed in. We include it, however, to show a typical complete key sequence:

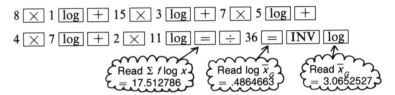

Notice that if we try to compute $\bar{x}_G$ directly, before taking the thirty-sixth root we would have 3.2568×10^{17} displayed. Clearly, if we had more data, we would very likely overflow the calculator. Using the logarithmic method overcomes this. The midrange is simply $(1 + 11)/2 = 6$, far from the other means.

9. Compute the mean, variance, and standard deviation of the following population data: 1.2, 3.4, 3.7, 3.8, 5.2, 6.1, 9.2, 10.0. Also compare the standard deviation with the range.

We shall show the calculation both without and with built-in statistical functions. It is helpful to view the data in a tabular form to guide in the calculation of $\bar{x} = \Sigma x/n$ and $\sigma^2 = 1/n \, \Sigma (x - \bar{x})^2 = 1/n \, (\Sigma x^2 - n\bar{x}^2)$.

X	X^2
1.2	1.44
3.4	11.56
3.7	13.69
3.8	14.44
5.2	27.04
6.1	37.21
9.2	84.64
10.0	100.00

We need the X and X^2 columns in the table. With a calculator with memory, the individual squares need not be recorded but are shown here so that the intervening quantities computed during the calculation may be identified by the reader. In order to get $\Sigma\ x$ and $\Sigma\ x^2$ simultaneously, key

1.2 [STO] [x²] [+]

3.4 [SUM] [x²] [+]

3.7 [SUM] [x²] [+]

3.8 [SUM] [x²] [+]

5.2 [SUM] [x²] [+]

6.1 [SUM] [x²] [+]

9.2 [SUM] [x²] [+]

10 [SUM] [x²] [=]   and read $\Sigma\ x^2$:   [290.02]

Now key [EXC] and read $\Sigma\ x$: [42.6]. Then key [÷] 8 [=] and read $\bar{x}$: [5.325]. To compute $\sigma^2 = 1/n\ (\Sigma\ x^2 - n\bar{x}^2)$, remember that $\Sigma\ x^2$ is still in memory and $\bar{x}$ is displayed, so key (AOS system)

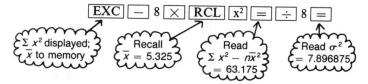

and then key [√x̄] in order to compute σ: [2.8101379]. The range is just $x_{max} - x_{min} = 10 - 1.2 = 8.8$. This is about three standard deviations.

If you have a statistical calculator, the calculations are much easier. Just start by entering the data:

1.2 [Σ+] 3.4 [Σ+] 3.7 [Σ+] 3.8 [Σ+] 5.2 [Σ+] 6.1 [Σ+] 9.2 [Σ+]
10 [Σ+]

and read $n = 8$. To compute $\bar{x}$, key [2nd] [x̄] (or possibly [2nd] [mean]). To compute the population standard deviation σ, key [2nd] [σ_n] and then square the result by keying [x²] to obtain the corresponding variance.

10. Compute the sum of squares $\displaystyle\sum (x - \bar{x})^2 = \Sigma\ x^2 - n\bar{x}^2$ for the data of Problem 9.

We have already computed the answer during the calculation without the statistical functions on the calculator. However, if we wish to obtain this quantity from the automatically computed functions, we observe that $\Sigma(x - \bar{x})^2 = n\sigma^2$. Thus, multiply the variance by $n = 8$. It may be necessary to clear statistical registers by keying $\boxed{\text{2nd}}$ $\boxed{\text{CSR}}$ to unlock the $\boxed{\times}$ key on some calculators. Do not clear the display! For example, the key sequence, after the data have been entered, might look like this:

$$\boxed{\text{2nd}} \; \boxed{\sigma_n} \; \boxed{x^2} \; \boxed{\text{2nd}} \; \boxed{\text{CSR}} \; \boxed{\times} \; 8 \; \boxed{=}$$

and the result should be the sum of squares, in this example, 63.175.

11. Compute both s and σ for the data 5, 6, 7, 10, and 15 using the statistical functions on the calculator.

First enter the data:

$$5 \; \boxed{\Sigma+} \; 6 \; \boxed{\Sigma+} \; 7 \; \boxed{\Sigma+} \; 10 \; \boxed{\Sigma+} \; 15 \; \boxed{\Sigma+} \quad \text{and read } n = 5$$

To compute σ, key $\boxed{\text{2nd}}$ $\boxed{\sigma_n}$ or possibly $\boxed{\text{2nd}}$ $\boxed{\sigma}$. You may have to key $\boxed{\text{VAR}}$ $\boxed{\sqrt{x}}$ if your calculator computes the variance first with the denominator n, so that you must take the square root in order to obtain the standard deviation. In any event, the result is $\sigma = 3.611094$. To compute s, key $\boxed{\text{2nd}}$ $\boxed{\sigma_{n-1}}$ or $\boxed{\text{2nd}}$ $\boxed{s}$ or possibly $\boxed{\text{2nd}}$ $\boxed{\text{SD}}$, depending on the key configuration, and read $s = 4.0373258$.

12. Compute the coefficient of variation for the data in Problem 11 using the statistical functions on the calculator.

After entering the data using the $\boxed{\Sigma+}$ key, as described in Problem 11, compute the mean $\bar{x}$ and store it in memory by keying $\boxed{\text{2nd}}$ $\boxed{\bar{x}}$ $\boxed{\text{STO}}$; then compute s by keying $\boxed{\text{2nd}}$ $\boxed{\sigma_{n-1}}$ (or equivalent keys). Since the coefficient of variation CV $= s/\bar{x}$, we must divide the value of s displayed by the value of $\bar{x}$ stored in memory. It may be necessary on some calculators to clear statistics registers (not the display) at this point in order to unlock the division key. This is done by keying $\boxed{\text{2nd}}$ $\boxed{\text{CSR}}$ on some calculators. Try to do the division without doing this to see if it is necessary on your calculator. If it is, the entire key sequence, from the point after the data are entered, would be

$$\boxed{\text{2nd}} \; \boxed{\bar{x}} \; \boxed{\text{STO}} \; \boxed{\text{2nd}} \; \boxed{\sigma_{n-1}} \; \boxed{\text{2nd}} \; \boxed{\text{CSR}} \; \boxed{\div} \; \boxed{\text{RCL}} \; \boxed{=}$$

and we find that CV $= .4694565$. If your calculator does not require the clearing, omit that operation.

STATISTICS FOR SAMPLING

13. For the following sample of nine data points, compute the mean $\bar{x}$, the sample standard deviation s_x, and the standard error of the mean

$s_{\bar{x}}$. The data are 1.2, 3.0, 4.5, 4.6, 5.7, 5.8, 5.9, 6.2, and 9.8. Use the statistics functions built into your calculator. First enter the data:

$$1.2 \;\boxed{\Sigma+}\; 3 \;\boxed{\Sigma+}\; 4.5 \;\boxed{\Sigma+}\; 4.6 \;\boxed{\Sigma+}\; 5.7 \;\boxed{\Sigma+}$$

$$5.8 \;\boxed{\Sigma+}\; 5.9 \;\boxed{\Sigma+}\; 6.2 \;\boxed{\Sigma+}\; 9.8 \;\boxed{\Sigma+}$$

The number of data points entered will be displayed. Now compute $\bar{x}$ by keying $\boxed{\text{2nd}}\;\boxed{\bar{x}}$ and read $\boxed{5.1888889}$.

Compute the standard deviation s_x by keying $\boxed{\text{2nd}}\;\boxed{\sigma_{n-1}}$ and then read s_x: $\boxed{2.370361}$ (*Note*: If you don't have statistical functions, you can use the methods of Problem 9 to compute these quantities.) To compute the standard error of the mean, use the formula

$$s_{\bar{x}} = \frac{s_x}{\sqrt{n}} = \frac{2.37036}{\sqrt{9}}$$

Since $s_x = 2.370361$ is still displayed, the calculation is simple, but you may have to key $\boxed{\text{2nd}}\;\boxed{\text{CSR}}$, which clears the statistical registers and unlocks the division key; then key $\boxed{\div}\; 9 \;\boxed{\sqrt{x}}\;\boxed{=}$ and read the standard error of the mean: $\boxed{0.7901203}$.

14. For the data of Problem 13, use the results of the statistical functions and modify them to derive the values of $\Sigma\, x$ and $\Sigma\, x^2$.

Since $\bar{x} = \Sigma\, x/n$, we know that $\Sigma\, x = n\bar{x}$. Moreover, $\sigma_x^2 = (\Sigma x^2 - n\bar{x}^2)/n$ and thus $\Sigma\, x^2 = n(\sigma_x^2 + \bar{x}^2)$. After the data are entered (as in Problem 13), first compute σ_x, store it, then compute $\bar{x}$. This has both main quantities available, since it may be necessary to clear statistics registers in order to complete calculations. We compute as if this were the case:

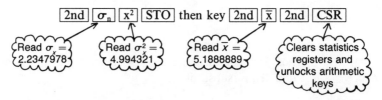

Now with $\bar{x}$ still displayed, multiply by $n = 9$ by keying $\boxed{\times}\; 9 \;\boxed{=}$ and read $\Sigma\, x = 46.7$. Now we need $\bar{x}$ back again to compute $\Sigma\, x^2 = n(\sigma_x^2 + \bar{x}^{\,2})$ so divide by 9 and proceed with the calculation:

$$\boxed{\div}\; 9 \;\boxed{=}\;\boxed{x^2}\;\boxed{\text{SUM}}\;\boxed{\text{RCL}}\;\boxed{\times}\; 9 \;\boxed{=} \quad \text{and read } \Sigma\, x^2 = 287.27$$

(*Note*: Some multimemory calculators give these sums automatically so that this process becomes unnecessary. It may be handy to know, however, if it ever becomes necessary to reconstruct these quantities.)

15. A sample of 25 observations has a mean of 10.5 and a sample standard deviation of 3.8. Compute $s_{\bar{x}}$, the standard error of the mean.

$$s_{\bar{x}} = \frac{s_x}{\sqrt{n}} = \frac{3.8}{\sqrt{25}}$$

So key 3.8 $\boxed{\div}$ 25 $\boxed{\sqrt{x}}$ $\boxed{=}$ and read $s_{\bar{x}}$ = .76. Notice that the mean $\bar{x}$ had nothing to do with this calculation and was only a "red herring."

16. A sample of 25 observations from a population with mean $\mu_x = 8.2$ produces a sample mean of 10.5. If the population has a standard deviation $\sigma_x = 3.8$, compute the z score corresponding to $\bar{x}$.

Now $\mu_{\bar{x}} = \mu_x = 8.2$ and $\sigma_{\bar{x}} = \sigma_x/\sqrt{n}$; so

$$z = \frac{\bar{x} - \mu_{\bar{x}}}{\sigma_{\bar{x}}} = \frac{10.5 - 8.2}{3.8/\sqrt{25}} = \frac{(10.5 - 8.2)\sqrt{25}}{3.8}$$

Thus, to compute z, key

10.5 $\boxed{-}$ 8.2 $\boxed{=}$ $\boxed{\times}$ 25 $\boxed{\sqrt{x}}$ $\boxed{\div}$ 3.8 $\boxed{=}$ and read $\boxed{3.0263158}$

which we round to two decimal places: $z = 3.03$.

17. A simple random sample from a normal population produces a mean $\bar{x} = 8.1$. If the population standard deviation is $\sigma_x = 1.3$, compute a 95% confidence interval for μ_x if (a) $n = 20$, and (b) $n = 80$.

The formula for the required confidence interval is

$$\bar{x} \pm \frac{z\sigma_x}{\sqrt{n}}$$

For 95% confidence, $z = 1.96$ from tables of the normal distribution. Thus, substituting:

(a) $8.1 \pm \frac{(1.96)(1.3)}{\sqrt{20}}$,   (b) $8.1 \pm \frac{(1.96)(1.3)}{\sqrt{80}}$

Computing each of these:
(a) 1.96 $\boxed{\times}$ 1.3 $\boxed{\div}$ 20 $\boxed{\sqrt{x}}$ $\boxed{=}$ $\boxed{STO}$
8.1 $\boxed{+}$ $\boxed{RCL}$ $\boxed{=}$ and read the upper limit: $\boxed{8.6697501}$
8.1 $\boxed{-}$ $\boxed{RCL}$ $\boxed{=}$ and read the lower limit: $\boxed{7.5302499}$
Thus rounded to two decimal places the 95% confidence interval is (7.53, 8.38).

(b) The calculation is exactly the same as in part (a), except that the 20 is replaced by 80.

$1.96 \boxed{\times} 1.3 \boxed{\div} 80 \boxed{\sqrt{x}} \boxed{=} \boxed{\text{STO}}$

$8.1 \boxed{+} \boxed{\text{RCL}} \boxed{=}$ and read the upper limit: $\boxed{\quad 8.3848751}$

$8.1 \boxed{-} \boxed{\text{RCL}} \boxed{=}$ and read the lower limit: $\boxed{\quad 7.8151249}$

Thus for $n = 80$, a 95% confidence interval for μ_x is (7.82, 8.38), rounded to two decimal places. Notice that *quadrupling* the sample size had the effect of cutting the confidence interval length in *half*.

18. Use the algebraic fact that $(a + b) - 2b = a - b$ to shorten the calculation of a 95% confidence interval for μ_x if $\bar{x} = 45.7$, $\sigma_x = 5$, and $n = 30$.

The limits are given by $\bar{x} \pm z\sigma_x/\sqrt{n} = 45.7 \pm (1.96)(5)/\sqrt{30}$.
First compute and store $z\sigma_x/\sqrt{n} = (1.96)(5)/\sqrt{30}$.

$$1.96 \boxed{\times} 5 \boxed{\div} 30 \boxed{\sqrt{x}} \boxed{=} \boxed{\text{STO}}$$

Then add $\bar{x}$: $\boxed{+} 45.7 \boxed{=}$, and read the upper limit: $\boxed{\quad 47.489227}$. Now to get the lower limit subtract *twice* $z\sigma_x/\sqrt{n}$ from the displayed value (the upper limit). The technique for doing this varies depending on whether your calculator has an AOS or an arithmetic entry system. For AOS systems, key

$$\boxed{-} 2 \boxed{\times} \boxed{\text{RCL}} \boxed{=} \text{ reading the lower limit: } \boxed{\quad 43.910773}$$

For arithmetic systems, with parentheses, key

$$\boxed{-} \boxed{(} 2 \boxed{\times} \boxed{\text{RCL}} \boxed{)} \boxed{=}$$

and if you don't have parentheses, key

$$\boxed{\text{EXC}} \boxed{\times} 2 \boxed{+/-} \boxed{+} \boxed{\text{RCL}} \boxed{=}$$

19. A sample produces the following data: 2.2, 3.1, 3.7, 4.3, and 4.4. Compute a 90% confidence interval for the population mean μ. The limits for the confidence interval have the form

$$\bar{x} \pm \frac{t(4)s_x}{\sqrt{5}}$$

where the (4) denotes the degrees of freedom of t. We look up the value at the 95th percentile since we want 5% in each tail, leaving 90% for the confidence level. Read in a table of the Student t distribution the value $t_{.95}(4) = 2.132$. Using the statistical functions, enter the data and compute $\bar{x}$ and s_x as follows:

$2.2 \boxed{\Sigma+} 3.1 \boxed{\Sigma+} 3.7 \boxed{\Sigma+} 4.3 \boxed{\Sigma+} 4.4 \boxed{\Sigma+}$ (read $n = 5$)

Now key $\boxed{\text{2nd}}$ $\boxed{\bar{x}}$ $\boxed{\text{STO}}$ and read $\bar{x} = 3.54$ (now stored) and then key $\boxed{\text{2nd}}$ $\boxed{\sigma_{n-1}}$ and read $s_x = .9126883$. If necessary, clear the statistical registers by pressing $\boxed{\text{2nd}}$ $\boxed{\text{CSR}}$. Now s_x is displayed, $\bar{x}$ is in memory, so we key

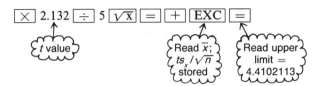

and then key $\boxed{-}$ 2 $\boxed{\times}$ $\boxed{\text{RCL}}$ $\boxed{=}$ and read the lower limit = 2.6697887. Note that we have used the shortcut described in Problem 19: $a - b = a + b - 2b$. The last key sequence is for AOS systems. (For other ways, see Problem 17, and see Problem 18 for using other systems.) Thus a 90% confidence interval for μ is (2.67, 4.41) rounded to two decimal places.

20. A sample of size $n = 10$ gives the point estimate $s_x^2 = 8.46$. Compute a 95% confidence interval for σ_x^2 and σ_x.

    The confidence interval depends on the chi-square distribution and is given by the formula

    $$\frac{s_x^2}{\chi_{1-\alpha/2}^2/df} < \sigma_x^2 < \frac{s_x^2}{\chi_{\alpha/2}^2/df}$$

    where $\chi_{1-\alpha/2}^2 = \chi_{.975}^2(9) = 19.02$ and $\chi_{\alpha/2}^2 = \chi_{.025}^2(9) = 2.70$ from a table of percentage points of the χ^2 (chi-squared) distribution, $df = 9$. The lower limit is

    8.46 $\boxed{\div}$ 19.02 $\boxed{\times}$ 9 $\boxed{=}$ reading $\boxed{4.0031546}$

    and the upper limit is

    8.46 $\boxed{\div}$ 2.7 $\boxed{\times}$ 9 $\boxed{=}$ reading $\boxed{28.2}$

    Take the square roots of these to get limits for σ_x.

21. A seed company samples 50 seeds from a harvest and finds that 42 of them germinate within 10 days after planting. Compute (a) a point estimate $\hat{p}$ of p, the proportion of seeds from the harvest that will germinate within 10 days of planting, and (b) a 99% confidence interval for p.

    (a) $\hat{p} = x/n = 42/50$, so key 42 $\boxed{\div}$ 50 $\boxed{=}$, which give $\hat{p} = .84$; that is, we estimate that 84% of the seeds will germinate.

(b) Since $n > 30$, we can use a normal approximation. Thus with a ½ % upper and lower tail, we have $z = 2.576$ from a table of the normal distribution, and the confidence interval is given by

$$\hat{p} - z\sqrt{\frac{\hat{p}\hat{q}}{n}} \le p \le \hat{p} + z\sqrt{\frac{\hat{p}\hat{q}}{n}}$$

with $n = 50$, $\hat{p} = .84$, $\hat{q} = 1 - \hat{p} = 1 - .84 = .16$. So first compute the radical, then multiply by z, and finally add (and subtract) that result from $\hat{p}$.

.84 $\boxed{\times}$ .16 $\boxed{\div}$ 50 $\boxed{=}$ $\boxed{\sqrt{x}}$ $\boxed{\times}$ 2.576 $\boxed{=}$ $\boxed{\text{STO}}$ $\boxed{+}$ .84 $\boxed{=}$
and read the upper limit: $\boxed{0.973555}$

.84 $\boxed{-}$ $\boxed{\text{RCL}}$ $\boxed{=}$ and the lower limit: $\boxed{0.7064449}$

Thus, approximately, $.706 \le p \le .974$ is a 99% confidence interval for the population proportion p.

INFERENCE (HYPOTHESIS TESTING)

22. A sample of size $n = 50$ is randomly selected from a normal population with $\sigma = 2.5$. A sample mean $\bar{x} = 45.3$ is observed. Test the hypothesis $H_0 : \mu = 48$ against the alternative $H_1: \mu \ne 48$, using $\alpha = .01$.

The test statistic is

$$z = \frac{\bar{x} - \mu}{\sigma_{\bar{x}}} = \frac{\bar{x} - \mu}{\sigma_x/\sqrt{n}} = \frac{45.3 - 48}{2.5/\sqrt{50}}$$

We change it for computational convenience into the form

$$z = \frac{(45.3 - 48)\sqrt{50}}{2.5}$$

Thus, to compute z, key 45.3 $\boxed{-}$ 48 $\boxed{=}$ $\boxed{\times}$ 50 $\boxed{\sqrt{x}}$ $\boxed{\div}$ 2.5 $\boxed{=}$ and read $\boxed{-7.6367532}$. Since $\alpha = .01$, the critical values are $z_{\alpha/2} = z_{.005} = -2.576$ and $z_{1-.005} = z_{.975} = +2.576$ from a table of the normal distribution. Since $z_{\text{observed}} = -7.6 < z_{.005} = -2.576$, we reject H_0 in favor of the alternative and conclude that the sample is unlikely to have been drawn from a population with mean $\mu = 48$, $\sigma = 2.5$.

23. A random sample of size $n = 18$ is taken from a normal population with variance $= 3$. If we observe $\bar{x} = 20.5$, test the hypothesis H_0: $\mu = 20$ against the (one-sided) alternative $H_1: \mu > 20$ at the 5% significance level.

Since the variance $\sigma^2 = 3$, $\sigma = \sqrt{3}$, and thus the test statistic is

$$z = \frac{\bar{x} - \mu}{\sigma/\sqrt{n}} = \frac{20.5 - 20}{\sqrt{3}/\sqrt{18}} = \frac{(20.5 - 20)\sqrt{18}}{\sqrt{3}}$$

and we compute

$$20.5 \boxed{-} 20 \boxed{=} \boxed{\times} 18 \boxed{\sqrt{x}} \boxed{\div} 3 \boxed{\sqrt{x}} \boxed{=}$$

and read $z_{observed} = 1.2245449$. From tables, $z_{critical} = z_{.95} = 1.645$. Since $z_{observed} < z_{.95}$, we accept H_0 and conclude that there is insufficient evidence to conflict with $\mu = 20$.

24. A random sample is selected from a normal population. The x data are 27, 36, 52, 48, 25, and 42. Test the hypothesis H_0: $\mu = 40$ against the alternative hypothesis H_1: $\mu \neq 40$ at the 10% level of significance.

This requires a two-tailed test with $\alpha = .10$. Since σ is not given (or unknown), we must estimate it, as well as μ, from the sample data. Then we use the Student t as the test statistic:

$$z = \frac{\bar{x} - \mu_0}{s/\sqrt{n}} = \frac{\bar{x} - 40}{s/\sqrt{6}} = \frac{(\bar{x} - 40)\sqrt{6}}{s}$$

If you have a statistics calculator, compute $\bar{x}$ and s as follows (if not, use the method shown in Problem 9):

$$27 \boxed{\Sigma+} 36 \boxed{\Sigma+} 52 \boxed{\Sigma+} 48 \boxed{\Sigma+} 25 \boxed{\Sigma+} 42 \boxed{\Sigma+}$$
and read $n = 6$

Then key $\boxed{2nd}$ $\boxed{\sigma_{n-1}}$ $\boxed{STO}$ and read $s = 11.00303$, which is stored in memory. Now key $\boxed{2nd}$ $\boxed{\bar{x}}$ and read $\bar{x} = 38.333333$, which is left displayed. In order to compute t we must first (on some calculators) clear statistics registers by keying $\boxed{2nd}$ $\boxed{CSR}$, which also unlocks the arithmetic functions. Now $\bar{x}$ is displayed and s is in memory, so in order to compute t, key

$$\boxed{-} 40 \boxed{=} \boxed{\times} 6 \boxed{\sqrt{x}} \boxed{\div} \boxed{RCL} \boxed{=}$$

and read $t_{observed} = -.3710326$. The degrees of freedom is $df = n - 1 = 6 - 1 = 5$ and the critical value is $t_{1-\alpha}(5) = t_{1-.10}(5) = t_{.90}(5) = 1.476$ from a table of the t distribution. Since $t_{observed}$ is clearly less than the critical value, we cannot reject H_0 and must conclude that $\mu = 40$.

(*Note*: On some calculators you cannot use the memory when in statistics mode. In that case, write down $\bar{x}$ and s; then key the values in directly once you have taken the calculator out of the statistics mode.)

25. Ten compressors are checked and found to have an average maximum output of 135 CFM (cubic feet per minute). Another shipment of 12 of the same model compressor is found to have an average maximum of 128 CFM. The manufacturer reports that the standard deviation is 5 CFM. Assuming that to be correct, is the pressure of the second shipment lower than that which might be expected by chance? Use a 5% significance level.

We test the hypothesis $H_0: \mu_1 = \mu_2$ against the alternative $H_1: \mu_1 > \mu_2$ by using the test statistic

$$ z = \frac{\bar{x}_1 - \bar{x}_2}{\sigma \sqrt{\dfrac{1}{n_1} + \dfrac{1}{n_2}}} = \frac{133 - 128}{5 \sqrt{\dfrac{1}{10} + \dfrac{1}{12}}} $$

and the critical value is $z_{.95} = 1.645$. Compute the observed value of z by keying

$$ 10 \boxed{1/x} \boxed{+} 12 \boxed{1/x} \boxed{=} \boxed{\sqrt{x}} \boxed{STO} \; 135 \boxed{-} 128 \boxed{=} $$
$$ \boxed{\div} \boxed{RCL} \boxed{=} $$

and read z: $\boxed{\quad 3.2696956 \quad}$. Since $z > 1.645$, we reject the null hypothesis H_0 and conclude that the second shipment has a lower average than the first (at least more than one expects by chance).

26. A new type of cattle feed is compared with an accepted standard by randomly allocating 10 cows to each diet and comparing the weight gains. The weight gains are shown in the table. Test whether the new feed produces a greater weight gain that the old diet.

(1)	New feed	59	64	62	61	56	65	64	60	62	61
(2)	Old feed	58	59	60	56	59	54	61	58	62	59

First compute the means and standard deviations for each group. Enter data for group 1:

$$ 59 \boxed{\Sigma+} 64 \boxed{\Sigma+} 62 \boxed{\Sigma+} 61 \boxed{\Sigma+} 56 \boxed{\Sigma+} 65 \boxed{\Sigma+} 64 \boxed{\Sigma+} $$
$$ 60 \boxed{\Sigma+} 62 \boxed{\Sigma+} 61 \boxed{\Sigma+} $$

and then compute

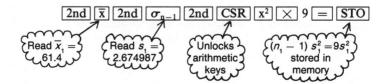

Read $\bar{x}_1 =$ 61.4   Read $s_1 =$ 2.674987   Unlocks arithmetic keys $(n_1 - 1) s_1^2 = 9s_1^2$ stored in memory

Enter data for group 2:

58 $\boxed{\Sigma+}$ 59 $\boxed{\Sigma+}$ 60 $\boxed{\Sigma+}$ 56 $\boxed{\Sigma+}$ 59 $\boxed{\Sigma+}$ 54 $\boxed{\Sigma+}$ 61 $\boxed{\Sigma+}$
58 $\boxed{\Sigma+}$ 62 $\boxed{\Sigma+}$ 59 $\boxed{\Sigma+}$

and then compute

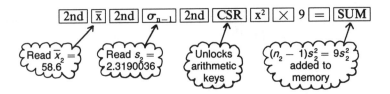

Now compute the pooled standard deviation

$$s_p = \sqrt{\dfrac{(n_1 - 1)s_1^2 + (n_2 - 1)s_2^2}{n_1 + n_2 - 2}}$$

Key $\boxed{\text{RCL}}$ $\boxed{\div}$ 18 $\boxed{=}$ $\boxed{\sqrt{x}}$ $\boxed{\text{STO}}$ and read $s_p = 2.5033311$, which is stored. Now that we have all the required values, we compute the statistic

$$t = \dfrac{\bar{x}_1 - \bar{x}_2}{s_p\sqrt{\dfrac{1}{n_1} + \dfrac{1}{n_2}}}$$

by first finishing the calculation of the denominator and then dividing it into the difference of the means computed earlier:

10 $\boxed{1/x}$ $\boxed{+}$ 10 $\boxed{1/x}$ $\boxed{=}$ $\boxed{\sqrt{x}}$ $\boxed{\times}$ $\boxed{\text{RCL}}$ $\boxed{=}$ $\boxed{\text{STO}}$ 61.4 $\boxed{-}$
58.6 $\boxed{=}$ $\boxed{\div}$ $\boxed{\text{RCL}}$ $\boxed{=}$ and read $t = 2.5010636$

The critical value of t is $t_{.95}(18) = 1.734$ from a table. Since the observed (computed) value of t exceeds the critical value, we reject the hypothesis of no difference and conclude that the new feed produces a greater weight gain than the old feed.

27. A certain drug is claimed to lower blood pressure within 20 minutes; thus as part of the data the systolic blood pressure is measured on 10 men both before the drug is administered and 20 minutes afterward. From the following data, test whether the drug appears to do as claimed with $\alpha = 5\%$.

BEFORE	AFTER	$d_i = $ AFTER $\boxed{-}$ BEFORE $\boxed{=}$
152	148	−4
146	132	−14
140	140	0
142	130	−12
168	145	−23
138	140	+2
150	129	−21
135	140	+5
145	140	−5
144	128	−12

The test statistic is

$$t = \frac{\overline{x}_{after} - \overline{x}_{before}}{s_{\overline{d}}}$$

$$= \frac{\overline{d}}{s_d/\sqrt{n}} = \frac{\overline{d}\sqrt{n}}{s_d}$$

Since we have first computed the differences d_i, just enter them as data. Then the calculator will automatically give $\overline{d}$ and s_d as needed. Also, since most of the differences are negative, it is a bit of a bother to key $\boxed{+/-}$ each time. You can enter the opposite sign (as if $d_i = $ before − after) and get the same result except for the sign of $\overline{d}$. Hence first enter the data d_i using the opposite sign:

$$4\,\boxed{\Sigma+}\,14\,\boxed{\Sigma+}\,0\,\boxed{\Sigma+}\,12\,\boxed{\Sigma+}\,23\,\boxed{\Sigma+}\,2\,\boxed{+/-}\,\boxed{\Sigma+}\,21\,\boxed{\Sigma+}$$
$$5\,\boxed{+/-}\,\boxed{\Sigma+}\,5\,\boxed{\Sigma+}\,12\,\boxed{\Sigma+}$$

and now complete the calculation of t (and don't forget that you must mentally change the sign of the result, since that is what was done to the data):

$$\boxed{2nd}\,\boxed{\sigma_{n-1}}\,\boxed{STO}\,\boxed{2nd}\,\boxed{\overline{x}}\,\boxed{2nd}\,\boxed{CSR}\,\boxed{\times}\,10\,\boxed{\sqrt{x}}\,\boxed{\div}$$
$$\boxed{RCL}\,\boxed{=}$$

and read the negative of t: $\boxed{2.7855934}$; thus $t = -2.7855934$. We have a one-sided test (at the left tail of the distribution) since we wish to test for lowering of blood pressure only. The critical value is $t_{.05}\,(9) = -1.833$ from tables. Since the computed value is farther into the tail of the distribution, we reject the no difference hypothesis and conclude that the drug apparently lowers systolic blood pressure as claimed. This test is known as the *paired t test*.

Statistics **28.** Using the χ^2 distribution, test the hypothesis H_0: $\sigma^2 = 10$ if a sample of size $n = 12$ produces a sample variance $s^2 = 18$. Use the one-sided alternative H_1: $\sigma^2 > 10$ at a 5% level of significance.

The test statistic is

$$\chi^2 = \frac{(n-1)s^2}{\sigma_0^2} = \frac{(12-1)18}{10}$$

and so key

$$11\ \boxed{\times}\ 18\ \boxed{\div}\ 10\ \boxed{=}\quad \text{and read } \chi^2 = 19.8\ (df = 11)$$

The critical value is $\chi^2_{.95}\,(11) = 19.68$ and the computed value just barely exceeds this. Thus, at the 5% level, we conclude that $\sigma^2 > 10$.

29. An experiment is performed to test whether certain characteristics occur in a ratio of 9 : 3 : 3 : 1. The experiment produces 256 objects with the observed frequencies shown in the table. The theoretical relative frequencies are $9/16$, $3/16$, $3/16$, and $1/16$, so the expected frequencies are these fractions of 256. Test whether the observed results fit the expected frequencies.

OBSERVED	EXPECTED
148	144
45	48
46	48
17	16

First compute the χ^2 statistic

$$\sum \frac{(O-E)^2}{E} = \frac{(148-144)^2}{144} + \frac{(45-48)^2}{48} + \frac{(46-48)^2}{48}$$
$$+ \frac{(17-16)^2}{16}$$

Since the subtractions are easily done *mentally* in this example, we compute (AOS system)

$$4\ \boxed{x^2}\ \boxed{\div}\ 144\ \boxed{+}\ 3\ \boxed{x^2}\ \boxed{\div}\ 48\ \boxed{+}\ 2\ \boxed{x^2}\ \boxed{\div}\ 48\ \boxed{+}\ 1\ \boxed{\div}\ 16\ \boxed{=}$$

(If you have a sequential-type entry system, either use parentheses or accumulate the sum in the memory.) The result is $\chi^2 = .4444444$. The degrees of freedom $df = 4 - 1 = 3$. With such a small value of χ^2, it is impossible to reject the null hypothesis, so we conclude that the observed frequencies fit the expected frequencies.

30. Fifty hip replacement patients were divided into two equal groups after surgery. One group was given low doses of heparin (an anticoagulant) and the other was given a placebo (nonactive substance). It was observed how many developed blood clots of the legs during the recuperative period. Test whether the treatment group (heparin) is the same as the control group (placebo) at the 5% level.

	PLACEBO	HEPARIN	TOTAL
Clots	18	14	32
No Clots	7	11	18
Total	25	25	50

We compute

$$\chi^2 = \frac{50 \, (18 \cdot 11 - 7 \cdot 14)^2}{25 \cdot 25 \cdot 18 \cdot 32}$$

by keying

$$18 \; \boxed{\times} \; 11 \; \boxed{-} \; \boxed{(} \; 7 \; \boxed{\times} \; 14 \; \boxed{=} \; \boxed{x^2} \; \boxed{\times} \; 50 \; \boxed{\div} \; 25 \; \boxed{x^2} \; \boxed{\div}$$
$$18 \; \boxed{\div} \; 32 \; \boxed{=}$$

and read $\chi^2 = 1.3888889 < \chi^2_{.95}(1) = 3.841$ from tables. Thus we have insufficient evidence to reject the null hypothesis of no difference.

31. Two blood pressure medications are to be tested to see if they have similar efficacy in lowering blood pressure. A group of 50 patients is randomly divided into two groups. Half will get drug A first; then after a washout period they will get drug B. The other group will get drug B first, then drug A. Thus all patients get to try both drugs. This is called a *crossover design*. Analyze the data in the table using a χ^2 test at the 5% level of significance.

		DRUG A		
		Lowers BP	Does not Lower BP	
DRUG B	Lowers BP	2	28	30
	Does Not Lower BP	8	12	20
	Total	10	40	50

Since all patients get both drugs, the two cells on the main diagonal (the 2 and the 12) contain no information about the difference of drug A versus drug B, so we omit them from the calculation. The χ^2 statistic for this design can be computed in two ways:

Method 1 First compute the expected values for the pertinent cells. If the drugs were alike (null hypothesis) we would expect the off-diagonal elements to be equal, in particular $\frac{1}{2}(8 + 28) = \frac{1}{2}(36) = 18$. Thus

$$\chi^2 = \frac{(28 - 18)^2}{18} + \frac{(8 - 18)^2}{18}$$

which is easily computed as

$$8 \boxed{-} 18 \boxed{=} \boxed{x^2} \boxed{STO} 28 \boxed{-} 18 \boxed{=} \boxed{x^2} \boxed{SUM}$$
$$\boxed{RCL} \boxed{\div} 18 \boxed{=}$$

and read $\chi^2 = 11.111111$. Notice that we divided by 18 last since both divisors were the same.

Method 2 McNemar's version of the test statistic is

$$\chi^2 = \frac{(b - c)^2}{b + c} = \frac{(28 - 8)^2}{28 + 8} = \frac{(20)^2}{36}$$

Since the sum and difference were easily computed mentally, key $20 \boxed{x^2} \boxed{\div} 36 \boxed{=}$ and again $\chi^2 = 11.111111$, which we compare with the table value $\chi^2_{.95}$ (1) $= 3.841$ and conclude that we reject the hypothesis of no difference and that drug B is the better of the two drugs. (Compare this problem with Problem 30.)

32. Compute the Yate's continuity corrected value of χ^2 for the data of Problems 30 and 31.

For Problem 30, the value is

$$\chi^2_{corrected} = \frac{50[\,|\, 8 \cdot 11 - 7 \cdot 14 \,| - \frac{1}{2}(50)]^2}{25 \cdot 25 \cdot 18 \cdot 32}$$

To compute this (AOS entry system), key

$$18 \boxed{\times} 11 \boxed{-} 7 \boxed{\times} 14 \boxed{=} * \boxed{-} 50 \boxed{\div} 2 \boxed{=} \boxed{x^2} \boxed{\times} 50 \boxed{\div}$$
$$25 \boxed{x^2} \boxed{\div} 18 \boxed{\div} 32 \boxed{=}$$

Read $\chi^2_{corrected} = .78125$.

*If display is $-$ here, key $\boxed{+/-}$ to get absolute value, which is $+$.

For Problem 31, McNemar's test has the continuity corrected formula

$$\chi^2_{corrected} = \frac{(|b - c| - 1)^2}{b + c} = \frac{(|28 - 8| - 1)^2}{28 + 8}$$

To compute this (AOS entry), key

$$28 \boxed{-} 8 \boxed{=} * \boxed{-} 1 \boxed{=} \boxed{x^2} \boxed{\div} \boxed{[(} 28 \boxed{+} 8 \boxed{=}$$

and read $\chi^2_{corrected} = 10.027778$.

33. Three teaching methods for acquiring a skill in a given period of time were tried on 90 people randomly allocated to each method so that all three groups were of equal size. A pass–fail test was administered with the following results:

METHOD	PASS	FAIL	TOTAL
I	20	10	30
II	17	13	30
III	24	6	30
Total	61	29	90

We use the formula

$$\chi^2 = N \left[\sum_{i=1}^{3} \frac{1}{R_i} \sum_{j=1}^{2} \frac{O_{ij}^2}{K_j} - 1 \right]$$

to test for homogeneity of the methods. To calculate this somewhat formidable expression, we compute terms corresponding to each row separately, and after adding them in the memory, divide the result by N.

The three terms for rows $i = 1, 2,$ and 3 are as follows:

$$\text{Row 1:} \quad \frac{1}{30} \left(\frac{20^2}{61} + \frac{10^2}{29} \right) = \frac{1}{R_1} \sum_{j=1}^{2} \frac{O_{1j}^2}{K_j}$$

$$\text{Row 2:} \quad \frac{1}{30} \left(\frac{17^2}{61} + \frac{13^2}{29} \right) = \frac{1}{R_2} \sum_{j=1}^{2} \frac{O_{2j}^2}{K_j}$$

$$\text{Row 3:} \quad \frac{1}{30} \left(\frac{24^2}{61} + \frac{6^2}{29} \right) = \frac{1}{R_3} \sum_{j=1}^{2} \frac{O_{3j}^2}{K_j}$$

*If display is − here, key $\boxed{+/-}$ to get absolute value, which is +.

In this illustration the row totals are all equal to 30, so by combining terms with the same denominator the sum simplifies to

$$\chi^2 = 90 \left[\frac{1}{30} \left(\frac{20^2 + 17^2 + 24^2}{61} + \frac{10^2 + 13^2 + 6^2}{29} \right) - 1 \right]$$

Thus we key

20 $\boxed{x^2}$ $\boxed{+}$ 17 $\boxed{x^2}$ $\boxed{+}$ 24 $\boxed{x^2}$ $\boxed{=}$ $\boxed{\div}$ 61 $\boxed{=}$ $\boxed{\text{STO}}$

10 $\boxed{x^2}$ $\boxed{+}$ 13 $\boxed{x^2}$ $\boxed{+}$ 6 $\boxed{x^2}$ $\boxed{\div}$ 29 $\boxed{=}$ $\boxed{\text{SUM}}$

$\boxed{\text{RCL}}$ $\boxed{\div}$ 30 $\boxed{-}$ 1 $\boxed{=}$ $\boxed{\text{x}}$ 90 $\boxed{=}$ and read $\chi^2 = 3.7648389$

The degrees of freedom $df = (r - 1)(k - 1) = (3 - 1)(2 - 1) = 2$, and from a table of critical values, $\chi^2_{.95}(2) = 5.99$. Since the computed value is less than this tabled value, we have insufficient data to conclude that there is any difference between the three methods. (*Note*: The computed value could also have been obtained by computing the expected value E for each cell frequency and then computing $\sum \frac{(O - E)^2}{E}$ directly.)

REGRESSION

34. A set of (X, Y) data produces the following summary statistics: $n = 8$, $\Sigma X = 44$, $\Sigma Y = 53.2$, $\Sigma X^2 = 284$, $\Sigma Y^2 = 385.8$, and $\Sigma XY = 327.4$. Use these statistics to compute, for the least-squares line $Y = a + bX$, the slope b, the Y intercept a, and the auxiliary quantities Σx^2 and Σxy.

First compute the sum of squares

$$\Sigma x^2 = \Sigma(X - \bar{X})^2 = \Sigma X^2 - (\Sigma X)^2/n = 284 - (44)^2/8$$

which we compute (AOS entry system)

284 $\boxed{-}$ 44 $\boxed{x^2}$ $\boxed{\div}$ 8 $\boxed{=}$ $\boxed{\text{STO}}$

and read $\Sigma x^2 = 42$, which is stored. If you have a sequential entry system, insert a left parenthesis in front of the 44 or use 44 $\boxed{x^2}$ $\boxed{\div}$ 8 $\boxed{=}$ $\boxed{+/-}$ $\boxed{+}$ 284 $\boxed{=}$ $\boxed{\text{STO}}$. The sum of products

$$\Sigma xy = \Sigma (X - \bar{X})(Y - \bar{Y}) = \Sigma XY - \Sigma X \Sigma Y/n = 327.4 - (44)(53.2)/8$$

so key

$$327.4 \boxed{-} 44 \boxed{\times} 53.2 \boxed{\div} 8 \boxed{=}$$

for AOS entry systems, and read $\Sigma \; xy = 34.8$. (*Note:* For sequential entry calculators use $44 \boxed{\times} 53.2 \boxed{\div} 8 \boxed{+/-} \boxed{+} 327.4 \boxed{=}$.) Now $b = \Sigma \; xy/\Sigma x^2$. Since $\Sigma \; xy = 34.8$ is now displayed and $\Sigma \; x^2 = 42$ is in memory, key $\boxed{\div} \boxed{RCL} \boxed{=} \boxed{STO}$ and read $b = .8285714$, which is stored. The Y intercept

$$a = \bar{Y} - b\bar{X} = \frac{\Sigma \; Y}{n} - b\frac{\Sigma \; X}{n} = \frac{\Sigma \; Y - b \; \Sigma \; X}{n} = \frac{53.2 - b(44)}{8}$$

where b is the slope that we stored in memory. Thus key

$$53.2 \boxed{-} \boxed{RCL} \boxed{\times} 44 \boxed{=} \boxed{\div} 8 \boxed{=}$$

(for AOS systems) and read $a = 2.092857$. (For sequential entry systems, $\boxed{RCL} \boxed{\times} 44 \boxed{\div} 8 \boxed{+/-} \boxed{+} 53.2 \boxed{=}$.)

35. Using the data of Problem 34 and any of the results obtained, compute the explained sum of squares, unexplained sum of squares, as well as the standard error of estimate $s_{y \cdot x}$ and the correlation r.

First we compute

$$\Sigma \; y^2 = \Sigma \; (Y - \bar{Y})^2 = \Sigma \; Y^2 - (\Sigma \; Y)^2/n = 385.8 - (53.2)^2/8$$

by keying

$$385.8 \boxed{-} 53.2 \boxed{x^2} \boxed{\div} 8 \boxed{=} \boxed{STO}$$

(AOS entry) and read $\Sigma \; y^2 = 32.02$.

The explained sum of squares $= (\Sigma \; xy)^2/\Sigma \; x^2 = (34.8)^2/42$, so simply key $34.8 \boxed{x^2} \boxed{\div} 42 \boxed{=}$ and read $SS_{explained} = 28.834286$. The unexplained sum of squares $=$ total SS $-$ SS$_{explained} = \Sigma \; y^2 -$ SS$_{explained}$. Since $\Sigma \; y^2$ is in memory and the explained sum of squares is still displayed, key $\boxed{+/-} \boxed{SUM} \boxed{RCL}$ and read SS$_{unexplained}$ $= 3.1857143$. Since $s_{y \cdot x}^2 =$ SS$_{unexplained}/(n - 2)$ and $n - 2 = 8 - 2 = 6$, divide the unexplained sum of squares by 6 and then take the square root to get the standard error of estimate $s_{y \cdot x}$: $\boxed{\div} 6 \boxed{=} \boxed{\sqrt{x}}$ and read $s_{y \cdot x} = .7286648$. The coefficient of correlation r is given by the formula

$$r = \frac{\Sigma \; xy}{\sqrt{\Sigma \; x^2 \; \Sigma \; y^2}} = \frac{34.8}{\sqrt{(42)(32.02)}}$$

and is computed as $42 \boxed{\times} 32.02 \boxed{=} \boxed{\sqrt{x}} \boxed{\div} 34.8 \boxed{=} \boxed{1/x}$ and
$r = 0.9489513$

Notice that we first computed the quotient in reverse and then took the reciprocal.

36. For the data and quantities computed in Problems 34 and 35, test the hypothesis H_0: $\beta = 0$ against the alternative H_1: $\beta \neq 0$ at the 5% level of significance.

The test statistic is

$$t = \frac{b s_x \sqrt{n-1}}{s_{y \cdot x}} = \frac{b \sqrt{\Sigma x^2}}{s_{y \cdot x}} = \frac{(.8285714) \sqrt{42}}{.7286648}$$

with $n - 2 = 8 - 2 = 6$ degrees of freedom. The substituted values were obtained from the previous problems. To calculate, key

$.8285714 \boxed{\times} \boxed{\sqrt{x}} \boxed{\div} .7286648 \boxed{=}$ and read t: $\boxed{7.3693094}$

Since the critical value on the upper tail of the distribution is $t_{.975}(6) = 2.45$ (from a table) and the computed value exceeds it, we reject H_0 and conclude that $\beta \neq 0$. Out best estimate of β is b.

37. A calculator with linear regression functions does not automatically compute $s^2_{y \cdot x}$. Using the values that are automatically computed, $r = .95$ and $s_Y = 2.14$ with $n = 8$, show how to compute $s^2_{y \cdot x}$.

Use the formula

$$s^2_{y \cdot x} = \frac{n-1}{n-2} s^2_Y (1 - r^2)$$

$$= \frac{8-1}{8-2} (2.14)^2 (1 - .95^2)$$

Computing the simple differences mentally, calculate by keying

$.95 \boxed{x^2} \boxed{+/-} \boxed{+} 1 \boxed{=} \boxed{\times} 2.14 \boxed{x^2} \boxed{\times} 7 \boxed{\div} 6 \boxed{=}$

and read $s^2_{y \cdot x} = .5209295$. [*Note*: If you wish to use this formula, as the correlation and variance of Y is being computed, utilize the memory. Yet another formula discussed in the text is

$$s^2_{y \cdot x} = \frac{n-1}{n-2} (s^2_Y - b^2 s^2_X)$$

38. Confidence Intervals: For the data in Problems 34 to 36, we found that $b = .8285714$ and $s_{y \cdot x} = .7286648$ with $\Sigma x^2 = 42$. Use this information to compute a 95% confidence interval for β.

The formula for a $(1 - \alpha)$ confidence interval for β is

$$b \pm \frac{t_{1-\alpha/2}(n-2)s_{y\cdot x}}{\sqrt{\Sigma(X-\bar{X})^2}} = b \pm \frac{t_{.975}(8-2)s_{y\cdot x}}{\sqrt{\Sigma x^2}}$$

where $n = 8$, $df = n - 2 = 8 - 2 = 6$ and hence $t_{.975}(6) = 2.45$ from a table. Thus, after making all substitutions, we must evaluate

$$.8285714 \pm \frac{(2.45)(.7286648)}{\sqrt{42}}$$

Thus we use the same technique as before for calculating confidence limits (AOS entry):

2.45 $\boxed{\times}$ .7286648 $\boxed{\div}$ 42 $\boxed{\sqrt{x}}$ $\boxed{+}$ $\boxed{STO}$ .8285714 $\boxed{-}$ 2 $\boxed{\times}$

$\boxed{RCL}\boxed{=}$

Read $b_U =$ 1.1040382   Read $b_L =$ .5531046

Thus a 95% confidence interval is $(b_L, b_U) = (.553, 1.104)$.

39. Consider the following data and using a calculator with linear regression statistics, (a) compute the slope and Y intercept of the fitted line $Y = a + bX$, and (b) compute the fitted value $\hat{Y}$ at $X = 6$.

X	2	3	4	5	6	7	8	9
Y	3.6	4.7	5.9	5.1	7.1	8.8	9.2	8.8

Step 1 In statistical (or linear regression) mode, enter the data:

2 $\boxed{x \leftrightarrows y}$ 3.6 $\boxed{\Sigma+}$ 3 $\boxed{x \leftrightarrows y}$ 4.7 $\boxed{\Sigma+}$ 4 $\boxed{x \leftrightarrows y}$ 5.9 $\boxed{\Sigma+}$

5 $\boxed{x \leftrightarrows y}$ 5.1 $\boxed{\Sigma+}$ 6 $\boxed{x \leftrightarrows y}$ 7.1 $\boxed{\Sigma+}$ 7 $\boxed{x \leftrightarrows y}$ 8.8 $\boxed{\Sigma+}$

8 $\boxed{x \leftrightarrows y}$ 9.2 $\boxed{\Sigma+}$ 9 $\boxed{x \leftrightarrows y}$ 8.8 $\boxed{\Sigma+}$

Step 2 Compute the intercept a and the slope b:

$\boxed{2nd}$ $\boxed{b/a}$ and read the Y intercept $a = 2.0928571$

$\boxed{x \leftrightarrows y}$ and read the slope $b = .8285714$

Thus the equation of the line is approximately $Y = 2.093 + .829$.

Step 3 To compute $\hat{Y}$ for $X = 6$, key the X value first; then $\hat{Y}$ can be computed automatically:

$$6 \boxed{\text{2nd}} \boxed{\text{y}'} \quad \text{and read} \quad \boxed{\quad 7.0642857 \quad}$$

(If your calculator does not have this key, substitute $X = 6$ into the equation.)

ANALYSIS OF VARIANCE

40. The yield in a chemical process is measured on five randomly select-ed samples of raw materials from each of three suppliers. (The given data is hypothetical.) Using the shortcut method described in the text, construct an ANOVA table and test the null hypothesis of identical suppliers.

SUPPLIERS		
I	II	III
12.3	11.2	14.2
8.2	13.7	10.0
9.5	8.1	7.9
7.7	8.1	12.8
10.4	9.3	11.5
Totals 48.1	50.4	56.4

First enter the X data:

$$12.3 \boxed{\Sigma+} 8.2 \boxed{\Sigma+} \ldots 11.5 \boxed{\Sigma+}$$

and read the number of data points $n = 15$. Now compute SST

$$\boxed{\text{2nd}} \boxed{\sigma_n} \boxed{x^2} \boxed{\text{2nd}} \boxed{\text{CSR}} \boxed{\times} 15 \boxed{=} \boxed{\text{STO}}$$
$$\text{reading} \quad \boxed{\quad 67.609333 \quad}$$

Then enter the column totals as data:

$$48.1 \boxed{\Sigma+} 50.4 \boxed{\Sigma+} 56.4 \boxed{\Sigma+} \quad \text{and read } k = 3$$

Since each column total is comprised of five X data entries, we com-pute SSC as follows:

$$\text{2nd} \boxed{\sigma_n} \boxed{x^2} \boxed{\text{2nd}} \boxed{\text{CSR}} \boxed{\times} 3 \boxed{\div} 5 \boxed{=} \boxed{+/-} \boxed{\text{SUM}}$$
$$\text{reading} \quad \boxed{\quad 7.3453333 \quad}$$

During these calculations, we have computed SST — SSC in the memory, so to get the error squares just press $\boxed{\text{RCL}}$ and read SSE: $\boxed{60.264}$. Thus we enter these into the complete ANOVA table, which looks like this:

SOURCE	SS	DF	$MS = \dfrac{SS}{DF}$	F RATIO
Suppliers	7.35	2	3.675	0.73 (nonsignificant)
Error	60.26	12	5.022	
Total	67.61	14		

Since the computed F ratio is clearly nonsignificant, we accept the null hypothesis and conclude that we cannot distinguish suppliers.

41. The air pollution level is measured from atop four different buildings on four different days as indicated in the data table. The buildings are located in the same general area but have different heights with building 1 being the shortest up to building 4, the tallest. Air pollution is measured on a scale from 1 to 5, with 5 being the worst. Using the methods of this text, create an ANOVA table and test the *main effects.*

Air Pollution Data

	DAY 1	DAY 2	DAY 3	DAY 4	TOTALS
Building 1	3.2	4.3	3.6	4.7	15.8
Building 2	3.0	3.5	3.1	4.2	13.8
Building 3	2.6	3.2	2.8	4.0	12.6
Building 4	2.6	3.0	1.7	3.7	11.0
Totals	11.4	14.0	11.2	16.6	

First enter the X data from the body of the table:

$$3.2 \boxed{\Sigma+} \ 4.3 \boxed{\Sigma+} \ldots 3.7 \boxed{\Sigma+} \quad \text{reading } n = 16$$

Now compute SST by keying

$$\text{2nd} \ \boxed{\sigma_n} \ \boxed{x^2} \ \text{2nd} \ \boxed{\text{CSR}} \ \boxed{\times} \ 16 \boxed{=} \text{ and read SST} = 8.57 \text{ (total sum of squares).}$$

Enter the row totals as data:

$$15.8 \boxed{\Sigma+} \ 13.8 \boxed{\Sigma+} \ 12.6 \boxed{\Sigma+} \ 11 \boxed{\Sigma+} \quad \text{and read } r = 4$$

Now we compute SSR. We have an additional shortcut here since we would have had to multiply σ_R^2 by $r = 4$ and then divide by $k = 4$ (the same value!); we conclude that SSR $= \sigma_R^2$ and compute:

$$\boxed{\text{2nd}}\ \boxed{\sigma_n}\ \boxed{x^2}\ \text{ and read } \sigma_R^2 = \text{SSR (for this example)} = 3.07$$

Prepare to enter the column totals as data by first clearing statistical registers: $\boxed{\text{2nd}}\ \boxed{\text{CSR}}$. Now enter those totals:

$$11.4\ \boxed{\Sigma +}\ 14\ \boxed{\Sigma +}\ 11.2\ \boxed{\Sigma +}\ 16.6\ \boxed{\Sigma +}\ \text{and read } k = 4$$

Again, by similar reasoning, conclude that $\sigma_C^2 = \text{SSC}$, since we know that SSC $= \sigma_C^2 \times k \div r$ and here $k = r = 4$.
Thus to compute SSC for this example, simply key

$$\boxed{\text{2nd}}\ \boxed{\sigma_n}\ \boxed{x^2}\ \text{and read SSC} = 4.85$$

The ANOVA table is given next. The quantity SSE $=$ SST $-$ SSR $-$ SSC, which could have been accumulated in memory or done separately.

SOURCE OF VARIATION	DF	SUM OF SQUARES	MEAN SQUARES $= \dfrac{SS}{DF}$	F RATIO
Buildings	3	3.07	1.023	14.169*
Days	3	4.85	1.617	22.385*
"Error"	9	0.65	0.07	
Total	15	8.57		

The critical value $F_{.99}(3, 9) = 10.6$, so that both F ratios are significant even at the 1% level. This is denoted by an asterisk next to the values in the ANOVA table. The tests are valid only if we assume no interaction. (A better experiment would have been to take multiple readings so that we could better estimate experimental error and actually test whether there was any interaction. If there is, general conclusions are limited.)

42. Five teachers teach the same course, each using a different textbook in each of two classes. Three students are selected at random from each class to take a common final exam. Compute a partial ANOVA table giving the sums of squares with degrees of freedom.

		TEACHERS				
		A	B	C	D	E
		81	87	70	86	89
	I	80	85	68	97	100
		84	90	77	75	92
TEXT		56	79	63	88	73
	II	72	81	66	81	74
		76	72	68	77	77

First form a summary table giving row, column, and cell totals:

	A	B	C	D	E	TOTAL
I	245	262	215	258	281	1261
II	204	232	197	246	224	1103
TOTAL	449	494	412	504	505	

Make certain that statistical registers are cleared. Then enter the X data:

81 [Σ+] 87 [Σ+] 70 [Σ+] . . . 77 [Σ+] reading $n = 30$

Now compute SST, the total sum of squares, by keying

[2nd] [σ_n] [x^2] [2nd] [CSR] [×] 30 [=] [STO]
reading SST = 2894.8

Next enter the cell data:

245 [Σ+] 262 [Σ+] . . . 224 [Σ+] and read $rk = 10$

Since each cell total is comprised of three ($p = 3$) X values, SS(cells) is computed as follows:

[2nd] [σ_n] [x^2] [2nd] [CSR] [×] 10 [÷] 3 [=]
reading SS(cells) = 2170.1333

We subtract this value from SST in memory by keying [+/−] [SUM] [+/−] [the last sign change was to make SS(cells) positive again]. Now key [EXC] and read the error sum of squares, SSE = 724.66667, which was computed in memory and has now been replaced by SS(cells), from which SSR and SSC will be subtracted as we compute them to ultimately get SSI, the interaction.

Enter the row totals as data:

$$1261 \boxed{\Sigma+} 1103 \boxed{\Sigma+} \text{ and read r} = 2.$$

Now each row total is comprised of kp = (5)(3) = 15 X-values, so SSR is computed like this:

$$\boxed{\text{2nd}} \boxed{\sigma_n} \boxed{x^2} \boxed{\text{2nd}} \boxed{\text{CSR}} \boxed{\times} 2 \boxed{\div} 15 \boxed{=} \text{ and read SSR} =$$
$$832.13333$$

which we subtract from memory by keying $\boxed{+/-}$ $\boxed{\text{SUM}}$. Next enter the column totals as data:

$$449 \boxed{\Sigma+} 494 \boxed{\Sigma+} 412 \boxed{\Sigma+} 504 \boxed{\Sigma+} 505 \boxed{\Sigma+} \text{ reading } k = 5$$

Each column is comprised of rp = (2)(3) = 6 X data points, so we compute SSC as follows:

$$\boxed{\text{2nd}} \boxed{\sigma_n} \boxed{x^2} \boxed{\text{2nd}} \boxed{\text{CSR}} \boxed{\times} 5 \boxed{\div} 6 \boxed{=} \text{ and read SSC} =$$
$$1120.4667$$

which we subtract from the quantity in memory by keying $\boxed{+/-}$ $\boxed{\text{SUM}}$.

Finally, retrieve the interaction sum of squares SSI [or SS($R \times C$)] from the memory where it was computed by subtraction by keying $\boxed{\text{RCL}}$ and reading SSI = 217.53333. This is all organized in the following partial ANOVA table:

SOURCE OF VARIATION	DF	SUM OF SQUARES
Books (SSR)	1	832.13
Teacher (SSC)	4	1120.47
Interaction	4	217.53
Subtotal (cells)	9	2170.13
Error	20	724.67
Total	29	2894.80

We shall not discuss further analysis of this example here as our purpose was to illustrate the calculation of the sums of squares.

43. Consider an experiment where three types of corn are planted in three types of soil using three different types of fertilizer. This is done in a *Latin-square design* according to the cyclic pattern given in the table. We compute the sums of squares associated with this design and arrange them in the standard ANOVA format.

	I	II	III	TOTAL
1	305 (A)	380 (B)	300 (C)	985
2	310 (C)	285 (A)	350 (B)	945
3	412 (B)	325 (C)	290 (A)	1027
Total	1027	990	940	

Roman numeral, soil type; Arabic numeral, fertilizer; Latin letters, corn type. The numbers in the cells are the yield in bushels per acre. The table shows the Arabic (row) and Roman (column) totals. We also need the Latin totals:

$$A = 305 + 285 + 290 = 880$$

$$B = 412 + 380 + 350 = 1142$$

$$C = 310 + 325 + 300 = 935$$

With the basic data plus the summary data, commence to compute the various sums of squares as follows:

1. Enter the cell data:

$$305 \boxed{\Sigma+} \ 380 \boxed{\Sigma+} \ 300 \boxed{\Sigma+}$$
$$310 \ \Sigma+ \ \ 285 \boxed{\Sigma+} \ 350 \boxed{\Sigma+}$$
$$412 \boxed{\Sigma+} \ 325 \boxed{\Sigma+} \ 290 \boxed{\Sigma+}$$

and read $n = 9$. Now compute the total sum of squares by keying

$$\boxed{2nd} \ \boxed{\sigma_n} \ \boxed{x^2} \ \boxed{2nd} \ \boxed{CSR} \ \boxed{\times} \ 9 \ \boxed{=} \ \boxed{STO}$$

and read SST = 15180.222, which is stored in the memory.

2. Now enter the Roman (column) totals

$$1027 \boxed{\Sigma+} \ 990 \boxed{\Sigma+} \ 940 \boxed{\Sigma+} \quad \text{and read } k = 3$$

the number of columns. Since each column is comprised of $r = 3$ of the cell entries, we would compute

$$\text{SS(Roman)} = \sigma^2_{\text{Roman}} \times k \div r$$

and in this example $k = r = 3$, so the sum of squares will equal the variance here. Hence we simply compute $\boxed{2nd} \ \boxed{\sigma_n} \ \boxed{x^2}$ and read SS(Roman) = 1270.8889, which is subtracted from SST in the memory by keying $\boxed{+/-} \ \boxed{SUM}$. Clear statistical registers: $\boxed{2nd} \ \boxed{CSR}$.

3. Now enter the Arabic (row) totals:

$$985 \boxed{\Sigma+} \; 945 \boxed{\Sigma+} \; 1027 \boxed{\Sigma+} \quad \text{and read } r = 3$$

Notice that

$$SS(\text{Arabic}) = \sigma^2_{\text{Arabic}} \times r \div k$$

but $k = r = 3$ because of the symmetry, so simply key

$$\boxed{\text{2nd}} \; \boxed{\sigma_n} \; \boxed{x^2} \quad \text{and read } SS(\text{Arabic}) = 1120.8885$$

which is subtracted from the quantity in memory by keying $\boxed{+/-}$ $\boxed{\text{SUM}}$, and then key $\boxed{\text{2nd}} \boxed{\text{CSR}}$ to clear statistics registers.

4. Now enter the Latin totals as data:

$$880 \boxed{\Sigma+} \; 1142 \boxed{\Sigma+} \; 935 \boxed{\Sigma+}$$

For analogous reasons $SS(\text{Latin}) = \sigma^2_{\text{Latin}}$, so again simply key

$$\boxed{\text{2nd}} \; \boxed{\sigma_n} \; \boxed{x^2} \quad \text{and read } SS(\text{Latin}) = 12724.222$$

which is also subtracted from the quantity in memory by keying $\boxed{+/-}$ SUM ·

5. Finally, the residual sum of squares (estimate of error) is now in the memory, so retrieve it by keying $\boxed{\text{RCL}}$. The partial ANOVA table will look like this:

SOURCE	DF	SUM OF SQUARES
Roman	2	1270.889
Arabic	2	1120.889
Latin	2	12724.222
Residual	2	64.222
Total	8	15180.222

5

The Mathematics of
Business and Finance

Percent

The word *percent* means "per hundred." The symbol % indicates that the number preceding it is to be divided by 100. On a calculator a percent is usually expressed in decimal form, except when using special business functions on some business calculators.

The $\boxed{\%}$ key has several functions:

1. (Number) $\boxed{\%}$ divides the number by 100, hence changing a percent into decimal units.
2. (Number) $\boxed{\times}$ (r) $\boxed{\%}$ $\boxed{=}$ takes $r\%$ of a number.
3. (Number) $\boxed{+}$ (r) $\boxed{\%}$ $\boxed{=}$ takes $r\%$ of a number and then adds it to the original number.
4. (Number) $\boxed{-}$ (r) $\boxed{\%}$ $\boxed{=}$ takes $r\%$ of a number and then subtracts it from the original number.
5. (Number) $\boxed{\div}$ (r) $\boxed{\%}$ $\boxed{=}$ divides the number by $r\%$.

(Some calculators work a little differently, but the system described is the most common and is quite convenient. If your calculator does not use this system, most of the discussion of calculator use in this chapter will not apply.)

There are three basic components to a percentage problem, the base (B), the rate (R), and the percentage (P). The rate is given in % units. The "percentage" is just a "part" of the base (although it can be bigger than the base if the rate is more than 100%). They are related by the following three formulas:

$$P = R \times B, \qquad R = P \div B, \qquad B = P \div R$$

These can either be memorized or derived from the first by simple algebra.

Example **(1)** Find 48% of 25. $B = 25$, $R = 48\%$. Compute $P = 48\% \times 25$. $\boxed{48}\boxed{\%}$ $\boxed{\times}\boxed{25}\boxed{=}$ or alternatively $\boxed{25}\boxed{\times}\boxed{48}\boxed{\%}\boxed{=}$ The result is 12.

(2) 200 is what percent of 8000? $P = 200$, $B = 8000$. Compute R. $R = 200 \div 8000$, using the second formula.

$$\boxed{200}\boxed{\div}\boxed{8000}\boxed{=} \quad \text{giving the result} \quad \boxed{0.025}$$

This can be translated mentally as 2.5%. If, however, you wish to have the calculator perform this change into percent units, either key $\boxed{\times}\boxed{100}\boxed{=}$ or $\boxed{\div}\boxed{1}\boxed{\%}\boxed{=}$.
Caution: The $\boxed{\%}$ key will *not* change decimal units into percent. It does just the opposite.

(3) 12 is 25% of what number? $R = 25\%$, $P = 12$, $B = ?$

$$B = P \div R = 12 \div 25\%, \qquad \boxed{12}\boxed{\div}\boxed{25}\boxed{\%}\boxed{=}$$

The result is 48.

Markup, Discount, and Gross Profit Margin

The *gross profit* is the net selling price minus the gross cost. When this quantity is expressed as a percentage of cost, we have a *cost markup.* When gross profit is expressed as a percentage of the selling price, this is known as the *gross profit margin.* Thus markup is given by the formula

$$M = \frac{S - C}{C}$$

expressed as a percent, where $C =$ cost and $S =$ selling price.
The gross profit margin (GPM) is given by a similar formula:

$$\text{GPM} = \frac{S - C}{S} \quad \text{also expressed as a percent}$$

The only difference is the denominator. This slight difference, however, makes the calculations quite different in terms of special functions on some business calculators. The markup can be computed by using the $\boxed{\Delta\%}$ function, whereas the profit margin can utilize the triad of keys $\boxed{\text{CST}}$, $\boxed{\text{SEL}}$, and $\boxed{\text{MAR}}$.

Example An item that costs \$40 is sold for \$50. Compute (a) the cost markup and (b) the gross profit margin.

(a) $M = (50 - 40)/40$, computed as $50 \boxed{-} 40 \boxed{=} \boxed{\div} 40 \boxed{=}$. If your calculator has arithmetic entry, the first equals may be omitted. The result is .25, which is interpreted as 25%. On a business calculator, or any calculator with a change in percent key, this may also be computed as

$$40 \boxed{\text{2nd}} \boxed{\Delta\%} 50 \boxed{=} \quad \text{(on the Business Analyst I)}$$

which computes the change in percent from 40 to 50. This equals the markup but is displayed in percent units as 25. (On the Business Analyst II, reverse the 40 and 50, entering the 50 first for the same calculation.)

(b) $GPM = (50 - 40)/50$, which is computed as $50 \boxed{-} 40 \boxed{=} \boxed{\div} 50 \boxed{=}$, and the result is .20, which is interpreted as 20%. If you use the special set of keys on a business calculator, the key sequence looks like this (in the appropriate mode):

$$40 \boxed{\text{CST}} 50 \boxed{\text{SEL}} \boxed{\text{2nd}} \boxed{\text{MAR}}$$

The result is 20., which is already in percent units, whereas the direct calculation gives the result in decimal form.

For convenience, equivalent forms of the basic equations for markup and profit margin are given in Table 5-1.

TABLE 5-1.

MARKUP	GROSS PROFIT MARGIN
$M = \dfrac{S - C}{C} = \dfrac{S}{C} - 1$	$MAR = \dfrac{SEL - CST}{SEL} = 1 - \dfrac{CST}{SEL}$
$S = C(1 + M)$	$CST = SEL(1 + MAR)$
$C = \dfrac{S}{1 + M}$	$SEL = \dfrac{CST}{1 + MAR}$

In all these formulas, when calculated arithmetically, the quantities M and MAR are entered in decimal form. When using the special business functions, percentage units are used. For gross profit margin the special keys are used by entering the known quantities followed by the corresponding special key; then the quantity to be computed is produced by keying $\boxed{\text{2nd}}$ before pressing the key that corresponds to the desired quantity.

A *discount* is simply a deduction. A *trade discount* is expressed as a percentage of list price. The key sequence to compute the discount and the resulting net price at the same time is

(list) $\boxed{-}$ (discount rate) $\boxed{\%}$ $\boxed{=}$

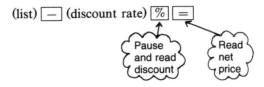

Example A $50 item is discounted at 7%. What is the discount and net price?

$$50 \boxed{-} 7 \boxed{\%} \quad \text{(read discount)} \quad \boxed{3.5}$$

$$\boxed{=} \quad \text{(read net price)} \quad \boxed{46.5}$$

Thus the discount is $3.50 and the net price is $46.50.

Series discounts or *chain discounts* are successively applied discounts. These are usually applied to the list price. If L = the list price and there are, for example, three series discounts at rates r_1, r_2, and r_3, then the net price N is given by the formula

$$N = L(1 - r_1)(1 - r_2)(1 - r_3)$$

This expression could be computed as written. If the rates can easily be subtracted from 1 mentally, then the formula is just a chain multiplication. A more efficient way, using the automatic discount function of the $\boxed{\%}$ key, is this:

$$L \boxed{-} r_1 \boxed{\%} \boxed{-} r_2 \boxed{\%} \boxed{-} r_3 \boxed{\%} \boxed{=}$$

Example A $45 item is discounted at 15%, 10%, and 4%. Find the net price.

$$45 \boxed{-} 15 \boxed{\%} \boxed{-} 10 \boxed{\%} \boxed{-} 4 \boxed{\%} \boxed{=} \quad \text{which gives} \quad \boxed{33.048}$$

The net price, rounded to the nearest cent, is $33.05.

The *equivalent single discount rate* is the ratio $(L - N)/L$ expressed as a percent and is computed as

$$L \boxed{-} N \boxed{=} \boxed{\div} L \boxed{=}$$

In the preceding example the equivalent single discount rate is

$$45 \boxed{-} 33.048 \boxed{=} \boxed{\div} 45 \boxed{=} \quad \text{which gives} \quad \boxed{0.2656}$$

Thus the equivalent single discount rate is 26.56%. Notice that the rate is given in decimal form on the display and must be converted to percent units.

Simple Interest and Discount

Interest is consideration for the use of invested or loaned capital expressed in monetary units. Interest depends on *principal* (*P*), the amount invested, *rate of interest* (*r*), the percent of principal paid for its use for one period of time, and the *time* (*t*), the number of periods during which the principal is used, usually expressed in years. The *amount* (*S*) is the sum of the principal and interest.

The formulas relating these quantities, together with appropriate key sequences, are given in Table 5-2 for both arithmetic entry and AOS system entry calculators. Where no AOS entry method is shown, the same sequence will work.

TABLE 5-2. Summary of Simple Interest Formulas

FORMULA	KEY SEQUENCE (ARITHMETIC AND AOS)
$I = Prt$	$P\ \boxed{\times}\ r\ \boxed{\times}\ t\ \boxed{=}$
$S = P + I$	$P\ \boxed{+}\ I\ \boxed{=}$
$S = P + Prt$	$P\ \boxed{\times}\ r\ \boxed{\times}\ t\ \boxed{+}\ P\ \boxed{=}$ $P\ \boxed{+}\ P\ \boxed{\times}\ r\ \boxed{\times}\ t\ \boxed{=}$ (AOS system)
$S = P(1 + rt)$	$r\ \boxed{\times}\ t\ \boxed{+}\ 1\ \boxed{\times}\ P\ \boxed{=}$ $P\ \boxed{\times}\ \boxed{(}\ 1\ \boxed{+}\ r\ \boxed{\times}\ t\ \boxed{=}$ (AOS system)

The number *r* should be expressed as a decimal, or key $r\ \boxed{\%}$ instead.

Some alternative forms of these formulas, which are useful if *P*, *r*, or *t* needs to be computed, are given in Table 5-3.

TABLE 5-3.

FORMULA	KEY SEQUENCE
$P = \dfrac{I}{rt}$	$I\ \boxed{\div}\ r\ \boxed{\div}\ t\ \boxed{=}$ or $I\ \boxed{\div}\ \boxed{(}\ r\ \boxed{\times}\ t\ \boxed{=}$
$r = \dfrac{I}{Pt}$	$I\ \boxed{\div}\ P\ \boxed{\div}\ t\ \boxed{=}$ or $I\ \boxed{\div}\ \boxed{(}\ P\ \boxed{\times}\ t\ \boxed{=}$
$P = \dfrac{S}{1 + rt}$	$S\ \boxed{\div}\ \boxed{(}\ r\ \boxed{\times}\ t\ \boxed{+}\ 1\ \boxed{=}$ or $r\ \boxed{\times}\ t\ \boxed{+}\ 1\ \boxed{=}\ \boxed{\div}$ $S\ \boxed{=}\ \boxed{1/x}\ S\ \boxed{\div}\ \boxed{(}\ 1\ \boxed{+}\ r\ \boxed{\times}\ t\ \boxed{=}$ (AOS system)
$t = \dfrac{I}{Pr}$	$I\ \boxed{\div}\ P\ \boxed{\div}\ r\ \boxed{=}$ or $I\ \boxed{\div}\ \boxed{(}\ P\ \boxed{\times}\ r\ \boxed{=}$
$t = \dfrac{S - P}{Pr}$	$S\ \boxed{-}\ P\ \boxed{\div}\ P\ \boxed{\div}\ r\ \boxed{=}$ or $S\ \boxed{-}\ P\ \boxed{\div}\ \boxed{(}\ P\ \boxed{\times}\ r$ $\boxed{=}\ S\ \boxed{-}\ P\ \boxed{=}\ \boxed{\div}\ P\ \boxed{\div}\ r\ \boxed{=}$ or $S\ \boxed{-}\ P\ \boxed{)}$ $\boxed{\div}\ \boxed{(}\ P\ \boxed{\times}\ r\ \boxed{=}$ (AOS system)

Before using any of the formulas of Tables 5-2 and 5-3, the number t must be expressed in years and the rate r must be expressed as a decimal. This can also be accomplished by keying the sequence $r\boxed{\%}$ in some cases.

The amount S is also known as the *future value*; P is also called the *present value*. The amount $D = S - P$ is called the *simple discount*. Other forms of this expression are $S = D + P$ and $P = S - D$.

The terminology for *bank discounts* (D) is slightly different. The quantity S is called the *maturity value*, t is called the *period of discount*, and the percentage discount d is called the *discount rate*. The relationships among these quantities as well as the corresponding key sequences are given in Table 5-4.

TABLE 5-4. Summary of Simple Discount Formulas

FORMULA	KEY SEQUENCE (ARITHMETIC AND AOS)
$D = Sdt$	$S\boxed{\times}d\boxed{\times}t\boxed{=}$
$D = S - P$	$S\boxed{-}P\boxed{=}$
$P = S - Sdt$	$S\boxed{\times}d\boxed{\times}t\boxed{=}\boxed{+/-}\boxed{+}S\boxed{=}$ or $S\boxed{-}\boxed{((}S\boxed{\times}d\boxed{\times}t\boxed{=}$
$P = S(1 - dt)$	$S\boxed{-}S\boxed{\times}d\boxed{\times}t\boxed{=}$ (AOS system)
	$d\boxed{\times}t\boxed{-}1\boxed{=}\boxed{+/-}\boxed{\times}S\boxed{=}$
	$S\boxed{\times}\boxed{((}1\boxed{-}d\boxed{\times}t\boxed{=}$ (AOS system)
$S = \dfrac{P}{1 - dt}$	$d\boxed{\times}t\boxed{-}1\boxed{=}\boxed{+/-}\boxed{\div}P\boxed{=}\boxed{1/x}$
	$P\boxed{\div}\boxed{((}1\boxed{-}d\boxed{\times}t\boxed{=}$ (AOS system)

The quantity d is entered as a decimal and t is entered as years.

Moreover, the simple interest rate r and the discount rate d are related by the two formulas of Table 5-5.

TABLE 5-5.

FORMULA	KEY SEQUENCE
$r = \dfrac{d}{1 - dt}$	$d\boxed{\div}\boxed{((}1\boxed{-}\boxed{((}d\boxed{\times}t\boxed{=}$ or $d\boxed{1/x}\boxed{-}t\boxed{=}\boxed{1/x}$ *
	$d\boxed{\div}\boxed{((}1\boxed{-}d\boxed{\times}t\boxed{=}$ (AOS system)
$d = \dfrac{r}{1 + rt}$	$r\boxed{\div}\boxed{((}r\boxed{\times}t\boxed{+}1\boxed{=}$ or $r\boxed{1/x}\boxed{+}t\boxed{=}\boxed{1/x}$ †
	$r\boxed{\div}\boxed{((}1\boxed{+}r\boxed{\times}t\boxed{=}$ (AOS system)

*Since $d/(1 - dt) = 1/(1/d - t)$.
†Since $r/(1 + rt) = 1/(1/r + t)$.

The formulas of Tables 5-4 and 5-5 illustrate the basic computational strategies. Variations can of course be implemented, such as use of the memory or taking advantage of some of the properties of the calculator. This is illustrated in the following example.

Example At what rate should a note be discounted to be equivalent to 8% interest for three months? The correct formula is $d = \dfrac{r}{1 + rt}$, where $r = .08$ and $t = {}^3/_{12} = {}^1/_4 = .25$. Thus we compute

$$.08 \; \boxed{\text{STO}} \; \boxed{\div} \; \boxed{(\!(} \; \boxed{\text{RCL}} \; \boxed{\times} \; .25 \; \boxed{+} \; 1 \; \boxed{=}$$

This gives the result $\boxed{\;.07843137\;}$. This is approximately 7.8%. Notice that the interest rate was stored and then recalled when needed. Compare this with the last formula in Table 5-5.

As a shortcut, you don't even have to use the memory to avoid reentering the rate. Just key the following:

$$.08 \; \boxed{\div} \; \boxed{(\!(} \; \boxed{\times} \; .25 \; \boxed{+} \; 1 \; \boxed{=}$$

This works because the .08 is still on the display when the multiplication key is pressed. This can be varied slightly by making use of the percent key:

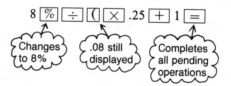

Notice that the right parenthesis $\boxed{)\!)}$ was not needed. If you did key it, the value of the expression in the parenthesis would be completed. Keying the $\boxed{=}$ does this plus completes all the rest.

Compound Interest

When interest earned in a given period is added to the principal, it is said to be *converted* into principal or *compounded*. The *frequency of conversion* is the number of times interest is converted in one year (m). The interest rate for each period is denoted by i, and the nominal annual rate is denoted by j ($i = j/m$). The number of compounding periods is denoted by n, where $n = m \times t$ and t is the number of years. For example, if interest is converted m times per year for 3 years, then $n = 3m$. The effective rate r is the rate equivalent to simple interest for one year.

The formulas relating principal invested (present value), amount due in n periods, and the interest rate, as well as related expressions, are given in Table 5-6. The key sequences are for *arithmetic entry systems* only and for business calculators. *Do not use these on an AOS entry system.* Key sequences for AOS systems are given in Table 5-7.

223

TABLE 5-6. Summary of Compound Interest Formulas

TERMINOLOGY	FORMULA	KEY SEQUENCES (ARITHMETIC OR BUSINESS FUNCTIONS)
Amount	$S = P(1 + i)^n$	1 [+] i [y^x] n [×] P [=] n [N] i [%i] P [PV] [2nd] [FV]
Present value	$P = S(1 + i)^{-n}$	1 [+] i [y^x] n [+/−] [×] S [=] n [N] i [%i] S [FV] [2nd] [PV]
Effective rate	$r = (1 + i)^m - 1$	1 [+] i [y^x] m [−] 1 [=] (r = decimal) m [N] i [%i] 1 [PV] [2nd] [FV] 1 [N] [2nd] [%i] (r = % form)
Compound discount factor	$v^n = (1 + i)^{-n}$	1 [+] i [y^x] n [+/−] [=] n [N] i [%i] 1 [FV] [2nd] [PV]
Accumulation factor	$s = (1 + i)^n$	1 [+] i [y^x] n [=] n [N] i [%i] 1 [PV] [2nd] [FV]
Computing time (n)	$n = \dfrac{\ln (S/P)}{\ln (1 + i)}$	S [÷] P [=] [lnx] [÷] [(] i [+] 1 [)] [lnx] [=] i [%i] P [PV] S [FV] [2nd] [N]
Periodic and nominal rate	$i = \sqrt[n]{S/P} - 1$ $j = mi$	S [÷] P [2nd] [$x\sqrt{y}$] [−] 1 [=] (read i) [×] m [=] (read j) both decimals n [N] P [PV] S [FV] [2nd] [%i] (read i) 1 [N] [2nd] [%i] (read j) both % units
Continuous effective rate	$r = e^j - 1$	j [2nd] [e^x] [−] 1 [=] (j is entered as a decimal)

Note: In arithmetic calculations, rates are entered as decimals, but when using special business functions, rates are entered in percent units.

TABLE 5-7. Summary of Compound Interest Formulas for Calculation with AOS Entry System

TERMINOLOGY	FORMULA	AOS KEY SEQUENCE
Amount	$S = P(1 + i)^n$	i $+$ 1 $=$ y^x n $\times$ P $=$
Present value	$P = S(1 + i)^{-n}$	i $+$ 1 $=$ y^x n $+/-$ $\times$ S $=$
Effective rate	$r = (1 + i)^{-m} - 1$	i $+$ 1 $=$ y^x m $+/-$ $-$ 1 $=$
Compound discount factor	$v^n = (1 + i)^{-n}$	i $+$ 1 $=$ y^x n $+/-$ $=$
Accumulation factor	$s = (1 + i)^n$	i $+$ 1 $=$ y^x n $=$
Computing time (n)	$n = \dfrac{\ln (S/P)}{\ln (i + 1)}$	S $\div$ P $\ln x$ $\div$ $(($ 1 $+$ i $))$ $\ln x$ $=$
Periodic and nominal rate	$i = n\sqrt{S/P} - 1$ $j = mi$	S $\div$ P $=$ INV y^x $-$ 1 $=$ (read i) $\times$ m $=$ (read j) both decimal
Continous effective rate	$r = e^j - 1$	j INV $\ln x$ $-$ 1 $=$

Note: All rates are expressed in decimal form.

Annuities

An *annuity* is a sequence of equal payments made at equal intervals of time. The amount of each payment is called the *periodic rent* or *periodic payment*. The *rent period* or *payment interval* is the time interval between two successive payments. The *term* of the annuity is the time from the beginning of the first rent period to the end of the last one. When the payment is made at the end of the rent period, we have an *ordinary annuity*. When payment is made at the beginning of each rent period, it is called an *annuity due*. A *deferred annuity* is an ordinary annuity whose term begins a fixed number of periods from the present time, with payments made at the end of each period after the term begins. These are all examples of an *annuity certain* since they begin and end on fixed dates.

Other classes of annuities are a *perpetuity*, which begins on a fixed date, but payments continue forever, and a *contingent annuity*, where either the first or the last payment is at a time that depends on some event, the time of which is uncertain. Contingent annuities will not be considered. They are topics in the mathematics of life insurance.

The *amount, final value,* or *future value* of an annuity is the sum of the compound amounts of all payments to the end of the term. This concept can be seen in the following time diagram, a device that is of great assistance in the analysis of annuities.

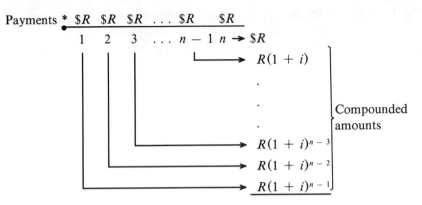

$$\text{Final value} = S = \text{sum of above terms}$$

The sum of the compounded amounts of the payments illustrated on the time line is the sum of a geometric series $\Sigma\ ar^k$, where

$$a = R, \quad r = (1 + i)$$

where i is the interest rate for each period, $k = n - 1$. Thus

$$S = a\frac{1 - r^{k+1}}{1 - r} = R\frac{1 - (1 + i)^n}{1 - (1 + i)} = R\frac{1 - (1 + i)^n}{-i}$$

$$= R\frac{(1 + i)^n - 1}{i}$$

This formula is also written as $S_n = R \cdot s_{\overline{n}|i}$, where the symbol

$$s_{\overline{n}|i} = \frac{(1 + i)^n - 1}{i}$$

and is the future value of an annuity with rent of $1 per period.

The symbol S or S_n denotes the *amount* or *final value* of an annuity. It is also referred to as the *future value* of the annuity. (Do *not* call it the "sum of an annuity." That has no meaning.) On most calculators this quantity can be computed making use of the $\boxed{y^x}$ key. Business calculators have an annuity mode that makes use of the following five keys:

$$\boxed{N}\ \boxed{\%i}\ \boxed{PMT}\ \boxed{PV}\ \boxed{FV} \quad \text{in conjunction with the } \boxed{2nd}\ \text{key}$$

Data are entered by keying the appropriate key when the number to be entered is on the display. Then the amount desired is computed by keying $\boxed{2nd}$, followed by the key corresponding to the desired quantity. This sometimes takes the calculator several seconds, especially when the periodic rate is to be computed. While the calculator is computing internally, do not press any keys.

The *present value* of an annuity A_n or A is the single sum of money that, when invested now at the given rate, will, when compounded, amount to the final value (future value) of the annuity. This is also known as the *cash equivalent of the annuity.* Thus we require

$$A_n (1 + i)^n = R \cdot s_{\overline{n}|i} = R \cdot \frac{(1 + i)^n - 1}{i}$$

Solving this equation for A_n gives

$$A_n = R \cdot \frac{1 - (1 + i)^{-n}}{i}$$

which is symbolized as

$$A_n = R \cdot a_{\overline{n}|i}$$

The quantity

$$a_{\overline{n}|i} = \frac{1 - (1 + i)^{-n}}{i}$$

is also the present value of an annuity with a rent of $1 per period.

There are many formulas relating the quantities $a_{\overline{n}|i}$ and $s_{\overline{n}|i}$ for various combinations of n and i, but they are useful primarily where tables of these factors are used. The calculator reduces the basic formulas to a smaller set. They are shown in the summary table. A time diagram for an ordinary annuity is shown next, indicating payment times and where the quantities A_n and S_n occur.

$$
\begin{array}{l}
\quad \$ \quad \$ \quad \$ \ldots \$ \quad \$ \\
\hline
A_n \qquad\qquad\qquad S_n = R s_{\overline{n}|i} \\
\quad\longrightarrow \quad\quad = A_n (1 + i)^n
\end{array}
$$

In an annuity due, the payments are made at the beginning of each period. This is shown, as well as present and final values, in the following time diagram:

$$
\begin{array}{l}
\qquad\quad \text{term} \\
\$R \quad \$R \quad \$R \ldots \$R \\
\;1 \quad\; 2 \quad\; 3 \ldots n \\
A_n \text{ (due)} \qquad\qquad S_n \text{ (due)}
\end{array}
$$

The formulas for an annuity due are as follows:

$$S_n \text{ (due)} = R \cdot (s_{\overline{n+1}|i} - 1) = R \cdot s_{\overline{n}|i} (1 + i)$$

$$A_n \text{ (due)} = R \cdot (a_{\overline{n-1}|i} + 1) = R \cdot a_{\overline{n}|i} (1 + i)$$

The amount or final value of a deferred annuity for n periods, deferred for m periods, is the same as for an ordinary annuity for n periods. The present value however is shifted back m periods. This is shown in the time diagram:

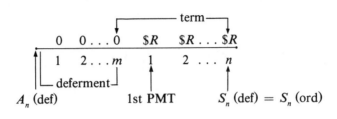

There are two basic equivalent formulas for deferred annuities:

$$A_n \text{ (def)} = R \cdot (a_{\overline{m+n}|\,i} - a_{\overline{m}|\,i})$$

$$A_n \text{ (def)} = R \cdot a_{\overline{n}|\,i} (1 + i)^{-m}$$

There are basically two kinds of perpetuities:

Type I R dollars payable at the end of each period, the first payment due one period from the present time. Let the rate be i per period. The *present value,* A_∞ is the sum, which if invested now at rate i per period would yield R dollars at the end of each period, with the original principal remaining intact. The formula is

$$A_\infty = \frac{R}{i}$$

Type II If W dollars is payable at the end of every k periods, with the first payment due k periods from now with rate i per period, then the present value is

$$A_{\infty,\,k} = \frac{W}{i}\frac{1}{s_{\overline{k}|\,i}}$$

The handling of annuities due, deferred annuities, and perpetuities is shown in the solved problems. Table 5-8 illustrates the basic computational strategies. The sequences shown work for both arithmetic and AOS systems; however, some parentheses could have been eliminated with the AOS system. The sequences are therefore not the most efficient. Variations on these methods are also illustrated in the problems.

TABLE 5-8. Summary of Basic Ordinary Annuity Formulas

FORMULA	DIRECT CALCULATION (I = DECIMAL FORM) ARITHMETIC OR AOS	BUSINESS CALCULATOR (I = % FORM) SET TO ANNUITY MODE
$S = R \cdot s_{\overline{n}|i}$ $= R \cdot \dfrac{(1+i)^n - 1}{i}$	i [STO] [+] 1 [=] [y^x] n [−] 1 [=] [÷] [RCL] [×] R [=]	n [N] i [%i] R [PMT] [2nd] [FV]
$A = A_n = R \cdot a_{\overline{n}|i}$ $= R \cdot \dfrac{1 - (1+i)^{-n}}{i}$	i [STO] [+] 1 [=] [y^x] n [+/−] [=] [+/−] [+] 1 [=] [÷] [RCL] [×] R [=]	n [N] i [%i] R [PMT] [2nd] [PV]
$R = S \cdot \dfrac{1}{s_{\overline{n}|i}}$ $= S \cdot \dfrac{i}{(1+i)^n - 1}$	S [×] i [÷] [(] [(] [(] i [+] 1 [)] [)] [y^x] n [−] 1 [)] [=]	n [N] i [%i] S [FV] [2nd] [PMT]
$R = A \cdot \dfrac{1}{a_{\overline{n}|i}}$ $= A \cdot \dfrac{i}{1 - (1+i)^{-n}}$	A [×] i [÷] [(] [(] 1 [−] [(] [(] [(] 1 [+] i [)] [)] [y^x] n [+/−] [=]	n [N] i [%i] A [PV] [2nd] [PMT]
$n = \dfrac{\ln\left(\dfrac{Si}{R} + 1\right)}{\ln(i + 1)}$	S [÷] R [×] i [+] 1 [=] [lnx] [÷] [(] [(] 1 [+] i [)] [lnx] [=]	i [%i] R [PMT] S [FV] [2nd] [N]
$n = -\dfrac{\ln\left(1 - \dfrac{Ai}{R}\right)}{\ln(1 + i)}$ $(Ai < R)$	1 [−] [(] [(] A [×] i [÷] R [=] [lnx] [÷] [(] [(] 1 [+] i [)] [lnx] [=] [+/−] Error if $Ai \not< R$	i [%i] R [PMT] A [PV] [2nd] [N] Error if $Ai \not< R$

A comparison of payment times and present and future values for deferred, ordinary, and annuities due is illustrated in the following combined time diagram:

m periods

It is a good habit to draw the time diagram for each problem as you read it. Do not rely on formulas alone to understand the situation.

Amortization and Sinking Funds

The *amortization* of an interest-bearing debt refers to the extinction of the debt by a sequence of equal payments at equal time intervals, with each payment including a portion of the principal and interest on the outstanding principal. Since the payments form an annuity with present value equal to the principal of the debt, the payment is the periodic rent of the annuity. The principal remaining is the present value of the rent with k payments remaining. This is summarized in the following formulas:

(payment) $\quad R = A_n \cdot \dfrac{1}{a_{\overline{n}\mid i}}, \quad$ where $A_n = $ principal, $i = $ periodic rate, $n = $ number of periods

(amount of debt left $\quad A = R \cdot a_{\overline{n-k}\mid i}$
after k periods)

The last amount is usually computed in the course of generating an *amortization schedule,* which shows how each payment is distributed into reduction of principal with interest paid. Subtract the periodic interest on the previous balance from the current payment to get the current reduction of principal. (Thus the payment must be more than the current interest or no principal reduction would occur.) An example is shown in Problem 44. A general amortization schedule is shown in Table 5-9.

TABLE 5-9. Typical Amortization Schedule at Periodic Rate i with Payment R for n Periods

BALANCE AT BEGINNING OF PERIOD	INTEREST AT END OF PERIOD	PAYMENT	BALANCE REDUCED BY
$Ra_{\overline{n}\mid i}$	$R(1 - v^n)$	R	Rv^n
$Ra_{\overline{n-1}\mid i}$	$R(1 - v^{n-1})$	R	Rv^{n-1}
$\vdots$	$\vdots$	$\vdots$	$\vdots$
$Ra_{\overline{1}\mid i}$	$R(1 - v)$	R	Rv

$v^n = (1 + i)^{-n}$

The values in an amortization schedule are better computed sequentially according to the scheme shown in Table 5-10. The periodic payment is computed first according to the basic annuity formula, and then the rest of the schedule is multiplications by the periodic rate i and successive subtractions.

TABLE 5-10. General Amortization Schedule:
An Iterative Formulation

BALANCE AT BEGINNING OF PERIOD	INTEREST AT END OF PERIOD	PAYMENT	BALANCE REDUCED BY
$P_1 = P$	$i \times P_1$	R	$R - iP_1 = Red_1$
$P_2 = P_1 - Red_1$	$i \times P_2$	R	$R - iP_2 = Red_2$
$P_3 = P_2 - Red_2$	$i \times P_3$	R	$R - iP_3 = Red_3$
.	.	.	.
.	.	.	.
.	.	.	.

Continue this process until balance is reduced to zero.

i = periodic rate; P_k = remaining principal at beginning of kth period; Red_k = reduction in principal by k^{th} payment.

The tabular formulation of Table 5-9 is useful if some specific entry in the table is to be computed without having to compute the entire table. The iterative formulation of Table 5-10 is more useful for generation of an amortization schedule on a calculator.

When a debt is to be extinguished by the *sinking fund method,* the debtor pays the interest regularly at an agreed upon rate and also makes payments into an interest-bearing account that is to accumulate to equal the total principal at some future date. This amount would then be paid to the holder of the note. The account is called a *sinking fund.*

It will be assumed that payments are made at equal time intervals and in equal amounts on the same day that interest payments are made to the creditor. The *total periodic charge* is the sum of payments to the creditor and to the sinking fund. The sinking fund forms an ordinary annuity where the future value should equal the borrowed principal. A general formulation of a sinking fund schedule is shown in Table 5-11.

TABLE 5-11. Sinking Fund Schedule Earning Interest
at Rate i per Period with Payment R

K	PAYMENT	INTEREST	CHANGE IN FUND	FUND BALANCE
1	R	0	R	$R \cdot s_{\overline{1}|i}$
2	R	$R((1 + i) - 1)$	$R(1 + i)$	$R \cdot s_{\overline{2}|i}$
3	R	$R((1 + i)^2 - 1)$	$R(1 + i)^2$	$R \cdot s_{\overline{3}|i}$
.	.	.	.	.
.	.	.	.	.
n	R	$R((1 + i)^{n-1} - 1)$	$R(1 + i)^{n-1}$	$R \cdot s_{\overline{n}|i}$

The periodic payment R is computed from the formula

$$R = P \cdot \frac{1}{s_{\overline{n}|i}}$$

The expressions given in Table 5-11 could be used to generate the table, but are best used if specific isolated quantities are desired without generating entire table. To generate the table on a calculator, an iterative approach is easiest. A scheme for this is given in Table 5-12 and is illustrated in Problem 45.

TABLE 5-12. Sinking Fund Schedule: An Iterative Approach

K	PAYMENT	INTEREST	CHANGE IN FUND	FUND BALANCE
1	R	$I_1 = 0$	$CF_1 = R$	$Bal_1 = R$
2	R	$I_2 = i \times Bal_1$	$CF_2 = R + I_2$	$Bal_2 = Bal_1 + CF_2$
3	R	$I_3 = i \times Bal_2$	$CF_3 = R + I_3$	$Bal_3 = Bal_2 + CF_3$
.	.	.	.	.
.	.	.	.	.
.	.	.	.	.

Continue this process until balance equals borrowed principal.

The symbols I_k = interest for k^{th} period, CF_k = change in sinking fund at the end of the kth period, and Bal_k = balance in fund at end of period. Notice that all that is required is multiplying i times the old balance and then adding I_k plus the current payment R to obtain the new balance upon adding that result to the old balance.

Depreciation

Fixed assets such as machinery, other kinds of equipment, and buildings are diminished in value by wear and tear, exposure, and obsolescence— in short, time. The decrease in value that cannot be retrieved by making repairs is called *depreciation*. The value of the asset at the end of its useful life is called the *salvage* (or *scrap*) *value*. The difference between the original cost and the salvage value is the *total depreciation* (or *wearing value*) of the asset.

Since capital in an enterprise should be kept intact (according to a basic principle of economics), in order to offset the depreciation, part of the profits produced by using the assets is put into a *depreciation fund* periodically (usually on an annual basis). This amount is the *annual contribution*. The *annual depreciation charge*, however, may be more than the annual contribution, if the fund earns interest. The *book value* of an asset is the difference between the original cost and the amount in the depreciation fund.

We shall consider four basic methods of depreciating an asset: the straight-line (or linear) depreciation method, the sum-of-digits method, the constant percentage (declining balance) method, and the sinking fund method.

In the discussion that follows, let C = original cost, n = useful life (in years), t = any intermediate time (in years), W = total depreciation (wearing value), R = annual contribution to depreciation fund, V = book value of the asset, and S = salvage value.

Straight Line Method This method assumes that equal contributions are made annually to the depreciation fund and that the fund earns no interest. The annual contribution is

$$R = \frac{C - S}{n} = \frac{W}{n}$$

This can be viewed graphically as a straight line. The slope is negative and in absolute value equals the annual depreciation R. The equation of the line is $V = C - Rt$. The y intercept is at the original cost (see Figure 5-1) and the y axis is the book value, V.

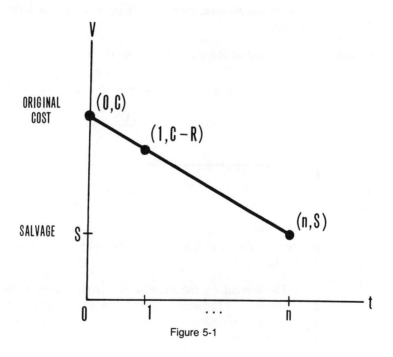

Figure 5-1

If your calculator has a linear regression capability, the depreciation line can be easily calculated by entering the two end points $(0, C)$ and (n, S) as data. Otherwise, the annual contribution can be computed directly and successively subtracted from the original cost to produce a depreciation schedule. The general format is shown in Table 5-13.

TABLE 5-13. Straight-Line Depreciation

END OF YEAR	ANNUAL CONTRIBUTION	FUND BALANCE	BOOK VALUE
0	0	0	C
1	R	R	$C - R$
2	R	$2R$	$C - 2R$
.	.	.	.
.	.	.	.
.	.	.	.
n	R	nR	$C - nR = S$

Sum-of-Digits Method   This method is an accelerated depreciation with successively decreasing contributions to the fund. If the useful life is n years, the sum of digits is

$$\sum_{k=1}^{n} k = 1 + 2 + \cdots + n = \frac{n(n + 1)}{2}$$

This sum can be computed directly or by using the formula on the right-hand side.

Example   Find the sum of the digits from 1 to 10.

$$1 + 2 + 3 + 4 + 5 + 6 + 7 + 8 + 9 + 10 = \frac{10(10 + 1)}{2} =$$
$$\frac{10(11)}{2} = 55$$

This can be calculated as

$$10 \boxed{\times} 11 \boxed{\div} 2 \boxed{=}$$

or even done mentally. Notice that the addition of 1 is not worth doing on the calculator, and so is done mentally and calculated as "10 times 11 divided by 2."

The annual contribution is the original cost C times the fraction k/N, where N is the sum of digits previously calculated. The numerator k starts as n and decreases by 1 each year until n years have passed, when $k = 1$; that is,

$$\frac{n}{N} C, \frac{n - 1}{N} C, \ldots \frac{2}{N} C, \frac{1}{N} C$$

Referring to the previous example, for ten years, the successive depreciations would be

$$^{10}/_{55} C, \, ^{9}/_{55} C, \, ^{8}/_{55} C, \, \ldots, \, ^{2}/_{55} C, \, ^{1}/_{55} C$$

A general form of a depreciation schedule, based on the sum-of-digits method, is given in Table 5-14.

TABLE 5-14.

END OF YEAR	ANNUAL CONTRIBUTION	BOOK VALUE
0	—	C
1	$\dfrac{n}{N} C$	$V_1 = C - \dfrac{n}{N} C$
2	$\dfrac{n-1}{N} C$	$V_2 = V_1 - \dfrac{n-1}{N} C$
.	.	.
.	.	.
.	.	.
$n-1$	$\dfrac{2}{N} C$	$V_{n-1} = V_{n-2} - \dfrac{2}{N} C$
n	$\dfrac{1}{N} C$	$V_n = 0$

The iterative approach is emphasized here. The salvage value is zero. An efficient way to calculate the sequence of annual contributions is to store the quantity C/N (i.e., the cost divided by the sum of digits) in memory. Then successively multiply it by n, $(n-1)$, . . . , 3, 2, 1 by recalling it as each multiplication is to be performed (see Problem 48).

The Constant Percentage of Book Value Method The annual contribution in this method is achieved by multiplying a fixed percent times the book value at the end of the preceding year. It is assumed that the fund earns no interest. (A variation of this method is known as the *declining balance* method, and often a factor of 125% to 200% is used to accelerate the process even more, but then the salvage value cannot be taken into account.) The constant percentage r is called the *rate of depreciation*. Thus the sequence of book values is

$$C, C(1 - r), C(1 - r)^2, \ldots$$

We want the last value of this sequence to equal the salvage value S, and hence we require

$$C(1 - r)^n = S$$

Solving this for r, we get

$$r = 1 - \sqrt[n]{\frac{S}{C}}$$

This rate is computed by either using the nth root sequence 2nd $\boxed{x\sqrt{y}}$ or $\boxed{\text{INV}}$ $\boxed{y^x}$, depending on which calculator you have. Typically, the calculation can be done like this:

$$S \boxed{\div} C \boxed{=} \boxed{\text{2nd}} \boxed{x\sqrt{y}} n \boxed{=} \boxed{+/-} \boxed{+} 1 \boxed{=}$$

This sequence will work on both an arithmetic entry and an AOS entry system. On the arithmetic system, the first $\boxed{=}$ could be omitted. Once the depreciation rate r is calculated, one can use the automatic discount feature of the $\boxed{\%}$ key to get the depreciation and book value at the same time (see Problem 49). After all, this method is just a series of discounts from the original cost.

The Sinking Fund Method This method accumulates equal annual contributions in an interest-bearing depreciation fund. The result is that the depreciation charge is increasing due to the accumulated interest. The ultimate goal is that the fund accumulate the total depreciation (wearing value) W. Hence the annual contribution, if the periodic rate is i, is simply

$$R = W \cdot \frac{1}{s_{\overline{n}|\,i}}$$

The depreciation charge at the end of year k is

$$\frac{W(1 + i)^{k-1}}{s_{\overline{n}|\,i}} = R(1 + i)^{k-1}$$

It is useful to give a sinking fund schedule showing these amounts. The change in the fund each year (depreciation) is just the interest earned on the previous balance plus the current contribution (see Problem 50).

Bonds

A *bond* is a promise to pay a specified sum, the *redemption price*, at some future date. Equal dividends are paid at a fixed rate at equal intervals until redemption. The *dividend* is periodic interest based on the *face value (par)* of the bond. There are many different types of bonds used for various purposes. Only coupon bonds and annuity bonds will be considered.

The *yield rate* is the rate of return that the purchaser expects to realize when the bond matures (is redeemed). If the bond is purchased for less than par (discount), the yield will be higher than the coupon rate; if bought at more than par (premium), the yield will be lower than the coupon rate.

The formula relating the pertinent quantities is

$$V = C(1 + i)^{-n} + R \cdot a_{\overline{n}|i}$$

where V = purchase price
C = redemption price (usually par)
i = yield rate
n = number of payments until redemption
R = periodic dividend = face value $\times$ periodic coupon rate

Notice that the first term on the right-hand side resembles a compound interest formula. It is in fact the present value of the money one would receive from the bond when redeemed. The second term is the present value of an annuity where the rent (payments) are just the periodic dividends. The sum of these is the present value of the bond, which is the amount for which it should be purchased to achieve the yield rate i.

These two terms can be computed directly, or by using compound discount factor tables and annuity tables, or by using the compound interest and annuity functions built into a business calculator.

If a bond is *not* redeemable, then the first term cannot be taken into account until the bond is actually sold, since we cannot predict the market price. At that time, C would represent the market price. Until then, all that can be computed is the internal yield based on the purchase price and dividend rate.

Finding the yield to maturity is difficult. One method is to interpolate in bond tables (see Problem 54). Another method is to use numerical techniques (specifically, linear iterations) to solve the basic equation numerically for the yield rate i. One possible formulation is developed in Problem 55 and illustrated in Problem 56.

An *annuity bond* is a promise to pay a debt in equal periodic installments, principal together with interest, at a fixed rate. Thus the periodic installment is

$$R = A \cdot \frac{1}{a_{\overline{n}|i}}$$

where A = face value, n = number of periods, and i = periodic rate.

If the bond has k payments left, when it is purchased, then the value of the bond is

$$V = R \cdot \frac{1}{a_{\overline{k}|i}}$$

This is the present value of an annuity of k periods with periodic rent R.

Solved Problems

PERCENT

1. Last year's gross sales were \$158,255. This year's were 7% higher. Compute the increase and the current year's gross sales.

Method 1   First compute the increase: 7% × \$158,255.

$$7 \boxed{\%} \boxed{\times} 158255 \boxed{=} \quad \text{Result:} \boxed{11077.85}$$

Then add this to last year's sales:

$$\boxed{+} 158255 \boxed{=} \quad \text{Result:} \boxed{169332.85}$$

Thus there was an increase of \$11,077.85, bringing the gross sales up to a total of \$169,332.85.

Method 2   Use the add-on feature of some calculators.

$$158255 \boxed{+} 7 \boxed{\%} \quad \text{(read increase)}$$
$$\boxed{=} \quad \text{(read total)}$$

2. A buyer is bragging that he bought an item for only 40% of its current wholesale price on a special sale. If he paid \$300 per thousand, what is the current wholesale price per thousand? The unit cost?

This is a simple percent problem in which we want to compute the base $B = P/R$. Thus we compute $300 \div 40\% = 300 \div .40$. This can be calculated as written above either way. If you have a percent key, then use $300 \boxed{\div} 40 \boxed{\%} \boxed{=}$. Thus the wholesale price is \$750 per thousand. The unit cost is \$750 ÷ 1000 = \$.75, which you should do easily mentally.

3. An item sells for \$2.99 plus 6% sales tax. (a) What is the tax and the final cost? (b) What would these be if the item sells for \$2.05?

(a) Key $2.99 \boxed{+} 6 \boxed{\%}$ (read tax) $\boxed{=}$ (read final cost). Thus the tax would be \$.1794 rounded to \$.18, and the final cost is \$3.1694 rounded to \$3.17.

(b) Key $2.05 \boxed{+} 6 \boxed{\%}$ (read tax) $\boxed{=}$ (read final cost). The tax you read is \$.123, which should be rounded *up* to \$.13 (even though the digit 3 is less than 5, because sales taxes are charged a full cent for *any* amount over an even cent). The final cost read is \$2.173, which we round *up* to \$2.18 for the same reason.

4. You are computing your income tax and find that your taxable income is \$32,500. A look at the tax computation tables indicates that your tax is \$6201 plus 37% of any amount over \$29,900. What is your income tax?

The tax is ($32,500 − $29,900) × 37% + $6201. To compute this, key

$$32500 \boxed{-} 29900 \boxed{=} \boxed{\times} 37 \boxed{\%} \boxed{+} 6201 \boxed{=}$$

(If you have an arithmetic operating system, the equals after the 29,900 could be omitted. Parentheses could be used in either case, but are clearly unnecessary.)

MARKUP, DISCOUNT, AND GROSS PROFIT MARGIN

5. A store adds a 40% markup to an item that costs the store $4.12. There is also a 5% sales tax. What is the final cost of the item to the customer?

The retail price is $4.12 + 40% of $4.12. Then an additional 5% of this result is added. The calculation is

$$4.12 \boxed{+} 40 \boxed{\%} \boxed{+} 5 \boxed{\%} \boxed{=}$$

The result is $6.0564. This is rounded up to $6.06.

6. A store discounts a $250 coat by 25%. There is no sales tax on clothing. What is the amount of the discount? What is the actual sale price?

Key 250 $\boxed{-}$ 25 $\boxed{\%}$ (read discount) $\boxed{=}$ (read price). $\boxed{62.5}$ means $62.50, $\boxed{187.5}$ means $187.50.

7. A car is listed for $7254. You have read that the list is an average markup of 21% of cost. What did the car cost the dealer?

The correct formula is C = S/(1 + M), where C = dealer cost, S = selling price, and M = cost markup rate. The calculation, in general, is

$$S \boxed{\div} \boxed{(} 1 \boxed{+} M \boxed{)} \boxed{=}$$

However, it is easier to add the 1 mentally to the decimal equivalent of M = 21% = .21 and just compute 7254 $\boxed{\div}$ 1.21 $\boxed{=}$ yielding $\boxed{5995.0413}$, which we round to $5995 to the nearest dollar.

8. Another manufacturer sells a vehicle similar to that in Problem 7 for $7254 also. However, he works on a 21% *profit margin* (percent of list). What do the dealers pay for the vehicle?

The correct formula is cost = sell (1 − mar), where here cost = dealers cost, sell = list price, and mar = profit margin. The calculation is

$$7254 \boxed{\times} \boxed{(} 1 \boxed{-} 21 \boxed{\%} \boxed{)} \boxed{=} \quad \text{giving} \quad \boxed{5730.66}$$

or $5731, to the nearest dollar.

If you have a "business calculator" that does this automatically, key

$$7254 \boxed{\text{SEL}} \; 21 \boxed{\text{MAR}} \boxed{\text{2nd}} \boxed{\text{CST}}$$

giving the same result. Compare the result with Problem 7. Notice that profit margin is different than a cost markup.

9. A gift-shop owner works on a constant gross profit margin (GPM) of 35%. If three items cost $42, $35, and $56 per dozen, what should the selling price of each of these items be?

First we compute the selling price per dozen and then divide by 12 to get the per item price. The formula is

$$\text{sell} = \frac{\text{cost}}{(1 - \text{mar})}$$

Since the margin is constant, we use the constant key $\boxed{\text{K}}$, if your calculator has one. First key 1 $\boxed{-}$ 35 $\boxed{\%}$ $\boxed{=}$ $\boxed{\div}$ $\boxed{\text{K}}$ $\boxed{=}$. This sets up the division by (1 − mar). Then key

42 $\boxed{=}$ (read $64.62 and record)

35 $\boxed{=}$ (read $53.85 and record)

56 $\boxed{=}$ (read $86.15 and record)

These are the prices per dozen. Now we divide each by 12. To set this up, key 12 $\boxed{\div}$ $\boxed{\text{K}}$ $\boxed{=}$; then reenter each of the recorded prices per dozen followed by an equals:

64.62 $\boxed{=}$ (read $5.39)

53.85 $\boxed{=}$ (read $4.49)

86.15 $\boxed{=}$ (read $7.18)

These are the prices for each item rounded to the nearest whole cent. Notice the use of the constant avoided reentering the constant divisors. If you had to do this with 50 items, it would be a real time saver.

Remark: It is recommended, when possible, that the quantity 1 − mar be computed *mentally* to save time. In this example it is simply 1 − 35% = 1 − .35 = .65. Then you can set up the constant divisor simply as .65 $\boxed{\div}$ $\boxed{\text{K}}$ $\boxed{=}$. (If you don't have a constant key, do the divisions in the usual way.)

If you have a business calculator, then key

35 [MAR]   (sets up margin as a constant)

42 [CST] [2nd] [SEL] [÷] 12 [=]

35 [CST] [2nd] [SEL] [÷] 12 [=]

56 [CST] [2nd] [SEL] [÷] 12 [=]

Read the per item prices after each [=].

10. An item that costs $25 is sold for $35. What is the cost markup? What is the gross profit margin?

The formulas are

$$\text{(a) Cost markup} = \frac{\text{sell} - \text{cost}}{\text{cost}}$$

$$\text{(b) GPM} = \frac{\text{sell} - \text{cost}}{\text{sell}}$$

Formula (a) can be computed directly as in

Method 1   35 [−] 25 [=] [÷] 25 [=]   (read 0.4 = 40%)

or, using the △% key, if available,

Method 2   25 [2nd] [△%] 35 [=]   and read 40

indicating 40%. (Reverse order of numbers on BA II.) Formula (b) can be computed directly as

Method 1   35 [−] 25 [=] [÷] 35 [=]   (read .28571429 ≐ 28.6%)

or, if you have a business calculator,

Method 2   25 [CST] 35 [SEL] [2nd] [MAR]   (read 28.571429, approximately 28.6%)

11. Illustrate why a gross profit margin *cannot* be over 100% by trying to compute the selling price of an item costing $12 at a 150% margin.

The gross profit margin (GPM) = $(S - C)/S$. Thus

$$150\% = \frac{S - C}{S} = 1 - \frac{C}{S}$$

Solving this for S, we get

$$S = \frac{C}{1 - 150\%} = \frac{12}{1 - 150\%}$$

which we compute as

$$12 \boxed{-} \boxed{(} 1 \boxed{-} 150 \boxed{\%} \boxed{)} \boxed{=}$$

yielding -24. Thus we would have to "sell" the item for $-\$24$, that is, pay (?) the customer $24 to take the item off our hands! This is nonsense. *Never* enter a GPM of 100% or greater.

12. Graph the gross profit margin (GPM) as a function of the ratio S/C. Interpret the various regions of the graph.

If we let $S/C = k$, then

$$\mathbf{GPM} = \frac{S - C}{S} = 1 - \frac{C}{S} = 1 - \frac{1}{(S/C)} = 1 - \frac{1}{k}$$

We merely graph the expression $1 - (1/k)$ for various values of k. This is a hyperbola, reflected in the horizontal axis and translated vertically $+1$ units. It looks like Figure 5-2.

Figure 5-2

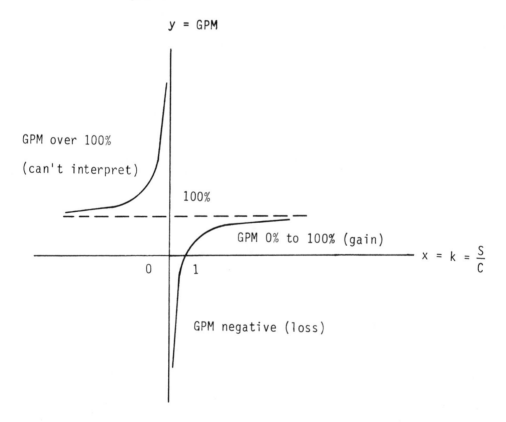

Notice that the usual region is when GPM is from 0% to 100% and $k = S/C$ is more than 1; that is, S is more than C, which means that something sells for more than it costs. When S is less than C, k is less than 1 and we have a loss—the GPM is negative. The only time GPM is more than 100% is when $k = S/C$ is negative, which is not possible under normal circumstances.

13. An item that costs \$14.05 is sold for \$18.95. Compute the GPM (gross profit margin).

$$\text{GPM} = \frac{\text{sell} - \text{cost}}{\text{sell}} = \frac{\text{sell}}{\text{sell}} - \frac{\text{cost}}{\text{sell}} = 1 - \frac{\text{cost}}{\text{sell}}$$

Thus we compute

1 $\boxed{-}$ 14.05 $\boxed{\div}$ 18.95 $\boxed{=}$ giving $\boxed{0.2585752}$

and round to 25.9%.

(*Caution*: If your calculator has sequential entry, rather than AOS, parentheses should be used after the $\boxed{-}$. Another way is to use the first form of the formula, which requires entry of the selling price twice: S $\boxed{-}$ C $\boxed{\div}$ S $\boxed{=}$; but this will *not* work for AOS systems. If you want to be safe, use this: S $\boxed{-}$ C $\boxed{=}$ $\boxed{\div}$ S $\boxed{=}$.)

If you have a business calculator, you can use

14.05 $\boxed{\text{CST}}$ 18.95 $\boxed{\text{SEL}}$ $\boxed{\text{2nd}}$ $\boxed{\text{MAR}}$ and read $\boxed{25.85752}$

which is already in percent form. Round to 25.9%.

14. Use the $\triangle\%$ function to compute the percentage increase in an automobile price that rose from \$6807 to \$6954.

Different calculators implement the $\triangle\%$ in different ways. These are the three most common methods:

(a)   6807 $\boxed{\text{2nd}}$ $\boxed{\triangle\%}$ 6954 $\boxed{=}$ (TI Business Analyst I)

(b)   6954 $\boxed{\text{2nd}}$ $\boxed{\triangle\%}$ 6807 $\boxed{=}$ (TI Business Analyst II)

(c)   6954 $\boxed{-}$ 6807 $\boxed{\text{2nd}}$ $\boxed{\triangle\%}$ (Some Sharp models)

Try your calculator to see which way is right. The result is 2.1595416%, which is 2.2% to the nearest tenth of a percent.

15. Compute the simple interest at 14.12% on 2700 dollars borrowed for three months.

$$P = 2700, \qquad r = .1412, \qquad t = \frac{3}{12} = \frac{1}{4} = .25$$

$$I = Prt = (2700)(.1412)(.25)$$

Compute this product directly, or the percent key can be used and the reduction of t to a decimal can be done on the calculator as follows:

$$2700 \;\boxed{\times}\; 14.12 \;\boxed{\%}\;\boxed{\times}\; 3 \;\boxed{\div}\; 12 \;\boxed{=}$$

The result is $95.31.

16. Compute the interest and payback amount on $500 borrowed at 17% *exact* simple interest for 100 days.

$$I = Prt = 500(17\%)(\frac{100}{365}); \qquad 500 \;\boxed{\times}\; 17 \;\boxed{\%}\;\boxed{\times}\; 100 \;\boxed{\div}\; 365$$
$$\boxed{=} \quad \text{(read interest)}$$

$$S = P + I; \;\boxed{+}\; 500 \;\boxed{=} \quad \text{(read total payback)}$$

The interest is $23.29 and hence the payback is $523.29.

17. After 120 days a man pays back a loan at 7% *ordinary* simple interest totaling $500. How much was the principal? The interest?

Since $S = P(1 + rt)$, substitution gives

$$500 = P[1 + 7\%\left(\frac{120}{360}\right)]$$

Thus solving for P gives

$$P = \frac{500}{[1 + 7\%(120/360)]}$$

Or just substitute in the formula for P; that is, $P = S/(1 + rt)$.

$$500 \;\boxed{\div}\;\boxed{(}\; 1 \;\boxed{+}\; 7 \;\boxed{\%}\;\boxed{\times}\; 120 \;\boxed{\div}\; 360 \;\boxed{)}\;\boxed{=} \quad \text{giving}$$
$$\boxed{488.59935}$$

If you have an arithmetic (sequential) entry system, you must add the 1 in reverse order:

$$7 \;\boxed{\%}\;\boxed{\times}\; 120 \;\boxed{\div}\; 360 \;\boxed{+}\; 1 \;\boxed{\div}\; 500 \;\boxed{=}\;\boxed{1/x}$$

Notice that we have divided by 500 and then inverted, which avoids the use of parentheses. (To use this on AOS systems, use $\boxed{=}$ after the 1.) The principle was $488.60. The interest is $500 − $488.60, calculated as 500 $\boxed{-}$ 488.6 $\boxed{=}$, read $\boxed{11.4}$, that is, $11.40.

18. On April 5, 1980, ABC loan company sold the following note to Big Bank:

> January 10, 1980
>
> One year after the above date I promise to pay to the order of ABC loan company the sum of $1000 plus simple interest at 11.2% per annum.
>
> (signed) Mr. Poor

If Big Bank used a 12% interest-in-advance rate, what were the proceeds? What interest rate does the bank realize on its investment?

Method 1 The note matures on January 10, 1981 for $1112. From April 5 to January 10 is 280 days, so $S = \$1112$, $t = 280/360$, and $d = 12\%$. The discount formula is $D = Sdt$, computed as

$$1112 \boxed{\times} 12 \boxed{\%} \boxed{\times} 280 \boxed{\div} 360 \boxed{=}$$

Result: $\boxed{103.78667}$, which we round to $103.79, the discount. The effective principal then is $P = S - D = 1112 - 103.79 = 1008.21$. The amount discounted is the proceeds, which becomes the bank's interest. Thus the interest rate is

$$r = \frac{I}{Pt} = \frac{103.79}{1008.21(280/360)}$$

which is computed as follows:

$$103.79 \boxed{\div} \boxed{(} 1008.21 \boxed{\times} 280 \boxed{\div} 360 \boxed{)} \boxed{=}$$

The result is $\boxed{.13235763}$, which is approximately 13.24%.

Method 2 Use the formula

$$r = \frac{d}{1 - td} = \frac{.12}{1 - (280/360)(.12)}$$

and compute

$$.12 \boxed{\div} \boxed{(} 1 \boxed{-} \boxed{(} 280 \boxed{\div} 360 \boxed{\times} .12 \boxed{=}$$

The result displayed is .13235294, which differs slightly from the result obtained using method 1 because of the rounding of the discount D in method 1.

19. Mr. Schmidt intends to borrow $3000 from Little Bank for 90 days. If the bank charges 9% interest in advance, how much should Mr. Schmidt actually request in order to end up with $3000? What is the ordinary simple interest rate?

$$S = \frac{P}{1 - dt} = \frac{3000}{1 - 9\%(90/360)}$$

To compute this (AOS),

$$3000 \;\boxed{\div}\;\boxed{(}\; 1 \;\boxed{-}\; 9 \;\boxed{\%}\;\boxed{\times}\; 90 \;\boxed{\div}\; 360 \;\boxed{)}\;\boxed{=}$$

Result: $\boxed{3069.0537}$. Mr. Schmidt should borrow $3069.05.
Caution: If you have arithmetic entry, do *not* use this sequence. Instead use

$$3000 \;\boxed{\div}\;\boxed{(}\; 9 \;\boxed{\%}\;\boxed{\times}\; 90 \;\boxed{\div}\; 360 \;\boxed{+/-}\;\boxed{+}\; 1 \;\boxed{)}\;\boxed{=}$$

What this does is to compute the expression as if it were written

$$\frac{3000}{-9\%(90/360) + 1}$$

If you don't do this, an arithmetic (sequential) entry system would have subtracted the 9% from the 1 in the first sequence given, which would give the wrong answer.

The interest rate actually earned by the bank is

$$r = \frac{I}{Pt} = \frac{69.05}{3000(90/360)}$$

$$69.05 \;\boxed{\div}\;\boxed{(}\; 3000 \;\boxed{\times}\; 90 \;\boxed{\div}\; 360 \;\boxed{)}\;\boxed{=}$$

Result: $\boxed{.09206667}$, which is 9.2% approximately.

COMPOUND INTEREST

20. Compute the compound amount on $2000 for one year at 9% compounded (converted) monthly.

The formula is $S = P(1 + i)^n$, where $P = 2000$, $i = 9\%/12$, and $n = 12$.

$$9 \boxed{\%} \boxed{\div} 12 \boxed{+} 1 \boxed{=} \boxed{y^x} 12 \boxed{\times} 2000 \boxed{=}$$

Read: $\boxed{\quad 2187.6138 \quad}$, which should be rounded to $2187.61.

If you have a business calculator this can be done automatically in three stages:

Stage 1 Put calculator in compound interest mode.

Stage 2 Enter data: $9 \boxed{\div} 12 \boxed{=} \boxed{\%i}$ Monthly rate entered
               $12 \boxed{N}$ Number of periods
               $2000 \boxed{PV}$ Principal

Stage 3 Compound amount is automatically done: $\boxed{2nd}$ $\boxed{FV}$. Computes future value.

This looks long, but once you become accustomed to the key sequence, it is actually quite easy.

21. A man has $1350 in a bank. In 5 years he will need $1000 to satisfy an obligation. If he expects the bank to continue paying $5^{3}/_4\%$ interest compounded daily, how much can he withdraw today, leaving the rest to accumulate.?

The solution is to discount $1000 for 5 years at the stated rate. There are two complications: (1) During any 5-year term there is always one leap year, giving an extra day, and (2) banks compute the rate per conversion period (day) by dividing by 360 and then compounding for 365 (or 366) days. The correct formula is

$$P = \frac{S}{(1 + i)^n} = S(1 + i)^{-n}$$

where $S = \$1000$, $i = 5.75\%/360$, and $n = 5(365) + 1$. (The 1 is the extra leap-year day.)

(a) Compute n and store in memory: $5 \boxed{\times} 365 \boxed{=} \boxed{+} 1 \boxed{=}$ $\boxed{STO}$ (the first $\boxed{=}$ may be omitted on an AOS calculator).

(b) Compute i, the daily interest rate: $5.75 \boxed{\%} \boxed{\div} 360 \boxed{=}$.

(c) Add 1 and raise to the nth power. Multiply by 1000. $\boxed{+} 1 \boxed{=}$ $\boxed{y^x} \boxed{RCL} \boxed{\times} 1000 \boxed{=}$.

The result is $\boxed{\quad 747.04564 \quad}$. Thus he can leave $747.05 in the account, which will become $1000 in 5 years. Thus he can withdraw $1350 - \$747.05 = \$602.95$ ($1350 \boxed{-} 747.05 \boxed{=}$).

Comment: Over an extended period such as 5 years, interest rates may actually fluctuate. Moreover, it is conceivable that the bank rules for compounding could change, although that is less likely.

If you have a business calculator, the same calculation may be done as follows:

(a) Set to compound interest mode:

(b) Enter time in days: $5 \fbox{$\times$} 365 \fbox{$+$} 1 \fbox{$=$} \fbox{N}$.

(c) Enter daily rate in %: $5.75 \fbox{$\div$} 360 \fbox{$=$} \fbox{%i}$.

(d) Amount required in 5 years: $1000 \fbox{FV}$.

(e) Compute amount left today: $\fbox{2nd} \fbox{PV}$.

(f) Amount to be withdrawn: $\fbox{$+/-$} \fbox{$+$} 1350 \fbox{$=$}$.

If you ignore the leap day and the bank divides by 365 to get the daily rate, then $750.15 must be left in the account and you can withdraw only $599.85. This can be computed easily in addition to the above if you have not yet cleared the calculator by keying

$$5.75 \fbox{$\div$} 365 \fbox{$=$} \fbox{%i} 1825 \fbox{N} \fbox{2nd} \fbox{PV}$$

22. What is the effective rate equivalent to (a) 8% compounded quarterly, (b) 8% compounded daily (theoretical), (c) 8% compounded daily (Banker's rule), (d) 8% compounded continuously, and (e) the force of interest equivalent to 8% continuous compounding?

(a) The effective rate is $r = (1 + i)^m - 1$, where $m = 4$ and $i = 8\%/4 = 2\% = .02$. Thus $r = (1 + .02)^4 - 1 =$ (mentally) $(1.02)^4 - 1$, and calculate $1.02 \fbox{$y^x$} 4 \fbox{$-$} 1 \fbox{$=$}$ which gives the result $\fbox{.08243216}$ which is interpreted as approximately 8.24%. (*Note*: the $\fbox{$-$}$ 1 could have been deleted and 1.0824322 would have been displayed. Then one just ignores the initial 1.) On a business calculator, if we realize that the effective rate is just the interest on $1, we can compute it as

$$2 \fbox{%i} 4 \fbox{N} 1 \fbox{PV} \fbox{2nd} \fbox{FV} * \fbox{$-$} 1 \fbox{$=$}$$
(gives interest in decimal form)

(b) For 8% compounded daily, $m = 365$ and $i = 8\%/365$; then compute $8 \fbox{%} \fbox{$\div$} 365 \fbox{$+$} 1 \fbox{$=$}$, which is $(1 + i)$; then continue with $\fbox{$y^x$} 365 \fbox{$-$} 1 \fbox{$=$}$, which is $(1 + i)^{365} - 1$, the effective rate in decimal form $\fbox{.08327733}$, which we round and interpret as approximately 8.3%. On a business calculator the method is similar to that in part (a) except that the daily rate $8 \div 365$ must be computed before keying $\fbox{%i}$, and of course N

---

*An alternate method at the last step is to change m (i.e., $\fbox{N}$) to 1 and compute the effective rate r as follows: $1 \fbox{N} \fbox{2nd} \fbox{%i}$. The result is expressed in percent form as 8.2432158, which is rounded to 8.24%.)

is now 365. For completeness, after putting the calculator in compound interest mode, the key sequence is

$$8 \boxed{\div} 365 \boxed{=} \boxed{\%i} \; 365 \boxed{N} \; 1 \boxed{PV} \boxed{2nd} \boxed{FV} \quad \text{read}$$
$$\boxed{1.0832773}$$

This is the future value of $1. The interest rate equals the amount earned, which is just the decimal part of the number. Thus ignore the initial 1 and interpret the decimal part, .0832773, as approximately 8.3%. This technique works as long as the rate is less than 100%, which is rarely otherwise. If for some unusual reason the rate is more than 100%, you would see an integer bigger than 1 and you just subtract 1.

(c) Banks use 360 as the divisor and then compound for 365 days. Thus compute as before, except that $i = 8\% \div 360$ and $m = 365$.

$$8 \boxed{\%} \boxed{\div} 360 \boxed{+} 1 \boxed{=} \boxed{y^x} \; 365 \boxed{-} 1 \boxed{=} \quad \text{yielding}$$
$$\boxed{.08448143}$$

We have just computed $[1 + (8\%/360)]^{365} - 1$, which equals 8.45% approximately. For business calculators, the calculation is the same as in part (b), except use for the rate $8 \boxed{\div} 360 \boxed{=} \boxed{\%i}$.

(d) The effective rate for continuous compounding is $r = e^j - 1$, where $j = $ nominal rate $= 8\%$. The calculation may look slightly different on different calculators. Here are two key sequences that are essentially the same except for the way 8% is entered and the appearance of the way the exponential function is activated:

$$.08 \boxed{INV} \boxed{1nx} \boxed{-} 1 \boxed{=} \quad \text{on some scientific calculators}$$

$$8 \boxed{\%} \boxed{2nd} \boxed{e^x} \boxed{-} 1 \boxed{=} \quad \text{on some business calculators}$$

In both cases the result is $\boxed{.08328707}$, or approximately 8.33%.

(*Note*: The e^x function is usually the second function above the $1nx$ key. If it is reversed and you can key e^x immediately, just omit the 2nd.)

Notice that the interest compounded continuously is not much different from the theoretical daily rate but is less than using the usual Banker's rule.

(e) To compute the force of interest, which is the nominal rate j that will produce the given effective rate r (in this case 8%), we solve the continuous compounding formula for j and then calculate: $r = e^j - 1$ so that $(r + 1) = e^j$. Taking natural logs of both sides, we get $j = \ln(r + 1)$. Since $r = 8\%$, we compute

$$8 \boxed{\%} \boxed{+} 1 \boxed{=} \boxed{\ln x} \quad \text{which gives} \quad \boxed{.07696104}$$

That is, a nominal rate of about 7.696% (the force of interest) gives a continuously compounded effective rate of 8%.

23. Compute the compound discount factor $(1 + i)^{-n}$ for the following situations: (a) 6% quarterly for 3 years, (b) 14% semiannually for 2½ years, and (c) 5½% daily for 3 years.

(a) $i = 6\%/4$, $n = 4 \times 3 = 12$ quarters; thus we compute

$$6 \boxed{\%} \boxed{\div} 4 \boxed{+} 1 \boxed{=} \boxed{y^x} 12 \boxed{+/-} \boxed{=}$$
$$\text{(read discount factor)} \quad \boxed{.83638743}$$

On a business calculator, think of this as the present value of $1 at 1.5% per quarter for 12 quarters. Thus enter (in compound interest mode)

$$12 \boxed{N} \; 1.5 \boxed{\%i} \; 1 \boxed{FV} \boxed{2nd} \boxed{PV}$$

(b) $i = 14\% \div 2 = 7\%$, $n = 2 \times 2\tfrac{1}{2} = 5$. Compute $(1 + .07)^{-5}$:

$$1.07 \boxed{y^x} 5 \boxed{+/-} \boxed{=} \quad \text{and read} \quad \boxed{.71298618}$$

Notice that it was easier to compute $1 + .07 = 1.07$ mentally before computing the discount factor.

On a business calculator (in compound interest mode), key

$$5 \boxed{N} \; 7 \boxed{\%i} \; 1 \boxed{FV} \boxed{2nd} \boxed{PV}$$

(c) $i = 5\tfrac{1}{2}\% \div 365$, $n = 3 \times 365$ (which are computed during entry).

$$5.5 \boxed{\%} \boxed{\div} 365 \boxed{+} 1 \boxed{=} \boxed{y^x} \boxed{(} 3 \boxed{\times} 365 \boxed{)} \boxed{+/-} \boxed{=}$$

The result is $\boxed{.84790481}$.

On a business calculator (in compound interest mode) we also calculate the quantities before entering them:

$$3 \boxed{\times} 365 \boxed{=} \boxed{N} \; 5.5 \boxed{\div} 365 \boxed{=} \boxed{\%i} \; 1 \boxed{FV} \boxed{2nd} \boxed{PV}$$

Notice that when it is possible to do the evaluation of i, $1 + i$, or n mentally it cuts down the time for calculator entry. It is a good idea to get in the habit of taking advantage of simple numbers for combining mental calculation with the power of the calculator.

24. Compute the value of $2500 if money is worth 6% (a) 5 years from now and (b) 3 years ago.

(a) $S = P(1 + i)^n = 2500(1 + 6\%)^5 = 2500(1.06)^5$:

$$1.06 \boxed{y^x} \; 5 \boxed{\times} \; 2500 \boxed{=} \quad \text{and the result is} \quad \boxed{3345.5639}$$

which is interpreted and rounded to $3345.56. Notice that $1 + 6\%$ is computed as 1.06 mentally. When $1 + i$ is more complex, it should of course be calculated.

(b) $P = S(1 + i)^{-n} = 2500(1 + 6\%)^{-3} = 2500(1.06)^{-3}$:

$$1.06 \boxed{y^x} \; 3 \boxed{+/-} \boxed{\times} \; 2500 \boxed{=} \quad \text{and the result is}$$
$$\boxed{2099.0482}$$

which is rounded to $2099.05. Notice that the multiplication by $2500 was performed last. If you have an AOS entry system it could be performed first. If your entry system is sequential then you either would need parentheses or you would get the wrong result. Try it, seeing what happens on your display after each function is performed.

Note: As an alternative for part (b), one could also have taken the result of part (a) and multiplied it by $(1.06)^{-8}$, since 8 years back from 5 years in the future equals 3 years back from today.

25. A student borrows $3000, agreeing to pay it in 10 years with accumulated interest at 7% for the last 5 years only. At the end of 7 years he wishes to discharge the debt and money is worth 8%. What should he pay to settle the debt?

The maturity value of the loan in 10 years would be $3000(1 + 7\%)^5$ since he is only paying interest for 5 years. Compute this as

$$1.07 \boxed{y^x} \; 5 \boxed{\times} \; 3000 \boxed{=}$$

and leave the result, 4207.6552 displayed. Since he wants to pay the debt 3 years early, the maturity value is discounted at 8% for 3 years by multiplying by $(1.08)^{-3}$:

$$\boxed{\times} \; * \; \boxed{(}\; 1.08 \boxed{y^x} \; 3 \boxed{+/-} \boxed{)} \; * \boxed{=} \quad \text{read} \quad \boxed{3340.1723}$$

Thus he can discharge the debt for $3340.17.

26. How long will it take $15,000 to amount to $40,000 at 8½% interest compounded monthly?

---

*If you are using a scientific calculator with hierarchial logic (i.e., AOS), the parentheses can be omitted.

If you solve the compound interest formula $S = P(1 + i)^n$ for n using natural logarithms, you get the formula

$$n = \frac{\ln (S/P)}{\ln (1 + i)}$$

where, in this example, $S = 40,000$, $P = 15,000$, and $i = 8\frac{1}{2}\%/12$. We compute as follows:

$$40000 \boxed{\div} 15000 \boxed{=} \boxed{\ln x} \boxed{\div} \boxed{(} 8.5 \boxed{\%} \boxed{\div} 12 \boxed{+} 1 \boxed{)} \boxed{\ln x} \boxed{=}$$

which gives 138.95985, the number of *months*. To convert to years, do not clear the display; divide by 12 by keying

$$\boxed{\div} 12 \boxed{=} \quad \text{and read the result} \quad \boxed{11.579987}$$

which is about 11.6 years, or 11 years, 7 months (139 months). The actual amount accrued in 139 months is \$40,011.34, which is slightly over the goal, but interest is converted on a monthly basis.

On a business calculator this is easily computed (in compound interest mode):

$$15000 \boxed{PV}\ 40000 \boxed{FV}\ 8.5 \boxed{\div} 12 \boxed{=} \boxed{\%i} \boxed{2nd} \boxed{N} \quad \text{(read}$$
months)

Then divide by 12 to compute years.

ANNUITIES

27. Compute $s_{\overline{32}|\,4\%}$ and $a_{\overline{32}|\,4\%}$.

$$s_{\overline{n}|\,i} = \frac{(1 + i)^n - 1}{i} = \frac{(1 + 4\%)^{32} - 1}{4\%} = \frac{(1.04)^{32} - 1}{.04}$$

which we compute as follows:

$$1.04 \boxed{y^x} 32 \boxed{-} 1 \boxed{=} \boxed{\div} .04 \boxed{=} \quad \text{giving the result} \quad \boxed{62.701468}$$

On a business calculator (annuity mode) $s_{\overline{n}|\,i}$ is just the future value of an annuity with a \$1 payment for n periods at rate i per period, so it is computed as follows:

$$32 \boxed{N}\ 4 \boxed{\%i}\ 1 \boxed{PMT} \boxed{2nd} \boxed{FV}$$

$$a_{\overline{n}|\,i} = \frac{1 - (1 + i)^{-n}}{i} = \frac{1 - (1 + 4\%)^{-32}}{4\%} = \frac{1 - (1.04)^{-32}}{.04}$$

$$1 \boxed{-} \boxed{(} 1.04 \boxed{y^x} 32 \boxed{+/-} \boxed{)} \boxed{=} \boxed{\div} .04 \boxed{=} \quad \text{which gives}$$
$$\boxed{17.873551}$$

Since $a_{\overline{n}|i}$ is just the present value of an annuity with a $1 payment for n periods at rate i per period, it can also be calculated on a business calculator (annuity mode) as

$$32 \boxed{N} \; 4 \boxed{\%i} \; 1 \boxed{PMT} \boxed{2nd} \boxed{PV}$$

28. If you save $100 at the end of every month at 5½% compounded monthly, how much will be accumulated at the end of two years? How much interest was earned?

$S = R \cdot s_{\overline{n}|i}$ where $R = \$100$, $n = 2 \times 12 = 24$, and $i = 5\frac{1}{2}\%/12$. Thus

$$S = 100 \frac{[1 + (5\frac{1}{2}\%/12)]^{24} - 1}{5\frac{1}{2}\%/12}$$

To compute this, first compute i and store in memory for recalling when you are ready to divide by it:

$$5.5 \boxed{\%} \boxed{\div} 12 \boxed{=} \boxed{STO}$$

and continue the calculation with

$$\boxed{+} 1 \boxed{=} \boxed{y^x} 24 \boxed{-} 1 \boxed{=} \boxed{\div} \boxed{RCL} \boxed{\times} 100 \boxed{=} \quad \text{Result:}$$
$$\boxed{2530.8556}$$

On a business calculator (in annuity mode), key

$$24 \boxed{N} \; 5.5 \boxed{\div} 12 \boxed{=} \boxed{\%i} \; 100 \boxed{PMT} \boxed{2nd} \boxed{FV}$$

enters	computes	enters	enters	computes
n	i	i	R	amount

If you had not earned any interest at all, you would have had only $24 \times \$100 = \$2400$. The difference $\$2530.86 - \$2400 = \$130.86$ represents the total interest earned.

29. If you invest $1500 per year in a pension plan that guarantees 8% per year, what is the pension plan worth in 30 years? What is its present value?

$$S = R \cdot s_{\overline{n}|i} = 1500 \cdot s_{\overline{30}|8\%} = 1500 \cdot \frac{(1 + .08)^{30} - 1}{.08}$$

computed as

$$1.08 \boxed{y^x} 30 \boxed{-} 1 \boxed{=} \boxed{\div} .08 \boxed{\times} 1500 \boxed{=} \quad \text{which gives}$$
$$\boxed{169924.82}$$

Do not clear! To find the present value, discount this amount at 8% compounded annually:

$$\boxed{\times}\ \boxed{(}\ 1.08\ \boxed{y^x}\ 30\ \boxed{+/-}\ \boxed{)}\ \boxed{=}\quad \text{which gives}\quad \boxed{16886.675}$$

Thus the future value is $169,924.82 in 30 years, which has a present value of $16,886.68 rounded to the nearest cent.

An alternative method is to compute

$$A = R \cdot a_{\overline{n}|i} = R \cdot \frac{1 - (1 + i)^{-n}}{i} = 1500 \cdot \frac{1 - (1 + .08)^{-30}}{.08}$$

using the following key sequence:

$$1.08\ \boxed{y^x}\ 30\ \boxed{+/-}\ \boxed{=}\ \boxed{+/-}\ \boxed{+}\ 1\ \boxed{=}\ \boxed{\div}\ .08\ \boxed{=}$$

which gives the same result as discounting the future value.

If you have a business calculator, both of these can be computed easily in the annuity mode as follows:

$30\ \boxed{N}\ 8\ \boxed{\%i}\ 1500\ \boxed{PMT}$ (this enters the data)

$\boxed{2nd}\ \boxed{FV}$ (this computes the future value)

$\boxed{2nd}\ \boxed{PV}$ (this computes the present value)

30. If you put $4000 into an annuity that gives 10% per year, how much will accumulate at the end of 35 years? If the inflation rate averages 15% per year (and we treat it as if it were constant), what is that future amount worth in terms of today's dollars?

$$S = R \cdot s_{\overline{n}|i} = R \cdot \frac{(1 + i)^n - 1}{i} = 4000 \cdot \frac{(1.10)^{35} - 1}{.10}$$

$$1.1\ \boxed{y^x}\ 35\ \boxed{-}\ 1\ \boxed{=}\ \boxed{\div}\ .1\ \boxed{\times}\ 4000\ \boxed{=}\quad \text{which gives}$$
$$\boxed{1084097.5}$$

If the inflation rate is 15%, discount the result at 15% per annum for 35 years:

$$P = S(1 + i)^{-n} = 1084097.5(1 + .15)^{-35}$$

$$1084097.5\ \boxed{\times}\ \boxed{(}\ 1.15\ \boxed{y^x}\ 35\ \boxed{+/-}\ \boxed{)}\ \boxed{=}\quad \text{which gives}$$
$$\boxed{8140.3657}$$

(This calculation could have been shortened by starting with the $\boxed{\times}$ while leaving the result of the previous calculation on the display, rather than reentering it as was done.)

Thus you would have \$1,084,097.50 in 35 years, but inflation would make it worth only \$8,140.37!

On a business calculator this can be done in two stages as follows: first, in annuity mode, key

$$35 \boxed{N} \ 10 \boxed{\%i} \ 4000 \boxed{PMT} \boxed{2nd} \boxed{FV} \quad \text{(read future value)}$$

Second, without disturbing the results, change to compound interest mode; then reenter the future value displayed for this calculation by keying the $\boxed{FV}$ key again. The continuing calculation is

$$\boxed{FV} \ 15 \boxed{\%i} \boxed{2nd} \boxed{PV}$$

and read the same present value as before, \$8140.37.

31. If money can be invested at 8% compounded quarterly for 30 years, how much should be invested at the end of each quarter if an annuity with a present value of \$50,000 is required?

$$R = A \cdot \frac{1}{a_{\overline{n}|i}} = A \cdot \frac{i}{1 - (1 + i)^{-n}} = 50,000 \cdot \frac{.02}{1 - (1 + .02)^{-120}}$$

Notice that $i = 8\%/4 = 2\%$, $n = 4 \times 30 = 120$, and $A = 50,000$. The calculation is done with the multiplication by 50,000 done last:

$$.02 \boxed{\div} \boxed{(} 1 \boxed{-} \boxed{(} 1.02 \boxed{y^x} 120 \boxed{+/-} \boxed{)} \boxed{)} \boxed{\times} 50000 \boxed{=}$$

The result displayed is $\boxed{1102.4048}$. Thus \$1102.40 should be set aside each quarter. On a business calculator this can be computed as follows:

$$120 \boxed{N} \ 2 \boxed{\%i} \ 50000 \boxed{PV} \boxed{2nd} \boxed{PMT}$$

32. If money is converted at 9% semiannually, how much should be set aside semiannually to create an annuity worth \$500,000 in 25 years?

$$R = S \cdot \frac{1}{s_{\overline{n}|i}} = S \cdot \frac{i}{(1 + i)^n - 1} = 500,000 \cdot \frac{4.5\%}{(1 + 4.5\%)^{50} - 1}$$

Notice that $i = 9\%/2 = 4.5\% = .045$, $n = 2 \times 25 = 50$, and $S = 500,000$; so we compute the quantity

$$500000 \cdot \frac{.045}{(1.045)^{50} - 1}$$

as follows:

$$500000 \boxed{\times} .045 \boxed{\div} \boxed{(} 1.045 \boxed{y^x} 50 \boxed{-} 1 \boxed{)} \boxed{=} \quad \text{which gives}$$
$$\boxed{2801.0728}$$

Thus $2801.07 should be set aside twice a year. On a business calculator, this can be computed as

$$50 \boxed{N} \; 4.5 \boxed{\%i} \; 500000 \boxed{FV} \boxed{2nd} \boxed{PMT}$$

33. If you can afford an annual contribution of $500, at 6% per year how long will it take to accumulate $5000?

This asks for the term of an annuity. If we solve $S = R \cdot s_{\overline{n}|i}$ for n using natural logarithms, we get the formula

$$n = \frac{\ln[(Si/R) + 1]}{\ln(1 + i)}$$

where $S = 5000$, $R = 500$, $i = .06$, and we compute n as follows:

$$5000 \boxed{\div} \; 5000 \boxed{\times} \; 6 \boxed{\%} \boxed{+} \; 1 \boxed{=} \boxed{\ln x} \boxed{\div} \; 1.06 \boxed{\ln x} \boxed{=} \quad \text{giving}$$
$$\boxed{8.0661135}$$

It will take just over 8 years.

(Notice how $1 + i = 1 + 6\% = 1 + .06 = 1.06$ was computed mentally before taking the second logarithm. This simplified the computational sequence somewhat. This procedure could also have been done at the beginning of the calculation, but keying 6 followed by $\boxed{\%}$ actually required one less keystroke than keying .06. Saving one keystroke in an isolated calculation is not really important. The purpose of this discussion is to illustrate the flexibility in the way many calculations of this sort can be handled.)

On a business calculator this can be calculated as follows:

$$6 \boxed{\%i} \; 500 \boxed{PMT} \; 5000 \boxed{FV} \boxed{2nd} \boxed{N}$$

In 8 years the amount actually accumulated is $4948.73. If another contribution is made, the sum exceeds the goal of $5000. If instead this sum is left to accumulate for about 2+ months at 6%, the goal will be reached. The problem here is the practical one of dealing with the fractional part of the conversion period. This must always be considered when applying theoretical results.

34. A man buys a lawn mower from a catalog and agrees to pay the mail order company 10% down and $14 a month for 24 months. If the cash price is $329, at what interest rate, converted monthly, is he paying?

(The problem of finding the rate of an annuity is difficult and tedious to do accurately by hand. This is such a problem. Various numerical techniques can be used for successive approximations of the rate i, but are not really practical except for rough approximations.

However, several business calculators have a method prepro-
grammed. The method, as it applies to this problem, follows.)

Make certain that your business calculator is in annuity mode. First
compute the principal to be paid and enter it as present value:

$$329 \boxed{-} 10 \boxed{\%} \boxed{=} \boxed{PV}$$

Then enter the number of payments and the installment payment; 24
$\boxed{N}$ 14 $\boxed{PMT}$, and compute the monthly rate: $\boxed{2nd}$ $\boxed{\%i}$. (This takes
the calculator a little time. Imagine doing all of that manually.) The
result of this step should be 1.0370426. Now get the annual rate by
multiplying that result by 12:

$$\boxed{\times} 12 \boxed{=} \quad \text{giving the result} \quad \boxed{12.444511}$$

Thus he is paying off his debt on the lawn mower at an annual interest rate of about 12.44% compounded monthly.

35. A couple buys a house for $89,500 making a down payment of 20%.
The remainder is financed for 30 years at 11½% in equal monthly
payments. What are the monthly payments?

The amount financed (mortgage) is just the present value of an ordinary annuity and the monthly "rent" must be calculated using the
formula

$$R = A \cdot \frac{1}{a_{\overline{n}|i}} = A \cdot \frac{i}{1 - (1 + i)^{-n}}$$

where $n = 30 \times 12 = 360$, the monthly rate $i = 11\frac{1}{2}\%/12$, and
the present value is 80% of $89,500. Calculate

11.5 $\boxed{\%}$ $\boxed{\div}$ 12 $\boxed{=}$ $\boxed{STO}$	(i computed and stored)
$\boxed{+}$ 1 $\boxed{=}$ $\boxed{y^x}$ 360 $\boxed{+/-}$ $\boxed{=}$ $\boxed{+/-}$ $\boxed{+}$ 1 $\boxed{=}$	(denominator of $\dfrac{i}{1 - (1 + i)^{-n}}$)
$\boxed{EXC}$ $\boxed{\div}$ $\boxed{RCL}$ $\boxed{=}$ $\boxed{STO}$	(above expression com-puted, stored)
80 $\boxed{\%}$ $\boxed{\times}$ 89500 $\boxed{\times}$ $\boxed{RCL}$ $\boxed{=}$	(calculation of R com-pleted)

This keystroke sequence illustrates how the annuity factor can be
computed without the use of parentheses if the various features of
the memory are exploited.

If you have a business calculator, then the computation can be readily done in annuity mode as follows:

$$360 \boxed{\text{N}}\ 11.5 \boxed{\div}\ 12 \boxed{=} \boxed{\%\text{i}}\ 80 \boxed{\%} \boxed{\times}\ 89500 \boxed{=} \boxed{\text{PV}} \boxed{\text{2nd}} \boxed{\text{PMT}}$$

Using either method, the result is $\boxed{\ \ 709.04866}$. That is, the monthly payment of principal and interest is $709.05 rounded to the nearest cent. (This does not include of course other costs of property, such as insurance and real estate taxes.)

36. Find the amount of an *annuity due* that has a payment of $200 per month for 10 years at 7% converted monthly.

$$S_n(\text{due}) = S_{n+1}(\text{ord.}) - R = R \cdot s_{\overline{n+1}|\,i} - R = (s_{\overline{n+1}|\,i} - 1) \cdot R$$

where $R = 200$, $n = 10 \times 12 = 120$, and $i = 7\%/12$. Substituting these,

$$(s_{\overline{n+1}|\,i} - 1)R = [\ \frac{(1+i)^{n+1} - 1}{i} - 1] \cdot R =$$

$$[\ \frac{[1 + (7\%/12)]^{121} - 1}{7\%/12} - 1\ ] \times 200$$

In order to keep track of the calculation, it will be presented in stages. This is not the most efficient in terms of keystrokes, but it will make things easier to follow. The memory is used to store the computed value of i and recalled as needed.

(a) Compute, store i: $\ 7 \boxed{\%} \boxed{\div}\ 12 \boxed{=} \boxed{\text{STO}}$

(b) Compute $s_{\overline{121}|\,i}$: $\boxed{+}\ 1 \boxed{=} \boxed{\text{y}^{\text{x}}}\ 121 \boxed{-}\ 1 \boxed{=} \boxed{\div} \boxed{\text{RCL}} \boxed{=}$

(c) Subtract 1, multiply by 200: $\boxed{-}\ 1 \boxed{=} \boxed{\times}\ 200 \boxed{=}$

The result should be $\boxed{\ \ 34818.899}$, which can be rounded to $34,818.90.

If you have a business calculator it will make things easier to realize that an annuity due is just an ordinary annuity with an extra period of interest. This is shown in the equivalent formula:

$$S_n(\text{due}) = S_n(\text{ord.}) \cdot (1 + i)$$

Thus we just compute as if we have an ordinary annuity and multiply by $(1 + i)$. This can also be accomplished by using the compound interest feature for 1 period after computing the value of the annuity.

$$7 \boxed{\div}\ 12 \boxed{+} \boxed{\%\text{i}}\ 120 \boxed{\text{N}}\ 200 \boxed{\text{PMT}} \boxed{\text{2nd}} \boxed{\text{FV}} \boxed{\text{STO}}$$

$$7 \boxed{\%} \boxed{\div}\ 12 \boxed{+}\ 1 \boxed{=} \boxed{\times} \boxed{\text{RCL}} \boxed{=}$$

The second step can also be accomplished by a change to the compound interest mode and compounding for 1 period by keying

$$\boxed{PV}\ 1\ \boxed{N}\ \boxed{2nd}\ \boxed{FV}$$

37. Solve Problem 36 by using tabled values of $s_{\overline{n}|i}$ combined with calculator computations.

Since

$$S_n(\text{due}) = R(s_{\overline{n+1}|\,i} - 1) = 200\,(s_{\overline{121}|\,i} - 1)$$

where $i = 7\%/12$, look up (in most finance math texts) the value of $s_{\overline{n}|\,i}$ in the $7/12\%$ column next to $n = 121$ and find the value 175.09446881. *Mentally* subtract the 1 and enter 174.09447 (rounded value) into the calculator, and then multiply by $R = 200$:

$$174.09447\ \boxed{\times}\ 200\ \boxed{=}\quad \text{and the result is}\quad \boxed{34818.894}$$

Notice that when this is rounded to the nearest cent, \$34,818.89, it differs by 1 cent from the value computed in Problem 36. This is *not* due to the fact that we rounded the table value, but due to the way the 121st power is computed internally in the calculator.

It is possible to enter the entire 11 digits into the calculator due to the 3 guard digits that the calculator stores internally. To do this, enter the value as a sum, that is, 174.0944 + .00006881 by keying 174.0944 $\boxed{+}$ .00006881 $\boxed{=}$. The number displayed will not *look* any different, but the extra digits are now held internally. Multiplying this number on display will produce the same answer as before.

38. Compute the present value of an annuity due of \$100 per quarter for 5½ years at 10% converted quarterly.

$$A_n(\text{due}) = R(a_{\overline{n-1}|\,i} + 1)$$

where $R = 100$, $n = 5\frac{1}{2} \times 4 = 22$, and $i = 10\%/4 = 2.5\%$. Thus

$$A_{22}(\text{due}) = 100\,(a_{\overline{21}|\,2.5\%} + 1) = 100\,[\frac{1 - (1 + 2.5\%)^{-21}}{2.5\%} + 1]$$

$$= 100\,[\frac{1 - (1.025)^{-21}}{.025} + 1]$$

which is computed as

$$1\ \boxed{-}\ \boxed{(\!(}\ 1.025\ \boxed{y^x}\ 21\ \boxed{+/-}\ \boxed{)}\ \boxed{\div}\ .025\ \boxed{+}\ 1\ \boxed{=}\ \boxed{\times}\ 100\ \boxed{=}$$

and the result is $\boxed{1718.4549}$.

(Notice that $(1 + i) = 1.025$ was computed mentally before attempting to compute $A_{22}(\text{due})$. It can certainly be calculated and stored in the memory and recalled as needed, or it can be computed as you proceed with a calculation within parentheses. Always use whichever technique makes the flow of the calculation easiest for you.)

To compute this on a business calculator, use the fact that

$$A_n(\text{due}) = R(a_{\overline{n-1}|\,i} + 1) = R \cdot a_{\overline{n}|\,i}(1 + i)$$

Thus we can compute this present value as if we had an ordinary annuity and then multiply by $(1 + i)$:

$$22 \boxed{\text{N}}\ 2.5\ \boxed{\%\text{i}}\ 100\ \boxed{\text{PMT}}\ \boxed{\text{2nd}}\ \boxed{\text{PV}}$$

and then multiply by $(1 + i)$:

$$\boxed{\times}\ 1.025\ \boxed{=}$$

The present value of the annuity due is \$1718.45.

39. Solve Problem 38 using tables of $a_{\overline{n}|\,i}$ as well as a calculator.

Since

$$A_n(\text{due}) = R(a_{\overline{n-1}|\,i} + 1) = 100\,(a_{\overline{21}|\,i} + 1)$$

where $i = 2.5\%$ look in the 2½ % column in a table of values of $a_{\overline{n}|\,i}$ next to $n = 21$ and find 16.18454857. Mentally add the 1. Enter a value rounded to 8 significant digits into the calculator and multiply by $R = 100$ (which for this value of R you could actually do mentally).

$$17.184549\ \boxed{\times}\ 100\ \boxed{=}\quad \text{and the result is}\quad \boxed{1718.4549}$$

On the Business Analyst II (BA II), simply key

$$22\ \boxed{\text{N}}\ 2.5\ \boxed{\%\text{i}}\ 100\ \boxed{\text{PMT}}\ \boxed{\text{DUE}}\ \boxed{\text{PV}}$$

and read $A_n(\text{due})$.

40. The rent on a storefront on a busy street is \$7000 for 2 years payable biennially in advance. What would be an equivalent monthly rent in advance if money is worth 8%?

This is asking for the payment (rent) of an annuity due with present value (\$7000) known. We solve the formula for R:

$$R = \frac{A_n(\text{due})}{a_{\overline{n-1}|\,i} + 1} = \frac{7000}{a_{\overline{23}|\,i} + 1}$$

where $A_n(\text{due}) = 7000$, $n = 2 \times 12 = 24$, and $i = 8\%/12 = 2/3\%$. Four approaches to computing this are presented. Read them all and then select the one that seems to suit your situation.

Method 1 If you have tables, look up $a_{\overline{23}|\,2/3\%} = 21.25794723$. Round to 8 digits and compute

$$\frac{7000}{21.257947 + 1} = \frac{7000}{22.257947} = \$314.49441$$

7000 $\boxed{\div}$ 22.257947 $\boxed{=}$

Method 2 Compute $a_{\overline{23}|\,2/3\%}$ directly, add 1, and divide the result *into* 7000 as in method 1. Since 2/3% contains many digits in decimal form, we compute it first and store in memory to use as needed. The calculation is presented in three stages:

(a) Compute *i*: 2 $\boxed{\div}$ 3 $\boxed{=}$ $\boxed{\%}$ $\boxed{\text{STO}}$

(b) $a_{\overline{23}|\,i} + 1$: 1 $\boxed{-}$ $\boxed{(}$ $\boxed{(}$ 1 $\boxed{+}$ $\boxed{\text{RCL}}$ $\boxed{)}$ $\boxed{y^x}$ 23
$\boxed{+/-}$ $\boxed{)}$ $\boxed{\div}$ $\boxed{\text{RCL}}$ $\boxed{+}$ 1 $\boxed{=}$

(c) Compute *R*: $\boxed{\text{STO}}$ 7000 $\boxed{\div}$ $\boxed{\text{RCL}}$ $\boxed{=}$ The result is $\boxed{314.49439}$.

Method 3 On a business calculator recall that $A_n(\text{due}) = A_n(\text{ord.})$ $(1 + i)$. Thus first we discount the value of the annuity due for 1 period to get an equivalent $A_n(\text{ord.})$, which we enter in the annuity mode as present value. Then we compute the payment.

7000 $\boxed{\div}$ $\boxed{(}$ 2 $\boxed{\%}$ $\boxed{\div}$ 3 $\boxed{+}$ 1 $\boxed{)}$ $\boxed{=}$ $\boxed{\text{PV}}$

24 $\boxed{\text{N}}$ 2 $\boxed{\div}$ 3 $\boxed{=}$ $\boxed{\%i}$ $\boxed{\text{2nd}}$ $\boxed{\text{PMT}}$

The result is: $\boxed{314.49439}$ (If you have a BA II, with a $\boxed{\text{DUE}}$ key, use

7000 $\boxed{\text{PV}}$ 24 $\boxed{\text{N}}$ 2 $\boxed{\div}$ 3 $\boxed{=}$ $\boxed{\%i}$ $\boxed{\text{DUE}}$ $\boxed{\text{PMT}}$)

Method 4 Use the compound interest mode to discount the $7000 for 1 month; then switch to the annuity mode and compute the rent.

Compound interest mode:

1 $\boxed{\text{N}}$ 2 $\boxed{\div}$ 3 $\boxed{=}$ $\boxed{\%i}$ 7000 $\boxed{\text{FV}}$ $\boxed{\text{2nd}}$ $\boxed{\text{PV}}$

Switch to annuity mode:

$$24 \boxed{\text{N}} \boxed{\text{2nd}} \boxed{\text{PMT}}$$

(Notice that we did not have to reenter the rate i or the discounted present value). The approach mathematically is the same as method 3. Only the method of achieving it on the calculator varies.

41. Find the present value of 22 semiannual payments of \$750 at 6½% converted semiannually, with the first payment due in three years.

This is a deferred annuity. The annuity is deferred 5 periods (m); $m + n = 5 + 22 = 27$. The time diagram is shown next:

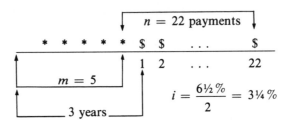

Notice that the annuity is considered in effect one period before the first payment. This is so that it can be treated as an ordinary annuity, which is simpler than looking at it as if it were annuity due beginning 6 periods after the starting point. The * indicates the end of a period with no payment, whereas the \$ indicates a payment.

Method 1 $A_n \text{ (def)} = R(a_{\overline{m+n}|\,i} - a_{\overline{m}|\,i}) = 750\,(a_{\overline{27}|\,i} - a_{\overline{5}|\,i})$

Since the interest is semiannual, the rate i is half of 6½% or 3¼%. If your table has a 3¼% column, look up the values and substitute. Many tables do not, so you may be forced to compute the values. The direct calculation of the annuity factors is illustrated in Problems 27 and 29, so we shall do this only for a business calculator (set to annuity mode). First compute $a_{\overline{5}|\,i}$ and store in memory:

$$5 \boxed{\text{N}} \; 3.25 \boxed{\%\text{i}} \; 1 \boxed{\text{PMT}} \boxed{\text{2nd}} \boxed{\text{PV}} \boxed{\text{STO}}$$

Then compute $a_{\overline{27}|\,i}$. (Notice that only n need be changed.)

$$27 \boxed{\text{N}} \boxed{\text{2nd}} \boxed{\text{PV}}$$

Now subtract $a_{\overline{5}|\,i}$, which was stored in memory:

$$\boxed{-} \boxed{\text{RCL}} \boxed{=}$$

Finally, multiply by R.

$$\boxed{\times}\ 750\ \boxed{=}$$

The result is $\boxed{9935.7748}$. The last step could have been avoided by entering the payment of $750 in the first step instead of $1. That would be like using the equivalent formula

$$A_n(\text{def}) = R \cdot a_{\overline{m+n}|\,i} - R \cdot a_{\overline{m}|\,i}$$

Method 2 Use the equivalent formula $A_n(\text{def}) = R \cdot a_{\overline{n}|\,i} \cdot (1 + i)^{-m}$, where $R = 750$, $i = 3.25\%$, $n = 22$, and $m = 5$. This can either be computed directly, or discount by using the compound interest mode. When you turn the calculator on, you are in the annuity mode; compute

22 $\boxed{\text{N}}$ 3.25 $\boxed{\%i}$ 750 $\boxed{\text{PMT}}$ $\boxed{\text{2nd}}$ $\boxed{\text{PV}}$ (this is $Ra_{\overline{n}|\,i}$)

$\boxed{\text{2nd}}$ $\boxed{\text{AN}-\text{CI}}$ $\boxed{\text{FV}}$ 5 $\boxed{\text{N}}$ $\boxed{\text{2nd}}$ $\boxed{\text{PV}}$ again read $\boxed{9935.7748}$

(On a BA II for a compound interest mode, use $\boxed{\text{FV}}$ 0 $\boxed{\text{PMT}}$ 5 $\boxed{\text{N}}$ $\boxed{\text{2nd}}$ $\boxed{\text{PV}}$ for the second part of the calculation.)

The present value is $9935.77 rounded to the nearest cent.

42. In order to have an additional working capital of $300 each quarter, a man wishes to invest a sum at $6\frac{1}{2}\%$ converted quarterly and preserve the principal. How much should he invest?

This is a *perpetuity* and we compute $A_\infty = R/i$, where $R = 300$ and $i = 6\frac{1}{2}\%/4$.

300 $\boxed{\div}$ $\boxed{(\!(}$ 6.5 $\boxed{\%}$ $\boxed{\div}$ 4 $\boxed{)}$ $\boxed{=}$ which yields $\boxed{18461.538}$

He should invest $18,461.54.

43. What sum should be invested at $7\frac{3}{4}\%$ converted quarterly to produce a payment of $3000 annually?

This is a perpetuity where the payments occur at the end of every four conversion periods (quarters). The formula is

$$A_{\infty,\,k} = \frac{W}{i} \frac{1}{s_{\overline{k}|\,i}}$$

where $W = 3000$, $k = 4$, and $i = 7\frac{3}{4}\%/4$. Thus

$$A_{\infty,\,4} = \frac{3000}{7.75\%/4} \frac{1}{s_{\overline{4}|\,7.75\%/4}}$$

This can be done by two methods. The first is direct calculation; the second takes advantage of the business functions on a business calculator.

Method 1 Compute $s_{\overline{4}|i}$ (as illustrated in Problem 27). The result should be 4.1177588; store it in memory. Then compute the quantity

$$A_{\infty,4} = \frac{3000}{s_{\overline{4}|i} \cdot i}$$

3000 $\boxed{\div}$ $\boxed{\text{RCL}}$ $\boxed{\div}$ $\boxed{(}$ $($ 7.75 $\boxed{\%}$ $\boxed{\div}$ 4 $\boxed{)}$ $\boxed{=}$

The result is $\boxed{\quad 37602.666\quad}$.

Method 2 Realize that the expression $(W/i)/(1/s_{\overline{n}|i})$ looks like the formula for the rent of an annuity with future value W/i for n periods with rate i per period. Thus on a business calculator compute

7.75 $\boxed{\div}$ 4 $\boxed{=}$ $\boxed{\%i}$ $\boxed{\%}$ $\boxed{\text{STO}}$ 4 $\boxed{\text{N}}$

3000 $\boxed{\div}$ $\boxed{\text{RCL}}$ $\boxed{=}$ $\boxed{\text{FV}}$

$\boxed{\text{2nd}}$ $\boxed{\text{PMT}}$

and once again we get $\boxed{\quad 37602.666\quad}$.

Notice that 7.75%/4 was entered into $\boxed{\%i}$ in percentage units and then converted into decimal form by keying $\boxed{\%}$ and then stored in memory, ready to divide into 3000 when recalled.

Whichever method is used, the sum to be invested is $37,602.67 to the nearest cent, which will provide unlimited annual payments of $3000 per year (assuming that the rate of interest is maintained.)

AMORTIZATION AND SINKING FUNDS

44. A debt of $500 is to be amortized at 10% converted monthly for two years. (a) Find the monthly payment. (b) Set up an amortization schedule showing the balance, interest paid, and principal paid each month for the first three months.

(a) The payment is just the payment on an annuity with a present value of $500 and is given by the formula

$$R = A \cdot \frac{1}{a_{\overline{n}|i}} = 500 \cdot \frac{1}{a_{\overline{24}|i}}$$

where $n = 2 \times 12 = 24$ and $i = 10\%/12$.

A similar calculation was done in Problem 35 as a direct calculation, which is somewhat cumbersome. Refer to this if you don't have a business calculator.

On a business calculator the monthly payment R is computed as

$$10 \; \boxed{\div} \; 12 \; \boxed{=} \; \boxed{\%i} \; 24 \; \boxed{\text{N}}$$

$$500 \; \boxed{\text{PV}} \; \boxed{\text{2nd}} \; \boxed{\text{PMT}}$$

The result is $\boxed{23.072464}$. Thus the monthly payment is $23.07. We need this to generate the amortization schedule.

(b) The amortization schedule is as follows. The column headings indicate how the column entries were computed. The specific calculations follow the table.

Amortization Schedule

MONTH	(I) BALANCE AT 1ST OF MONTH OLD (I) − (IV)	(II) INTEREST AT MONTH'S END $I \times$ (I)	(III) MONTHLY PAYMENT R	(IV) BALANCE IS REDUCED BY (III) − (II)
1	500.00	4.17	23.07	18.90
2	481.10	4.01	23.07	19.06
3	462.03	3.85	23.07	19.22
.	.	.	.	.
.	.	.	.	.
.	.	.	.	.

The $23.07 is constant from part (a). Store 10%/12 in memory:

$$10 \; \boxed{\%} \; \boxed{\div} \; 12 \; \boxed{=} \; \boxed{\text{STO}}$$

For month 1 $500 \; \boxed{\times} \; \boxed{\text{RCL}} \; \boxed{=}$ (record col II) $\boxed{+/-}$

$\boxed{+} \; 23.07 \; \boxed{=}$ (record IV)

For month 2 $\boxed{+/-} \; \boxed{+} \; 500 \; \boxed{=}$ (record I) $\boxed{\times} \; \boxed{\text{RCL}} \; \boxed{=}$ (record II)

$\boxed{+/-} \; \boxed{+} \; 23.07 \; \boxed{=}$ (record IV)

For month 3 $\boxed{+/-} \; \boxed{+} \; 481.10 \; \boxed{=}$ (record I) $\boxed{\times} \; \boxed{\text{RCL}} \; \boxed{=}$ (record II)

$\boxed{+/-} \; \boxed{+} \; 23.07 \; \boxed{=}$ (record IV)

To complete the entire table, you continue this pattern until you get to the last payment, the 24th. Adjust it if necessary so that a zero balance is left. The adjustment is necessary due to roundoff error.

45. A debt of $4000 due in 5 years is to be discharged by the sinking fund method. Equal payments will be made into the sinking fund earning 8% annually. Suppose that the interest on the debt is 10% annually. (a) What is the payment into the sinking fund? (b) What interest is paid to the debtor annually? (c) What is the total annual charge? (d) Construct a sinking fund schedule for the 5 years. Show the book value of the debt in the schedule.

(a) The payment is given by $R = S \cdot \dfrac{1}{s_{\overline{n}|i}} = 4000 \cdot \dfrac{1}{s_{\overline{5}|\,8\%}}$

While in annuity mode, key

$$5 \;\boxed{N}\; 8 \;\boxed{\%i}\; 4000 \;\boxed{FV}\; \boxed{2nd}\; \boxed{PMT}$$

The result is $\boxed{681.82582}$. Thus $681.83 is to be deposited into the fund annually.

(b) $I = \$4000 \times 10\% = \$400$. Key $4000 \;\boxed{\times}\; 10 \;\boxed{\%}\; \boxed{=}$.

(c) The total annual charge is (a) + (b) = $681.83 + $400 = $1081.83, of which $400 is to be paid to the debtor at the end of each year and the remainder is paid into the sinking fund.

(d) The sinking fund schedule is given below. The column headings indicate how the entries were computed. The calculation method is given afterward.

Sinking Fund Schedule

YEAR	(A) PAYMENT R	(B) INTEREST AT 8% 8% × OLD (D)	(C) FUND INCREASE (A) + (B)	(D) FUND BALANCE (C) + OLD (D)	(E) BOOK VALUE OF DEBT 4000 − (D)
1	681.83	0	681.83	681.83	3318.17
2	681.83	54.55	736.38	1418.21	2581.79
3	681.83	113.46	795.29	2213.49	1786.51
4	681.83	177.08	858.91	3072.40	927.60
5	681.83	245.79	927.62	4000.02	−.02

To compute this schedule, write 681.83 in each row of the payment column. No interest is earned the first year since payments are made at the end of the year. Thereafter, the fund balance earns 8%. The book value is the debt minus the fund balance, that is, $4000 − balance. The entry for the first year is self-evident. During the calculation, the fund balance will be accumulated in the memory.

At the end of year 2,

$$681.83 \;\boxed{STO}\; \boxed{\times}\; 8 \;\boxed{\%}\; \boxed{=} \quad \text{(write interest)} \quad \boxed{+}\; 681.83 \;\boxed{=}$$
$$\text{(write increase)}$$

$$\boxed{SUM}\; \boxed{RCL} \quad \text{(write balance)} \quad \boxed{+/-}\; \boxed{+}\; 4000 \;\boxed{=}$$
$$\text{(write book value)}$$

At the end of year 3,

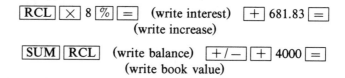
(write increase)
(write book value)

At the end of year 4,

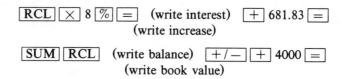
(write increase)
(write book value)

At the end of year 5,

$\boxed{\text{RCL}}\,\boxed{\times}\,8\,\boxed{\%}\,\boxed{=}$ (write interest) $\boxed{+}\,681.83\,\boxed{=}$
(write increase)

$\boxed{\text{SUM}}\,\boxed{\text{RCL}}$ (write balance) $\boxed{+/-}\,\boxed{+}\,4000\,\boxed{=}$
(write book value)

Notice that the fund balance exceeds the debt by \$.02. This is due to rounding during the writing of the schedule. This is adjusted by paying 2 cents less into the fund at the end of the last (fifth) year.

46. A sinking fund paying 7% per annum is accumulated for 8 years with an annual contribution of \$950 at the end of each year. Find the fund balance at the end of the third year without making a schedule.

The fund balance at the end of year k is given by $R \cdot s_{\overline{k}|\,i}$, where i is the annual rate. Thus simply compute the quantity

$$950 \cdot s_{\overline{3}|\,7\%}$$

This is done on a business calculator as follows:

$$3\,\boxed{\text{N}}\,7\,\boxed{\%i}\,950\,\boxed{\text{PMT}}\,\boxed{\text{2nd}}\,\boxed{\text{FV}}$$

The result is $\boxed{\quad 3054.155\quad}$, since the quantity represents the future value of an ordinary annuity after three periods. Thus the fund contains \$3054.16 after the third year.

47. A refrigeration unit that costs $3000 has an estimated life of 8 years. The salvage value is $300. Using the straight line method of depreciation, find (a) the annual depreciation, (b) the book value at the end of 3 years, and (c) the time when the book value is equal to $1000.

Method 1 Straightforward Calculation

(a) The depreciation per year is $R = (\text{cost} - \text{salvage})n$.

$$3000 \boxed{-} 300 \boxed{=} \boxed{\div} 8 \boxed{=} \boxed{\text{STO}} \quad \text{which gives}$$
$$\boxed{337.5}$$

The annual depreciation, $337.50, is stored in memory for the next calculation.

(b) At the end of 3 years the book value is $V = C - Rt = 3000 - 337.5(3)$.

$$3000 \boxed{-} \boxed{(}\boxed{\text{RCL}} \boxed{\times} 3 \boxed{=} \quad \text{which gives}$$
$$\boxed{1987.5}$$

The book value after 3 years is $1987.50. Notice that a parenthesis was needed after the minus, but it was not necessary to close the parenthesis on the right; the equals takes care of this. If you have an AOS entry system, the parenthesis can be omitted.

(c) Let $V = 1000$ and then solve $1000 = C - Rt$ for t after substituting the values for C and R.

$$t = \frac{3000 - 1000}{337.5}$$

$$3000 \boxed{-} 1000 \boxed{=} \boxed{\div} \boxed{\text{RCL}} \boxed{=} \quad \text{which gives}$$
$$\boxed{5.9259259}$$

Thus it takes (theoretically) slightly less than 6 years. At the end of the sixth year the book value will actually be slightly less than $1000.

Method 2 Using Linear Regression

If you have a business calculator with a linear regression feature that can give you slope and estimated x and y values, realize that the slope m of the line is the annual depreciation. Use the cost at time $t = 0$ and the salvage value at the end of the last year as two points to define the line. With this in mind, the calculation is as follows:

$\boxed{\text{2nd}}\ \boxed{\text{LR}}$ (or just STAT)	this sets the linear regression mode
$0\ \boxed{\text{x : y}}\ 3000\ \boxed{\Sigma\ +}$	enters the point (0, 3000)
$8\ \boxed{\text{x : y}}\ 300\ \boxed{\Sigma\ +}$	enters the point (8, 300)
$\boxed{\text{2nd}}\ \boxed{\text{m}}$ (or $\boxed{\text{2nd}}\ \boxed{\text{b/a}}\ \boxed{\text{x : y}}$)	(a) read -337.5, the depreciation
3 2nd $\boxed{y'}$	(b) read 1987.5, the third year value
1000 $\boxed{\text{2nd}}\ \boxed{x'}$	(c) read time when $V = 1000$

48. An office machine that costs $1165 is to be depreciated by the sum-of-digits method for 5 years. Assume that the salvage value is zero. Calculate a depreciation schedule.

The sum of digits for 5 years is $1 + 2 + 3 + 4 + 5 = 15$. A quick way to compute the sum of digits is to use the formula

$$1 + 2 + \cdots + n = \frac{n(n + 1)}{2} = \frac{5(6)}{2} = \frac{30}{2} = 15$$

The amounts depreciated each year are 5/15, 4/15, 3/15, 2/15, and 1/15 of the initial cost. To calculate these amounts quickly, store cost $\div$ 15 = 1165 $\div$ 15 in the memory. Then we multiply successively by 5, 4, 3, 2, and 1.

	Annual Depreciation	Book Value
1165 $\boxed{\div}$ 15 $\boxed{=}$ $\boxed{\text{STO}}$		
5 $\boxed{\times}$ $\boxed{\text{RCL}}$ $\boxed{=}$	388.33	777.67
4 $\boxed{\times}$ $\boxed{\text{RCL}}$ $\boxed{=}$	310.67	466.00
	233.00	233.00
3 $\boxed{\times}$ $\boxed{\text{RCL}}$ $\boxed{=}$	155.33	77.67
2 $\boxed{\times}$ $\boxed{\text{RCL}}$ $\boxed{=}$	77.67	0
$\boxed{\text{RCL}}$ $\boxed{=}$		

The amounts computed are the annual depreciations. To get the corresponding book values, subtract each of these amounts successively from the initial cost:

$$1165 \boxed{-} 388.33 \boxed{-} \text{(read book value)} \ 310.67 \boxed{-} \text{(read book value)}$$

$$233 \boxed{-} \text{(read book value)} \quad 155.33 \boxed{-} \text{(read book value)}$$

$$77.67 \boxed{=} \text{(read book value)}$$

The final book value is zero.

49. A machine that costs \$20,000 with a salvage value of \$5000 is to be depreciated over 5 years by the constant percentage method. Find the constant percentage r that will reduce the initial cost to the salvage value at the end of year 5, and create the corresponding depreciation schedule.

We require that $(1 - r)^n \cdot C = S$. That is, $(1 - r)^5 \cdot 20,000 = 5000$. Solving for r we get

$$r = 1 - \sqrt[5]{\frac{5000}{20,000}}$$

This is computed by keying

$$5000 \boxed{\div} 20000 \boxed{=} \boxed{\text{2nd}} \boxed{x\sqrt{y}} \ 5 \boxed{=} \boxed{+/-} \boxed{+} 1 \boxed{=}$$

This gives $\boxed{.24214172}$. Now key $\boxed{\times}$ 100 $\boxed{=}$ $\boxed{\text{STO}}$. This stores the rate in percentage, rather than decimal form, and we are ready to compute the depreciation schedule, as follows:

KEY SEQUENCE	DISPLAY	EXPLANATION
20000 $\boxed{-}$ $\boxed{\text{RCL}}$ $\boxed{\%}$	4842.83	Depreciation for year 1
$\boxed{=}$	15157.17	Book value at end of year 1
$\boxed{-}$ $\boxed{\text{RCL}}$ $\boxed{\%}$	3670.18	Depreciation for year 2
$\boxed{=}$	11486.98	Book value at end of year 2
$\boxed{-}$ $\boxed{\text{RCL}}$ $\boxed{\%}$	2781.48	Depreciation for year 3
$\boxed{=}$	8705.51	Book value at end of year 3
$\boxed{-}$ $\boxed{\text{RCL}}$ $\boxed{\%}$	2107.97	Depreciation for year 4
$\boxed{=}$	6597.54	Book value at end of year 4
$\boxed{-}$ $\boxed{\text{RCL}}$ $\boxed{\%}$	1597.54	Depreciation for year 5
$\boxed{=}$	5000.00	Book value at end of year 5 which also equals salvage value

The values are usually displayed in a table with the depreciations in one column and the book values in a parallel column. As these values are generated by the calculator, they should be transcribed into such a format.

50. Depreciate the machine described in Problem 49 using the sinking fund method over 5 years; assume a 6% interest rate for the fund.

The annual contribution to the sinking fund is given by the formula

$$R = W \cdot \frac{1}{s_{\overline{n}| i}}$$

where, in this case, $n = 5$, $i = 6\%$, and $W = 20{,}000 - 5000 = 15{,}000$. The calculation will be shown only for business calculators. (Otherwise use tables of $s_{\overline{n}| i}$ and divide into W.) In annuity mode,

5 $\boxed{\text{N}}$ 6 $\boxed{\%\text{i}}$ 15000 $\boxed{\text{FV}}$ $\boxed{\text{2nd}}$ $\boxed{\text{PMT}}$ which gives $\boxed{2660.946}$

Thus the annual contribution to the sinking fund is $2660.95. The schedule is now computed as illustrated in Problem 45. The result is shown next. The change in the fund each year is the depreciation to be charged against the item in question.

Sinking Fund Schedule

ANNUAL CONTRIBUTION	INTEREST AT 6%	CHANGE IN FUND (DEPREC.)	FUND BALANCE	BOOK VALUE
2660.95	0	2660.95	2,660.95	17,339.05
2660.95	159.66	2820.61	5,481.56	14,518.44
2660.95	328.89	2989.84	8,471.40	11,528.60
2660.95	508.28	3169.23	11,640.63	8,359.37
2660.95	698.44	3359.39	15,000.02	4,999.98

The book value is $20,000 — fund balance. To get these values, subtract the change in the fund successively from 20,000. The 2-cent difference is again due to accumulated roundoff error. This can be adjusted by contributing 2 cents less to the fund than prescribed by the formula at the end of the last (fifth) year.

BONDS

51. Compute the value of a $1000 bond paying 6% quarterly, redeemable at par in 5 years, if the purchaser wishes an 8% yield to maturity.

The formula is

$$V = C(1 + i)^{-n} + R \cdot a_{\overline{n}|i}$$

where $C = 1000$, $n = 5 \times 4 = 20$, $i = 8\% \div 4 = 2\%$, and $R = \frac{1}{4} \cdot 6\% \cdot C = 1\frac{1}{2}\% \times 1000 = $ quarterly dividend. The calculation will be illustrated using tables and also using a business calculator in lieu of tables.

Method 1   Look up the value of $v^n = (1 + i)^{-n}$ in tables for the values $n = 20$, $i = 2\%$, and find .67297133. Multiply by 1000 and store in memory. Then look up $a_{\overline{20}|2\%}$ and find 16.35143334, which is multiplied by R, the quarterly dividend. This value is then summed in the memory and the total recalled.

.6729133 $\boxed{\times}$ 1000 $\boxed{=}$ $\boxed{\text{STO}}$

16.351433 $\boxed{\times}$ 1.5 $\boxed{\%}$ $\boxed{\times}$ 1000 $\boxed{=}$ $\boxed{\text{SUM}}$ $\boxed{\text{RCL}}$

The result displayed is $\boxed{\quad 918.2415}$. Thus the price that should be paid for the bond to achieve the desired yield is $918.24.

Method 2   Using a business calculator, start in the annuity mode and then switch to compound interest mode, as shown:

1.5 $\boxed{\%}$ $\boxed{\times}$ 1000 $\boxed{=}$ $\boxed{\text{PMT}}$ 20 $\boxed{\text{N}}$ 2 $\boxed{\%i}$ $\boxed{\text{2nd}}$ $\boxed{\text{PV}}$
$\boxed{\text{STO}}$

Now switch to compound interest mode: $\boxed{\text{2nd}}$ $\boxed{\text{AN}-\text{CI}}$ (or 0 $\boxed{\text{PMT}}$ on the BA II) 100 $\boxed{\text{FV}}$ $\boxed{\text{2nd}}$ $\boxed{\text{PV}}$ $\boxed{\text{SUM}}$ $\boxed{\text{RCL}}$, which gives $\boxed{\quad 918.24283}$.

In this case the difference in the two methods is due to the fact that we did not enter all the digits of the annuity factor found in the table. This could be remedied if desired by entering $a_{\overline{n}|i}$ as a sum (i.e., 16.3514 $\boxed{+}$ .00003334 $\boxed{=}$) before proceeding with the multiplication. We would then get exactly the same result as using method 2.

52. An 8-year annuity bond for $15,000 with interest at 8% payable quarterly is to be sold at the end of the third year. If the purchaser desires a 7% yield, what should be paid for the bond?

The periodic installment is $A \cdot 1/a_{\overline{n}|i}$, where $A = 15{,}000$, $n = 8 \times 4 = 32$, and $i = 8\%/4 = 2\%$. The payment is then

$$15{,}000 \cdot \frac{1}{a_{\overline{32}|\,2\%}}$$

Method 1 In a table, look up $1/a_{\overline{32}|\,2\%} = .04261061$; then multiply by 15,000

$$.04261061 \;\boxed{\times}\; 15000 \;\boxed{=}\; \quad \text{which gives} \quad \boxed{639.15915}$$

This is the quarterly installment. But the buyer will receive only $5 \times 4 = 20$ payments. If he wants a 7% yield, then the present value is given by

$$V = R \cdot a_{\overline{n}|\,i}, \text{ where } R = \$639.16 \text{ (from the last calculation)}$$

$$n = 20, \; i = \frac{7\%}{4} = 1\tfrac{3}{4}\%$$

Look up $a_{\overline{20}|\,1\frac{3}{4}\%} = 16.75288130$ and multiply by the payment:

$$16.752881 \;\boxed{\times}\; 639.16 \;\boxed{=}\; \quad \text{which gives} \quad \boxed{10707.771}$$

The price should be \$10,707.77 at the 7% desired yield.

Method 2 Using a business calculator (in annuity mode), first compute the installment payment:

$$32\;\boxed{\text{N}}\;2\;\boxed{\%\text{i}}\;15000\;\boxed{\text{PV}}\;\boxed{\text{2nd}}\;\boxed{\text{PMT}}$$

Now compute the present value of this amount at the desired yield of 7% converted quarterly:

$$\boxed{\text{PMT}}\;7\;\boxed{\div}\;4\;\boxed{=}\;\boxed{\%\text{i}}\;20\;\boxed{\text{N}}\;\boxed{\text{2nd}}\;\boxed{\text{PV}}\;\text{which}$$
$$\text{gives} \quad \boxed{10707.757}$$

The difference in the two methods is due to the rounding of both the payment and the annuity factor in method 1.

53. Compute the annual yield of a 5% *irredeemable* bond quoted at 102.

The annual dividend is proportional to 5% $\times$ 100 = 5. The yield if bought at 102 is just 5/102, which is computed as

$$5 \boxed{\div} \ 102 \boxed{=} \quad \text{the result is} \quad \boxed{.04901961}$$

which is approximately 4.9%. The bond itself may be sold at some future date for a price either more or less than its purchase price. At that time the actual yield achieved is different, either more or less than 4.9%, respectively. What has been computed is an internal rate of return.

54. A $1000 bond, with dividends payable semiannually at 6%, is purchased for $1065. If the bond is redeemable at par ($1000) in 10 years, use a bond table, linear interpolation, and a calculator to compute the yield to maturity.

Find a bond table of purchase prices 10 years before redemption. The appropriate section of the table should look something like the following:

Purchase Price 10 Years before Redemption

NOMINAL YIELD RATE	NOMINAL DIVIDEND RATE, PAYABLE SEMIANNUALLY, 6%
.	.
.	.
.	.
5.00	107.79
5.10	106.98
5.20	106.18
5.30	105.38
.	.
.	.
.	.

In the terminology of the table, the purchase price is 106.50. This price is between two tabled values. This information can be viewed like this:

Nominal % Yield	Price at 6%
5.10	106.98
x	106.50
5.20	106.18

Linear interpolation will provide an approximate value of the yield. The method assumes that the ratio of the differences indicated are equal:

$$\frac{a}{b} = \frac{A}{B}$$

The difference $a = 5.10 - x$, where x is the unknown yield that is being interpolated. Hence

$$\frac{a}{5.20 - 5.10} = \frac{106.98 - 106.50}{106.98 - 106.18} = \frac{.48}{.80}$$

(The result of the subtractions, shown last, can be done mentally or on the calculator.) Thus we have

$$\frac{a}{.10} = \frac{.48}{.80}$$

or, solving for a,

$$a = .10 \frac{.48}{.80}$$

Thus we compute a as follows:

$$.1 \boxed{\times} .48 \boxed{\div} .8 \boxed{=} \quad \text{which gives} \quad \boxed{0.06}$$

This amount $a = .06$ when added to the lower of the two known table values; that is, 5.10 gives the desired result:

$$5.1 \boxed{+} .06 \boxed{=} \quad \text{which gives} \quad \boxed{5.16}$$

Thus the yield is approximately 5.16%.

55. Devise a method of computing the yield to maturity given the redemption value C, purchase price V, periodic dividend R, and the number of periods n.

The basic formula is $V = C(1 + i)^{-n} + R \cdot a_{\overline{n}|i}$, which we wish to solve for i. This cannot be done explicitly. However, an iteration formula will be derived. Recall that

$$a_{\overline{n}|i} = \frac{1 - (1 + i)^{-n}}{i}$$

and thus

$$(1 + i)^{-n} = 1 - ia_{\overline{n}|i}$$

Substituting this last expression in the basic formula gives

$$V = C(1 - ia_{\overline{n}|i}) + R \cdot a_{\overline{n}|i}$$

$$V = C - iCa_{\overline{n}|i} + Ra_{\overline{n}|i}$$

$$iCa_{n\ i} = C - V + Ra_{\overline{n}|i}$$

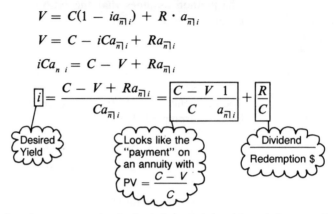

Notice that i appears on both the left and right sides of the equation (in $a_{\overline{n}|i}$). Thus the equation has the functional form

$$i = f(i)$$

so we can possibly get a numerical solution if the sequence of linear iterations

$$i_{k+1} = f(i_k)$$

actually converges (which it does). A schematic of the procedure looks like this:

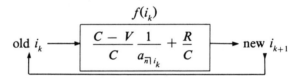

Substitute new value back into
formula. Continue this process.

This process continues until desired accuracy is achieved. The calculation of $f(i)$ is quite complicated. It is practical only on a business calculator (or a programmable calculator). A few tricks will be helpful to you.

1. Notice that the quantity $(C - V)/C$ looks like the gross profit margin with CST $= V$ and SEL $= C$.

2. The quantity

$$\frac{C - V}{C} \frac{1}{a_{\overline{n}|i}}$$

is just the PMT on an annuity if present value is the ratio $(C - V)/C$ with periodic rate i for n periods.

3. R/C is a constant, so it can be stored in memory and added to each new estimate of PMT.

Putting these thoughts together, the calculation procedure is as follows:

$$
\begin{aligned}
\text{Data:} \quad V &= \text{price paid for bond} \\
C &= \text{redemption price (usually par)} \\
R &= \text{periodic dividend} \\
n &= \text{number of periods} \\
i_k &= \text{periodic yield, } k\text{th estimate}
\end{aligned}
$$

Set calculator to annuity mode first.

Step 1 Compute $(C - V)/C$; then treat as a present value.

$$V \boxed{\text{CST}}\ C \boxed{\text{SEL}}\ \boxed{\text{2nd}}\ \boxed{\text{MAR}}\ \boxed{\text{PV}}$$

Step 2 Enter the number of payments.

$$(\text{years}) \boxed{\times} (\text{no. of annual payments}) \boxed{=} \boxed{\text{N}}$$

Step 3 Compute R/C, store, and also use as initial estimate i_0.

$$R \boxed{\div}\ C \boxed{\times}\ 100 \boxed{=} \boxed{\text{STO}}\ \boxed{\%\text{i}}$$

Step 4 Now proceed to compute successive estimates as "payments" plus the value stored in the previous step.

$$\boxed{\text{2nd}}\ \boxed{\text{PMT}}\ \boxed{+}\ \boxed{\text{RCL}}\ \boxed{=} \qquad \text{read } i_1$$

$$\boxed{\%\text{i}}\ \boxed{\text{2nd}}\ \boxed{\text{PMT}}\ \boxed{+}\ \boxed{\text{RCL}}\ \boxed{=} \qquad \text{read } i_2$$

$$\boxed{\%\text{i}}\ \boxed{\text{2nd}}\ \boxed{\text{PMT}}\ \boxed{+}\ \boxed{\text{RCL}}\ \boxed{=} \qquad \text{read } i_3$$

$$\vdots \qquad\qquad\qquad \vdots$$

Repeat this process until display value does not change (to desired accuracy).

Step 5 The value computed in step 4 is the periodic yield. To get the annual yield, multiply by m, the number of periods per year.

$$i_k \boxed{\times}\ m \boxed{=} \qquad \text{read annual yield}$$

The general method outlined is illustrated in Problem 56.

56. Use the method outlined in Problem 55 to compute the yield on the bond described in Problem 54, a $1000, 6% bond purchased for $1065, dividends payable semiannually, maturing in 10 years.

$$V = 1065, \quad C = 1000, \quad R = \frac{6\%}{2} \times 1000 = 3\% \times 1000 = 30$$

$$n = 10 \times 2 = 20, \quad i = \text{to be computed}$$

Start in the appropriate mode.

Change to FIN mode here

Step 1   1065 CST 1000 SEL 2nd MAR PV   which gives   -6.5

This is negative because the bond will be sold for less than was paid for it.

Step 2   10 × 2 = N   which gives   20.

Step 3   30 ÷ 1000 × 100 = STO %i   and read   3.

(Notice that the value obtained in step 3 is equal to 6%/2 = 3%, the periodic rate. This is only true if the redemption value C equals the face value, as it does in this example. This fact could be used to shorten step 3.)

Step 4   2nd PMT + RCL = $i_1 = 2.5630979$

        %i 2nd PMT + RCL = $i_2 = 2.5805544$

                            . $i_3 = 2.5798643$

                            . $i_4 = 2.5798916$

                            . $i_5 = 2.5798905$

                            . $i_6 = 2.5798906$

Important: After keying PMT wait a few seconds to allow the calculator to complete its work. If you were to repeat the sequence again, you would just see the same value repeated. It is not necessary to do as many iterations as shown here. This was done to illustrate what would happen if you continued.

Step 5   The value displayed last in step 4 is the periodic (in this case, semiannual) rate. We now multiply by the number of periods.

× 2 =   5.1597812

If we round this to two decimal places, we get 5.16. Thus the yield is approximately 5.16%, the same value that we got from interpolating in the bond tables. This method is useful if the tables do not contain the values in question, or if you need a more precise answer. Otherwise, the tables give two-place accuracy upon interpolation in most cases.

Index

A

Algebra, 31–83
  AOS system equivalents and, 34
  arithmetic system equivalents and, 34
  basic functions, 5, 31–33, 55–56
  calculator equivalents for, 33–35
  calculator key sequence for computing
    fractional powers, 38–39
  calculator key sequence for computing
    logarithms, 50
  calculator key sequence for computing
    powers and roots, 36
  calculator key sequence for computing
    the constant with powers and roots,
    37
  chi squared and, 167, 168, 170
  constant K, 34–35, 36–37, 51, 52, 53,
    58–59
  elementary, 31–83
  exponents and radicals, 44–46, 68–72
  fractional powers, 38, 39, 46
  imaginary numbers, 38
  indeterminate form, 35
  integer powers, 38
  inverse functions, 31
  linear equations, 39–41, 61–64
  logarithms, 47–50, 72–76
  negative numbers, 32, 37–38
  positive integer powers, 35
  powers and roots, 35–38, 60–61
  progressions, 50–55, 76–83
  proportions, 39–41, 61–64
  quadratic equations, 41–44, 64–68
  reciprocal, 32–33, 56
  solved problems, 53–83
  square root, 31, 55
  squares, 31, 55
  substitutions in simple expressions and
    formulas, 57–59
  transposing terms, 39–41
  zero and reciprocal, 32
Algebraic operating system. *See* AOS
Amortization, 230–32, 264–67
  definition of, 230
  iterative formulation and, 231, 232
  sinking funds and, 231, 232
  typical schedule for, 230, 231

Angles, measure, 84–87, 108–11
Annuities, 225–29, 252–64
    annuity due, 225, 227
    AOS entry systems and, 228–29
    arithmetic entry systems and, 228–29
    bonds and, 236, 237
    cash equivalent of, 227
    contingent, 225
    deferred, 225, 228, 229
    definitions of, 225
    future value and, 226
    ordinary, 225, 229
    perpetuity, 225, 228
    present value and, 227
ANOVA. *See* Variance
AOS entry system, 4–5
    algebraic expressions and 33–34, 51, 59
    annuities and, 228–29
    basic operations and, 20, 21, 22
    chi squared and, 168, 169, 202, 204, 205
    combined operations and, 10, 26, 27
    compound interest and, 225, 246, 251
    depreciation and, 236
    exponents and radicals and, 68, 69, 70
    gross profit margin and, 243
    hierarchy of, 7–9
    laws of exponents and 44, 45, 46
    parentheses and, 12, 60, 70
    powers and roots and, 60
    progressions and, 54
    quadratic equation and, 65, 66
    regression (least squares) and, 171, 174, 206, 207, 209
    simple discount and, 222
    simple interest and, 221, 222, 245
    statistics and, 189, 195, 196
    trigonometry and, 85, 109
APs. *See* Arithmetic progressions
Arc notation, 98–99
Arithmetic entry system, 4, 5, 6
    algebraic expressions and, 33–34, 57, 59, 63
    annuities and, 228–29
    basic operations and, 20, 21, 22
    chi squared and, 168, 169, 202
    combined operations and, 10, 26, 27
    compound interest and, 224, 246, 251
    cost markup and, 219
    depreciation and, 236
    exponents and radicals and, 68, 69, 70
    gross profit margin and, 219, 243
    hierarchy of, 7, 8
    laws of exponents and, 44, 45, 46
    linear equations and proportions and, 63
    parentheses and, 12, 56, 57, 59, 66–67, 70
    powers and roots and, 60–61
    quadratic equations and, 65, 66–67
    simple discount and, 222
    simple interest and, 221, 222, 244
    statistics and, 195, 206, 207
    trigonometry and, 85

Arithmetic mean, 148, 186–87, 188–89
    formula for, 148
    formula for adding new or additional values, 149
Arithmetic progressions, 51–52, 55, 77–79
Automatic scientific notation, 15
Average deviation. *See* Mean absolute deviation
Averages and variability, 148–57, 186–92
    arithmetic mean, 148–49, 186–87, 188–89
    calculation of basic statistics without statistical functions, 155
    calculation of basic statistics with special statistics functions, 154
    coefficient of variation, 151, 156
    common measures of variability, 151
    geometric mean, 148, 149–50, 187–89, 190
    harmonic mean, 148, 150–51, 187–88
    key configurations for, 152
    mean absolute deviation, 151, 156–57
    median, 148, 151, 186
    midrange, 148, 151, 189, 190
    mode, 148, 151
    range, 151
    types of common averages, 148
    variance, 151–53

B

Basic arithmetic, 1–30
    arithmetic operations, 3
    calculator displays, 1–2
    chain operations, 6–7
    combined operations, 10–11
    entry systems, 4–5
    hierarchy, 7–9
    parentheses, 11–13
    scientific notation, 13–17
    signed numbers, 9–10
    simple percentage, 17–19
    solved problems, 20–30
    using the constant K, 3–4
Bonds, 236–37, 271–79
    annuity, 236, 237
    coupon, 236
    definition of, 236
    yield rate and, 236
Business Analyst I. *See* TI Business Analyst I
Business Analyst II *See* TI Business Analyst II
Business and finance, 217–79
    amortization and sinking funds, 230–32, 264–67
    annuities, 225–29, 252–64
    bonds, 236–37, 271–79
    compound interest, 223–25, 246–52
    depreciation, 232–36, 268–71
    discount, 218–20, 239–43, 244–46
    gross profit margin, 218–20, 239–43
    markup, 218–20, 239–43

percent, 217–18, 238–39
simple interest, 221–23, 244–46
solved problems, 238–79

C

Calculators
    add-on capabilities, 17
    algebraic functions and, 5, 31–83
    AOS entry system, 4–5, 7
    arithmetic entry system, 4, 5, 6, 7, 8
    arithmetic operations and, 3, 10–11
    automatic constant and, 3–4
    basic arithmetic and, 1–30
    built-in conversion functions and, 105,
        106, 115, 152
    business use and, 217–79
    chain operations and, 6–7
    combined operations and, 10–11, 26–27
    constant K and, 3–4
    discount capabilities, 17
    entry systems and, 4–5, 159
    finance and, 217–79
    floating-point display, 1–2
    hierarchy and, 5, 7–9
    kinds of displays, 1–2
    LCD and, 6, 89
    LED and, 6, 88
    linear regression capability and, 6
    logarithmic functions and, 5
    manual constant and, 4, 5
    memory, 5
    parentheses and, 5, 6, 11–13
    percent and, 5, 17–19, 27–28, 217–18
    power function and, 5
    RPN, 4
    scientific notation and, 1–2, 5, 13–17, 23–25
    signed numbers and, 9–10, 22–23
    solved problems through, 20–30
    stat functions and, 6
    statistics and, 6, 147–216
    trigonometric functions and, 5, 84–146
Chain operations, 6–7
Chi squared, 166–70, 196, 202–6
    AOS entry systems and, 168, 169, 202,
        204, 205
    arithmetic entry systems and, 168, 169
    contingency table, 168
    equal proportions test, 168–70
    example of, 166–67
    goodness-of-fit tests, 166–67
    McNemar's test statistic, 204, 205
    use of algebra for, 167, 168, 170
    uses for, 166
    Yate's continuity correction, 169, 204
Coefficient of variation, 151
    definition of, 156
    way to compute, 156
Combined operations, 10–11, 26–27
Compound interest. *See* Interest
Confidence interval, 158–60, 194–97, 208–9
    way to compute, 159

Constant, automatic, 3–4
Constant K, 3–4, 5, 25–26
    algebra and, 34–35, 36–37, 51, 52, 53,
        58–59, 78
Constant, manual, 4, 5
Contingency table, 168, 169
Correlation. *See* Statistics
Cosecant, 89, 99, 100
Cosine function, 88, 89, 91–93, 97, 99, 112,
    113, 119–26
Cotangent, 89, 100

D

DATA key, 147, 152
Decimal degrees, 84, 85–86, 109
df. *See* Degrees of freedom
Degree-minute-second. *See* DMS
Degrees of freedom (df), 159–60, 165, 166,
    184, 195, 198, 206, 208
Depreciation, 232–36, 268–71
    AOS entry system and, 236
    arithmetic entry system and, 236
    constant percentage of book value meth-
        od of, 235–36
    declining balance method of, 235
    definition of, 232
    salvage value, 232
    sinking fund method of, 236, 271
    straight-line (linear) method of, 233–34,
        268
    sums-of-digits method of, 234–35, 269
    total, 232
Discount, 218–20, 239–43, 244–46
    chain, 220
    definition of, 220
    series, 220
    simple, 222
    trade, 220
DMS scale, 84, 85, 86, 109, 114–15, 124
DRG key, 88, 89, 96, 101, 105, 113, 129,
    130, 131, 133, 136, 138, 142

E

Entry systems, 4–5, 159
    See also names of individual systems
Euler's notation, 47
Exponent, 13–17
Exponential function, 35, 36
Exponential notation, 16
Exponents
    laws of, 44–45, 68–72
    roundoff error, 71

F

Finance. *See* Business and finance
Floating-point
    display, 1–2
    notation, 17, 59, 61
Fractional powers, 38, 39, 46

G

Geometric mean, 148, 187–89, 190
  formula for, 149–50
  logarithms and, 150, 187, 190
  ways of computing the, 150
Geometric progressions, 51, 52–55, 79–82
GM. *See* Geometric mean
GPM. *See* Gross profit margin
GPs. *See* Geometric progressions
Grads, 84, 89
Gross profit margin, 218–20, 239–43
  AOS entry system and, 243
  arithmetic entry system and, 243
  definition of, 218
  formulas for, 218, 219, 241

H

Harmonic mean, 148, 187–88
  formula for, 150
  ways of computing the, 150–51
Heron's formula, 94, 127–28
HM. *See* Harmonic mean
Hierarchy, 5, 7–9
Hypothesis testing, 160–66, 197–201
  background information, 161
  common statistical tests of, 162–63
  degrees of freedom, 165, 198
  left tail of a normal distribution, 161
  paired t test, 201
  two-sided (two-tailed) test, 164, 165, 198

I

Imaginary numbers, 38
Inference. *See* Hypothesis testing
Integer powers, 35, 38
Interest
  compound, 223–25, 246–52
  discount and, 222
  formulas for AOS entry system and, 221, 222, 225, 245, 246, 251
  formulas for arithmetic entry system and, 221, 222, 224, 244, 246, 251
  formulas for simple discount and, 222
  simple, 221–23, 244–46
Inverse functions
  algebra, 31
  trigonometry, 97–101, 133–36
Iterative formulation, 231, 232, 235

L

LCD, 6, 89
Least-squares regression, 147
LED, 6, 88
Light-emitting diode. *See* LED
Linear equations, 39–41, 61–64
Linear regression capability, 6, 233
Linear regression model, 170, 208, 209, 268–69

Liquid-crystal display. *See* LCD
Logarithms, 47–50, 72–76
  base 10 logarithm key, 47, 72
  calculator key sequence for computing logarithms, 50
  change of base formula, 48–49, 74
  definition of, 47
  Euler's notation, 47
  functions, 5
  geometric mean and, 150, 187, 190
  inverse log, 49–50, 73, 187
  lnx key, 48, 49, 72, 74, 75
  log key, 48, 49, 72, 74, 75
  natural logarithm key, 47, 73, 75, 76
  properties of, 47–48

M

Machin's formula, 133
McNemar's test statistic, 204, 205
Mantissa, 13–17
Markup, 218–20, 239–43
  cost markup, 218, 241
  definition of, 218
  formulas for, 219, 241
Mean absolute deviation, 151
  formula for, 156–57
Mean (statistics), 147
  standard error of the, 157
Median, 148, 186
  definition of, 151
Midrange, 148, 189, 190
  formula for, 151
Mode, 148
  definition of, 151

O

Operands, 3

P

Parentheses, 5, 6, 11–13
  algebra and, 33, 34, 44, 45, 54, 55, 56, 57, 59, 60, 66–67, 70
  statistics and, 168
  trigonometry and, 85
Percent, 5, 217–18, 238–39
  definition of, 217
  formulas for, 218
  % key functions, 217
  simple percentage, 17–19, 27–28
Point estimate, 157
Polar coordinates, 103–8, 144–46
Power funciton, 5, 35, 36
Powers and roots, 35–38, 60–61
Progressions, 50–55, 76–83
  arithmetic, 51–52, 55, 77–79
  geometric, 51, 52–55, 79–82
  recursive formulation, 51–52
Proportions, 39–41, 61–64
Pythagorean theorem, 92–93, 116

Q

Quadratic equations, 41–44, 64–68, 122, 139

R

Radians, 84, 86–87, 95–96, 98, 101, 105, 107, 109–11, 128–29
Radicals
  laws of, 44–45, 68–72
  roundoff error, 71
Radicands, 36, 71
Range, formula for, 151
RCL key, 5
  algebra functions and the, 54, 66, 67
  business and finance and the, 223, 229, 247, 253, 258, 261, 262, 264, 265, 266, 267, 268, 269, 270, 272, 277, 278
  statistics and the, 156, 157, 159, 165, 167, 168, 175, 177, 178, 182, 183, 184, 189, 191, 192, 193, 194, 195, 196, 197, 198, 199, 200, 201, 204, 206, 207, 209, 211, 214, 216
  trigonometry and the, 92, 94, 96, 97, 105, 108, 110, 115, 120, 123, 125, 127, 128, 129, 132, 133, 136, 138, 142, 144, 146
Reciprocal relations, 89, 112
Regression (least squares), 170–79, 206–10
  AOS entry system and, 171, 174–75, 206, 207, 209
  background information, 170
  common notations for, 171
  common textbook notations versus common calculator notations, 171
  confidence intervals, 208–9
  correlation problem, 170, 207–8
  formulas for, 170, 172
  linear regression model, 170, 208, 209
  predicted value, 179
  roundoff error and, 175
  sequential entry system and, 206, 207
  using a calculator without regression functions, 174–75
  using a calculator with regression functions, 176–78
Results, 3
Reverse Polish notation. *See* RPN
Roots, 35–38, 60–61
Roundoff error
  exponents and, 71
  regression statistics and, 175
  trigonometry and, 125
RPN, 4

S

Sampling distribution, 157
Scientific notation, 1–2, 5, 13–17, 23–25, 55, 59, 70

Secant, 89, 100, 112
Sequential entry system, 159
  See also Arithmetic entry system
Signed numbers, 9–10, 22–23, 65
Simple interest. *See* Interest
Simple random sample. *See* SRS
Sine function, 88, 89, 91–93, 97–99, 112, 113, 119–26
Sinking funds
  amortization and, 231–32, 264–67
  depreciation and, 236, 271
Square root, 31, 55
Squares, 31, 55
SRS, 157
Standard deviation, 147, 151
  common key configurations for, 152
  formulas for, 152
  ways of computing, 153
Standard error of the mean, 157, 194
Standard normal (Gaussian) distribution, 158, 166
Stat functions, 6
Statistics, 6, 147–216
  analysis of variance, 179–86, 210–16
  averages and variability, 148–57, 186–92
  background information, 147
  chi squared, 166–70, 196, 202–6
  correlation, 147, 170
  data entry key, 147
  inference (hypothesis testing), 160–66, 197–201
  mean, 147
  regression (least squares), 170–79, 206–10
  solved problems, 186–216
  standard deviation, 147, 151–53
  statistics for sampling, 157–60, 192–97
STO key, 5
  algebra functions and the, 54, 67
  business and finance and the, 223, 229, 247, 253, 258, 261, 262, 264, 265, 266, 268, 269, 272, 277, 278
  statistics and the, 156, 157, 159, 165, 167, 168, 175, 176, 177, 178, 182, 183, 184, 189 , 191, 192, 193, 194, 195, 196, 197, 198, 199, 200, 201, 204, 206, 207, 209, 210, 213, 215
  trigonometry and the, 92, 94, 96, 105, 108, 110, 115, 120, 123, 125, 126, 128, 129, 131, 133, 136, 138, 142, 143, 144, 146
SUM key, 5, 155, 157, 167, 168, 177, 182, 183, 184, 191, 193, 200, 204, 204, 206, 207, 210, 213, 214, 215, 216, 266, 267, 272

T

Tangent function, 88, 89, 97, 99, 112, 113
Texas Instruments, 2, 4, 5,
TI Business Analyst I, 6, 219, 243
TI Business Analyst II, 6, 219, 243, 260, 261, 263, 272

TI-30, 2, 5
TI-35, 5
Triangles, right, 90–91, 113–19
Trigonometry, 84–146
    angular measure, 84–87, 108–11
    arc notation, 98–99
    areas, 93–96, 126–30
    basic trigonometric functions, 87–90,
        112–13, 136–44
    conversion between rectangular and polar
        coordinates, 105–9
    cosecant, 89, 99, 100
    cosine, 88, 89, 91–93, 97, 99, 112, 113,
        119–26
    cotangent, 89, 100
    decimal degrees, 84, 85–86, 109
    determining the hypotenuse, 114
    DMS scale, 84, 85, 86 109, 114–15, 124
    DRG key, 88, 89, 96, 101, 105, 113, 129,
        130, 131, 133, 136, 138, 142
    functions, 5
    grads, 84, 89
    Heron's formula, 94, 127–28
    inverse functions, 97–101, 133–36
    key configurations for inverse functions,
        99, 100
    Machin's formula, 133
    polar coordinates, 103–8, 144–46,
    Pythagorean theorem, 92–93, 116
    quadratic formula, 122, 139
    radians, 84, 86–87, 95–96, 98, 101, 105,
        107 109–11, 128–29

reciprocal relations, 89, 112
roundoff error, 125
secant, 89, 100, 112
sine, 88, 89, 91–93, 97–99, 112, 113,
    119–26
solved problems, 108–46
solving right triangles, 90–91, 113–19
tangent, 88, 89, 97, 99, 112, 113
trigonometric equations, 101–3

V

Variance, 151, 179–86, 210–16
    ANOVA, degrees of freedom, sum of
        squares table, 184
    ANOVA theory, 179–86
    common key configurations for, 152
    computational procedure, 186
    key sequence for ANOVA, 180
    one-way ANOVA, 180–82
    SSC, 181, 182, 183, 184, 186, 210, 211,
        212, 213, 214
    SSE, 181, 182, 183, 186, 211, 213
    SSR, 183, 186, 212, 213, 214
    SST, 181, 182, 183, 186, 210, 211, 212,
        213, 215
    two-way ANOVA, 182–84, 185
    ways of computing, 153

Y

Yate's continuity correction, 169, 204